Commercial Law

Commercial Law
Essential Terms and Transactions

An adaptation for law students of
Fundamentals of Commercial Activity:
A Lawyer's Guide

Second Edition

John F. Dolan
Professor of Law
Wayne State University

ASPEN LAW & BUSINESS
A Division of Aspen Publishers, Inc.

ISBN 1-56706-505-8

This publication is designed to provide accurate and authoritative
information in regard to the subject matter covered. It is sold with the
understanding that the publisher is not engaged in rendering legal,
accounting, or other professional services. If legal advice or other
professional assistance is required, the services of a competent professional
person should be sought.

—From a *Declaration of Principles* jointly adopted by
a Committee of the American Bar Association and
Committee of Publishers and Associations.

Permissions
Aspen Law & Business
A Division of Aspen Publishers, Inc.
1185 Avenue of the Americas
New York, NY 10036

1 2 3 4 5

For Jim, Ben, and Sarah

Summary of Contents

PART I

SALES   1

PART II

SECURED LENDING   91

PART III

PAYMENTS SYSTEMS   215

PART IV

TRANSPORT AND STORAGE   299

Contents

PART I

SALES   1

Contents

Contents

Contents

PART IV

TRANSPORT AND STORAGE   299

Contents

Table of Figures

Table of Documents

Preface

This is not a law book but a book about commercial activity that commercial law governs. Its purpose is to provide sufficient introduction to commercial activity to enable students taking courses in commercial law or contracts to study the Uniform Commercial Code efficiently — with a maximum of learning and a minimum of pain. Study of the Uniform Commercial Code is often more difficult than it needs to be. By introducing the reader to the commercial practices that the statute governs, this book attempts to make that study simpler.

The book consists of four Parts that correspond to four areas of law study: Sales (Contracts), Payments Systems, Secured Lending, and Transport and Storage (Bailments). Given the traditional nature of law texts, most textbook authors are unable to spend sufficient time explaining the underlying transaction, and most teachers cannot spend enough classroom time on the subject. Students often find themselves working through cases that involve activity foreign to their experience.

A case involving the manufacture of a specially designed printing press for the wine label industry makes a little more sense if the student knows what a specialty manufacturer is and how it differs from General Motors or IBM. Cases growing out of the construction of a power plant make more sense when the student understands something about the construction industry and its multitude of players. A lawsuit arising out of the collection of a wire transfer payment under a contract for the international shipment of goods will make more sense to the student who understands the way banks collect international payments, what international buyers and sellers do, and why an international carrier operates the way it does than to the student who is struggling without that understanding.

Study of legal subjects, moreover, is normative. Students and faculty ask whether rules are "fair," "efficient," or "good." Yet, students, or any person for that matter, cannot fully appreciate the success or failure of a rule without understanding the activity the rule governs and the reasonable expectations of the participants engaging in the activity. Thus, in many cases, the student must decide whether rules of law should be prescriptive or descriptive. Should the law tell people how to behave in a given context, or should the conduct of the parties in that context dictate the rules of law? The practicing lawyer and the business person complain most often about rules of law on the grounds that they are not realistic — that they do not rest on an understanding of the practices in question.

Using the Book

In each of the book's Parts, the first chapter serves to introduce the subject matter and the chapters that follow deal with specific practices. Most chapters have figures and illustrative documents. Documents are for you to skim or examine closely, as you see fit. They should help you understand what the parties are doing. Bear in mind, however, that this is not a form book, and there is no attempt to provide the latest forms available. These are forms, however, that parties are using.

The chapters are generally short, and the text of the chapters and of the Parts tends to move from the less complex to the more complex. It will benefit many students to start with the first two or three chapters of a Part and then to look at the Contents again to determine what additional chapters merit reading. The Tables of Figures and of Documents and the comprehensive index are also helpful.

The glossary has four parts corresponding to the four Parts of the text. Commercial law is a subculture, and it must have a language. Commercial law and commercial activity have their own vocabulary. But the glossary is not merely for reference. On the contrary, it is worth reading by itself. Some readers may find it helpful to review the Sales portion of the glossary right after reading the introductory Sales chapter. The same practice should prove helpful for the Secured Transactions, the Payments, and the Transport and Storage Parts. There are terms and explanations in the glossary that do not appear in the substantive chapters. Once read, the glossary resumes its role as a handy reference defining terms that recur in the substantive chapters. The four parts of the glossary are somewhat long, but they are written in essay fashion. Textual explanations follow many of the dictionary definitions. The definitions in Part I may not be helpful to the reader of Part II. Thus, each part of the glossary is fashioned for the book's Part to which it corresponds.

Acknowledgments

I could not have written this book without the generous assistance of friends and colleagues. Captions to the documents reproduced here acknowledge the help of corporations and banks that their people so kindly supplied. A number of friends spent significant amounts of time on my behalf. I thanked them in the preface to the first edition. This time, special thanks go to my dean, James Robinson, who provided research support for this second edition; to my secretary, Nancy A. Shafer; to Georgia Clark, Law Librarian at Wayne State University and to her staff; and finally to my faculty colleagues at Wayne State University Law School for their cheerful encouragement.

John F. Dolan

February 1997

Commercial Law

PART I

SALES

1

Scope

§1.1 Subject Matter
§1.2 Exclusions

§1.1 SUBJECT MATTER

This Part covers those commercial activities that generally fall under the typical law school courses that we denominate Contracts and Sales. There is bound to be some overlap in any arbitrary classification of commercial activity. Merchants and consumers do not confine their activity to law school course headings. Most lawyers are comfortable with these classifications or at least are familiar with them, so they serve as a good starting point.

While consumers are key players in Sales law and important players in Contract law, chapters in this Part generally emphasize the *commercial* aspects of Sales and Contract law. Law study at times emphasizes *consumer* aspects. While there is nothing wrong with attention to consumer transactions, the fact is that the law surrounding consumer sales and consumer contracts tends to be fashioned with considerations peculiar to the consumer, and to limit study to the consumer setting distorts the study. Virtually all readers, moreover, are familiar with sales and contract activity in the consumer setting. The purpose of this book is to explain the unfamiliar transaction, not the familiar one. Finally, the commercial aspects of sales and contracts are richer in diversity than consumer transactions. In short, the commercial aspects of Sales and Contract law are the primary concern of this Part, though we begin with the familiar consumer sale and give some attention from time to time throughout to the consumer trans-

action. The focus is narrowed further by the effort to include here contract activity that involves or relates to the sale of goods or services.

§1.2 EXCLUSIONS

Some features of Contract and Sales law are either too broad or too
specialized to fit here. Real estate contracts and collective bargaining
agreements are sufficiently broad to merit books of their own. The former
appear here rarely and the latter not at all. Contracts peculiar to the activity of corporations, partnerships, and joint ventures fall into a similar
class, as do government contracts. Contracts for a celebrity's services,
agreements for the transfer of a liquor license, prenuptial contracts, and
agreements between federal and local agencies are rather specific for a
work whose focus is general. Other contracts, such as those peculiar to
bailments (Part IV), secured lending (Part II), or international sales (Part
IV), appear in other parts where they seem more appropriate and where
study of them is easier by virtue of their place in an industry or legal
classification.

2

Consumer Sales

§2.1 CASH

In the simplest and probably oldest sales transaction, the buyer either bar-ters one **chattel** for another or pays "cash on the barrelhead" for the goods. In these transactions, there is no **contract** for the sale of the goods, there is simply a *sale*, which consists of the passing of **title** to the goods from the seller to the buyer for a price. There are a number of reasons to distinguish these **cash sales** from **credit sales,** and the Uniform Commer-cial Code warns that an **agreement** between the parties for delay in pay-ment by even one day turns the transaction into one for credit.

Prior to the advent of consumer credit, consumer purchases followed the cash-sale model. With the rise of **Fordism** and the creation of con-sumer markets for relatively high-priced durables such as automobiles and appliances, the cash sale could not serve many consumer purchases. In many **consumer** sales at the counter of a retail store, it is true that the buyer will still pay for the goods against immediate delivery in a cash-sale transaction. Credit sales, however, now comprise a significant part of sales activity. Most **merchant**-to-merchant sales are on credit, and the number of consumer sales on credit has grown at a dizzying pace. In fact, the credit card industry has introduced credit into many small consumer purchases, those for meals, items of clothing, gasoline, and groceries. Ironically, a recent advance in payments mechanisms, the debit card, which Chapter 27 discusses, is reintroducing cash features to the consumer sale.

§2.2 SALES CONTRACT

We know that the consumer sale for cash will not involve any explicit contract of **purchase,** but we can say in theory that the cash-on-the-barrelhead sale involves an implicit contract, and the law reads into that contract a number of terms. If a buyer approaches a sales counter and gives the sales clerk a **check,** the law will impose on the buyer a contractual duty to pay the seller if the check bounces. That duty exists in addition to obligations the buyer has under the law of negotiable instruments as the drawer of an instrument that is dishonored. By the same token, the law reads into the cash-sale transaction seller **warranties** of merchantability and good title.

In some consumer large-dollar, cash-sale transactions, the parties will enter into a written contract. If a consumer agrees to purchase a new automobile, the seller, an automobile **dealer,** will usually prepare a contract of purchase. Note, however, that this transaction usually involves a period during which the promises of the parties are executory. The consumer picks the automobile on Monday and promises to pay for it on Thursday. The dealer agrees to sell the vehicle at the negotiated price and promises to prepare the vehicle for delivery on Thursday, when the buyer returns with the purchase price. In the true cash-on-the-barrelhead sale there is no executory phase. The customer orders the coffee and gives the purchase price to the clerk, as the clerk hands the coffee to the customer.

§2.3 CREDIT

The rise of Fordism and the mass marketing of consumer durables created a need for consumer credit. Ordinary consumers can pay cash for clothing and food but not for automobiles and washing machines. Consumer credit, like all credit, is information sensitive. Retailers do not afford credit to strangers, but in any mature consumer market, most of a retailer's customers will be strangers, at least to the extent of their creditworthiness. While a banker knows much about her customer's creditworthiness, a retailer will not. Most consumer credit traditionally came from retailers, not from bankers, though that situation eventually reversed itself when bank credit cards replaced retailer credit cards and the retail installment sales contract.

Consumer credit first became available when retailers established reliable credit reporting facilities. Initially, the local chamber of commerce or retail credit organization in a market began maintaining credit histories, on consumers and made those histories, or a rating computed on them, available to merchants. Those ratings were accessible by mail or telephone, but tended to be stale. Either the agency was not up to date because late credit events had not been reported, or the merchant was not up to date because he had not received late information from the agency. The regime worked tolerably well, however, though it sometimes took days for a merchant to decide whether to extend credit. Modern communications technology now ensures that credit information is current: Agencies learn quickly of a consumer's "loading up" on credit purchases or of his defaults and merchants have virtually immediate access to an agency's records.

With the development of reliable consumer credit reporting agencies and the recognition by merchandisers that the consumer will buy more if he can obtain credit, retailers began actively campaigning to promote consumer credit sales. In these transactions, the seller can grant credit to the buyer directly, or the seller can arrange to have a third party grant the credit. Initially, in both transactions, the seller took a contract of sale from the customer. That contract, a **retail installment sales contract**, usually calls for a down payment and for deferred payments, the total of which equals the "cash price" plus interest charges variously referred to as the *time price differential* or the *finance charge*. In most instances, state law regulates the consumer credit contract under a Retail **Installment** Sales Act that protects the consumer by requiring, among other things, that the seller disclose credit terms clearly.

The retail installment sale often stretches the dealer's capital to its limits or beyond. An automobile dealer that sells half of the cars on its lot under retail installment contracts will be concerned that it cannot pay with the retail contracts its salespeople or taxing bodies or its manufacturer supplier that is providing new inventory. Salespeople, local governments, the IRS, and General Motors want cash or bank credit from the dealer, not retail installment sales contracts. Thus, dealers must "sell" or "discount" their installment paper or consumer paper with a **financial intermediary**, a bank or finance company.

Dealers are always anxious to make sales. That is their primary business. They are aware, furthermore, that easy credit for their customers will increase sales, so they are willing to make credit available even when they do not have the capital to finance the buyer's purchase and, therefore, must pay a discount to the financial intermediary. In this two-stage transaction, the financial institution makes an indirect loan to the consumer. The dealer grants credit to the consumer in stage one but does so knowing that the financial institution will make credit available to the dealer in stage two.

Often, the loan from the financial institution is direct. The customers

Figure 2-1. Direct Consumer Loan

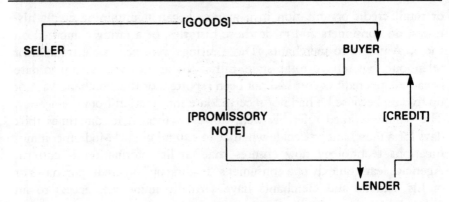

arrange their own credit. The buyer can obtain financing through his credit union or through a local bank or finance company. Frequently, it is in the buyer's best interest to arrange a loan, say, from a financial institution with which he regularly does business, since direct loans from these institutions to the consumer are often less expensive than an indirect loan under a retail installment sales agreement, the retailer's charge plan, or a bank-issued credit card.

In the indirect loan, the seller takes the installment sales contract from the consumer and assigns it to his financing institution, his bank or his finance company. In some cases, though these are rare in the consumer setting, the retailer sells under its own charge account plan and takes no contract from the buyer other than the contract the buyer signs when he opens the credit account. In these cases, the retailer has no "paper" to sell to or discount with the financial institution, but the institution will take his credit account receivables and extend credit to the retailer.

Figures 2-1 and 2-2 illustrate the direct and indirect credit arrangements.

In the retailer charge-plan transaction, the retailer ostensibly grants credit to the consumer under the retailer's own charge account plan. Thus, a buyer may purchase luggage and simply tell the sales clerk to charge it, that is, to charge the amount of the purchase to the buyer's revolving charge account with the seller. In fact, most retailers that maintain their own charge accounts do not have the resources to carry those accounts and finance those accounts at a bank or other commercial lender. Chapter 15 explains the retailers' account financing.

The buyer in this luggage example may prefer to use a bank credit card to finance the purchase. Bank credit card arrangements have grown dramatically in the last 25 years. The two national credit card systems have worked remarkably well despite the fact that there is little regulatory law on the subject and that there are several parties involved.

In a typical bank card system, commercial banks or other financial

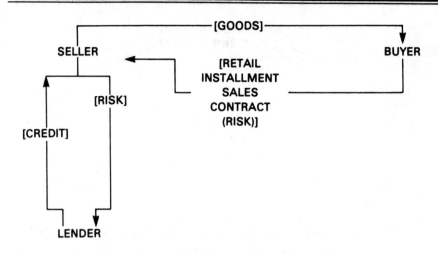

Figure 2-2.   Indirect Consumer Loan

institutions enter into an agreement with the system itself for the purpose of being able to issue cards and to use the national bank card collection network. Each bank member, in turn, enters into cardholder agreements with its customers. In a second role, banks in the credit card network enter into contracts with merchants in their market under which (1) the merchants agree to accept charges by cardholders and (2) the banks agree to take the charges from the merchants.

When the cardholder purchases luggage from a merchant member, the merchant notes a description of the goods on the familiar sales slip, which records the transaction. Sometimes, the merchant uses the slip, which banks call an *item* — the term banks use for checks and other instruments that pass through the check-collection system — to obtain credit (less a **discount**) from its bank. The bank uses the slip to charge the cardholder's account at the card issuer bank, which gives credit for the sales slip through the system. More often, the merchant bank captures the credit transaction data from a terminal at the retailer's counter and manipulates the data to (1) credit the merchant with the amount of the purchase (less the discount) and (2) obtain payment from the issuing bank. The issuing bank, in turn, uses the same data, all of this electronically, to charge the consumer when the bank mails her the periodic statement.

Under bank credit card arrangements, the cardholder does not have to pay off the entire monthly **statement** but has the option of paying only a portion of the outstanding balance each month plus interest on the balance remaining unpaid. Figure 2-3 illustrates the bank credit card relationships.

There is a second species of credit card that consumers use and that differs from the bank credit card. For a long time, some national or large regional retailers have used credit cards in connection with their market-

Figure 2-3.   Bank Credit Card Sales Relationships

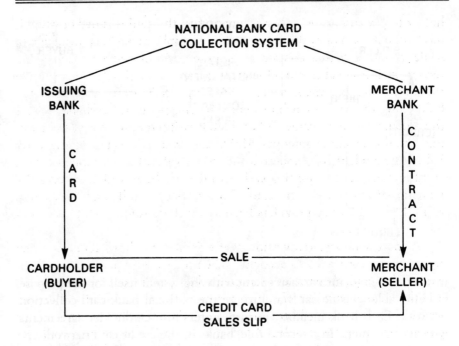

ing. These credit cards are in the nature of open-account arrangements whereby, for example, a customer may purchase gasoline from the oil company's dealer with the understanding that the customer will pay his bill periodically. Under these credit card agreements, installment credit is not available to the customer, as it is under bank card agreements, and the merchandiser does not use the bank collection system to obtain payment for charges but bills the consumer directly.

Other nonbank credit card issuers, such as Diners Club and American Express, issue similar cards, called *travel and entertainment cards*, that permit cardholders to charge purchases at merchant establishments that agree to take such cards.

Recently, national retailers have blended the aspects of bank cards and merchant cards to permit cardholders to pay card balances in installments and to permit retailers to use the bank collection system to collect on the sales slips or the sales data they generate through the sales of their goods and services.

§2.4 DEBIT CARDS

Debit cards differ from credit cards by virtue of the fact that they either require prepayment or effect an immediate or nearly immediate debit to the cardholder's account with the card issuer. Prepaid cards require the holder to pay cash or debit her account when the card is issued or when it has "run out" of money. Universities, for example, make cards available to students and staff that contain a computer chip or magnetic stripe that records its initial value and subsequent debits. In the simplest transaction, the cardholder purchases a card with, say, $5.00 of value. When the holder uses the card, a machine debits the charge on the card and reduces the amount of stored value. When a student inserts the card at the parking lot, the machine removes $1.00, say, from the value of the card. When the student has exhausted the stored value, he can replenish it at another machine by inserting cash into the machine, which encodes the replenished amount on the card. Transit systems, toll road authorities, and telephone service providers have found these simple debit cards useful.

A more sophisticated version of the debit card allows retailers direct access to the card holder's account. When a consumer purchase groceries with such a card, the retailer's terminal relays the amount of the purchase and the account number of the customer to the customer's bank or to a clearinghouse, which debit's the customer's account and credits the grocer's account. The familiar ATM card is a debit card. Chapter 30 describes in more detail debit cards and credit cards and the way they function in the bank collection system.

§2.5 HOMEMADE CONTRACTS

There is an abundance of case law, most of it the subject of study in the Contracts course, that deals with the homemade contract that is the product of pencil scratching on a pad of paper or the back of an envelope done at the kitchen table. These horrors are not significant to the national economy, but they frequently are significant to the parties that enter into them, and the courts have sometimes stuffed square pegs into round holes and otherwise punched the law of contract out of shape to effect a modicum of justice in these settings. No one can quarrel with these efforts, but the student and the lawyer must recognize them for what they are — ad hoc jurisprudence that should not extend to the regular and sophisticated transactions that are described in the first four sections of this chapter and surely should not apply to commercial contracts and transactions.

3

Open Account Sales

§3.1 THE TRANSACTION

As all students who have taken the Contracts course know, contracts fall into two categories. The first category includes the recurring transaction, e.g., insurance arrangements, retail installment sales agreements, loan agreements, collective bargaining agreements, and real estate sales contracts. The second category includes everything else. Many of the standard agreements in commercial law appear at one place or another in this book. The non-standard agreement, that is, the agreement tailored for a relationship obviously cannot be the subject of this book, which treats the recurring transactions of commercial law. It may be important to keep in mind, however, that the law of the recurring transaction often differs from the law that applies to the unique transaction. When courts construe an installment sales contract, they cannot but be mindful of the fact that the rule they fashion will govern not just the parties before them but thousands or millions of parties not before them. It is also the case that the transactions that this book describes, and especially the open account sale, usually relate to discrete transactions. That is to say, the disputes that usually arise under an open account sale, and the transactional planning in that context in which the merchant buyer and the merchant seller engage, relate to a single sale. That fact notwithstanding, there may be, as you learn in your study of Contracts, a relationship between the buyer and the seller; and the court may take account of relational facts when it interprets the open account sale arrangements. This chapter's focus is on the sale itself, however; and it leaves to you the task of remembering that the open account sale may or may not be part of a broader relationship between the two merchants that are parties to it.

For the purposes of introducing readers to commercial activity the hard part is the "everything else" category. The fact is that no teacher can cover that category, for while one teaches, the merchants and consumers that comprise the players on the commercial field are inventing new commercial devices and new contracts. Nowhere is that fact more evident than in the sales context. For while there are a number of recurring patterns in sales, many sales are unique.

This book generally attempts to deal with recurring commercial transactions. In sales those include, among others, retail installment contracts (*see* Section 2.3); consumer purchases on open credit (*see* Section 2.3); documentary draft transactions (*see* Chapter 4); imports and exports (*see* Chapter 5); consignments (*see* Chapter 6); and sales disguised as leases (*see* Chapter 9).

In domestic merchant-to-merchant sales there has also emerged an efficient and standard practice known as the *open account sale*. With the exception of those transactions described elsewhere in this chapter, the open account sale dominates domestic sales transactions between merchants when one of the merchants sells out of inventory to another.

The significant exception to that domination arises in the agricultural sector, where farm producers often sell their inventory to **brokers** or large corporate purchasers. The farmer selling his crop might do so not on open account but under a **futures contract**. Many agricultural sales follow the open account paradigm, however, such as those covering milk, eggs, poultry, some vegetables, and livestock, all of which are often subject to sale on open account.

This is probably as good a place as any to make the point that farmers are really merchants, most of them quite sophisticated. Even the small farmer who does not use computer terminals to gain access to markets, modern drip irrigation techniques, or scientific advances for soil testing will know as much about the agricultural enterprise as any small business entrepreneur knows about bank credit, markets, supply **costs,** taxes, and all the other areas of commerce and learning from which any business enterprise will benefit. The nation has long enjoyed something of a romance with the farm producer. There is allure in that romance, which a drive through the countryside on a fine summer evening inevitably nurtures. That romance must not mask the facts of agricultural commerce, however. It is best to think of the farmer as a merchant; the farmer has earned that respect.

Farmers and other merchants who sell to nonconsumer buyers have devised the open account sale as an efficient sales mechanism. It involves massive amounts of goods and billions of dollars of sales yearly in the domestic economy. Significantly, the open account sale is a credit transaction, and the existence of inexpensive, accurate, and easily accessible credit reporting has helped make the open account sale possible with all its attendant savings and its advantages for the small, thinly capitalized enterprise. In the overwhelmingly large percentage of merchant-to-merchant sales transactions, the parties will resort to the cheap, efficient device of the open account sale. A bit of history is helpful.

There was a time when merchants were not often able to sell on open account. Credit reporting was slow and often unreliable. A New York manufacturer in the nineteenth century was not willing to ship on credit to a buyer way off in Tennessee unless the manufacturer had hard facts supporting the buyer's credit standing. The manufacturer certainly would not extend credit (i.e., ship on open account) on the basis of an order on the buyer's letterhead. Some manufacturers, however, were large enough to support a network of sales personnel ("drummers" who "drummed" up business). Drummers would visit the buyer's establishment, talk to local merchants about the buyer, and report back to the manufacturer with a recommendation on credit. That system was expensive, and the volatile nature of many industries and many local economies rendered it imprecise and rendered the information generated by it of doubtful validity after short periods of time.

The day of the drummer is over. We encounter him in Meredith Wilson's catchy lyrics from *The Music Man* or in tired jokes modernized into stories about "traveling salesmen." Time has transmuted that commercial personage into a "marketing analyst" or the like. Armed with the information provided by accurate, reliable credit reporting agencies, sellers are in a better position to know the current state of a potential buyer's economic strength and, especially, to know when danger (usually foretold by late payments on current accounts) lurks. Specialized *credit agencies* accumulate data on customers in an industry and report that information for a fee that is far less than the cost of maintaining a cadre of drummers. Document 3-1 is an illustration of a modern commercial credit report.

In the past, sellers had to acquire periodic, written credit reports from the credit-reporting agencies. That process was slow enough that the information could lose its value as circumstances changed and the report's data became dated. The advent of computerized communications, however, has generally guarded against data obsolescence and has rendered the credit-reporting process more immediate and therefore more reliable. Today, any high-volume, open account seller will have access to the credit-reporting agency's database. When a seller needs information about an account, a clerk in the seller's credit department may access the base by satellite or by telephone wire and see on a computer terminal up-to-date credit information on the account in question.

The development of such credit reporting, faster communications methods, and the general standardization of transaction terms in many industries permitted sellers to do away with their costly in-house system of monitoring accounts and permitted them to sell to a vastly greater number of potential buyers. By the same token, the open account sale gives buyers tremendous advantages to the extent that it encourages sellers to sell on industry credit terms to new accounts and to new ventures that have in some way established a good credit rating.

It is important to understand that the open account sale is a credit sale. At the very least, the seller is giving the buyer credit during the time it takes for the seller's **invoice** to arrive at buyer's office and for buyer's purchasing people to forward payment to seller. In most industries, the credit terms are longer. Sellers in these industries ship on the understanding that payment is not due until the end of the month or 30 or even 60 days after the invoice date or after the end of the month. Many sellers, moreover, quote their prices in terms of discounts to those buyers that pay early.

§3.2 THE PARTIES

The efficiency of the typical open account sale is reflected in its simplicity. There are only two parties, the buyer and the seller, so there are no bank or broker fees; and documentation is often minimal. Figure 3-1 illustrates the simplicity of the open account sale.

Figure 3-1. Open Account Sale

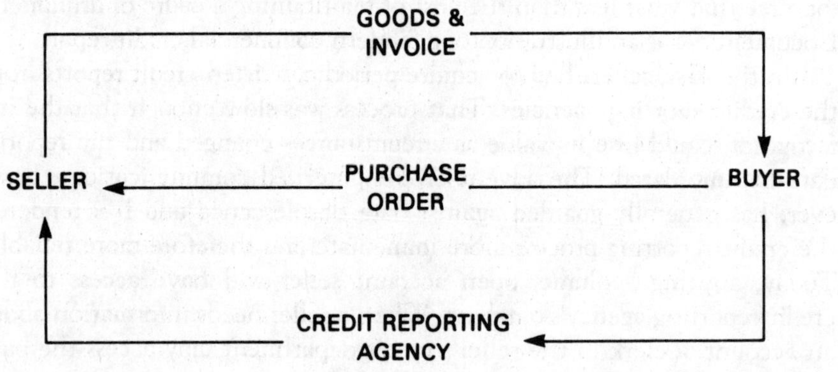

§3.3 DOCUMENTATION

In the open account sale, there may be little documentation. For example, a buyer in Tennessee may order merchandise from a New York seller by telephone. The seller's salesperson will book the order for internal purposes but probably will not send any acknowledgment, other than the sales invoice, to the buyer. Upon approval of the order by the seller's credit department, the shipping instructions, usually contained in a carbon copy of the invoice, or the document that will become the invoice, go to the shipping department, which in the course of a few days or less will ship the merchandise to the buyer. In many sellers' offices, internal documentation is paperless. The sales clerk enters the sales data into the firm's computer memory and generates invoices, purchase orders, and shipping documents electronically or not at all. In transactions that both parties conclude electronically, there is even less paper and less data input, as Section 3.6 explains.

At the same time that the shipping information goes to shipping, billing information goes to the credit department, which invoices the buyer without delay. Document 3-2 is a typical invoice, sometimes referred to as a *commercial invoice*.

Note that the invoice includes significant information, enough to satisfy the Statute of Frauds certainly, and note the economy of the document. By using computer technology, sellers with any significant volume of open account sales generate all of the information they need concerning the sale from the invoice itself, copies or records of which will serve as shipping tickets, sales records, and account records.

Briefly, then, the open account sale involves four simple steps. First, the sales department must determine that the sale is in the house, that is, that the buyer and the seller have agreed to a contract for the sale of the goods. Lawyers should be wary of importing into this determination their own legal culture. Business people may not always know whether the correspondence or telephone communications between the parties rise to the level of an enforceable contract. They do know, usually much better than the lawyers, what activity in the trade is sufficient for the seller to act. It is true that many times a court will subsequently decide that there was no contract. That **risk** is usually minimal in the minds of open account sellers, however. They act on the basis of commercial considerations that may not influence the court, and they are usually right. They may lose a lawsuit once in awhile, but they do not fashion their business with lawsuits in mind. A lawyer can tell a seller client that her documentation is insufficient to sustain a legal claim against a buyer that refuses to take delivery of goods, but many such sellers will respond that they don't care. The losses they sustain from such defaulting buyers are less than the costs of substantiating a legal case in every sale.

17

The second step involves the credit evaluation. The credit department may make periodic preauthorizations, so that the sales people can skip this step in the process unless the order takes the account over the preauthorized limit. If there is no preauthorization, the credit department must look in the reporting agency's database and determine whether the account merits credit under the seller's standards. If the credit department decides that the customer is worthy of customary industry credit terms, the department gives its approval to the order and initiates the invoicing process.

The third step is for the shipping department to arrange to ship the goods. The final step is to send the invoice.

§3.4 FURTHER DOCUMENTATION

In many cases, parties are not willing to rely on the telephone method of initiating an open account sale that is described in the foregoing paragraphs. Some buyers invariably follow the practice of issuing **purchase orders** in all of their purchase transactions or in those above a certain dollar amount or those from certain suppliers. Contractors that engage subcontractors, for example, frequently issue purchase orders to the sub. Document 3-3 is a purchase order.

Some sellers resort to documentation in the form of **order acknowledgments**. As all law students know, more often than not, the terms of the purchase order and the order acknowledgment differ in some respects. Those differences give rise to the famous "battle of the forms" that Contracts law teachers have so much fun with in the basic Contracts course. In real life, those battles are less significant than they are in the classroom. Most merchants do not rely on the boilerplate provisions that they incorporate into their forms. (At least they do not rely on them until the matter reaches litigation.) The disputes arise not because of the variances in the forms but because one or the other of the parties to the contract of sale no longer values it. In most cases, the buyer and the seller whose forms conflict go merrily on their way, often with no knowledge of the conflict; and if there are problems, say over the time period within which a buyer must examine goods and report defects, they work them out in a manner that is satisfactory to both. Only their lawyers worry about it.

§3.5 AN IMPORTANT VARIATION

In some industries, a growing number it would appear, and in all industries to some extent, sellers refuse to sell on open account without some assurance that the buyer will pay. There are two reasons for the seller's reluctance. First, if money is tight and interest rates are correspondingly high, some sellers find it difficult to finance their accounts. The open account sale leaves sellers with significantly high levels of accounts receivable. The seller can borrow on those accounts. (*See* Chapter 15 for a description of account financing.) The cost of that borrowing may be significant, however, and the seller can reduce its borrowing costs and be able to borrow more if the accounts are secured by a financially strong guarantor of some kind. Second, in some cases, a buyer's credit rating will not qualify it for open account credit. In that case, the buyer may resort to some kind of **guaranty** arrangement in order to qualify for industry credit terms.

The invoice **letter of credit** provides an efficient device for satisfying both the seller's needs and the buyer's lack of creditworthiness. In this three-party variation of the open account sale, the buyer's bank or other financial institution issues a standby letter of credit in favor of the seller. The bank is willing to issue the credit either because the buyer has financial resources that the buyer uses to secure the bank or because the buyer has secured the bank with independent guarantees or collateral owned by third persons. If the bank pays the seller under the credit, the bank looks to the buyer or the collateral to reimburse itself.

Banks that issue standby credit charge a fee, but by virtue of the fact that the bank is often the buyer's bank and, therefore, knowledgeable about the buyer's financial condition, the bank can secure itself more easily and at lowers costs than the seller could secure itself in the open account sale. Seller's are not usually as intimately involved with the buyer's business as the buyer's bank is. In the **middle market**, where most of these standby credits arise, the buyer's bank may already have granted the buyer a line of credit against which the buyer draws when he asks the bank to issue the standby. In short, it is much less expensive for the buyer's bank to issue the credit than it is for the seller to obtain some kind of collateral from the buyer. Figure 3-2 illustrates the transaction. For further discussion of the benefits of the standby to the seller when he seeks to borrow against his open accounts, *see* Section 15.9.

After the buyer causes the letter of credit to be established, the open account sale proceeds as usual. The buyer submits orders, and the seller ships on open account with customary terms. The seller resorts to the letter of credit only in the event that the buyer fails to pay the invoice when it is due.

The standby, carefully drawn, incorporates as an exhibit the certificate that the seller must execute in order to draw on the letter of credit. Also the letter of credit contains a definite expiry, as all letters of credit should. The expiry, however, is often subject to what merchants and bankers call an *evergreen clause*, which renders the credit automatically

Figure 3-2.   Invoice Standby Letter of Credit Transaction

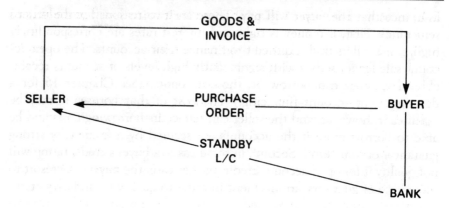

renewed in the event that the issuer of it does not give the seller 60 days' notice that it will not be renewed. When the seller receives notice of nonrenewal, it will stop selling on open account unless the buyer obtains a new credit from another issuer.

Invoice letters of credit are common in the automobile industry where the sellers, automobile manufacturers, are typically strong and the buyers, automobile dealers, are relatively weak. Automobile manufacturers have used their market strength to require dealers to obtain invoice standby credits, though they do not call them such. Such letters of credit are appearing with increasing frequency in other industries. They facilitate the open account sale and take full advantage of the knowledge a bank obtains in a typical middle market borrower/bank relationship. Chapter 12 discusses that relationship in more detail.

§3.6 ELECTRONIC DATA INTERCHANGE

Recently, buyers and sellers have been experimenting with computer technology in an effort to reduce the amount of costly paper work. **Electronic data interchange** (EDI) is one innovation that effects that reduction, and although it is still in its infancy, some buyers and sellers have adapted it to the open account sale and have been able to reduce the use of purchase orders and invoices.

EDI is the transmission by modern communications methods of business forms in a standardized format. In order to utilize EDI, therefore, parties in an industry must establish a trade organization that will undertake to standardize forms. Because of the advanced technology involved, progress in the area is slow. Parties must have computer capabilities and sophisticated computer personnel. The equipment and education costs are considerable, and because only a small segment of any industry is ready for

EDI, those with the capability must retain their paper-based procedures to service non-EDI customers or suppliers.

To date, EDI has achieved some success in the sales transaction by standardizing invoices and purchase orders. Under the trade group's standardization procedures, a party preparing a purchase order, for example, provides a minimum amount of information to the computer in language defined in a data dictionary. A buyer would need to enter a description of the merchandise, the price and **delivery terms**, and the identity of the parties. Much of the input is in codes, which the computer translates into a purchase order that appears on the prospective seller's computer terminal.

If the parties engage in frequent buy-sell transactions, the arrangement has obvious advantages. First, it is speedy. By using telecommunications technology, the parties can transmit the purchase orders or invoices instantly. The parties, moreover, have eliminated paper, so that there is no need to store or transport documents. Finally, because the information is in the parties' computers, they can gain access to it quickly, manipulate it (e.g., change quantity or **price terms** or call for periodic or account summaries), and retrieve it instantly, even at locations distant from the office that initially received it.

Electronic data interchange (EDI) has developed both in connection with proprietary standards and public standards. Proprietary standards are those worked out by a set of trading partners for their own use. For example, if an automobile manufacturer determines that it will require its suppliers to use EDI for bidding, accepting purchase orders, and invoicing, it might create its own standards for the computer operations involved. These standards would be proprietary. If an entire industry, on the other hand, such as the international banking industry, decides to utilize EDI, it may have a trade arm or independent trade organization fashion standards for the entire industry.

EDI is creating a new lexicon of EDI terms. A "transaction set" is what commercial lawyers would call a document. Thus, in the automobile manufacturer example described above, there would be one transaction set for a bid, one for a purchase order, and yet others for the order acknowledgement and invoice. Transaction sets are comprised of "data segments," which, in turn, are comprised of "data elements." In all probability, such a proprietary system would also call for payment by wire transfer, with the bank instructions themselves being issued as a transaction set. Document 3-4 is a purchase order generated from an EDI format.

Parties using EDI need a communications network. SWIFT and SWIFT-2, explained in Section 26.7, are communications networks created by the international banking industry for their own use. Automated clearinghouses, explained in Section 27.5, comprise a system of commercial-bank-owned and Federal-Reserve Bank-owned network facilities that permit any bank customer to use EDI.

Computer fraud is a potentially disastrous problem for EDI, since a system that permits dishonest parties or interlopers to falsify delivery or payment instructions, for example, would be useless. The parties that have fashioned EDI standards and the networks that carry EDI transmissions have gone to great lengths to avoid the consequences of such fraud by using codes, key words, message encryption, and algorithms. They have taken these and additional sophisticated measures to protect confidentiality and to give users reliable methods for authenticating messages and verifying content.

Experience to date seems to justify the high hopes some merchants and bankers harbor for EDI. Usage is growing, and problems remain manageable. Some of those problems may require the rethinking of legal requirements such as those involving "signatures," the keeping of records, and "writings." So far, the courts have been hospitable to these commercial innovations and have adapted current statutory and regulatory language to the new devices. Statutory revisions currently underway in the commercial area, including efforts to revise Uniform Commercial Code articles, have not ignored EDI.

The notion that EDI will replace paper transactions entirely is unrealistic, in the short term at least. Transaction paper continues to be with us and continues to grow; but the use of EDI is growing as well, with encouraging results. Some industries report remarkable cost savings after they install EDI capabilities. One seller reported that its cost of receiving orders under EDI was 11 percent of its cost under the paper-based system that EDI replaced.

The more complex the industry, the greater the savings, it would seem. The federal government has become a major user of EDI, as have large corporate enterprises such as General Motors and Sears. The U.S. Department of Defense procurement practices under EDI allow computers to order supplies automatically when inventory levels, also monitored by computer, are low.

Document 3-1.   Commercial Credit Report

Dun & Bradstreet
a company of The Dun's Bradstreet Corporation

ANALYTICAL SERVICES

GORMAN

GORMAN MANUFACTURING CO INC
492 KOLLER STREET
SAN FRANCISCO CA 94110
D&B OFFICE 052

DUNS 00-007-7743
SIC 2752
STARTED 1965
EMPLOYS 105

LAST INDUSTRY UPDATE: 01/199-   DATE PRINTED: 03/239-
SALES 13,007,229
WORTH 2,125,499
INDUSTRY ASSET RANGE: OVER $5 MILLION   WEST

	FISCAL DEC. 31, 1991 (46 FIRMS)				FISCAL DEC. 31, 1990 (22 FIRMS)				FISCAL DEC. 31, 1989 (27 FIRMS)		
	Value	% CHANGE	SUBJECT %	INDUSTRY %	Value	% CHANGE	SUBJECT %	INDUSTRY %	Value	SUBJECT %	INDUSTRY %
CASH	925,000	(17.6)	12.1	6.6	1,123,018	15.1	17.8	7.4	975,321	16.0	6.7
ACCOUNTS RECEIVABLE	1,725,814	41.1	22.7	30.2	1,223,128	22.0	19.4	28.7	1,002,381	16.4	25.3
NOTES RECEIVABLE	—	—	—	0.5	—	—	—	0.5	—	—	0.8
INVENTORY	1,643,311	60.6	21.6	11.7	1,023,311	2.8	16.2	13.1	995,221	16.3	12.9
OTHER CURRENT	1,131,000	(22.3)	14.8	3.2	1,456,154	(12.8)	23.1	4.7	1,670,898	27.3	3.7
TOTAL CURRENT	5,425,125	12.4	71.2	52.2	4,825,611	3.9	76.5	54.4	4,643,821	76.0	49.4
FIXED ASSETS	1,667,918	12.3	21.9	37.9	1,485,440	1.2	23.5	34.4	1,468,291	24.0	38.1
OTHER NON CURRENT	523,772	—	6.9	9.9	—	—	—	11.2	—	—	12.5
TOTAL ASSETS	7,616,815	20.7	100.0	100.0	6,311,051	3.3	100.0	100.0	6,112,112	100.0	100.0
ACCOUNTS PAYABLE	2,125,114	39.2	27.9	12.7	1,526,181	1.9	24.2	10.7	1,498,321	24.5	9.3
BANK LOANS	1,100,000	44.7	14.4	0.1	760,000	52.0	12.0	0.3	500,000	8.2	0.3
NOTES PAYABLE	450,000	28.6	5.9	5.7	350,000	0.0	5.5	3.9	350,000	5.7	5.7
OTHER CURRENT	450,604	(54.4)	5.9	14.0	988,819	(20.7)	15.7	17.0	1,247,500	20.4	15.4
TOTAL CURRENT	4,125,718	13.8	54.2	32.5	3,625,000	0.8	57.4	31.9	3,595,821	58.8	30.7
OTHER LONG TERM	1,365,598	76.4	17.9	28.9	773,939	21.5	12.3	26.0	636,840	10.4	25.4
DEFERRED CREDITS	—	—	—	0.9	—	—	—	0.8	—	—	1.7
NET WORTH	2,125,499	11.2	27.9	37.7	1,912,112	1.7	30.3	41.3	1,879,451	30.7	42.2
TOTAL LIABILITY/WORTH	7,616,815	20.7	100.0	100.0	6,311,051	3.3	100.0	100.0	6,112,112	100.0	100.0
NET SALES	13,007,229	26.0	100.0	100.0	10,325,582	10.8	100.0	100.0	9,321,118	100.0	100.0
GROSS PROFIT	3,777,675	65.3	29.0	27.6	2,285,112	4.7	22.1	28.2	2,181,712	23.4	29.3
NET PROFIT AFTER TAX	26,014	(87.8)	0.2	4.5	213,387	553.3	2.1	5.2	32,661	0.4	5.3
DIVIDENDS/WITHDRAWALS	—	—	—	3.7	—	—	—	6.6	—	—	2.7
WORKING CAPITAL	1,299,407	8.2			1,200,611	14.6			1,048,000		

GORMAN MANUFACTURING CO INC
492 KOLLER STREET
SAN FRANCISCO CA 94110
DUNS NO. 00-007-7743

ANALYTICAL SERVICES

PREPARED FOR

GORMAN

Dun & Bradstreet
a company of The Dun & Bradstreet Corporation

LAST INDUSTRY UPDATE: 01/199-   DATE PRINTED: 03/23/9-

RATIOS

1991 (46 FIRMS) —INDUSTRY QUARTILES—

	SUBJECT	% CHANGE	UPPER	MEDIAN	LOWER
(SOLVENCY)					
QUICK RATIO . . (TIMES) . . .	0.6	0.0	1.7	0.9	0.8
CURRENT RATIO . . (TIMES) . .	1.3	0.0	2.3	1.5	1.2
CURR LIAB TO NW . . (%) . .	194.1	2.4	42.2	104.6	175.8
CURR LIAB TO INVT . . (%) . .	251.1	(29.1)	207.5	281.2	392.3
TOTAL LIAB TO NW . . (%) . .	258.4	12.3	93.5	234.4	292.0
FIXED ASSETS TO NW . . (%)	78.5	1.0	75.9	148.3	209.9
(EFFICIENCY)					
COLL PERIOD . . (DAYS) . . .	48.4	12.0	44.8	52.9	67.9
SALES TO INVT . . (TIMES) . .	7.9	(21.8)	24.4	16.6	10.7
ASSETS TO SALES . . (%) . .	58.6	(4.1)	49.2	59.0	72.1
SALES TO NWC . . (TIMES) . .	10.0	16.3	20.0	10.0	5.0
ACCT PAY TO SALES . . (%)	16.3	10.1	4.0	6.5	8.5
(PROFITABILITY)					
RETURN ON SALES . . (%) . .	0.2	(90.5)	6.2	1.9	0.2
RETURN ON ASSETS . . (%) . .	0.3	(91.2)	7.5	3.2	0.3
RETURN ON NW . . (%) . . .	1.2	(89.3)	20.8	9.9	1.0

1990 (22 FIRMS) —INDUSTRY QUARTILES—

	SUBJECT	% CHANGE	UPPER	MEDIAN	LOWER
(SOLVENCY)					
QUICK RATIO . . (TIMES) . . .	0.6	0.0	1.4	1.0	0.8
CURRENT RATIO . . (TIMES) . .	1.3	0.0	2.5	1.5	1.1
CURR LIAB TO NW . . (%) . .	189.6	(0.9)	40.4	92.1	170.8
CURR LIAB TO INVT . . (%) . .	354.2	(2.0)	155.7	284.8	355.0
TOTAL LIAB TO NW . . (%) . .	230.1	2.2	74.8	258.0	339.8
FIXED ASSETS TO NW . . (%)	77.7	(0.5)	64.9	174.1	204.7
(EFFICIENCY)					
COLL PERIOD . . (DAYS) . . .	43.2	9.9	43.4	48.5	56.9
SALES TO INVT . . (TIMES) . .	10.1	7.4	21.0	16.6	10.7
ASSETS TO SALES . . (%) . .	61.1	(6.9)	38.9	51.2	69.0
SALES TO NWC . . (TIMES) . .	8.6	(3.4)	24.2	8.1	4.9
ACCT PAY TO SALES . . (%)	14.8	(8.1)	3.6	5.0	5.8
(PROFITABILITY)					
RETURN ON SALES . . (%) . .	2.1	425.0	6.4	3.7	1.3
RETURN ON ASSETS . . (%) . .	3.4	580.0	9.6	8.3	2.6
RETURN ON NW . . (%) . . .	11.2	558.8	21.5	15.0	9.1

1989 (27 FIRMS) —INDUSTRY QUARTILES—

	SUBJECT	UPPER	MEDIAN	LOWER
(SOLVENCY)				
QUICK RATIO . . (TIMES) . . .	0.6	1.8	1.0	0.7
CURRENT RATIO . . (TIMES) . .	1.3	2.4	1.4	1.2
CURR LIAB TO NW . . (%) . .	191.3	23.5	49.8	213.0
CURR LIAB TO INVT . . (%) . .	361.3	147.2	235.9	338.2
TOTAL LIAB TO NW . . (%) . .	225.2	54.1	99.4	272.9
FIXED ASSETS TO NW . . (%)	78.1	55.9	94.6	168.0
(EFFICIENCY)				
COLL PERIOD . . (DAYS) . . .	39.3	45.9	58.8	65.7
SALES TO INVT . . (TIMES) . .	9.4	21.9	15.8	8.3
ASSETS TO SALES . . (%) . .	65.6	54.0	67.7	78.2
SALES TO NWC . . (TIMES) . .	8.9	17.4	7.0	5.1
ACCT PAY TO SALES . . (%)	16.1	4.8	6.0	7.8
(PROFITABILITY)				
RETURN ON SALES . . (%) . .	0.4	5.9	4.5	1.4
RETURN ON ASSETS . . (%) . .	0.5	10.4	6.4	2.3
RETURN ON NW . . (%) . . .	1.7	23.5	14.3	7.1

ORIGINAL INVOICE

INVOICE NO.

REMIT TO:

ITT
AUTOMOTIVE

SOLD TO

SHIP TO

INVOICE DATE	DATE SHIPPED	TERMS		VENDOR NUMBER	SHIPPING PLANT		F.O.B.
PREPAID OR COLL.	CARRIER		B/L NUMBER	TRAILER NUMBER	BOOK NO.	A.E.T.C.	CUST. OURS
CONTAINERS NO. TYPE	WEIGHT	TOTAL SHPD. TO DATE	QUANTITY SHIPPED	CUSTOMER PART NUMBER	CUSTOMER'S PURCHASE ORDER NO.	RELEASE NUMBER	SUPPLIERS NUMBER	PRICE	AMOUNT

SPECIMEN

We hereby certify that these goods were produced in compliance with the Fair Labor Standards Act.

F10021 REV 9 95

Front page of document only. Reprinted with the permission of ITT Automotive, Inc.

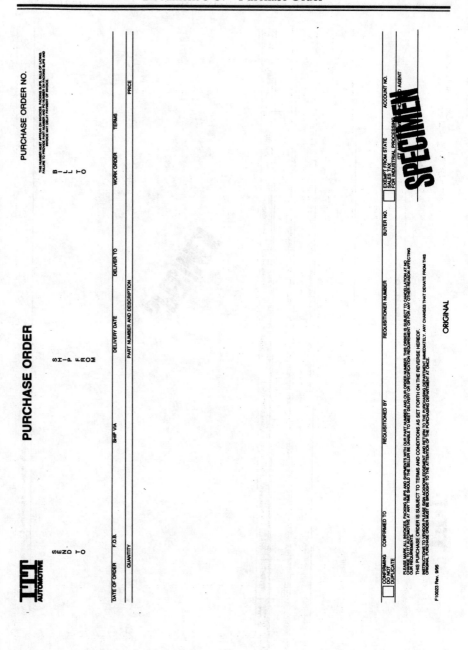

Front page of document only. Reprinted with the permission of ITT Automotive, Inc.

Document 3-4. Purchase Order (EDI Format)

PURCHASE ORDER: ABR01500

TO:
```
ABC COMPANY
850 STEPHENSON HWY.
TROY, MICHIGAN 48077
VENDOR NUMBER 123456789

WXYZ COMPANY
555 VENDOR LANE
FLINT, MICHIGAN 48557
```

SHIP TO:
```
ABC COMPANY
1962 14 MILE ROAD
TROY, MICHIGAN 48077
```

INVOICE TO:
```
ABC COMPANY
67802 RACINE
WARREN, MICHIGAN 48089
```

This Number Must Appear On All Invoices, Packing Slips, Packages and Bills of Lading.
(2) copies of your packing slip must accompany each shipment. Item Identification Number(s) must be shown on Packing Slips and Invoices.
Invoice Attn: Accounts Payable
Do not Declare Valuation of Express Shipments or Insure Parcel Post.

ORDER DATE	ALTERATION ISSUE DATE	ALTERATION EFFECTIVE DATE
02/28/92		

313-578-4926 Buyer

This order is not binding until accepted. Acceptance should be executed on acknowledgment copy which should be returned to Buyer.
On the reverse side hereof are the terms and conditions to which Seller agrees by acceptance of this order.
This order, including the terms and conditions on the face and reverse side hereof, contains the complete and final agreement between Buyer and Seller and no other agreement in any way modifying any of said terms and conditions will be binding upon the Buyer unless made in writing and signed by Buyer's authorized representative.
(If Government Contract Number is Shown Hereon, Additional Terms and Conditions Attached Herein Apply.

F.O.B. DESTINATION UNLESS OTHERWISE INDICATED   OUR PLANT

SHIP VIA UNITED PARCEL

PAYMENT TERMS 1.00% 10TH PROX

ITEM SEQUENCE	QUANTITY ORDERED	ITEM IDENTIFICATION NO.	NOUN NAME	DESCRIPTION	RFQ NUMBER	DATE REQUIRED	TAX CODE/ %	BASE UNIT PRICE	PRICE MULTIPLE	UNIT OF MEASURE
				THIS ORDER HAS BEEN ELECTRONICALLY TRANSMITTED						
				THIS IS A CONFIRMING ORDER – DO NOT DUPLICATE						
00001	125	654321	WIDGET 1	DESCRIPTION LINE 1 DESCRIPTION LINE 2		03/12/92	D 0.00%	ADVISE PRICE		BOX
				ACCT: 7000 05400		01				
00002	50.50	987661	PLASTIC GEM	DESCRIPTION LINE 1 DESCRIPTION LINE 2 DESCRIPTION LINE 3		03/12/92	F 100.00%	9.8800	1	LB
				ACCT: 7000 05400		01				

Document 3-4. (*continued*)

850 PURCHASE ORDER TRANSACTION

PURCHASE ORDER: ABRO1500

EDI FORMAT

ANSI VERSION 2 RELEASE 1

SEGMENTS/DATA ELEMENTS

```
ST*850*1005 N/L
BEG*06*SA*ABRO1500***920228 N/L
FOB*DF*****DE*OUR PLANT N/L
N1*SE*WXYZ COMPANY*1*123456789 N/L
N3*555 VENDOR LANE N/L
N4*FLINT*MI*48557 N/L
N1*BY*ABC COMPANY*92*05099PO1 N/L
N3*850 STEPHENSON HWY. N/L
N4*TROY*MI*48077 N/L
PER*BD*JOHN DOE*TE*313-578-4926 N/L
N1*ST*ABC COMPANY*92*05099S01 N/L
N3*1962 14 MILE ROAD N/L
N4*TROY*MI*48077 N/L
N1*BT*ABC COMPANY*92*05099I01 N/L
N3*67802 RACINE N/L
N4*WARREN*MI*48089 N/L
ITD*ZZ*3*1.00**999********10TH PROX N/L
TD5*O****UNITED PARCEL N/L
PO1*000001*125.00*BX***IN*654321 N/L
J2X***WIDGET 1    DESCRIPTION LINE 1 N/L
J2X***            DESCRIPTION LINE 2 N/L
NTE*LIN*TAX CODE: D    TAX PERCENT: 0.00% N/L
PO3*ZZ*****125.00*BX*ADVISE PRICE N/L
SCH*125.00*BX****002*920312 N/L
PO1*000002*50.50*LB*9.8800**IN*987661 N/L
J2X***PLASTIC GEM    DESCRIPTION LINE 1 N/L
J2X***            DESCRIPTION LINE 2 N/L
J2X***            DESCRIPTION LINE 3 N/L
NTE*LIN*TAX CODE: F    TAX PERCENT: 100.00% N/L:
SCH*50.50*LB****002*920312 N/L
CTT*2*175.50 N/L
SE*32*1005 N/L
```

NOTES: DATA ELEMENT SEPARATOR ASTERISK (*) IS USED WITHIN EACH SEGMENT.

NEW LINE CHARACTER "N/L" IS USED AT THE END OF EACH SEGMENT.

4

Sale by Documentary Draft

§4.1 CASH AGAINST DOCUMENTS

While the open account sale of Chapter 3 is the most common setting for sales between merchants, sellers have devised a number of ways to protect themselves against the uncreditworthy buyer. The first and easiest form of protection is for the seller to insist on payment in advance. Sellers who do not have confidence in a buyer can ask for a down payment or for a lump-sum cash payment against which the buyer's purchases will be charged. Down payments are not uncommon when merchants sell on credit to consumers, and some professional providers of services, such as lawyers, will require new accounts to pay a retainer in advance of rendering any services. Some sellers will ship C.O.D., that is, cash on delivery.

All of these methods entail risk on the part of the buyer that he may be unwilling to assume. Any buyer that pays for goods or services before delivery runs the serious risk of seller insolvency or nonperformance. In fact, it is safe to say that in most sale-of-goods transactions few professional buyers will ever pay in advance, and a transaction in which that practice appears may be an instance of fraud or other commercially baleful conduct. Sometimes prepayment is an attempt by the buyer to finance his seller, and in that case, the buyer is probably a lender attempting to take a security interest in goods and perhaps also attempting to hide it. In these circumstances, the **prepaying buyer** should be considered a secured lender

Figure 4-1.   Documentary Draft Transaction

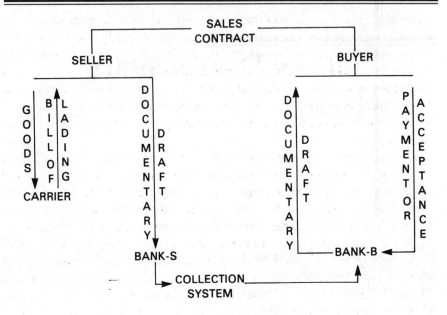

subject to the rules of Article 9, which are not hospitable to hidden security interests.

In order to avoid the risks and baleful commercial effects of prepayment, most buyers who confront a seller's unwillingness to ship on open account will suggest a sale for cash against documents or some variation thereof. Under this arrangement, which is illustrated in Figure 4-1, the buyer can assure himself with reasonable certainty before payment that the goods have in fact been shipped and that when they arrive in the buyer's city the carrier will deliver them.

§4.2 THE DOCUMENTS

Formerly, in the domestic sale and, today, in most international sales, two documents are necessary for the **documentary draft** transaction. The first is a negotiable **document of title** called an order **bill of lading**. Document 32-2 is a standard form order bill of lading.

The seller obtains the order bill from a common carrier, fills it out, and tenders it to the carrier along with the goods. The carrier then executes the bill, returns it to the seller (the "shipper" in transport language), and dispatches the goods to the buyer's city. Note that under the order bill, the carrier will deliver the goods only to the holder of the bill. Any delivery to another person is a violation of the carrier's obligation under the bill and under federal and state laws that govern bills of lading. Thus, when the seller's agent asks the buyer to pay against delivery of the bill, the buyer can rely on that obligation and can generally assume that if it has possession of the order bill, it will obtain delivery of the goods when they arrive at the destination specified in the bill. It is fair to say that a negotiable document of title stands for the goods themselves, which are "mere shadows" as long as the bill is outstanding. Chapter 32 discusses in more detail negotiable bills and the concept of **negotiability** for documents of title.

There is one important caveat for buyers and their lawyers who use order bills of lading. Merchandise is often shipped in cartons or other packaging, and even bulk cargo may be shipped in containers that are loaded at the seller's facility and remain sealed until they arrive at the buyer's facility. The containerization of shipments has done much to reduce pilferage and damage to cargo. It makes no sense to lose the efficiencies that are achieved by shipping in such fashion by insisting that carriers open the packages or containers to inspect the goods. Bills of lading traditionally contain disclaimers by the carrier concerning the contents of the packages. If the bill contains such a disclaimer, and it usually does, buyers generally do not rely and should not rely on the carrier's obligation to deliver goods that conform to the description in the underlying transaction or even in the bill of lading. Buyers who are concerned about the integrity of the seller or otherwise about the conformity of the goods should engage an independent inspector and should not pay against the bill of lading unless the inspector's certificate indicates that the goods conform.

In most domestic transactions, parties no longer use the negotiable bill of lading. While there are distinct advantages to the negotiable bill, primarily that the carrier will deliver only to the holder of it, there are disadvantages too. First, since it stands for the goods, if it becomes lost, the carrier will insist on indemnity (a **bond** of some kind) before it will release the goods. Second, because of the risk of losing the bill, the parties do not send it through the mail but use the bank collection chain. Indemnities and bank collection services cost money and increase the **transaction costs** for buyers and sellers. Third, goods transported by truck or air often arrive before the bill. In that case, someone must store the merchandise until the bill does arrive or must buy a bond. If the buyer is willing to trust the seller, it will pay the seller upon receipt of a nonnegotiable or "straight" bill of lading. Document 4-1 is a straight bill.

This straight bill does not stand for the goods, and there is a risk that the dishonest seller will stop delivery or redirect a shipment after the buyer pays in reliance on the straight bill as evidence that the goods have been "consigned" to it. The straight bill and the law governing it make it proper for the carrier to deliver the goods according to the seller's instructions after the bill issues and contrary to the original terms of the bill. Any buyer unwilling to trust the seller must insist on a negotiable bill.

In addition to the document of title, be it negotiable or nonnegotiable, the documentary draft transaction calls for a **draft**. Document 4-2 is a sight draft. This instrument is generally in negotiable form, i.e., is "bankable," so that the banks that collect it will be holders in due course and take it free of the underlying transaction's commercial equities. The draft is an order, similar to a check, reciting the seller's directions to the buyer. The seller is the drawer of the draft. He gives the order to the buyer (the drawee) demanding that the buyer pay the purchase price of the goods.

Drafts may be payable at sight, that is, on demand, or they may be credit instruments that are payable a specified period of time after a specified date or after sight. Sometimes sellers and buyers agree that the buyer must pay 30 days after the buyer receives the bill of lading — "30 days after sight" — or that the buyer must pay 30 days after the goods are shipped — "30 days after bill of lading date." Document 4-3 is a time draft, sometimes called a *usance draft*. It is payable at "90 days' sight," i.e., 90 days after the presenter **presents** it to the buyer for acceptance.

Sight drafts are payable on presentation, and the refusal of the drawee to pay the draft constitutes dishonor. Some time drafts, such as Document 4-3, are payable a number of days (30, 60, or 90 are common periods) after sight, that is, after the instrument is presented to the buyer, or a number of days after date. Time drafts are not payable until the time specified, e.g., 30 days after sight, but they are presented to the drawee for "**acceptance**" as soon as possible after they issue. The drawee (here, the buyer) accepts the draft by executing it on its face and dating the acceptance.

§4.3 MECHANICS OF THE TRANSACTION

In order to provide the buyer and the seller with the full protection of the documentary draft sales transaction, the parties will use the negotiable bill of lading and a negotiable draft, payable either at sight or at a given time, as the underlying contract stipulates. If the underlying contract provides for credit terms, the draft will be a time draft; if it calls for cash against documents, the parties will use a sight draft. If a seller in Detroit and a buyer in Fresno have entered into a contract for the sale of goods, payment against documents, the parties will proceed with the following steps.

First, the seller will prepare the goods for shipment and fill out the negotiable bill of lading form supplied by the carrier. Next, the seller (the shipper) will deliver the goods to the carrier and the carrier's agent will sign the bill and issue it to the seller's order. The seller will then indorse the bill of lading on its back and will draw a negotiable draft on the buyer for the amount of the contract purchase price. At that point the seller has created a documentary draft: the draft with the negotiable bill attached.

Second, the seller will take the draft and the bill to a financial institution in Detroit, probably the bank with whom she does business, and will ask the bank to collect the draft. The bank will give the seller provisional credit and often will let the seller draw on the credit. The bank feels safe in doing so (1) because it will require the seller to indorse the draft, so that if the buyer dishonors, the bank is a holder and the seller is liable to it in the seller's capacity as drawer and as indorser; (2) because the bank holds the negotiable bill of lading, which stands for the goods, to which the bank will have resort if the buyer dishonors and the seller defaults on her obligation to reimburse the bank in the event of dishonor; and (3) because often the seller is a valued customer of the bank whose drafts are invariably honored by buyers or invariably made good by the seller in the event the buyers do not honor.

Third, the Detroit bank will forward the documentary draft through the bank collection system to a bank in Fresno. The Fresno bank will notify the buyer that the draft and bill have arrived and will present the draft and ask the buyer to honor it. That presentation may be effected by calling the buyer and telling him the draft and bill of lading are at the Fresno bank. Recall that if the draft is a sight draft, the buyer honors it by paying the face amount. If it is a time draft, the buyer honors it by accepting the draft (signing its face), thereby creating a **trade acceptance**. The buyer later pays the face amount of the acceptance to the holder of it at maturity.

Fourth, upon the buyer's payment of the sight draft or acceptance of the time draft, the Fresno bank will surrender the properly indorsed bill of lading to the buyer, who will then hold a document that stands for the goods and who will be in a position to claim the goods from the carrier when they arrive in Fresno.

Note that the buyer achieves considerable protection under the negotiable bill. He has not paid for the goods in advance, even if the draft is a sight draft, since delivery of the bill to him, which is contemporaneous with his payment of the sight draft or acceptance of the time draft, is the virtual equivalent of delivery of the goods. At that point, the carrier will hold the goods for the buyer, not the seller. The carrier is the agent of the party holding the bill.

There are considerable transaction costs in the documentary draft sale. Many sellers are unwilling to pay those costs and find it more efficient to risk that the buyer will not pay. In domestic sales, the documentary draft transaction has largely fallen into disuse. In international commerce or in those cases where the value of the goods is high (e.g., the shipment of a super tanker of petrochemicals) the parties will pay the documentary draft transaction's costs and may incur even greater costs under the letter-of-credit variation of the documentary draft sale, which is described in the next section.

Note, however, that there are also some efficiencies in the documentary draft sale. Because the Detroit bank will make an advance against the seller's draft when she takes it to the bank for collection, the seller receives funds more quickly than she would under the open account sale. Note also that if insolvency or lack of interest prompts the buyer to dishonor the draft, the seller will still have control of the goods, since the Fresno bank will not surrender the bill of lading to the buyer that dishonors the draft. (Dishonor occurs upon one of three failures of the buyer: (1) failure to accept a time draft upon presentment for acceptance; (2) failure to pay a time draft upon maturity; or (3) failure to pay a sight draft upon presentment.) In the event of dishonor, the Fresno bank will notify the Detroit bank, which in turn will notify the seller to provide instructions for disposal of the goods. The seller can order the sale of the goods in Fresno, can direct their shipment elsewhere, or can ask that the goods be returned to Detroit. None of those choices are happy for the seller, since they inevitably result in increased sales costs and probably a sale at a price below the contract price; but all of the choices are better than having the buyer with the goods and the seller with no purchase price — the result that will obtain if the seller sells on open account to a buyer that does not pay the invoice. By the same token, the documentary draft sale protects the buyer, since he does not have to advance funds before he gets the bill of lading, which stands for the goods.

The documentary sale also facilitates the financing of the sale. Sometimes the buyer is a middleman that is going to resell the goods promptly. He needs financing during the brief period between the time he receives the goods and the time he receives payment from his subpurchaser. During that brief period, which might be 45 or 60 days, the buyer can avoid having to pay cash to anyone by bargaining with the seller for a documentary sale that involves a time draft. By negotiating for a sales contract that calls for a time draft due 60 days after sight, for example, the buyer can accept the draft (sign it on its face) and not have to come up with the cash to pay it until after the subpurchaser has paid the buyer.

At the same time, the seller achieves significant credit advantages from the documentary sale. Even when the draft calls for payment 60 days after sight, the Detroit bank will usually be willing to advance funds to the seller, less a discount for interest. The bank's willingness is increased by the fact that the draft is going to be accepted by the buyer. That acceptance renders the buyer liable on the instrument to the holder. If the seller is a small automobile parts manufacturer and the buyer is a General Motors Corporation facility in Fresno, the value of the trade acceptance goes up substantially upon the buyer's acceptance of it. In fact, such acceptances are attractive money-market instruments. Institutional investors often buy them for short periods if the interest yields are attractive.

By virtue of this feature of trade acceptances, banks themselves find them attractive, since there is a ready market for some of them in the event the bank wants to **liquidate** its investment in the trade acceptance in order to raise cash.

§4.4 LETTER OF CREDIT VARIATION

There is one gaping flaw in the documentary draft transaction. There is no way for the seller to insulate itself against the possibility that the buyer will dishonor the draft by refusing to accept or pay a time draft or refusing to pay a sight draft. In virtually all cases, that dishonor raises serious problems for the seller, and in some cases it has disastrous consequences. If, for example, the seller specially manufactures the goods for the buyer, or if the sale is international, the buyer's dishonor of the draft leaves the seller in a predicament. If it has specially manufactured goods for the buyer's unique requirements, the seller may not be able to find any buyer and will have to sell the merchandise for scrap. In international sales, if the buyer dishonors the draft, the seller will have goods in a distant market with which it may be entirely unfamiliar but in which it must dispose of the merchandise, often at distressed prices, the cost of returning them to the seller often being too great.

The commercial letter of credit is the obvious answer to the seller's problems, and by fashioning the transaction carefully, the parties can also achieve added protection for the buyer. Chapter 5 explains the use of the commercial letter of credit.

Document 4-1.   Straight Bill of Lading

Form 35-643 Printed and Sold by *UNZCO* 190 Baldwin Ave., Jersey City, NJ 07306 • (800) 631-3098 • (201) 795-5400

STRAIGHT BILL OF LADING—SHORT FORM—ORIGINAL—NOT NEGOTIABLE

RECEIVED, subject to the classifications and tariffs in effect on the date of the issue of this Bill of Lading, the property described above in apparent good order, except as noted (contents and condition of contents of packages unknown), marked, consigned, and destined as indicated above which said carrier (the word carrier being understood throughout this contract as meaning any person or corporation in possession of the property under the contract) agrees to carry to its usual place of delivery at said destination, if on its route, otherwise to deliver to another carrier on the route to said destination. It is mutually agreed as to each carrier of all or any of said property over all or any portion of said route to destination and as to each party at any time interested in all or any said property, that every service to be performed hereunder shall be subject to all the bill of lading terms and conditions in the governing classification on the date of shipment.

Shipper hereby certifies that he is familiar with all the bill of lading terms and conditions in the governing classification and the said terms and conditions are hereby agreed to by the shipper and accepted for himself and his assigns.

From _____

At _____ 19 ___ BY TRUCK ☐   FREIGHT ☐   Shipper's No. _____

DESIGNATE WITH AN (X)

Carrier _____ Agent's No. _____

(Mail or street address of consignee—For purposes of notification only.)

Consigned to _____

Destination _____ State of _____ County of _____

Route _____

Delivering Carrier _____ Vehicle or Car Initial _____ No. _____

No. Packages	Kind of Package, Description of Articles, Special Marks, and Exceptions	*Weight (Sub. to Cor.)	Class or Rate	Check Column	
					Subject to Section 7 of conditions of applicable bill of lading, if this shipment is to be delivered to the consignee without recourse on the consignor, the consignor shall sign the following statement: The carrier shall not make delivery of this shipment without payment of freight and all other lawful charges.
					Per _____ (Signature of Consignor.)
					If charges are to be prepaid, write or stamp here, "To be Prepaid."
					Received $ _____ to apply in prepayment of the charges on the property described hereon.
					Agent or Cashier
					Per _____ (The signature here acknowledges only the amount prepaid.)
					Charges Advanced:
					C.O.D. SHIPMENT Prepaid ☐ Collect ☐ $ _____ Collection Fee _____ Total Charges _____
					*If the shipment moves between two ports by a carrier by water, the law requires that the bill of lading shall state whether it is "Carrier's or Shipper's weight."
					†Shipper's imprint in lieu of stamp; not a part of bill of lading approved by the Department of Transportation.
					NOTE—Where the rate is dependent on value, shippers are required to state specifically in writing the agreed or declared value of the property.
					THIS SHIPMENT IS CORRECTLY DESCRIBED. CORRECT WEIGHT IS _____ LBS.
TOTAL PIECES					Subject to verification by the Respective Weighing and Inspection Bureau According to Agreement. Per _____

† The fibre containers used for this shipment conform to the specifications set forth in the box maker's certificate thereon, and all other requirements of Rule 41 of the Uniform Freight Classification and Rule 5 of the National Motor Freight Classification. †Shipper's imprint in lieu of stamp, not a part of bill of lading approved by the Interstate Commerce Commission.

If lower charges result, the agreed or declared value of the within described containers is hereby specifically stated to be not exceeding 50 cents per pound per article.

_____ Shipper, Per _____

_____ Agent, Per _____

Permanent post-office address of shipper

This is to certify that the above-named materials are properly classified, described, packaged, marked and labeled and are in proper condition for transportation according to the applicable regulations of the Department of Transportation. _____ SIGNATURE

Reprinted with the permission of Unz & Co., 700 Central Ave., New Providence, NJ 07974-1139.

Bank of America

Bill of Exchange

Place of Drawing

No.

Date

At ------------------- Sight Of This Bill Of Exchange

Pay To The Order Of

Value Received And Charge To Account Of

To

Drawer

At

Authorized Signature

FX-200   2-94   Bank of America   *(Reprint 5-94)

SPECIMEN

COPY

37

Bill of Exchange

Bank of America

Place of Drawing _____

Pay To The Order Of _____

Date _____

No. _____

At Ninety Days' Sight Of This Bill Of Exchange

Value Received And Charge To Account Of _____

To _____

Drawer

At _____

Authorized Signature

FX-200 2-94 Bank of America (Reprint 5-94)

COPY

SPECIMEN

5

Sale by Commercial Letter of Credit

§5.1 THE SETTING

There are circumstances in which the buyer and the seller are not willing to enter into the open account sale described in Chapter 3. The open account sale rests on a number of assumptions, not the least of which is that the seller has access to reliable credit information about the buyer. In addition, the open account seller assumes that the buyer values his credit rating. There is a measure of self help in the open account setting, for the disappointed seller can pressure her defaulting buyer. Open account buyers are aware that they risk much in defaulting on an open account obligation: They may jeopardize their all-important credit rating. In the event a buyer does default on his current obligations, he runs the risk that other open account sellers, having learned through credit reporting services of the default history, will not extend him credit. Such an eventuality can cause the demise of the buyer's enterprise, so important is open account credit to the vast majority of commercial buyers in the domestic economy.

In the international setting and in the event the buyer is an infrequent player in open account sales, the open account seller's assumptions may not be valid. First, there may not be reliable credit information on buyers in Portugal, Singapore, or Zimbabwe. The buyer may have a poor credit history, but the seller may not be able to learn of it or may not be able to learn of it without expensive credit inquiry. Second, the buyer may be a fictitious entity — a fact that the seller cannot discern easily or inexpensively without reliable credit reporting agencies. Third, the buyer may be a new entrant with little creditworthiness, not having established itself as an enterprise that will pay its debts. Fourth, the buyer may be situated in a country undergoing political turmoil. In short, there are a number of situations in which the seller cannot rely on credit reports, and if the seller cannot rely on the credit report, it is reluctant to sell on open account.

This discussion is not to suggest that there is no reliable international credit reporting. In fact, there is; and open account selling in well-established trading situations is growing. Yet, there are always new entrants, and there are always markets in political turmoil. Twenty years ago, trade with agencies of the Soviet Union were about as stable as international trade could be. Trade with entrepreneurs in Russia today is about as volatile as trade can get.

The failure of credit reporting in the international setting, in cases of new entities' entering the trade and in areas of political and commercial upheaval, should not prevent sellers from making sales to many buyers who do in fact have the financial resources to pay for goods, as many new entrants and many buyers in Portugal, Singapore, Zimbabwe, and Russia do. The seller who refuses to sell to these accounts will lose sales and profits. The fact is that these buyers are known to their banks, and to the extent the buyer can substitute the known credit of its bank for its own unknown credit and to the extent that bank is creditworthy or can itself use the services of a credit worthy bank, the buyer may be able to satisfy the seller. The commercial letter of credit is the device merchants and bankers have invented to cover these situations.

§5.2 THE PARTIES

In the simplest commercial letter of credit there are only three parties. The buyer, whom merchants and bankers variously call the account party (i.e., the one for whose account the credit is issued), the customer (i.e., the customer of the issuer of the credit), or the applicant (i.e., the party that applies for the letter of credit), asks a strong financial institution, usually its bank, to issue a credit in favor of the seller, the beneficiary of the credit. Figure 5-1 illustrates this simple commercial letter of credit.

In most international letter of credit transactions, the issuer opens the credit by **telex** or by the SWIFT network, as the next section explains. The telex is a common method of international communication that replaced the telegram. A telegram relies on the translation of a telegraph operator to render the message readable. A telex message, however, arrives at the receiver's place of business where a telex machine reads the signals emanating from the sender's place of business and automatically

Figure 5-1. Commercial Letter-of-Credit Transaction

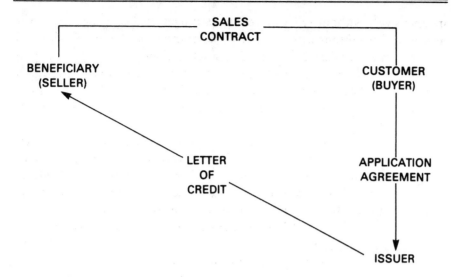

prints the message on paper stored in the machine. A telex machine with enough paper can read a night's or weekend's worth of traffic with no difficulty. The telex system is cheap and quick, but it is now being replaced by electronic data interchange (EDI). Under EDI, which is even quicker and cheaper than telex, computerized messages are transmitted globally at lightning speed and very little cost. Chapter 28 explains the use of this technology in international payments systems. Banks issuing international letters of credit now prefer the SWIFT network and the EDI technology to the telex.

In most transactions involving the international sale of goods, the parties use the services of a second financial institution, usually a commercial bank in the seller's market, to advise or confirm the letter of credit. The appearance in the transaction of this second bank, the advising bank (**adviser**) or the confirming bank (**confirmer**), facilitates the seller's use of the credit. Commercial letters of credit call for the presentation of certain documents on or before the letter of credit's expiry. It is problematic for a seller in Houston, for example, to present documents at a bank in the buyer's city, say, London. The documents may be lost or mangled in the mail, or one of the documents might contain an error or fail to bear a signature or a critical date. With a bank in its own market, the seller can submit its documents more easily and can submit them early and correct any defects that appear before the credit expires. Figure 5-2 illustrates the traditional four-party commercial letter of credit.

In addition, the issuer of a credit may designate some bank other than itself to honor the credit. The issuer may choose another bank as the *paying bank* (**nominated bank**), for example, when the issuer does not have sufficient amounts of the currency in which the credit is available. A Pakistani bank issuing a credit payable in U.S. dollars to a French seller

Figure 5-2. International Commercial Letter-of-Credit Transaction

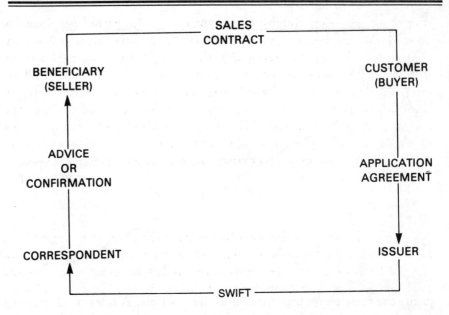

might designate a New York bank as the paying bank, since the New York bank will hold a dollar-denominated account for its Pakistani correspondent.

Often, though less frequently than in former times, the buyer's bank, being perhaps a country bank, has little familiarity with letters of credit. In that case, the buyer's bank will contact its big-city correspondent, a regional or money center bank with an international letter of credit department, that will issue the credit, not on behalf of the buyer alone, whom the issuer does not know, but on behalf of the buyer and the country correspondent, whom the issuer does know.

§5.3 PERFORMANCE OF THE COMMERCIAL CREDIT TRANSACTION

The following nine steps describe the complete performance of a typical commercial credit transaction.

Step 1

In the commercial letter of credit transaction, the first and indispensable act is the creation of a sales contract between a seller and a buyer. This contract is the underlying transaction that the letter of credit serves. Often, much of the activity of the parties is simultaneous, that is, while the buyer and the seller are settling the terms of the sales contract, the buyer is contacting its bank to have the credit issue, and the seller is getting the goods ready for shipment. Sometimes the parties get ahead of themselves. The buyer may cause the credit to issue before it has concluded all of the contract terms with the seller, or the seller may actually ship the goods before it sees the terms of the letter of credit. Lawyers cringe when merchants behave in such fashion, but it is naive to expect the busy merchant to be as concerned with details as lawyers are. The cautious lawyer would probably be an unsuccessful merchant. In any event, the transaction does not always proceed as this section describes it, but for optimal protection, the parties should proceed in this manner.

Step 2

After the buyer and the seller hammer out the terms of the underlying sales contract, the buyer should approach its bank and apply for the commercial letter of credit. The terms of the underlying contract dictate the terms of the credit: the description of the goods, the latest date of shipment, the credit's expiry, the requirement for insurance or inspection certificates, the amount of the credit, whether partial shipments are permitted, the mode of transport, the shipment destination, and so forth. Often these terms are not expressed in the underlying contract of sale but are incorporated into it by industry custom and practice or by course of dealing.

Step 3

The next step in the transaction is taken by the credit issuer, who will communicate via telex or SWIFT the terms of the credit to the advising bank (or confirming bank, as the case may be). The telex is a device that receives signals over telecommunications equipment and translates those signals into letters, spaces, and punctuation. The process requires an operator at the issuing bank to type each letter, space, and punctuation into telex sending equipment. At the advising bank, the receiving equipment then prints out the data that the issuing bank's clerk entered. Often, in telex originated credits, the advising bank copies the telex message and sends it to the seller/beneficiary as an attachment to its advice.

Facsimile equipment avoids the necessity of reentering each character and saves clerical time. Some letters of credit are now issued or advised via facsimile machines.

Since electronic data interchange technology made it possible to establish credits electronically, issuer use of the telex to communicate with the advising or confirming bank has diminished. Today, most international credits are issued via SWIFT, which stands for *Society for Worldwide Interbank Financial Telecommunications*, and which permits the parties to use the EDI technology. Under the SWIFT facility, the issuer's clerk enters relatively few keystrokes of coded information into the SWIFT system. The SWIFT computer translates that information into a formatted document that appears on the computer terminal of the advising bank. The process saves time and money on each transaction. Because the number of transactions is numerous, the savings to the banking industry and its customers are considerable.

Bank customers that issue credits in volume have resorted to computer technology that permits them to fashion the terms of the credit in-house and transmit it directly to the bank issuer's computers, where the issuer's clerks check it and then transmit it via SWIFT or telex to the foreign advising or confirming bank. Software providers have simplified these operations to the point that they are menu-driven and permit the customer's clerks to use either touch screen, keyboard, or mouse to fill in blanks that the software then translates into data that can be used in the bank issuer's telecommunications network.

Step 4

After it receives the telex or SWIFT message, the advising or confirming bank (the documents in this section assume that the correspondent will only advise the credit) will send the credit advice to the seller. Document 5-1 illustrates an advice.

Step 5

After it receives the advice, the seller-beneficiary should compare the terms of the credit with the terms of the underlying contract. Sometimes the advice will impose conditions that the underlying contract does not address. Industry practices may make those terms reasonable, but the seller should review the advice carefully to determine that it only contains terms with which the seller can comply. If there are any problems, the seller must insist at this point that the buyer and the issuer amend the credit, so that the terms of the credit do comply with the terms of the sales agreement and do not contain conditions that it is impossible for the seller to satisfy. Such an amendment will originate from the issuing bank and be advised by the advising bank to the seller.

Step 6

Once the credit is in order, the seller can begin its performance without risk. Note that the seller must act promptly, since the credit usually has a short expiry and often contains dates relating to the time within which the goods must be shipped or the bill of lading must be issued. The first step in the seller's performance is to generate the documents needed to satisfy the credit. The seller's billing department will prepare the invoice in as many copies as the credit requires. Its shipping department will prepare the goods for shipment and will deliver them to the carrier (or to a freight forwarder) and obtain a bill of lading that complies with the terms of the credit. Other agents of the seller, perhaps a freight forwarder or an in-house employee, will obtain the necessary insurance and inspection certificates and other documents. Finally, the seller will draw the all-important draft. Often, the credit will contain a requirement that the draft bear a legend identifying the credit under which it is drawn.

Step 7

After the seller has obtained the necessary documents from third parties and generated those documents that are prepared by its own personnel, the seller is ready to initiate presentation of the documents to the paying bank. The paying bank in this example is the issuer itself, and the seller will commence collection of the draft by taking it and the accompanying documents to a local bank for collection. The seller may take them to the advising bank. In any case, the seller will indorse the draft, and if the seller's credit with the local bank is good, the seller may be able to draw against the provisional credit that the local bank gives it, though there will be charges. If the draft is a time draft with a specified date for payment, the collecting bank may charge the seller by computing the interest until the date of payment and discounting the draft by that amount. In any event, the seller will normally be liable to the collecting bank if the issuer does not honor the draft.

Step 8

The collecting bank will present the draft and accompanying documents to the issuer through customary bank collection channels. Under most credits, which expire on a given date, that presentation must occur on or before the expiry.

Step 9

Once the draft and the documents arrive at the counters of the paying bank, document examiners begin the process of determining whether the presentation satisfies the documentary conditions of the credit. In that process, the examiners use banking industry practices that are codified in the Uniform Customs and Practice for Documentary Credits, a code that is drafted by the Commission on Banking Technique and Practice of the International Chamber of Commerce and is accepted by the international banking organizations of virtually all countries when they expressly incorporate the Uniform Customs into the terms of the credit. If a document appears to be nonconforming, the examiner will take it to a discrepancy clerk. If the clerk agrees that there is a discrepancy, the issuer will usually contact its customer, the buyer, and ask whether the buyer is willing to waive the discrepancy. If the buyer does waive it, as buyers do in a majority of cases, the issuer will honor the beneficiary's draft. If the buyer does not waive the defect, the issuer will promptly notify the presenting bank, which will give that notice to the seller, who will then attempt to cure the defect before the credit expires.

§5.4 DOCUMENTS

Unless the credit is "clean," that is, a credit that calls only for the beneficiary's draft, the credit will contain rather explicit terms relating to the documents that the paying bank must have before it will honor the beneficiary's draft. These documents are similar to the documents that a buyer will request in the documentary draft transaction that is the subject of Chapter 4, but the letter of credit transaction is usually more complicated and entails greater documentation than the documentary sale. Clean credits arise rarely in the commercial credit transaction and only a little more frequently in the standby credit transaction that is discussed in Section 3.5.

Invoice

The seller's invoice, sometimes referred to as a *commercial invoice*, presumably to differentiate it from a **pro forma invoice** (*see* Document 36-2), a customs invoice, or other government-regulated document, is a shorthand summary of the underlying sales agreement between the buyer (the applicant) and the seller (the beneficiary). Traditionally, letter-of-credit law puts great store by the description of the goods in the invoice and requires that description to track the description of the goods in the letter of credit. Descriptions of the goods in other documents need not be so precise, so long as they do not vary the description in the credit. An invoice description of goods that refers to them as "imported acrylic yarn" is not sufficient if the credit refers to the goods as "100% acrylic yarn"; nor is an invoice that refers to goods as "woolen knitwears" when the letter of credit described the goods as "ladies sweaters, dresses, pants, and skirts." The careful beneficiary will instruct his billing department that in drafting the invoice description of the goods it is essential to lift the description verbatim from the credit itself. From time to time, in the press of making prompt delivery, sellers will prepare their documents in advance of receiving the credit. They do so at their peril, for it may be too late to recall the invoice when the credit (with a short expiry) arrives containing a description the seller did not anticipate. Document 3-2 is a copy of a commercial invoice.

Bill of Lading

As Chapter 32 explains in more detail, the bill of lading, if it is negotiable, stands for the goods and plays an important role in the documentary sale and in the commercial letter of credit transaction. Courts and lawyers are apt to give it more credit than it deserves. The bill of lading is not a guaranty by the carrier that the goods described in it have, in fact, been shipped. Generally, the bill of lading contains disclaimer language that the law generally, though not without exception, respects. If the buyer is concerned about the contents of the seller's containers, it should insist on an inspection certificate and should expect to pay for it. The fact that inspection certificates are more common in international sales and less in domestic sales should not surprise anyone.

Some bill of lading forms are "on board" forms. Carriers will not issue these bills unless the goods are loaded on board a vessel. Often, bills of lading are in "received for shipment" form. This form merely recites that the carrier has received the goods. Carriers will execute such a bill, which the shipper prepares, upon the shipper's delivery of the goods to the carrier. Remember that the shipper is the seller, not the carrier, in transport parlance. Later, after the goods pass the ship's rail, the shipper resubmits the bill to the carrier's agent, who will affix an on board stamp to the bill and date and sign the stamped language. For the on board stamp to be missing would signal danger, since most insurance coverage does not commence until the goods are loaded on board.

In order to be acceptable to banks and buyers, moreover, a bill of lading should be "clean," that is, it should not contain any notation that the goods or containers are damaged. "Claused" bills are not clean. They are "dirty." Such clauses indicate, for example, that some containers are open or water damaged. Claused bills are another danger signal. Under letter of credit law, unless the credit expressly provides otherwise, a paying bank will not honor a draft accompanied by a claused bill or a "received for shipment" bill that fails to carry a properly signed and dated on board stamp.

Inspection Certificate

The buyer who is unwilling to trust the seller must ask for an inspection certificate. In the underlying transaction, the contract of sale between seller and buyer, the buyer will negotiate a term that specifies that payment will be by letter of credit calling for, among other documents, an inspection certificate. That certificate should specify the name of the inspecting agency and should indicate what the certificate should say. If the credit does not lay out the details of the certificate, the paying bank will accept any certificate, even one signed by the seller, or one saying that the inspector has examined one of 4,000 cartons of goods. In many industries, inspection criteria are standardized, and buyers can rely on the assertion of the inspector that the shipment contains 30,000 bushels of #2 yellow corn, without concern that the inspector may not have examined the corn adequately.

Insurance Certificate

Because under sales law the risk of loss often shifts to the buyer when the goods pass over the ship's rail, it is not only important that the bill of lading indicate that the goods are on board, it is also important that the buyer know that the goods are insured at that point. The insurance certificate is generally sufficient proof of that coverage, and most buyers under commercial letters of credit will require an insurance certificate unless they have some kind of broad insurance coverage that covers off-premises goods that are in transit from sellers.

Certificates of Origin

On occasion, a buyer may be concerned about the origin of goods that he is purchasing. He may, for example, be concerned about the quality of goods and not want the seller to supply it with goods that are manufactured in countries that do not have adequate standards for product quality or safety. In such cases, a certificate of origin is appropriate and may be called for in the credit. In other cases, certificates of origin may be utilized as devices to further politically motivated boycotts of a country's products. United States law generally renders it unlawful to participate in such boycotts against countries friendly to the United States. Banks and merchants must take care that they do not run afoul of these laws, which carry heavy fines.

Other Documents

It would be futile to attempt to set out in any book all of the certificates and documents that might arise in a commercial letter of credit transaction. Suffice it to say that the only limit on the documents that may arise is the imagination of the merchants and bankers that use commercial credits. There are a number of documents in addition to those described above that appear in the commercial letter of credit transaction with some frequency. Countries that have enacted foreign exchange laws or import regulations often use letters of credit to monitor the payment of currency out of the country and the importation of goods that may compete with domestic producers. These countries frequently require "customized" or "consularized" invoices or other documents. Those terms refer to the need for a customs or consular official to sign and stamp the document in question.

Often, letters of credit will refer to the need for a document to be "countersigned." That language requires the beneficiary of the credit to obtain the signature of some party on a document other than the party that issues the document or other than the party whose signature one would expect to find on the document. For example, if the credit calls for a commercial invoice "countersigned by the purchasing vice president of the buyer," the seller must present the paying bank with a copy of the invoice containing that signature. Note that such a requirement puts the seller-beneficiary at the buyer's mercy. If the vice president refuses to countersign the invoice, the seller cannot comply with the terms of the credit and will not get paid under it. Courts have indicated that they will order a buyer to countersign a document if the refusal is arbitrary and if the buyer does not have the right arbitrarily to refuse to countersign, but the time it takes to obtain such an order probably will run beyond the expiry of the credit. Remember that the credit is not the obligation of the buyer. It is the obligation of the bank issuer, and the courts have generally refused to reform a credit after a bank issues it. The documents are critical, therefore, and the seller beneficiary must be concerned with them. The common practice of submitting documents that do not conform with the credit's terms or of shipping goods before the seller receives the credit and knows its terms are dangerous. True, in most cases, buyers act in good faith and waive documentary discrepancies, but sometimes they do not, and bank document examiners are not in a position to waive discrepancies. They do not know enough about the underlying transaction to make the decision that a discrepancy is immaterial.

Document 5-1. Advice of Credit

 **Bank of America**

PAGE: 1

DATE:

ADVICE OF IRREVOCABLE DOCUMENTARY CREDIT

ISSUING BANK'S NUMBER:
OUR REFERENCE NUMBER:

ISSUING BANK

BENEFICIARY   APPLICANT

AMOUNT

EXPIRATION
                                        1996 OUR COUNTERS

AT THE REQUEST OF OUR CORRESPONDENT, WE HEREBY ADVISE THE ATTACHED
DOCUMENTARY CREDIT.

THIS CREDIT IS NOT CONFIRMED BY US AND THEREFORE CARRIES NO ENGAGEMENT ON
OUR PART.

DRAFT (IF REQUIRED) TOGETHER WITH THE DOCUMENTS MAY BE PRESENTED TO ANY
OF THE LOCATIONS SPECIFIED ON THE ENCLOSED FLYER.

THE ORIGINAL LETTER OF CREDIT (OPERATIVE CREDIT INSTRUMENT) MUST BE
SUBMITTED WITH EACH PRESENTATION OF DOCUMENTS. ADDITIONALLY, PLEASE
PROVIDE ONE COPY OF THE COMMERCIAL INVOICE FOR OUR FILES.

AN ADDITIONAL HANDLING FEE OF USD 75.00 WILL BE DEDUCTED FROM PROCEEDS
FOR DOCUMENTS PRESENTED WITH DISCREPANCIES.

SHOULD PAYMENT BE EFFECTED BY WIRE TRANSFER OR CHECK, A USD 35.00
HANDLING FEE WILL BE DEDUCTED FROM PROCEEDS.

SHOULD ANY OF THE TERMS OF THE CREDIT BE UNACCEPTABLE TO YOU, PLEASE
CONTACT YOUR CUSTOMER SO THEY CAN INSTRUCT THE ISSUING BANK TO AMEND THE
CREDIT.

IF YOU REQUIRE ANY ASSISTANCE OR HAVE ANY QUESTIONS REGARDING THIS
TRANSACTION, PLEASE CALL

BANK OF AMERICA NT & SA

AUTHORIZED SIGNATURE

Bank of America NT&SA Trade Operations Center 5655
333 South Beaudry Avenue, 19th Flr., Los Angeles, CA 90017
CABLE ADDRESS: Telex MCI 67652 BANKAMER SFO • SWIFT ADDRESS BOFAUS6S   (Reprint 3-96)   CORR-1041A 10-95

♻ Recycled Paper

6

Consigments and the Like

§6.1 THE BRIGHT IDEA

We do not know how property concepts evolved, but we suppose that at times "might made right" and that the person with the biggest fist or the biggest band of followers got the buffalo carcass when a dispute arose over such matters, just as that "rule" of property sometimes obtains today. At other times, kings or other rulers owned all or virtually all of the valuable property in a society. In some societies, no one owned anything, all property being owned in common and being available for those who needed or took it; in still others the tribal chieftain allocated property among the tribe's members, fairly or unfairly. Those legal systems for allocating resources have generally not survived in today's world, which tends to regard a system of personal property as more efficient or at least tending to cause less unrest and resentment than the older systems.

Eventually, any society works out one system or another for allocating property on its notions of fairness or efficiency. Schoolyard societies reflect the notion that possession connotes ownership. "Finders keepers" enjoys a certain amount of success in resolving ownership disputes over marbles. "Possession is nine points of the law" has attracted more than the schoolyard lawyer. Ultimately, many societies opt for notions of title — a purely metaphysical idea that often yields results contrary to the possessory rules of the schoolyard. Title sometimes generates a measure of comfort from lawlessness, the fear that some bully will come along and "steal"

51

(an idea that proceeds from the concept of title) our property. Cases that defend the notion of title often quote an old saw to the effect that "no man may be deprived of his property without his consent."

The success of title as a concept for allocating resources has not usurped the role of possession entirely. The possession rule, that is, the notion that possession connotes title and may even defeat title, is still very much alive, especially in commercial law, as the doctrines of void-able title and some buyer-in-ordinary-course rules suggest.

This discussion is necessary to understand what it is that merchants are doing when they enter into **consignments** and similar transactions. On the surface, when an owner (the consignor) consigns her property to another (the consignee), the parties agree quite simply that the owner does not part with title and has merely created a **bailment,** with the con-signee holding possession of the goods but having no interest other than a possessory interest.

While the law does not really care about such an arrangement insofar as it affects the consignor and the consignee, it should care very much about the effects of the agreement on third parties, such as buyers from and creditors of the consignee. If the consignment theory works, Owner (the consignor) will deliver the goods to Agent (the consignee) as agent. Sales transactions that Agent enters into with third parties will bind Owner only under the rules of agency law. If Agent exceeds his actual authority, under primitive agency rules, the third party takes nothing, since Agent has nothing to give unless he acts within the scope of his agency. Figure 6-1 illustrates the agency sale with the consignee acting as an agent, a conduit. The figure illustrates a quite successful fiction in property law.

Agency law, if its crafters want us to take it seriously, cannot persist with a foolish rule such as this one, and it eventually fashioned *estoppel*

Figure 6-1.   Consignment Fiction

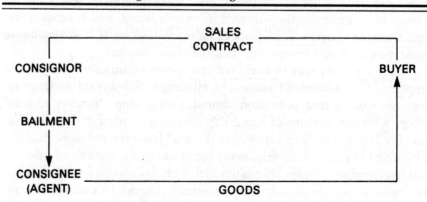

and *apparent authority* inconsistencies to the logically consistent result that an agent cannot give good title to a buyer if the buyer takes from an agent acting outside the scope of his agency. Under the exceptions, the transaction takes the form of Figure 6-2, rather than that in 6-1.

By the same token, property law fashioned exceptions to its title rules. Owner may argue that she never agreed to let Agent sell to Third Party under the terms of the sales contract Agent entered into with Third Party, but the law estops Owner. Lord Ellenborough once observed that "[i]f the owner of a horse send it to a repository of sale, can it be implied that he sent it hither for any other purpose than that of sale?"

During a period when a merchant's wealth often consisted of his stock in trade, many were concerned that consignments served to mislead creditors of the consignee. Owner, a woolen company, for example, would "consign" a large shipment of worsteds to Agent, a **distributor.** Agent's creditors would enter her premises and incorrectly assume that Agent was a solvent, going concern, given the large stock of valuable merchandise in her warehouse. If the fiction of the consignment worked, those creditors might suffer unfairly if they extended credit to Agent on the basis of the false impression her possession of the worsteds produced.

It is probably no longer true to say that creditors rely on a merchant's possession of merchandise, though buyers certainly do. But, the law remains quite chary of the consignment and has developed a number of rules that protect the buyer of goods from the consignee and, importantly, protect the creditors of the consignee. It is probably fair to say that all good-faith buyers from the consignee will defeat the **claim** of the true owner. Creditors of the consignee are not always so successful, though often they prevail. Secured transactions law is quite suspicious of the consignment, which resembles a loan secured by a security interest in inventory.

There remain for consideration in this chapter "true" consignments, that is, consignments that are not disguised secured transactions.

Figure 6-2.   Consignment Reality

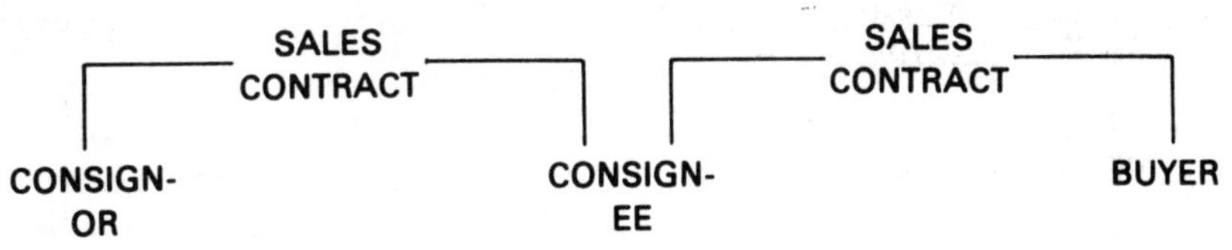

53

§6.2 THE CONSIGNMENT TRANSACTION

In the last century, **factors** (sometimes referred to as "old" factors to distinguish them from the "new" factor, who is basically an account lender and who is the subject of discussion in Chapter 15) would take merchandise or, sometimes, agricultural produce, and move it to markets where it could be sold. A Kentucky tobacco farmer might deliver his tobacco to such a factor, who would take it by river barge to New Orleans and sell it. Earlier in the century and probably for a long time before, merchants in maritime countries would deliver merchandise to ship captains who would take it abroad to trade in various ports.

In order to protect the farmers in the first example and the merchants in the second, the parties resorted to the idea that the delivery to the factor, as the agent came to be called, was a consignment with limits on the transfers of the merchandise that the factor could make. It was long-accepted doctrine, for example, that a factor could sell merchandise entrusted to him but could not pledge it to a lender as security. The world knew that these factors were holding the merchandise of others and had not paid for it, but the world could assume that the factor had the authority to sell the merchandise, such activity being consistent with the common consignment arrangement.

The advent of modern marketing techniques that include instant communication, commodity exchanges, and credit arrangements spelled doom for the old-time factor. Yet, as is so often the case in commercial transactions, where a device that once was an innovation enjoyed something of a heyday and then fell into disuse, but was reinvented or rediscovered, the consignment found new applications. At one time, vagaries in the antitrust laws permitted manufacturers to fix the resale prices of goods their consignees sold to customers. For years, General Electric delivered light bulbs to retail and wholesale establishments on consignment with instructions on the prices to be charged to buyers, who were in theory not the customers of the wholesaler or the retailer but of General Electric. Although the law did not permit a seller to fix resale prices on goods that it "sold," it did permit **resale price maintenance** when the goods were "consigned." Generally, such consignments no longer protect sellers from rules against price fixing, and the use of the consignment for that purpose has not survived as a widespread practice.

Consignments also appear in a few commercially unimportant areas. For example, artists and artisans frequently resort to consignment arrangements under which they entrust their work to a shop or theater for sale. The shopkeeper or theater may post signs indicating that the goods are consigned. The Uniform Commercial Code provides in Article 2 that such "true" consignments must take place in a way that creditors of the consignee will not be misled.

There are a few instances in which consumers or other favorites of the law run afoul of the consignment rules. For example, if a buyer of a mobile home decides she does not want to keep it, she might take it back to the dealer from whom she purchased it and ask the dealer to sell it for her. Although the consumer and the dealer do not think about it and do not say anything to each other about it, both of them assume that the title to the mobile home remains in the consumer and that the dealer is a mere agent for the purposes of arranging the sale for which he will receive some agreed-upon commission. In fact, the arrangement is a consignment, and the consumer may be trapped unfairly when her failure to comply with the rules of Article 2 leave her with a mobile home subject to the claims of the dealer's creditors. The law should probably fashion some exceptions for innocent consumers such as the one in this example, but so far in most jurisdictions no principled exception has emerged.

It is probably fair to say that all consignments are disguised lending arrangements. Even the consumer in the mobile home example and the artist who entrusts his paintings to the summer theater are providing inventory to a business enterprise on credit and retaining title to protect themselves. To the extent that the entruster is a commercial enterprise, the law has no trouble with the characterization: The arrangement is a secured transaction subject to Article 9 of the Uniform Commercial Code. To the extent that the consignor is a nonmerchant, the consequences of permitting him to use the consignment are probably of little commercial significance and should not offend anyone. Such arrangements will probably survive in the consumer and artist situations.

There is one other kind of consignment that has arisen from time to time. In certain industries, some large sellers will consign stock to a **commission merchant** or the like. These merchants travel from market to market much as the old factors did. Generally, they do not use their stock of goods as collateral for loans. In fact, they do not generally borrow from commercial lenders. The commission merchant arrangement, therefore, has generally escaped the attention of the law and its animus against the consignment.

§6.3 LIKE TRANSACTIONS

Sometimes, merchant or consumer sellers will invent other schemes to keep their buyers from obtaining title to the goods that are the subject of their agreement. Most of these inventions have been tried before, and most of them are disguised secured transactions. Some sellers or buyers, for example, have sold merchandise with the understanding that title does not pass to the buyer until the buyer pays. Others use **leases** under which the buyer is designated lessee and the seller lessor. The former reserved title transaction is known as a conditional sale, the latter as a lease-purchase arrangement. Both are disguised secured transactions, and the law is clear that they come within the scope of Article 9 of the Code. That clarity will not prevent some merchant or consumer in the future from fashioning a transaction with such ideas, and sometime, someplace an ill-advised court will accept the argument, and we will have a new device for selling goods without the immediate passage of title.

§6.4 MODERN USEFUL BAILMENTS

While some bailments are nothing more than obvious efforts to avoid secured lending requirements or claims of the bailee's creditors, there remain useful and quite innocent bailment devices. The personal property lease is perhaps the most common. Chapter 9 of this Part discusses leasing as a method of distribution and distinguishes that use of leases from leases as security agreements, which are the subject of Chapter 18 in Part II. The **pledge** is also a useful bailment, since it permits a borrower to use sometimes unique chattels (art work, jewels, and the like) to obtain credit. Chapter 14 in Part II describes this kind of bailment.

Other bailments arise in the manufacturing process. In one case a manufacturer of film discovered that the film was defective and wanted to send it off to a metals processor to remove the film's silver content. The film manufacturer, however, was not disposed to sell the defective film for fear that it might find its way into the market and damage the manufacturer's goodwill. It fashioned, therefore, a bailment arrangement under which the metals processor agreed to hold the film as bailee until the processing was complete. At that time, the processor purchased the recovered silver.

Some manufacturers engage in outsourcing — a method of purchasing manufacturing services. A heavy equipment manufacturer, for example, might want to avail itself of an aluminum fabricator's services. The manufacturer will deliver partially manufactured aluminum parts to the fabricator for one or two steps in the manufacturing process. The fabricator will perform the one or two steps and will then return the parts of the manufacturer for incorporation into the finished goods. In another instance, one food processor with inadequate plant capacity farmed out some of its processing to a competitor. The processor delivered agricultural commodities, cans, cartons, and labels to the competitor, which then processed them into finished product.

With increased activity between U.S. manufacturers and their foreign subsidiaries or independent foreign manufacturers, the practice of **production sharing** has become increasingly common. Production sharing involves exporting partially manufactured goods for further manufacture in a foreign country, usually followed by reimporting the parts or partially manufactured product to the United States. Thus an automobile manufacturer in Tennessee might begin manufacture of an automobile component, export it to Mexico for further manufacture, and import the component to a plant in California for completion of the equipment manufacturing process before the company sells the final product. Sometimes, the U.S. manufacturer completes the manufacturing process in the foreign country and simply imports the goods for resale.

In each of these cases, the parties are bailing goods as part of the purchase of services. Secured transactions lawyers, however, may contend that the arrangements are disguised secured loans. The law is not altogether clear in this area.

Merchants continue to use the bailment as a device to maximize efficiency, but commercial law has been burned by the bailment in the past, and the Code still casts a jaundiced eye on some of these arrangements. The imaginative lawyer, therefore, may find the practices susceptible to characterizations that the parties did not contemplate, and the bailor's lawyer must guard against the eventuality that a court might view a bailment as a disguised sale or a disguised secured transaction.

7 Distribution Arrangements

§7.1 MARKETING THROUGH THIRD PARTIES

Although many sellers to merchant buyers maintain a sales force that solicits accounts and arranges sales through the open account sale described in Chapter 3, many merchant sellers find it necessary to establish a more elaborate sales organization with local distributors, dealers, franchisees, or **wholesalers**. While a giant firm might choose to integrate the distribution function and establish firm-owned distributors and the like, most industries involve independent parties that play important warehousing, warranty service, credit, and delivery functions to the ultimate consumer or to intermediaries as the goods pass from manufacturer to consumer.

§7.2 THE PARTIES

In the simplest distribution arrangement, the manufacturer or other seller of a finished product or commodity will sell directly to the consumer.

Figure 7-1.   Distribution System (Finished Goods)

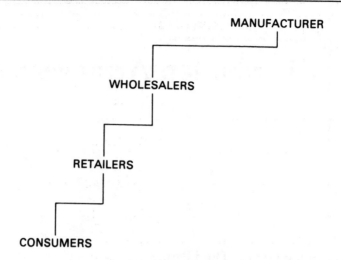

Mail-order houses, retailers, and farm stand operators make **direct sales.** Newspaper publishers, automobile manufacturers, and similar sellers need a distribution system. In a way, even a small parts manufacturer for the automobile industry or a small die and mold company will use an **original equipment manufacturer's** distribution system to move the small manufacturer's product from the manufacturer's plant to the ultimate consumer. In the same way, a raw materials supplier uses a manufacturer's distribution system. If we consider only finished goods, Figure 7-1 illustrates a typical distribution system.

In all probability, however, that finished-goods manufacturer buys parts from **vendors** and raw materials from suppliers, so that Figure 7-2 is a more accurate illustration of the movement of goods through the distribution system.

In fact, vendors and even some raw materials suppliers have received goods from their own vendors or suppliers, sometimes through a distribution chain, so that Figure 7-2 is a simplification of the usually more complicated process of moving goods through the **channel of distribution** from mines and farms to consumer.

It is not possible to describe all distribution systems. It is probably not possible even to know all of them, since merchants are continuously devising new methods of relating to their distributors and new modes of distribution. This chapter describes some common distribution arrangements.

§7.3 DISTRIBUTION THROUGH WHOLESALERS

In a classic wholesale distribution arrangement, the wholesaler performs warehousing and delivery functions for the manufacturer. If a brewery in-

Figure 7-2. Distribution System

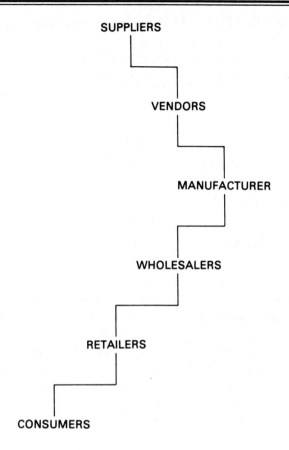

SUPPLIERS

VENDORS

MANUFACTURER

WHOLESALERS

RETAILERS

CONSUMERS

tends to market its products in a city, it needs warehousing facilities to take delivery from the manufacturer, probably at a rail siding; to store the product until retailers, who traditionally have small storage space, can take delivery; and to deliver the product when retailers order it. The investment in warehouse space, trucks, and personnel is considerable, and brewers may well not have the capital or the management needed to operate their own warehouses all over the country or all over the regions in which they market their products. The wholesaler can serve these functions and can save the brewer the cost of building the system.

Note also that the distributor plays a financing role for the brewer. By virtue of the fact that the wholesaler usually pays for product before its customers (the retailers) pay the wholesaler, the wholesaler cuts the period of time during which the brewer must finance inventory. The wholesaler will pay the brewer and finance its own inventory until the retailer pays, thereby shortening the time it takes for the brewer to receive cash for its product and reducing the interest charges that the brewer must pay its inventory lender. The wholesaler pays its bank for financing inventory at the wholesaler's warehouse.

§7.4 DISTRIBUTION THROUGH DEALERS

Dealers usually buy from manufacturers or wholesalers and resell to consumers. The dealer performs some of the same functions that the wholesaler performs. He provides some warehousing, though usually less than a wholesaler, and pays for goods before he receives payment from the consumer. Retailers also expend considerable effort in developing the market through sales promotion and advertising. Dealers may also perform a warranty service function. Customers with warranty complaints return defective products to dealers who service the complaint and charge the manufacturer for the work done. In some industries, such as the automobile industry, where manufacturers are strong, dealers play a key role in the financing of the manufacturer's product. In such an industry, the dealer may pay for the goods before they are delivered and may have to ask a bank to guaranty payment under a letter of credit. Manufacturers with the market strength to exact this kind of arrangement from dealers have an enormous benefit — they incur little credit risk and receive payment promptly, thereby achieving significant cash flow advantages not available to manufacturers in other industries.

In this rather sophisticated dealer arrangement, there is a key player in addition to the dealer and his supplier (the manufacturer). That player is the dealer's financer, often a bank or finance company. Chapter 17 explains in more detail the mechanics of the arrangement, but it is worth noting here that the lender, sometimes called a *floor planner*, is interested not only in lending money to the dealer to buy merchandise from the manufacturer but, often, is more interested in granting credit to the dealer's buyers. The volume of credit from those buyers and the all-important interest charges that the lender will earn on those loans is more significant than the volume of credit and interest on the loans to the dealer itself. A dealer with an inventory loan of $2 million may generate enough credit sales to his customers to give the lender $12 million in consumer paper, which bears interest rates in the range of 13 or 14 percent, compared to the modest 8.5 to 9.5 percent interest on the inventory loan.

Often, manufacturers are big enough to incorporate or acquire their own finance companies to play the lender role. In such a case, the manufacturer will ultimately make a profit on the sale of the automobile to the dealer, on the loan the finance company makes to the dealer to buy the vehicle from the manufacturer, and on the loan the finance company makes to the consumer to buy the car from the dealer.

§7.5 DISTRIBUTION THROUGH FRANCHISEES

Franchising is a very old idea. Whenever a party with a power or a right that he cannot fully exploit himself conveys a part of that power or that right to another, he has, in a sense, created a franchisee. Emperors granted **franchises** to vassals to govern in a given territory; governments sometimes grant franchises to accord privileges or to generate income. Thus the Queen of England once granted a franchise to import playing cards into England. A state might grant a franchise to build a bridge over the Charles River and collect tolls from travelers. Cities have granted franchises to street railways in the past and to cable television companies in the present. This section deals with commercial franchises, that is, franchises between private parties wherein one, the franchisor, gives something of value to another, the franchisee, usually for a fee based on the franchisee's volume of business or on the condition that the franchisee will buy product from the franchisor.

Despite its long history, franchising is the great commercial innovation of the last 30 years, as entrepreneurs adapted it to a host of new industries and, in some cases, used it to create new industries. For a long time, product franchise arrangements have been common, especially in the retail gasoline, automobile dealership, and wholesale soft-drink bottling trades. Under these product franchise arrangements, independent, local operators obtain franchises from national corporations.

The number of these "product" franchises has been declining somewhat, but that decline has witnessed the enormous growth of the "service" franchise, common to the fast-food restaurant, car rental, health spa, and similar industries. The number of product franchises is shrinking, while the number of retail service establishments is growing.

There are a number of features common to any franchise. First is a trade name or trademark. Under the franchise, the franchisee obtains the right to exploit that proprietary interest of the franchisor. Second is the exclusivity feature. Nearly all franchises contain some exclusivity feature, usually a prohibition against the franchisor's granting of additional franchises in a designated territory. Third is the requirement that the franchisee take steps to protect the quality of the franchisor's name or mark. In product franchises, the franchisee is usually restricted to sales of the franchisor's products. In service franchises, the franchisor must provide the franchisee with instructions and training, so that the franchisee will provide the service in a manner that enhances the service mark. The service franchisee may also be required, under the service franchise agreement, to carry the franchisor's products. Frequently, franchisees must engage in a minimum amount of local advertising and promotion and must use signs, uniforms, and even build facilities that comport with the franchisor's marketing schemes.

The franchise agreement's exclusivity provisions vary but usually are geographic in nature. Thus a franchise might provide that the franchisee has the exclusive right to exploit the franchisor's mark or brand in a given town or county, or the agreement might stipulate that the franchisor will not grant any other franchise to a party located within a certain radius of the franchisor's location. Often, franchisors that have trained one franchisee will grant the franchisee additional franchises in a market in order to minimize development costs for the franchisor and enhance the franchisee's return on investment of time and start-up costs. This type of "horizontal" extension of franchising is quite benign. It does not resemble the vertical proliferation of franchising that is evident in pyramid franchising.

Franchising is subject to considerable regulation under state and federal law. The definitions in these laws are not always consistent, and it is sometimes difficult to distinguish distributors and dealers from franchisees. In fact, of course, sometimes distributors and dealers are franchisees.

The franchise serves a number of purposes. First, it permits an entrepreneur with a good idea and some trade secret, trade name, or trademark to exploit the full potential of those trade advantages. Second, it does so without requiring a great deal of capital, since the franchisee, not the franchisor, must finance the local franchise. Third, it permits small business people to launch a business that they own with the advantages of the goodwill of the franchisor's name, mark, or secret. Fourth, it often permits the franchisor to market goods and make a profit on the goods as well as on the fees for the franchise itself.

In a typical product franchise, such as that involving an oil company and a local service station, there may be little control by the franchisor over the franchisee's method of doing business; while in the typical service franchise, such as a fast-food restaurant, the method of doing business is crucial to the protection of the franchisor's name or mark.

A typical service franchise agreement covers such matters as the hours that the franchisee's establishment is open, hiring practices, site selection, and facility design.

In the simplest territorial franchising arrangements, the franchisor is a national or regional organization that licenses retail operations at given locations with territorial restrictions. In a successful franchise operation, there may be as many as 10,000 franchisees. Figure 7-3 illustrates the simple territorial allocation.

In other franchising schemes, the franchisor may allocate large territories to a franchisee with the power in the franchisee to grant sublicenses. The original franchisor may obtain fees from its franchisees based in part on the fees the franchisees receive from their subfranchisees. If there are no limits on the number of franchisees and subfranchisees, a franchise scheme approaches the pyramid model with sub-subfranchisees to varying levels, such as that illustrated in Figure 7-4, a model suggesting that subfranchising and subinfeudation have something in common. Franchising laws and regulations generally prohibit such schemes, which are a classic violation of fairness in franchising and, often, of criminal statutes.

Figure 7-3. Franchise System

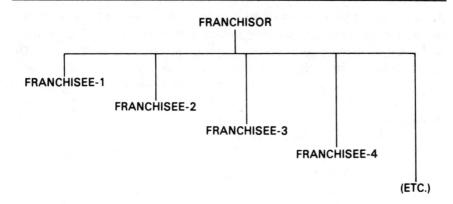

FRANCHISOR

FRANCHISEE-1

FRANCHISEE-2

FRANCHISEE-3

FRANCHISEE-4

(ETC.)

§7.6 DISTRIBUTION THROUGH SALES REPRESENTATIVES

A sales representative customarily takes possession of a manufacturer's or distributor's merchandise and sells it to retailers or consumers. In the simplest arrangement, a salesman, who may represent a number of manufacturers or distributors, either in the same line of products or complementary lines, puts merchandise in the trunk of his car and travels throughout his territory hawking the merchandise. At the other end of the scale is the broker who takes merchandise to the leased premises of a

Figure 7-4. Franchise Pyramid

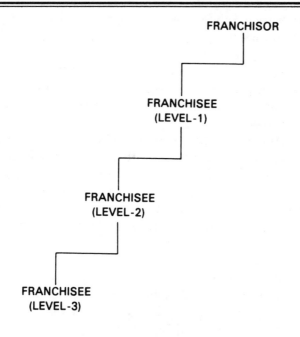

FRANCHISOR

FRANCHISEE
(LEVEL-1)

FRANCHISEE
(LEVEL-2)

FRANCHISEE
(LEVEL-3)

larger retail operation, usually a department store, and sells merchandise to walk-in customers. Often, the salesman who markets out of the trunk of his car has a loose relationship with his supplier, and the delivery of the goods to him is probably a consignment, subject to the problems that arise in consignment selling, problems that have not manifested themselves in this relationship in part because the consignments tend to be small and because the creditors of the broker tend not to rely on his stock in trade. Clearly, this merchandise broker is often at the margin of commercially important transactions. There are times, however, when merchandise brokers handle valuable stock, such as precious gems. Chapter 6 discusses consignments.

In the commercially more important transaction, the merchandise broker will take delivery of significant volumes of merchandise and will have a carefully drawn agreement with her supplier, for whom she acts as broker, and with the store in which she displays and sells the merchandise, the latter agreement being in the nature of a lease.

§7.7 DISTRIBUTION BY LICENSE

To a significant extent, franchise agreements entail licensing provisions that render the franchisee a licensee of a copyright or trademark. There are also licensees who serve as marketers of a licensor's secrets or registered name through licenses that are not franchises.

Patent licenses, for example, grant the licensee the right to make, use, or sell a patented invention. The invention may be a product that comprises a major part of the licensee's business, but more often it is a small part of that business and may be only a component of a small part of the business. Patent licenses may cover the right of an automobile manufacturer to use a piece of equipment on its assembly line, the right of a food processor to use paper bags in which it markets its products, or an earthmoving equipment manufacturer to incorporate a small roller bearing assembly in a road grader.

Sometimes, an inventor grants an exclusive patent, thereby granting to another, usually an organization with a distribution system or a manufacturer that is willing to pay high fees to obtain the patent monopoly, the sole right to exploit the patent. At other times, the inventor or owner of the patent grants nonexclusive patents to a number of licensees, either in a fashion that permits them to exploit the patent in a single territory or market, or as a means of generating license fees, that is, as a means of getting parties to use the patent. Patent licenses can take on many forms.

Frequently, an inventor assigns his rights as inventor to his employer or to another who desires to exploit the invention, and other inventors sometimes assign or even license their application rights.

Sometimes, a licensee has the right to sublicense. Thus a bag manufacturer with the right to manufacture a patented paper bag that it sells to the grain industry might sublicense a bag manufacturer that sells bags to the fertilizer industry.

Trademarks and copyrights are also frequently the subject of license. If, because of limited production capacity or limited distribution capacity, a manufacturer is unable to exploit its mark fully in some markets, it might license manufacturers to make and market products under the trademark. Such arrangements are potentially fatal for the trade name owner. Unless it retains the right to control the quality of the licensee's product, that mark might be significantly diluted to the point that the mark loses its value. Franchisees are often licensees of marks, and franchise agreements usually contain the grant of a license in them and invariably contain stiff requirements designed to protect the quality of the mark. Many licensees, of course, are not franchisees.

Trade secrets sometimes do not meet the requirements of patent, copyright, or trademark law and cannot be protected by registration or patent. In that case, parties that develop the trade secret may attempt to exploit it by contract, that is, by licensing the secret. Those attempts are often perilous, since the very disclosure of the trade secret tends to increase the risk that the cat will get out of the bag, leaving the licensor with nothing to license. Disclosure of secrets is also a problem for licensees, who may feel, after they learn the secrets, that they knew them already or would have learned them in the normal course of business in a short time. Disgruntled employees or former employees of licensors and licensees may destroy the secret intentionally or unintentionally.

Since licenses are, by their nature, anticompetitive, they sometimes run afoul of antitrust laws or other regulatory laws or rules. Parties to such agreements may have to prove to a government official or a jury that the secrets are indeed secret and are not fabricated for the purposes of restricting competition. The transfer of technology, which is the outcome under any trade secret license, is often a carefully regulated matter in third world and even western countries, and licensors may find their licenses unenforceable (and their license fees uncollectible) after disclosure, if a foreign tribunal decides that the information was in the public domain.

Inventors or people with ideas may ask an enterprise to enter into a nondisclosure agreement in advance of disclosure of a secret or invention. Those agreements are potential problems for the enterprise, since the invention or secret may already be in the public domain or may be known to the enterprise. After disclosure, the inventor will argue that any exploitation was a result of her disclosure, and the evidentiary battle is on. It is often difficult for an enterprise to prove that, in fact, it did have the information prior to the disclosure. Such disclosure arrangements are also a problem for the inventor, since she may have a difficult time proving that, in fact, the enterprise did not have knowledge of her invention or secret. Many parties avoid nondisclosure agreements altogether or water them down to the point that the inventor has no protection.

Copyrights protect tangible expressions in books, articles, films, and other reproductions of intellectual work. To a significant extent, a copyright protects the owner against commercial exploitation of the intellectual property by anyone not licensed and permits the owner to exploit the product fully. At times, the owner is not in a position to exploit the product. The author of a short story might grant a nonexclusive license to a magazine to publish the story and later grant an exclusive license to a publisher who tries to have the story published in anthologies or other collections. Studies of economic and social conditions often yield copyrighted material, which can be the subject of license.

§7.8 DISTRIBUTION THROUGH BROKERS

In some industries, sellers do not market their products to the ultimate consumer but store it or continue to use it until a broker finds a purchaser. Brokers differ from many other middlemen in that they do not take possession of the merchandise or real estate that they are attempting to sell. Frequently, brokers underwrite advertising costs and sometimes maintain their own publications with pictures and descriptions of the seller's property. The broker arrangement best known to consumers is the real estate broker, who lists a seller's property and attempts to find a buyer.

Commodity brokers describe their merchandise by industry standards, e.g., "Number 2 yellow corn," "West Texas intermediate crude." These brokers often sell goods that are stored with commercial **bailees** who have issued documents of title covering the commodity. The brokers can then sell the commodity by transferring the document in the fashion that is described in Chapter 4 and in Section 32.3. Some brokers buy occasionally for their own account, but most buy only for their clients. Raw materials sellers and agriculture producers frequently rely on brokers and often do so without any written agreement, it being understood in such arrangements that the broker does not have an exclusive listing and earns his commission only when the seller sells to a buyer.

§7.9 GROUP BUYERS

In industries where some retailers are small, and suppliers diverse, retailers band together for the purpose of saving on transaction costs in their purchases and to obtain quantity discounts. Small hardware outlets and grocery stores that compete with much larger operations have sometimes set up cooperatives or merchandise brokers to do their buying. These arrangements permit the small operator to avoid the cost of contacting all of the small manufacturers or even the large distributors that supply such an operation. Under the arrangements, the cooperative or the broker will contact the various sources of supply, negotiate price terms, contact the local operator to determine his needs and delivery requirements, and place the orders. Usually, the cooperative will not serve any wholesale function, that is, it will not take delivery of the goods but will cause them to be **drop shipped** directly to the local enterprise or will simply give the local operator information and let him place the order directly with the supplier.

§7.10 INVENTORY CONTROL

It is no secret to those who market their goods under the various systems outlined in this chapter that their customers (vendors, manufacturers, wholesalers, franchisees, licensees, and general retailers) strive to keep their inventory levels low. One hundred years ago, credit analysts viewed high inventory levels as a sign of fiscal strength. Today, such high levels often reflect weakness in an account. In the last century, inventory carrying costs, the interest that an enterprise paid its bank for inventory loans, were either nonexistent or low. Formerly, most enterprises did not borrow on inventory but used capital to buy it; and in the event they did borrow to finance the enterprise's acquisition of inventory, they were able to borrow that money at low rates.

Today, of course, the elimination of carrying charges is often critical. Cash managers know that small profit margins will disappear when inventory carrying costs are high. Thus efficiencies realized by a firm's competitors require it to reduce inventory carrying costs or face the inability to meet price competition. In short, the business enterprise has learned what the homemaker has always known: Don't buy it until you need it.

Another, equally devastating cost in carrying high inventory levels is the risk of obsolescence. Those who build high inventories of oil, ores, or agricultural commodities face moderate risks that alternate energy sources, ores, or commodities will supplant their reserves. In the manufacturing and retailing sectors, however, change is now alarmingly fast paced. The steel auto part of today gives way to the plastic part of tomorrow; and the plastic part of tomorrow gives way to the lighter, tougher, plastic part of the next day. The highly successful blue gel toothpaste of one month can face extinction in the market the next month when a heavy media advertising campaign introduces a better-tasting, green-mint paste.

Inventory users, of course, want inventory when they need it; and the firm's cash manager cannot prevail on inventory managers to reduce inventory to zero. They have, however, been able to induce the inventory manager to reform inventory practices to the point that we are now witnessing striking changes in them.

The first innovation, which is at least ten years old, is the just-in-time inventory practice. Under this inventory control reform, buyers insist that their vendors ship inventory so that it arrives just as the buyer needs it. An original equipment manufacturer may need plastic parts during a February production run. The manufacturer will not want to take delivery of the parts the preceding fall or even in January. Under traditional open account credit terms, the manufacturer knows that it will have to pay for those deliveries probably within 30 days after it receives them. The manufacturer does not want to pay early, however, for early payments increase the need to borrow. Early deliveries do not accelerate the time within which the manufacturer can turn the parts around by incorporating them into product and selling them. The manufacturer is also concerned with storage costs and the risk of obsolescence. Plant warehouse space is costly. The less inventory the manufacturer has on hand, the smaller amount of space it must dedicate to inventory storage. While obsolescence risks are less here than in other settings, they can arise. News of product tampering and media-prompted health scares can have a short-term, but potentially devastating, impact on a retailer's inventory. When a Hollywood starlet makes the nightly news proclaiming the poisonous effects of a fungicide thought hitherto (and subsequently) safe, many supermarket chains would like to cancel plans to purchase apples until the scare subsides; and the buyer that insists on just-in-time deliveries may be able to cancel or redirect some or all of those purchases thereby reducing inventory carrying and storage costs and loss on the non-saleable product.

The more surprising innovation in inventory control, and the one that is perhaps having the greatest impact on commercial practices, is found most often in retail establishments. Information storage technology and communications now permit a retailer, even one with a national chain of outlets, to keep virtual up-to-the-minute track of inventory and to respond quickly to changes in consumer preference or demand. This is the "quick response" mechanism of inventory management. Computerized checkout equipment not only allows automated calculation of sales prices stored in bar codes but also immediate translation to a centralized data bank of information on customer preferences and outlet inventory levels. When a heavy media campaign prompts consumers to alter hand soap preferences, a retailer with these information capabilities will know it instantly and will be able to track it to determine whether it is a permanent alteration or a momentary phenomenon. Retailers with this capability will know what product to order and can have a telling impact on a manufacturer's production schedules. If cleanser with a private label is outselling cleanser bearing the manufacturer's nationally recognized label, the retailer will know not to purchase more of the latter but to order more of the former; and the manufacturer will know, directly or indirectly, to increase production of the latter and reduce production of the former.

When the information storage and communication capabilities that give rise to quick response combine with just-in-time inventory practices, they effect considerable change not only in inventory and marketing, but also in financing practices. As the U.S. economy moved out of the recession of the late 1980s, economists were surprised by the low levels of inventory growth. Lenders were altering their inventory ratio parameters. It may be that even lower levels of inventory will be necessary for a firm to maintain its competitiveness in the future. Enterprises offering inventory capacity may find less demand for their services; and lenders that specialize in inventory lending may find that they will need to branch into other directions.

Lean manufacturing, as this just-in-time inventory practice is sometimes called, is a major change in the dominant manufacturing and inventory practices in the United States from the early decades of this century and in the world manufacturing industry from the end of the Second World War until the mid-1980s. Fordism, the practices of Henry Ford, involved the division of intellectual activity from repetitive assembly line work and rested on large inventories and multiple sources of supply. Lean manufacturing, on the other hand, assumes rapid response to manufacturing problems, high technology in the assembly process itself, smaller inventories, and fewer sources of supply, which are subject to stricter quality and delivery requirements.

One effect of lean manufacturing has been the reduction in inventories that manufacturers carry and a concomitant reduction in the cost of financing those inventories. A second and equally important effect is that many suppliers will go out of business. Automobile manufacturers in the United States have reduced the number of first tier suppliers — that is, suppliers who sell directly to the automobile producer — from the thousands to the hundreds. While some first tier suppliers have become second or even third tier suppliers, selling to suppliers higher in the pecking order, many have disappeared.

In short, one effect of lean manufacturing practices is consolidation in the automobile supply industry and the elimination of some automobile industry suppliers.

8

Bulk Sales

§8.1 THE TRAP

Bulk sales law is anachronistic; it rests on assumptions that are no longer valid. Yet, bulk sales law is still alive. At this writing, the Uniform Commercial Code's sponsoring agencies have approved two new approaches to bulk sales. One is to abolish the bulk sales law altogether. The other is to revise the law somewhat.

The effect of the bulk sales law is to make certain buyers of goods in bulk liable for the debts of the seller to the extent that those goods remain in the buyer's hands. The effect of the law is quite startling. Before the sale, the seller's creditors have no interest in the seller's goods; but after the sale, the goods, in the hands of the usually innocent buyer, are subject to the creditors' claims. Figure 8-1 illustrates the operation of the bulk sales law.

In short, the bulk sales rule fashions a trap for unwary bulk buyers, and, in all probability, for the buyer's lawyer who fails to advise her client properly.

§8.2 THE SETTING

In the past, there were unscrupulous merchants who engaged in fraudulent practices common enough that the law took notice of them. The

73

Figure 8-1. Bulk Sale Trap

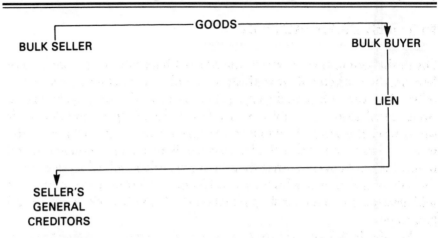

practices consisted of selling inventory out of the ordinary course of business in bulk, sometimes for less than a valuable consideration, and then disappearing or setting up a new business, all without paying unsecured creditors. The assumption of the proponents of bulk sales laws was that unsecured creditors of the bulk seller relied on his stock of merchandise and were caught off guard when he sold out quickly, denying them an opportunity to attach his merchandise and protect themselves. There may still be merchants that sell out quickly, in bulk, but the practice has lost its criminal allure. Today, unsecured creditors tend not to rely on their debtor's stock in trade. The modern unsecured creditors generally are open account sellers (the merchant's inventory suppliers), utilities, and the like. Nontrade creditors such as taxing authorities and tort victims are also unsecured creditors. To the extent that the merchant's unsecured creditors rely, they rely on the debtor's credit rating, not on the fact that it has shelves full of merchandise. Taxing authorities and tort claimants are classic examples of nonreliance creditors. It may be safe to say that they never rely on the debtor's stock in trade and that it is no surprise to them when the debtor sells out quickly. Concern for tort victims post-dates the bulk sales laws in any event. That concern cannot justify their existence ab initio and may not serve to justify them now. Inventory rarely funds the tort victim's recovery. Tort victims' recovery is usually a matter for liability insurance.

Generally, the nervous trade creditor now has a plethora of devices (security interests, especially purchase-money security interests, personal guaranties, and letters of credit) under which she can obtain security cheaply. Most unsecured creditors remain unsecured because they are not interested in incurring the expense or going to the trouble of (1) discerning which customers can and should give them security and (2) getting the security.

Thus, the bulk sales law is with us in many jurisdictions, and commercial lawyers need to understand the way it can trap their clients.

§8.3 THE TRANSACTION

Given the assumption on which the original bulk sales laws rested, those laws usually restricted their application to bulk sellers of inventory and to sellers that were substantially engaged in sales out of inventory. Hardware stores, retail clothing establishments, feed sellers, drapers, and dry goods stores were the kind of establishment that might be the subject of the fraudulent sellout and that the law covered. Barber shops, restaurants, and hotels were not covered, since their sales primarily involved services, with the sale of goods as a subsidiary consideration. Certainly no utility that sold electricity to a barber shop relied on the barber's stock of combs and hair tonic.

Yet the bulk sales law took on a life of its own and came to cover equipment sales when they were accompanied by bulk sales of inventory, and in some jurisdictions the law has been expanded to cover bulk sales by service enterprises.

Generally, the bulk sales laws do not apply unless there is a sale of more than half of the seller's inventory, but once the sale reaches that threshold, the rules apply to the equipment that the buyer purchases as well as the inventory. Thus, when an employee of a trendy jeans outlet buys the business from his boss, if he fails to comply with the bulk sales law, he takes the inventory and the equipment (shelving, mannequins, and cash register) subject to the claims of the seller's creditors. Similarly, the assistant manager of a restaurant who purchases the business from the retiring restaurant owner may, depending on the state's version of the bulk sales law, take the small inventory of food and the like (salt and pepper, coffee, ketchup, paper towels), and the equipment (ovens, refrigerators, silverware, tables, and chairs) subject to claims arising out of the seller's unpaid telephone bill, the amount she owed her wine distributor, and the dry cleaner's bill for linen napkins and tablecloths.

§8.4 THE "CURE"

Generally, though the versions of Uniform Commercial Code Article 6, both in its scope and its implementation, vary as the various states have adopted it, the bulk sales statutes require the bulk buyer to notify all creditors of the impending bulk sale. Note that, in most jurisdictions, the statute does not require the bulk buyer to reserve a portion of the purchase price for the unsecured creditors, it only requires notice, so that, theoretically, the creditors can take steps (unspecified in the statute) to protect themselves. Note also that all creditors, including categories that have not relied on the seller's stock in trade, or on any of his assets for that matter, are entitled to notice. In brief, the bulk sales law has become a **fraudulent conveyance** statute that applies against innocent buyers. It does not matter that the buyer fails to give the notice by virtue of innocent neglect. The bulk sales law imputes fault to the buyer and renders the subject of his purchase hostage to his neglect or fraud, as the case may be.

The bulk buyer cannot give the notice unless he has a list of the creditors. The statute requires the buyer to ask the seller for a sworn list. It does not matter that the seller gives the buyer an incomplete list. If the buyer notifies all of the creditors listed and unless the buyer knows or has good reason to believe that the list is incomplete, the buyer takes the goods free and clear of the claims.

§8.5 CONCLUSION

You may conclude from this discussion that the bulk sales law is a bad idea. It does not really protect creditors very much, since they often can do little to protect themselves without considerable transaction costs. The creditor can hire a lawyer and get a judgment or some kind of prejudgment relief, but that kind of action can rarely be obtained prior to consummation of the sale, given the fact that the notice might be given only ten days before the sale, and the relief is generally not available without proof of fraud — a notoriously difficult proof problem. The law also rests on the questionable assumption that the creditor is looking to the seller's inventory, even though few unsecured creditors, if any, rely on inventory these days and even though the statute frequently covers sellers of services who have little inventory to start with. The major effect of the law, in the view of some, is to catch the unwary buyer and permit the creditors to collect from an honest party as a matter of fortuity. Those problems with the bulk sales law aside, it remains a problem for the lawyer who represents the buyer in bulk.

9 Leasing

§9.1 DISTINGUISHING THE NONLEASE

This chapter deals with **leases** but does not deal with a common transaction that parties frequently refer to as a "lease," that is, the lease-purchase transaction. For a variety of reasons, installment sellers that want to hold "title" to the goods that are the subject of a sale will designate the transaction a "lease" when in law the arrangement is a secured transaction. It is not always easy to draw the line between the "true" lease and the secured transaction disguised as a lease. Article 2A of the Uniform Commercial Code and the modifications that the Code's sponsoring agencies adopted to the Article 1 definition of *security interest* cause the distinction to turn on the economic realities of the transaction rather than its form or the intent of the parties.

In general, if the lease and any extensions or renewals comprise the entire useful life of the property, or if the lessee must buy the property or has the option to buy the property at the termination of the lease period for a nominal consideration, the lease is in reality a secured transaction, not a lease. In leases with significant tax consequences, the parties must review Internal Revenue Service guidelines to determine the nature of the transaction. Part II deals generally with secured transactions; this chapter deals with the true lease.

§9.2 THE CONSUMER LEASE

In the simplest lease, familiar to any consumer, the lessor is an enterprise in the business of leasing equipment for a day or a few days. Travelers who lease automobiles for a weekend, the home gardener who leases a tiller for a Saturday afternoon, and the bride's parents who rent a green and white striped tent for a reception usually enter into this kind of short-term lease.

In recent years automobile leasing by dealers to consumers has become popular. These closed-end lease transactions assume that some consumers (and some businesses) prefer to lease new vehicles for fixed periods at charges that approximate the cost of the vehicle, less its value at the termination of the lease, plus interest charges. These leases are probably true leases, just as the weekend lease from Hertz is a true lease.

§9.3 THE EQUIPMENT LEASE

While the dealer-generated automobile lease has grown dramatically in recent years, of much greater commercial importance than consumer rentals is the industrial or commercial equipment lease. Today, users of industrial and commercial equipment are more likely to lease it than to purchase it. Purchasers of equipment in this multi-billion-dollar industry tend to be finance companies, banks, and their leasing subsidiaries or the leasing subsidiary of the equipment manufacturer itself.

There are a number of reasons that parties may want to enter into an equipment lease. First, some equipment leases are short-term arrangements under which the goods revert to the lessor at a time when they retain significant commercial value and can be leased again to other lessees. In these situations, it is less expensive for the lessee to enter into a short-term lease than to purchase equipment, use it for a brief time, and then let it sit idle or resell it. Second, equipment leases for longer terms often cover equipment that is subject to quick obsolescence by virtue of the fast pace of innovation in an industry. Third, sometimes the lessee is unsure that he wants to keep the equipment and enters into the lease in order to maintain his options to return the equipment after the initial lease term. Fourth, tax considerations may enter into the true lease transaction. Lessors with high gross revenues may want to retain ownership of equipment in order to reduce tax liabilities through investment tax credits or accelerated depreciation rules currently unavailable under federal law but formerly important tax considerations. Lessees that face unprofitable futures might prefer to lease property rather than own it, so that the lessor can enjoy the tax advantages and pass them on, or at least part of them on, to the lessee in the form of reduced lease payments. Fifth, some lessees will enter into an equipment lease under which the lessor must maintain the equipment, so that the lessee, who may not have the expertise or trained personnel to undertake that maintenance, can avoid the cost of investing in that expertise or personnel. This kind of lease is often referred to as a service lease. Finally, some equipment users prefer to carry lease obligations on their balance sheets than to incur long-term debt to acquire equipment.

Despite the current void in the tax laws for the investment tax credit, tax-oriented leases are attractive to many equipment users. Under the tax-oriented lease, the lessor and lessee can be confident that the Internal Revenue Service will treat the lessor as the owner of the equipment and the lessee as a true lessee, not as a disguised buyer. By virtue of the fact that the lessor is the owner of the equipment for tax purposes, the lessee may confidently deduct all lease payments on its income tax return, and the lessor may confidently depreciate the equipment on its income tax return. Equipment users that pay the alternate minimum tax may find it advisable to lease equipment under a tax-oriented lease. Tax rules for such taxpayers deny them certain accelerated depreciation benefits. It is often beneficial, then, for the parties to enter into a tax-oriented lease in order to ensure that the transaction enjoys the maximum benefits under the income tax laws.

Tax-oriented leases fall into two categories: guideline leases and TRAC leases. The former is a lease that satisfies the Internal Revenue Service's guidelines for true leases. Generally, those requirements exclude from the definition of a guideline lease any lease that is, in fact, a disguised secured transaction. Thus a lease that permits the lessee to acquire the equipment at the end of the lease term for nominal consideration would not qualify as a tax-oriented lease.

TRAC leases cover motor vehicles and contain terminal rental adjustment clauses under which the parties reduce or increase the lessee's rental obligation at the end of the lease. If the residual value of the equipment is higher than the TRAC figure in the lease, the lessee will receive a rebate of rent paid. If the residual value is less than the figure in the lease, the lessee must pay additional rent to the lessor.

Lessees may have additional incentives for entering into a true lease of equipment instead of acquiring the equipment under an installment sales arrangement. Bear in mind that equipment can be extraordinarily expensive. Drag lines for strip mining and aircraft command prices in the hundreds of millions of dollars. If the lessee acquires expensive equipment on credit, its balance sheet will reflect the acquisition, in part, by increasing the firm's debt. Because a firm, for perfectly legitimate reasons, may choose not to show increased debt on its balance sheet, it may elect to lease the equipment rather than purchase it. Similarly, taking on debt by acquiring equipment under a credit sale will have an unfavorable impact on a ratio that the lessee is obligated to maintain at a specified level in, say, its bank loan agreement or the terms of debt instruments. Loan agreements often require a borrower to maintain a current ratio — the ratio of current (convertible within one year) assets to current (due within one year) liabilities — at a level acceptable to the bank. Incurring debt to acquire equipment will have a negative impact on the buyer's current ratio. A true lease, however, will have an impact only to the extent of one year's rent.

While some of the foregoing justifications for leasing practices may strike the young lawyer as subterfuges designed to mislead bank lenders or investors, bankers and regulators generally claim that they appreciate the significance of the leasing arrangements and are not misled by it.

In all of these transactions, the parties must take care that the arrangement is a true lease and not a secured transaction. Ultimately, a lessee enters into a lease because he needs the equipment but does not want to buy it.

Note that in the lease situation, the lessor is using the lease to market products. An automobile dealer may sell a new car to a business enterprise and buy it back each year as part of a trade for a new purchase, or the dealer can lease a new vehicle each year to its customer. In both cases, the customer enjoys the use of a new car for a year, and the dealer must dispose of the used car at the end of the year. In the sale transaction, the dealer takes the car in trade; in the lease transaction, the car reverts to it when the lease expires. In both cases, the dealer disposes of the used car through its used-car lot or through its used-car broker.

Similarly, a computer manufacturer that markets products directly to businesses can use equipment leases to effect distribution. Often, under such a lease, when the manufacturer develops a modified product, the lessee will terminate the lease of the old product and enter into a new lease of the upgraded product. The manufacturer knows that if it does not keep its product competitive, the lessee will terminate and go with a competitor. The lessee knows that he will not be stuck with obsolete equipment. Some leases are "net" leases, that is, they provide that the lessee will pay all costs of maintaining, insuring, and servicing the equipment.

Commercial parties sometimes distinguish between open-end and closed-end leases. Under the open-end lease, the lessee guarantees that the equipment will have a specified residual value. The TRAC lease discussed above is an open-end lease. Leases in which the lessee does not guarantee a residual value is a closed-end lease.

Under a closed-end lease, the lessor undertakes risk that it does not undertake in the open-end lease. Assuming that the lessee is financially responsible, the lessor under an open-end lease does not face the risk that it will not be able to recoup the residual value the parties assumed for the equipment when they entered into the lease.

Sometimes leasing companies, especially those that are subsidiaries of a manufacturer, will enter into master lease agreements with a customer. Under the terms of a master lease, the customer leases additional equipment from time to time and adds the additional equipment to the lease by means of a schedule Thus, for example, a computer manufacturer's leasing subsidiary may enter into a master lease to cover equipment leased over a relatively long period. As the customer expands its operations or modernizes them, it will take additional equipment that will come under the master lease.

§9.4 BANKRUPTCY CONSIDERATIONS

There is a wrinkle in bankruptcy law that should give lessors pause when they decide whether to enter into a true lease, the subject of this chapter, or a credit sale disguised as a lease, which is the subject of Section 18.2. Under the Bankruptcy Code, the trustee in bankruptcy of a lessee may choose to reject a true lease. In the event of rejection, the trustee must return the equipment to the true lessor. In the event the trustee elects to continue the lease, as he has the right to do, the trustee must make the rental payments under the lease. If the lease is a disguised sale, however, the trustee has no right to disavow the lease, which is a secured transaction, but the trustee does have the power under the bankruptcy law's cramdown provision to force the lessor in the disguised sale to take a secured claim for what the court determines to be the market value of the equipment and an unsecured claim for the balance.

10

Construction Contracts

§10.1 THE INDUSTRY

The construction industry involves an ever-larger number of players as its activity becomes increasingly complex. Few industries embrace as many different processes, services, and products as this one, which comprises simple activity such as repairing a leaky garage roof and complex activity such as constructing a space center or a nuclear power facility. In most cases, the transaction begins when a purchaser, whom the industry generally calls the "owner," decides to buy construction services and, usually, materials. In any reasonably complex construction, the owner must express his requirements in some fashion. Unlike many sales transactions, construction sales are often unique or nearly so. This year's automobile assembly facility will be different from last year's. Contrary to the image of manufacturing in the popular media, that industry, like most industries, is subject to innovation that continues at a considerable pace.

In specifying their requirements, owners often seek the help of architects and engineers, and their specifications are recorded in excruciating detail. The contract documents and specifications for even a modest construction project can be a foot thick.

Construction activity differs from other sales in that it frequently requires a long period of time between the day the owner specifies what he wants and the day of completion when he finally gets what he ordered.

Finally, the construction industry itself consists of hundreds of separate industries. In the construction of a simple dwelling, there will be excavators, masons, carpenters, plumbers, electricians, roofers, and painters, whose suppliers will include equipment rental companies, lumberyards, pipe and fitting suppliers, hardware wholesalers, window manufacturers, insulation producers, and more.

In short, construction activity is not akin to the assembly line. Contractors cannot always rely on timely deliveries, weather, subsoil conditions, the absence of strikes or work disputes, the availability of skilled workers, the adequacy of materials supply, steady prices during construction, continued fiscal health among subcontractors and subsubcontractors, and the absence of specification changes by the owner.

The **prime contractor,** the contractor that agrees to complete the project in accordance with the owner's drawings and specifications, engages subcontractors, who may engage their own subcontractors to perform portions of the work. In such cases, subcontractors and their subsubcontractors (subsubs) may be working on a number of projects at one time. Delays on one project will tend to force delays on the subcontractor's other projects, since his employees (construction workers and management personnel) can only work on one project at a given time. One subcontractor's delays, furthermore, tend to delay everyone else. The pipe fitters cannot install pipe until the structural steel is in place; the carpet installers cannot lay the carpet while the painters are at work. One might marvel that anything ever gets built, and some owners complain that during the construction period, they wondered whether their project would ever see completion.

In fact, the system, ragged and complex as it is, works pretty well, but it is not always simple, and there are lots of traps and sometimes unhappy results.

§10.2 THE PLANNING PHASE

While an owner often knows what she wants her project to do, e.g., carry traffic over a gully, generate electricity, or house a tool and die works' expanded operation, she frequently does not know what it takes to achieve her desired objectives. Most commercial owners engage inside or outside construction experts, engineers, architects, and designers to create the specifications and drawings that will guide the construction of the facility. The product of this planning can be quite voluminous, so bulky and difficult to reproduce that often when the parties reach the bidding stage, potential bidders have to visit the owner's or the architect's premises to view the drawings, which may easily number in the hundreds, and specifications, which may easily comprise thousands of pages. Such drawings and specifications will include the dimensions of each doorway and window, the location of every power outlet for the plant's assembly area, the plywood grades and dimensions for interior and exterior surfaces, the diameter of steel reinforcing rods in the concrete footings, and the glazing compound for the windows.

Contracts with engineers, designers, and architects have been standardized to some extent. The American Institute of Architects publishes standard contract forms.

§10.3 THE BIDDING PHASE

After the owner and its architects, engineers, and other designers have completed the drawings and specifications for the project, it is time to let the contract. While some owners may act as their own "general" contractor, most owners, especially small and medium-sized commercial enterprises without engineering or construction experience, let the entire construction contract to a general contractor who subcontracts those portions of the project that he is not equipped to perform. The general contractor, for example, might have his own excavation equipment, carpenters, sheet metal workers, and laborers but subcontracts the mechanical work (plumbing, heating, and electrical) and some of the specialized work, such as the roofing, painting, and landscaping. At other times the prime contractor subcontracts all of the work, except for some general supervisory operations.

In government construction projects, the bidding procedure is usually governed by statutes and regulations, and any failure on the part of a bidder to comply with the governing rules will render the bid unacceptable to the municipal owner. In private projects, the owner has more leeway in soliciting bids. She might negotiate face-to-face with a single contractor or a few contractors and let the work on the basis of a cost-plus arrangement or might enter a contract at a fixed price for the completed work. She might invite sealed bids from a number of designated contractors or might open the bidding to contractors in general. Owners must take some care in specifying the terms of the bidding procedure. If the owner wants to reserve the right to reject the lowest bid if the reputation or financial integrity of a bidder is unsatisfactory, the invitation for bids should say so. Usually, the owner will want to accept the lowest bid and will want to ensure fairness in the bidding process in order to attract bidders. The greater the number of responsible bidders, the greater the chance that the bids will be competitive and that the owner will enjoy the full benefit of that competition.

The prime contractor cannot submit a bid to the owner until he knows what it will take to satisfy subcontractors. The prime will, therefore, solicit bids from potential subcontractors in advance of submitting that bid to the owner. The prime requires his subcontractors to leave their bids open until he knows whether the owner will award him the job. In the event she does, he can quickly accept the subcontractors' bids and bind them.

After the owner notifies the prime contractor that she has awarded him the job, the prime contractor notifies the subcontractors. Figure 10-1 illustrates the overall transaction in a small building construction project at the time the bids are accepted. Included in that diagram are the many suppliers from whom subcontractors purchase materials and supplies for the project. Supply of some materials may be sufficiently scarce or price sensitive that subcontractors assure themselves of sources before bidding, but other materials are in abundant supply and do not justify the transaction costs in obtaining bids and the fixed prices that result in the bidding process.

§10.4 THE ROLE OF THE BONDING COMPANY OR OTHER GUARANTOR

By insisting on bonds or their equivalent from bidders, prime contractors, subcontractors, and owners have reduced their exposure to risks of nonperformance. In the case of bids owners run the risk that a bidder might submit a bid and then, either because he no longer values the deal or is in financial difficulties, be unable to secure the necessary payment and performance bonds or refuse to enter into the contract after the owner accepts the bid. In that case, the owner must either accept the next-lowest bid, which may be significantly higher than the lowest bid, or relet the contract. The reletting process takes time, may occur after word of the prior bid has become public, and results in delay and higher costs for the project. Failure of the winning bidder to enter into the contract and post the required payment and performance bonds is a serious blow to the owner's interests. She can prevent some of the loss by looking to a bond in a liquidated amount and conditioned on such a breach by the successful bidder. Thus, if the winning bidder fails to enter into the contract and secure the **payment** and **performance bonds**, the owner makes a claim on the prime bidder's **bid bond**. For similar reasons, prime contractors and subcontractors seek bid bonds from their subcontractors.

The risk of nonperformance or misperformance does not confine itself to the bidding stage of the construction transaction. After the parties begin to perform, there is the danger that one or more of them will default. As a hedge against that eventuality, the owner may require the prime contractor and all subcontractors to obtain payment and performance bonds. These bonds require the bonding company to perform the insured

Figure 10-1. Construction Contract Model

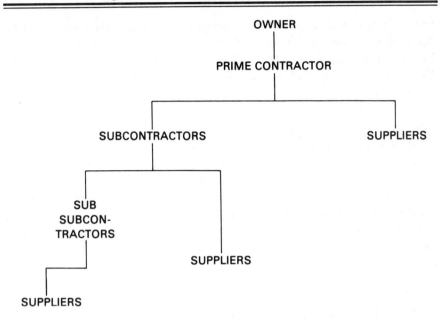

contractor's work in the event of default and to pay any subcontractor or supplier whom the defaulting contractor fails to pay. Companies that issue performance bonds do not perform the work of the defaulting contractor but hire another contractor to do the work.

Lately, some contractors have been complaining that the cost of bonds, especially bid bonds, is too great and that they sometimes cannot obtain them even when they are financially responsible. Since most large construction projects call for bid bonds, a contractor that cannot obtain a bid bond or its equivalent may have to go out of business. Some owners have agreed to permit bidders to use letters of credit issued by commercial banks in lieu of the fidelity company's bid bond. There are two significant differences between the letter of credit and the bond. First, letters of credit are the primary obligation of the issuer, while bonds are secondary obligations. Second, a letter of credit issuer pays funds to the beneficiary, while the bond issuer, depending on the nature of the bond, may perform or may hire another contractor to perform an obligation of a defaulting contractor.

As the banking industry encroaches on the insurance industry's turf, bank letters of credit and **independent guarantees,** a primary undertaking, are serving some of the functions of the insurance industry's bonds, which are secondary undertakings. In international construction projects, some buyers, especially those in the Middle East, require bid bonds and performance bonds in the form of bank guarantees. These guarantees are primary obligations of their issuers and most of the time call for payment against presentation of pieces of paper. They are redolent, then, of the standby letter of credit, and U.S. courts and commentators are inclined to apply letter of credit law to them.

At the moment, regulators are chary about recognizing the power of banks chartered in the United States, either as state banks or national banks, to issue such guarantees. Thus a U.S. seller of construction services may not be in a position to have its own U.S. bank issue the document that fills the role of the bid bond or the performance bond. The problem is exacerbated further for the U.S. seller by the fact that a foreign bank, which can issue the bank guarantees, is unfamiliar with the U.S. seller and is, therefore, disinclined to extend credit to the seller.

International bankers have fashioned the transaction in a way that permits U.S. banks and U.S. sellers to participate in foreign construction projects. Under this scheme, the U.S. seller's bank issues a standby letter of credit to a foreign bank, which in turn issues the guarantee. The standby is payable against the foreign bank's certification that it paid under the guarantee. The effect of the arrangement is that, in the event of a draw on the guarantee, the U.S. seller pays, because such a draw prompts a draw on the standby, and a draw on the standby prompts the U.S. bank to obtain reimbursement from the U.S. seller.

Figure 10-2 illustrates this transaction in a bid bond setting. The performance bond setting would be similar.

§10.5 THE PERFORMANCE PHASE

The owner must supervise performance of the construction contract. It would be wasteful to wait until the project is complete to determine whether the contractors have complied with the drawings and specifications, and, as any first-year law student knows, the courts are reluctant to force a contractor to rip a building apart to replace one brand of pipe with another. If the owner wants a special brand of pipe, she had better have someone present when the plumbers install it. The owner, furthermore, must make periodic payments to her contractors. Construction companies are not sufficiently capitalized that they can finance the construction project. Banks and other short-term lenders traditionally serve that function. Contractors cannot perform on credit for very long periods. By delaying payments to their subcontractors and suppliers, contractors can usually perform on credit for a week or two or perhaps a little longer, but, during the performance of the contract, they must be paid frequently.

The owner engages a manager, perhaps the architect or a firm specializing in the business, to supervise the construction at the job site. That supervision includes the keeping of records of material delivered to the site and of the work performed. The supervisor must determine that the materials delivered conform to the specifications and that the work done

Figure 10-2. Bank Guarantees in Foreign Construction Projects

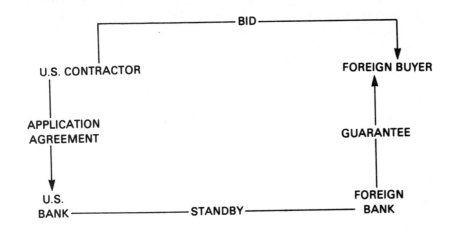

is also conforming. If the materials and work are conforming, the supervisor authorizes payment at the end of the payment interval. If everything goes according to plans, at the end of a payment period, each subcontractor submits an application for payment to the contractor. Accompanying that application is a statement of work done by the prime contractor and subcontractors. The owner then applies to the lender or the lender's agent, typically a title company, for an advance under the construction loan.

Under the law of most jurisdictions, persons who supply goods or services that are incorporated into real estate have a lien on that real estate and on the funds due under a contract for the construction of the improvement. In order to ensure that those liens do not cloud the title and impair its mortgage, the construction lender insists that each application be accompanied by partial lien waivers, executed by the subcontractors and their suppliers. The contractor asks the job supervisor to approve the applications. The owner then submits all of the applications to the construction lender, who pays the face amount of the applications, less any retainage specified in the contracts. Usually, the owner has the right to retain 10 percent of each application, the retainage to be paid when all of the work is satisfactorily completed. At the time of final payment, the owner or the construction lender's agent requires final lien waivers from the contractors.

PART II

SECURED LENDING

11

Introduction to Secured Lending

§11.1 SUBJECT MATTER

Part II (Secured Lending) deals with those transactions that generally fall within the coverage of the traditional law school course on Secured Transactions, that is, with activity governed by Article 9 of the Uniform Commercial Code. Any discussion of that activity must consider unsecured lending in order to place secured lending in context and to contrast the two kinds of lending activity. One of the problems these days in academic literature and to some extent in the cases lies in the failure to pay enough attention to the distinction between the secured lender and the unsecured lender. The secured lender is, in fact, if not in the theory of some law teachers, a very different animal from the lender that intentionally does not take security.

Before we treat the various secured transactions, it is also important to consider (1) the ways financial institutions and **commercial** sellers extend credit and (2) the complex process they traditionally utilize in making the decision to lend or not to lend.

§11.2 SOME HISTORY OF COMMERCIAL LENDING

Over the last century, commercial lending has changed dramatically, but for present purposes it is enough to know that in the recent past there were five basic lenders: (1) financing sellers, (2) **commercial banks,** (3) **finance companies,** (4) **small loan companies,** and (5) **thrifts**.

Financing sellers traditionally extended credit in two ways. As credit reporting became more and more reliable, they began to sell enormous amounts of **goods** and services on open **account,** that is, **short-term,** unsecured credit (30, 90, or 120 days, typically). Some sellers granted longer credit terms but took a discrete **security interest** in the goods they sold. This security interest is the **purchase-money security interest** to which commercial law often accords favored treatment. These two practices continue and probably constitute the greatest single category of commercial credit in the economy today. Note that only one of them involves secured lending; that one, moreover, is significantly less in volume than unsecured, open account credit. Chapter 3 discusses open-account selling.

Commercial banks traditionally targeted large industrial corporations and the **middle market** as sources for commercial bank loans. These loans were generally unsecured, but they involved **negative pledges,** that is, the borrower agreed not to grant security interests to any other lender or even to borrow from any other lender, with some exceptions, such as for purchases on open account. The net effect of the arrangement was to give the bank a favorable position in the event of bankruptcy, since other creditors were usually few in number with relatively low credit balances, and, in any event, the risk of insolvency was generally small for the all-important reason that commercial banks did not lend to marginal operations. Only the good credit risk, the industrial corporation with a healthy balance sheet, or the strong mid-level company with personal guaranties from wealthy individuals could get a bank loan.

There were exceptions to this pattern, and commercial banks, especially the larger ones in major financial centers, did engage in a significant amount of secured lending, most notably in connection with self-liquidating loans. These usually involved transactions that gave rise to valuable paper: **documents of title,** corporate securities, and the like.

The conservative nature of the commercial banker and his appetite for safe loans left considerable room for the more adventuresome lender. Commercial finance companies targeted the territory of the borrower who could not satisfy the commercial banker but who often did have assets available to collateralize the obligation and who would pay a somewhat higher rate of interest for credit than the bank charged. This is the area where secured lending advanced considerably. At first, the loans tended to be against discrete items of **collateral,** such as a loan to **purchase a** given shipment of merchandise or to buy a specific piece of **equipment.**

Eventually, the finance companies saw the benefit of revolving loans and **revolving collateral.** They granted loans to purchase **inventory** or equipment and took a security interest in that collateral as it existed at the time of the loan and as the borrower added to it or sold it off thereafter. Commercial bankers operated within the confines of a theory of banking under which each loan had to be self-liquidating, that is, each loan had a schedule of payments reducing the loan balance to zero over a fixed period of time. Finance companies advanced the notion that loan payments should be a matter subject to the debtor's cash flow, not preordained payment schedules of short-term lending custom. In brief, the signal advances in secured lending occurred in the commercial finance sector, not the commercial bank sector, of the lending industry.

Eventually, even before the advent of **deregulation** in the financial institutions industry, commercial bankers discovered the profitability of entering into secured lending. To some extent events forced them to venture into secured lending. First, they lost much of the industrial market when large borrowers were able to squeeze **financial intermediaries** such as banks out of the picture by borrowing directly from investors. Today, a national retailer may not seek credit from a bank but may borrow directly from the investing public. By asking a brokerage house to underwrite its offering of short-term notes (30-, 60-, or 90-day **paper**), for example, a large, well-regarded enterprise is able to market its notes (**commercial paper**) at lower rates of interest than banks would charge the same borrower. This method of borrowing removes the financial intermediary, the bank, and thereby saves the borrowing corporation money. By eliminating the bank, the borrower eliminates the bank's charges from the borrower's cost of raising funds.

Second, commercial bankers realized that secured loans were often as good as the unsecured loans they were accustomed to making and that such loans were often as profitable or more profitable than the unsecured loans they had traditionally made.

At the same time that bankers entered the asset-based lending field, they began to exploit the **consumer** market with installment loans. These loans are also secured, usually by the goods that the consumer has purchased.

One effect of this transformation of commercial banking has been a significant decline in the number of finance companies, with many of them now owned by commercial banks. The unique product of today's commercial finance company is often not its willingness to lend against collateral (banks being willing to do that) but its willingness to lend to the marginal borrower at higher rates and also to lend quickly, sometimes without first obtaining collateral. Thus in a curious way, finance companies now sometimes make unsecured loans, which later become secured.

Thrifts have not figured prominently in personal property secured lending, and small loan companies have restricted their activity to small consumer transactions. Until recent deregulation, thrifts were forbidden by law from making most commercial loans. They could lend to consumers only in connection with certain types of activity and were required by law to confine the bulk of their loans to real estate financing and development.

Although many of those strictures no longer apply to the thrift industry, savings institutions, as of this writing, have not acquired the expertise to make them feel comfortable in the commercial-lending area. This lack of confidence is subsiding, however, and the arrival of thrifts in the commercial-lending area may be only a matter of time. To some extent, commercial lending by thrifts has already begun. With much of the thrift industry presently recovering from the throes of fiscal and regulatory turmoil, no one can be certain what that industry will look like in the future.

Small loan companies traditionally have made loans for consumer purchases or emergencies. These institutions usually take a purchase-money security interest in the consumer durables (automobiles and appliances) that their customers buy. Small loan companies also take security interests in a consumer's furniture and other personal property. The small loan companies' share of the consumer market is relatively small.

Credit unions have a long history of making secured consumer loans and have done so at generally attractive interest rates. Automobile and home appliance financing have been an important part of their business.

Pawnshops are probably the oldest secured lenders. While they do not play a significant role in the consumer lending market, they do play a role; and recently they have enjoyed considerable growth. One scholar claims that there are over 8,000 pawnshops in the United States and that their loan activity has been increasing. Outstanding loans at pawnshops are in the $2 billion range and turn over quickly. By one estimate, these small, relatively unimportant secured lenders make more than 35 million loans annually. Pawnshops, which are classic pledgees, are no longer the small shops with a single clerk wearing a green eye-shade but may be part of a national chain whose stock is traded publicly. Their customers tend to be from low-income groups, often the unemployed; and their interest charges are on a level that venture capitalists charge their riskiest customers.

§11.3 DECIDING TO LEND

The decision to lend is usually the culmination of a subtle, complex evaluation process. Parents lending to their children do not customarily take security, neither does the local entrepreneur who launders shirts, but the reasons for these decisions not to take security are obviously different. Parents do not seek security often because their children do not have anything worth taking a security interest in. The local laundry does not take security from customers that pay their laundry bills monthly because (1) it relies on their favorable credit, (2) the frequency of losses is too rare to justify the cost of taking a security deposit or other security interest, or (3) its customers will take their dirty shirts somewhere else if they cannot get credit.

By the same token, the decisions of the bank loan officer to grant unsecured credit to Company A, to grant credit to Company B only on a secured basis, and to deny credit to Company C may rest on judgments that are difficult to ascertain and to explain. This discussion of that process is necessarily summary and may have the unfortunate effect of being misleading. Some courts have been misled in rendering judgments against lenders, under **lender liability** theories, because the lenders themselves could not adequately explain the process. In fact, it is true that the same loan officer may extend credit to one person without security and deny it to a similarly situated person who offers security (or extend a loan's term in the first case and deny it in the second), and in each case the decision may be rational and justified, though difficult to articulate.

There are instances when the law emphatically interdicts that process. It would not matter, for example, that persons who are divorced and have not remarried are statistically less likely to repay their loans than persons who have not been divorced or who have been divorced but are remarried. If those statistics are true, and this is not to say that they are, the law forbids lenders from taking marital status into account in making loan decisions. Similarly, other factors such as race, national origin, sex, religion, and residential location may be proscribed by state or federal law, no matter that they might, on a statistical basis, be relevant considerations.

Experience suggests that the most compelling consideration is not whether the borrower provides the lender with security but whether, on the whole, the lender judges that the borrower will repay the loan. The existence of security is but one among many factors on which that judgment rests. True, in some cases, the existence of security is determinative. If a borrower grants a bank a security interest in a $100,000 United States treasury obligation, virtually any loan officer will authorize a $50,000 loan, if the interest rate is fair. Yet, some loan officers will balk at such a loan if, say, the borrower is of unsavory character or one who has been unpleasant in prior business dealings. Lenders are not yet public utilities obliged to serve the public, and the federal courts have not found a constitutional right to borrow — yet.

In the vast majority of loan transactions, the strongest factor militating in favor of making a loan is the credit history of the borrower. Most lenders are not interested in foreclosing on collateral. They find **foreclosure** distasteful. Bankers are financial people; they deal with audited balance sheets and reports; they are interested in economic indicators and community trends. In short, they are comfortable at what nonbankers view as paper shuffling. They are not comfortable and are not interested in liquidating securities or grain futures contracts, let alone used factory equipment or (God forbid) hogs. Lawyers for defaulting borrowers often use that feature of the loan officer's personality in order to exact concessions from the lender. "Just lend us another $500,000, and we will make this loan good." It is an important fact of commercial lending that lenders resist the conclusion that they have made a bad loan. When a borrower is in financial difficulty, loan officers often feel helpless and regret that circumstances have transformed what began as a quite cheerful and optimistic relationship into a tense, adversarial one.

Commercial lenders victimized by the defaulting borrower's hard times exculpate themselves with the maxim: "No loan is bad when it is made." Loans go bad, but they start out good.

That maxim hints at an important facet of commercial lending that the commentators have overlooked. While it is true that lenders are profit maximizers and are at the same time risk averse, and while the economists and their imitators in the world of legal scholarship can create models to track those forces, they cannot track the very personal judgments that can be so compelling in loan decisions, especially in the all-important (for this is the locus of lender liability lawsuits) middle market. An economic model is incomplete unless it takes into account a simple yet enormously powerful scenario: On Monday the loan officer made a "safe" loan to a business wunderkind. On Tuesday, the wunderkind failed. On Wednesday the loan officer did not walk to the water cooler, even though he was thirsty, because in order to get there he had to walk past his colleagues desks.

Borrowers that "cheat" on a spouse, or wear white shoes, or are too ready to buy the drinks or not ready enough to buy lunch, or have too many "toys" (sporty car, power boat, etc.) can fail to win the confidence of certain loan officers but are the ready recipient of loans from other loan officers.

These may not sound like good reasons to deny credit (or to refuse credit extensions) to someone who has collateral and a history of earnings, but these are typical of the factors a loan officer considers. Ultimately, and especially in the middle market where secured lending predominates, the controlling consideration is the judgment of the loan officer or of the **loan committee** that the prospective borrower will repay the loan, and that judgment is often the product of years of experience, personal taste, and personal views of the world. In short, the loan officer's judgment may be visceral. That fact troubles senior loan vice presidents who rely on their loan officers' abilities to generate good loans, not bad ones; and it troubles courts that would like to see lenders justify their decisions with objective standards. Those who would like to change these facts of commercial lending should consider changing the law of gravity.

There have been, nonetheless, some attempts to objectify the loan evaluation process. The method some banks, especially larger ones, have used is called **loan scoring**. Loan scoring involves the process of assigning numerical values to certain features of a borrower's financial profile to determine whether a loan is bankable, how much of it is bankable, and what the interest rate should be. Among the features to which banks will assign point values are comparisons of a potential borrower's cash needs with those of others in the same industry, liquidity, debt service requirements, nature of collateral, assessment of management, comparisons of account and inventory levels with industry levels, and quality of internal and external audits. While the process has the trappings of objectivity, it involves considerable banker judgment.

§11.4 FUNCTION OF COLLATERAL

Lenders take collateral for one reason: to secure repayment of the loan. Lenders can use the collateral in two ways. First, in the event of **default,** they can sell the collateral and apply the proceeds to the loan balance. Second, they can use the threat of foreclosure to get the borrower's attention and induce her to resume payments or otherwise attend to her obligations under the **loan agreement**. A few commercially squeamish courts and commentators find something odious about the second use of collateral. Such conduct is oppressive: it forces people to do something they do not want to do, to allocate their resources in a fashion contrary to their wishes. Such conduct also resembles the habits of the loan shark and evokes images of beefy enforcers threatening to break legs or of unscrupulous bankers in the classic western film eyeing the family ranch or the favor of the rancher's daughter.

There is no excuse for the practices of loan sharks and the villains of Hollywood fiction, but efforts by secured lenders to use their security to enforce the terms of the loan agreement are, though not always dainty, quite harmless and, in fact, socially and economically beneficial. The defaulting borrower, at the least, raises the cost of credit to the nondefaulter and, at worst, endangers the credit system and the economy that rests upon it. Those few who object to the use of threats under **security agreements** are really objecting to secured credit, not to particular practices.

There are some who candidly acknowledge their objections to secured credit either on these grounds or on theories of efficiency. It is not our purpose to address the challenge on the latter grounds here. As to the former, one cannot deny that a market economy can exist without secured lending. One must admit, however, that the same number of people and the same class of people will not have access to credit under a system that does not allow it as will have access to credit in a system that does.

The raison d'être of secured lending is not to enhance the power of lenders. Ultimately, it is to increase the availability of credit to people who would otherwise not have it.

§11.5 BANK REGULATION AND STRUCTURE

It is helpful in studying secured lending to understand a little about bank regulation. Commercial banks are now a primary source of secured lending. Unlike credit sellers, commercial banks are heavily regulated. For a number of reasons, that regulation is rather Byzantine. First, under the American dual banking system, we have both state and federally chartered banks, with the result that there are federal and state regulators for the two types. The federal agency that regulates **national associations,** i.e., national banks, is the **Comptroller of the Currency.** State regulators go under a variety of names, such as the Superintendent of Banking in New York and the Director of the Financial Institutions Bureau in Michigan.

In addition, because state and national banks insure their deposits with the **Federal Deposit Insurance Corporation** (FDIC), the FDIC has important regulatory functions and is the primary federal regulator for state chartered banks that are not members of the Federal Reserve. The **Federal Reserve Board** is the chief federal regulator for state banks that are members of the Federal Reserve.

Under the Bank Holding Company Act, the Federal Reserve Board is also the regulator of **bank holding companies,** that is, corporations that own the stock of commercial banks, referred to as their *operating subsidiaries*. The **Office of Thrift Supervision** (OTS) acts as chief regulator of **savings and loan associations.** The FDIC also exercises such functions in its role of insurer of thrift deposits. The **National Credit Union Administration** (NCUA) is the chief regulator of federal credit unions.

The net effect of this crisscrossing of financial institution regulation can be complex and problematic. A bank holding company may own several operating subsidiaries. Some of them may be state **nonmember banks,** some national banks, and some state member banks. Lawyers for the holding company will deal with the Federal Reserve Board as regulator of the state member banks and the holding company, the Comptroller of the Currency as regulator of the national banks, the FDIC as regulator of the state nonmember banks, and a state agency as regulator of state banks.

Some holding companies exploited a loophole in the definition of *bank* in the Bank Holding Company Act by organizing nonbank banks that were not subject to any bank regulators until Congress put a moratorium on the practice. The chief executive officer of one large national association suggested that his bank could compete better against the insurance and securities industries, the biggest competitors of banks today, if the bank dissolved as a bank and became a business corporation. In that event, it would not have to deal with regulatory strictures against bank and bank holding company activity in the securities and insurance fields. Ultimately, however, that national bank took a different route, merging with another bank.

The traditional commercial bank allocates its activities among various departments. A typical bank might be organized into (1) operations, (2) commercial loans, (3) installment loans, (4) trust department, and (5) international banking. The operations division handles payments and **collections** (the payment system that is the subject of Part III) and administrative tasks. **Installment loan departments** are the source of consumer loans in the bank. The international bank department, if there is one, deals with international collections and payments and with letters of credit.

The banking industry divides banks into three categories: money-center banks, regionals, and country banks, all of which usually engage in commercial lending of one sort or another. With the advent of a relaxation of the laws against interstate banking, interstate acquisitions have created the super-regional bank. Some banks have traditionally emphasized retail banking, that is, dealing with small business enterprises or consumers; while other banks, fewer in number, have emphasized wholesale banking, that is, dealing with other, usually smaller banks, with multinational corporations and the like. Regional and money-center banks usually combine retail and wholesale banking.

§11.6 EXCLUSIONS

The material in this Part does not deal with real estate financing, except to the marginal extent that it deals with **fixtures,** and does not generally deal with consumer lending, except in purchase-money cases. Real estate lending is a subject for another book. Non-purchase-money consumer borrowing is seldom secured now, though many consumers borrow against home equity or **pledge** stock in order to raise money for home improvements, tuition, medical expenses, and other extraordinary consumer expenses.

Part II also does not discuss securitization, but a few words here about this new device are in order. Securitization is a rather recent phenomenon that raises more bank regulation and securities law issues for the practicing lawyer than secured transactions law issues.

Basically, securitization is the process whereby a financial institution packages and sells its loans (often after splitting them into "tranches") through the capital markets. A credit card bank, for example, generates significant amounts of receivables from customers who hold its credit cards. (Section 30.3 explains the role the credit card bank plays in the broad credit card industry.) For various reasons, the credit card bank may want to remove these assets form its balance sheet. Sometimes it simply wants to raise additional cash. Credit card banks have significant cash needs, since every time a cardholder makes a credit card purchase, the bank finances the purchase by paying the merchant seller. In any event, the bank can go directly to investors through the capital markets as a source of cash or as buyers for the assets it wants to sell.

There are additional advantages in securitization. Often, one part of the country may be in a development phase that gives rise to credit needs, while another part may have a dearth of some kind of investment opportunity. Traditionally, real estate lending has been local in the United States. When an area is developing, it may find funds insufficient to meet borrowers' needs. Because U.S. banking law has generally not permitted interstate banking, the local lender was not in a position to raise funds from parts of the country that had them. This resulted in inefficiencies in mortgage lending that the federal government addressed by creating agencies that would insure local mortgages and make them available for national investment.

The solution not only worked, it gave rise to the securitization phenomenon and signaled a sharp increase in the availability of credit for residential and, later, commercial construction and sales. The transaction is relatively simple. A mortgage originator, usually a bank or thrift, sells the mortgage notes and mortgages to a trustee. This transaction is called pooling. The trustee, in turn, issues certificates representing an ownership interest in the underlying pool and sells the certificates, usually through an underwriter, to investors on a national scale. The certificate holders are entitled to the principal and interest payments made by the mortgagees to the originator, which retains a small percentage of the payments as its servicing fee.

In the mortgage industry, moreover, securitization avoided a very nasty problem that confronted mortgage originators as interest rates rose. Thrifts, the largest source of mortgage lending, traditionally relied on deposits to fund their mortgage loans. Deposits, however, were and remain short term. The thrift depositor might make a 30-day time deposit or might buy a five-year certificate of deposit, but the thrift could not match those short-term deposits with the long-term (20- or 30-year) loans it made to its mortgage borrowers. Thus, when the interest rate on the time deposits rose, the thrifts were funding low-interest loans with high-interest deposits. This "interest rate risk" was one the thrift industry could not shoulder and is one of the reasons for the industry's decline in the 1980s and 1990s. Securitization permits the loan originator to pass interest rate risk to investors, often financial institutions with long-term investment needs (such as insurance companies and pension funds), who are willing to accept it.

These certificates are called pass-through certificates because the payments from the mortgagees are passed through to the certificate holders. There are investment disadvantages in the pass-through certificates, whose maturity and average payments are unpredictable. If interest rates fall, for example, many mortgagees will refinance their mortgages, and principal payments will accelerate. Thus originators have fashioned variations on the pass-through certificate, using pay-through bonds, for instance, which allow the separation of principal payments by tranches. Under a pay-through bond there might be three tranches providing that for the first five years all principal payments will be made to the holders of the first tranche, during the second five years to the holders of the second tranche, and during the final five years to the holders of the third tranche of bonds.

The credit card bank with a large portfolio of receivables — the sums due from cardholders at the end of the billing cycle — can use those receivables as security for its obligation, usually referred to as a certificate. Thus, when the bank sells the certificates, through underwriters or directly to investors, in effect it sells the cardholder loans and accompanies that sale by transferring the cardholders' obligations to pay, that is, by assigning the cardholders' accounts.

Financial institutions have used car loans secured by security interests in automobiles, mortgage obligations secured by interests in real estate, consumer installment loans secured by interests in consumer goods, chattel paper in the form of leases, and even secured commercial loans in this fashion. Sometimes, the original transaction, leasing of construction equipment, say, may not proceed until the institution knows that it has a customer for the obligations it will issue with the leases as security.

The securitized transaction has obvious Article 9 features. It is in part a secured transaction. It is nearly always the case that the bank will convey the assets to a trustee. That conveyance itself frequently will (in the case of accounts or chattel paper) be the creation of a security interest; or it will constitute the transfer of a security interest.

Figures illustrating various loan transactions and the evolving securitization process demonstrate the efficiency of securitization and its secured transaction component. Figure 11-1 illustrates the relationships in a simple loan transaction. If the loan is secured by the borrower's assets, the lender is a secured party and the borrower, the debtor.

Figure 11-1. Simple Loan

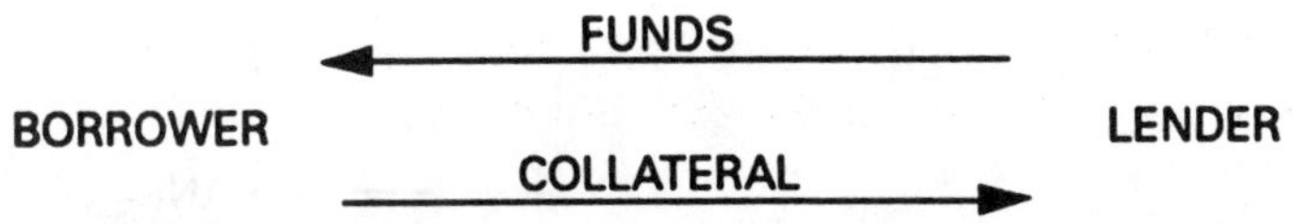

Figure 11-2. Loan Participation

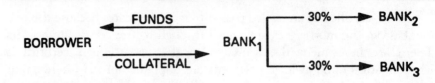

Lenders seeking to satisfy lending limit requirements or to avoid capital adequacy requirements might decide to "sell" a portion of a simple loan by participating a portion of it to one or more financial institutions. This early device for avoiding some of the problems that securitization addresses is illustrated in Figure 11-2.

Another early device for effecting some of these benefits is the loan syndication under which several banks together agree to lend to a single borrower. Figure 11-3 illustrates the loan syndication.

Note that in the three illustrations there is a single borrower that usually is borrowing a large sum. These devices involved considerable transaction costs and did not permit the originator, the original lender, to lay off small loans even though the small loans may have been considerable in the aggregate. Securitization permits the originator to lay off its small loans. A credit card bank, for example, with a hundred million dollars in credit card receivables may want to use a pass-through arrangement to remove the receivables from its balance sheet and to reduce capital requirements or make capital available for more profitable uses. The bank will pool the assets with a trustee (usually the trust department of another bank), which will issue certificates back to the credit card bank. The credit card bank, in turn, will sell the certificates through an underwriter to the investors. In this transaction, which is illustrated in Figure 11-4, there are two additional parties: a letter-of-credit issuer and a rating agency. The letter-of-credit issuer, a third bank, will enhance the marketability of the certificates by insuring a portion (for example, 10 percent) of them against default. The rating agency will give the certificates a rating that renders them investment grade, thereby making them acceptable to investors.

Asset securitization, then, is rather complex. The process usually involves substantial amounts of collateral. And, although tax and securities law considerations tend to dominate, note that there are clear secured

Figure 11-3. Syndicated Loan

```
                                          ┌───── BANK₁

          BORROWER ───────────────────────┼───── BANK₂

                                          └───── BANK₃
```

Figure 11-4. Asset Securitization

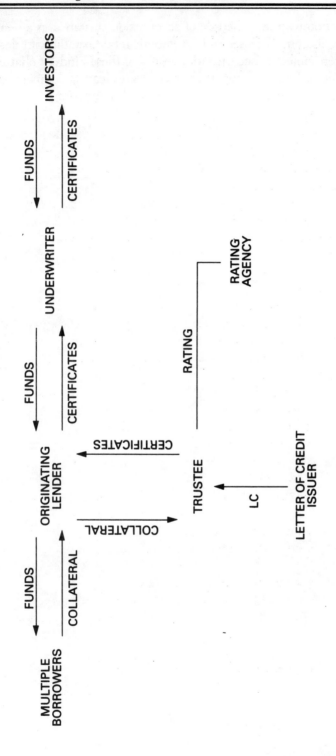

transaction features. The sale of accounts, for instance, is a secured transaction. Equipment leases and automobile retail installment sales contracts are often subject to securitization. Sales of these kinds of chattel paper by automotive finance companies or computer leasing company subsidiaries of computer manufacturers are also secured transactions.

12

The Basic Loan Agreement and the Working Capital Loan Concept

§12.1 INTRODUCTION

Prior to the adoption of the Uniform Commercial Code, the varied history of secured lending and the disparate origins of such lending yielded a mélange of secured lending practices and terminology. The signal achievement of the Code project was to standardize much of the practice, though a few vagaries survive. It is important for the student of secured transactions *law* to study that law with an eye to those features and to study that law in discrete fashion. In other words, the study should proceed along the lines of the various kinds of financing, e.g., inventory, accounts, equipment, and **dealer.** By the same token, our study here — the study of secured lending *practices* — uses the same approach by devoting separate chapters to those kinds of secured lending and the various practices that arise in them. This chapter deals with a few important, basic premises of good secured lending.

§12.2 NEED FOR THE LOAN AGREEMENT

The first, basic premise is the notion that most secured loan transactions, especially those involving a secured lender rather than a secured seller, should commence with a well-crafted loan agreement. There may be a tendency for the law teacher and the student to overemphasize in the study of secured transactions the note, security agreement, and **financing statement** — the **documents** that the Code defines and governs. Surely, secured lending documentation is incomplete until the parties consider whether those documents are necessary and, if so, until they are properly drafted and executed; nothing in this book suggests the contrary. In fact, the lawyer's role in secured lending is often clerical, just as it is in most other areas of the law.

The importance of those documents should not overshadow the importance of the loan agreement, which addresses the general relationship between lender and borrower and does far more than the note, the security agreement, and the financing statement are designed to do.

§12.3 PROMISSORY NOTE

Having said that the note, the security agreement, and the financing statement generally do not, by themselves, satisfy the needs of **loan documentation**, we must add that sometimes the **promissory note** does indeed perform the general function of the loan agreement by specifying in detail the relationship between the parties. Negotiable **instruments** law renders that approach problematic, since under that law, a note with "excess baggage" is not negotiable. It is either a curious tribute to the conservative nature of bank lenders or evidence of the power of tradition that most institutional lenders continue to take negotiable promissory notes from their borrowers. In a former era, banks negotiated their borrowers' notes, that is, they indorsed them to **correspondent banks** or other holders. The acceptability of those notes related directly to their negotiability, since the correspondent that took a negotiable note was a holder in due course that took free of **claims** and of important commercial defenses. Today, commercial banks generally do not negotiate their notes, except in some evolving areas of export finance. (*See* Section 19.7.) Virtually all of the notes that are executed in the domestic commercial loan industry sit in the files of the original lender and are never transferred to anybody. The one important exception to this domestic practice arises when a bank becomes insolvent. In that event, another bank or the Federal Deposit Insurance Corporation (FDIC) may acquire the failed bank's portfolio of promissory notes.

There is a considerable body of federal law that protects the FDIC in those situations, and it is probably fair to say that the FDIC does not need the benefit of the Code's holder-in-due-course rules. Perhaps the purchasing banks do need it, however. In any event, the practice of taking promissory notes in negotiable form survives in the banking industry. Document 12-1 illustrates a bank negotiable promissory note form.

§12.4 FORM OF LOAN AGREEMENT

While many institutional lenders will prepare form loan agreements for certain types of recurring transactions, some loan agreements will be tailored to the specific loan transaction. Document 12-2 is a standard form that a bank might use in connection with a number of loans. Note that in the loan agreement, there is no request for a security agreement, the loan in that case being an unsecured loan. Such unsecured loan agreements are not unusual in commercial banking, where, traditionally, banks make unsecured loans to good credit risks. Document 12-3 is the kind of note a bank might take under a working capital loan agreement. This note will bear a face amount equal to the full amount of the loan commitment. If the borrower's **line of credit** is $1 million, the note will be for that amount. The note stipulates, however, that the sum due under it is not the face amount, but the amount of all advances, less payments, plus interest.

§12.5 THE WORKING CAPITAL LOAN CONCEPT

This is the time to introduce the idea of the working capital loan. Much commercial lending relates to the type of collateral that the lender takes. The law of secured lending and the industry itself reflect that fact. The rules for purchase-money security interests in inventory are different from the rules for purchase-money security interests in other commercial collateral, for example.

In a similar way account lending can differ, depending on the nature of the account lender. Generally, lenders against accounts fall into one of three categories: banks, finance companies that lend against the accounts, and finance companies that buy the accounts (**factors**). Bankers that use accounts to secure the working capital loan will let the borrower collect the accounts and use the proceeds as he sees fit. The borrower may use the proceeds to pay off a portion of the loan or may use them to pay taxes and insurance. The commercial finance industry traditionally has been tougher in lending against accounts, may monitor them closely, and may insist that payments by the **account debtors** be used to reduce the loan balance. Some finance companies "buy" accounts, that is, they take the accounts and collect them themselves. In both of the latter cases, the lender is lending against discrete accounts and is not making a working capital loan. The bank's loan against accounts, however, is typical of the working capital loan.

Sometimes, especially in equipment lending, the loan is self-liquidating, that is, there is a set payment schedule that commences with the loan balance in the loan amount, gradually reduces the loan principal to zero, and does not exceed the life of the equipment. That type of loan is not a working capital loan either.

The working capital loan is more general in its treatment of the borrower and more flexible in meeting the borrower's cash needs. Under the working capital loan, the parties assume that the borrower will need capital during a period, often one calendar year, and that he will draw on the line of credit with the bank and will make repayments of principal from time to time during that period. In a business that has seasonal sales that peak in June, for example, the borrower may draw on the line all during the spring, as it builds inventory. During that period, expenses for raw materials, parts, payroll, and utilities will be relatively high and cash flow will be relatively low. After June, those costs will diminish, and cash flow will increase as customers begin paying for deliveries. In this ideal illustration, the borrower's annual cash needs will resemble a sine curve over the course of the year, as Figure 12-1 illustrates.

Typically, the working capital loan agreement will require the borrower to reduce its principal balance to zero at one time during the business cycle. The requirement reflects the fact that banks are short-term lenders and do not take an equity position in their borrower's business, that is, they lend to a company, they do not buy an interest in the company.

Figure 12-1.   Cash Need Graph

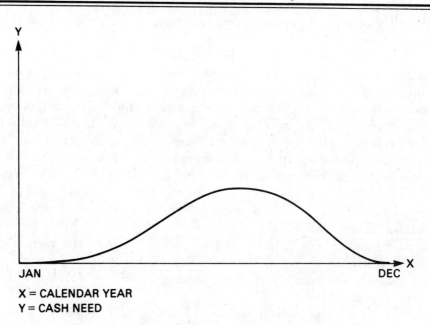

X = CALENDAR YEAR
Y = CASH NEED

§12.6 FURTHER LOAN DOCUMENTATION

In a loan transaction, there will be any number of documents in addition to the loan agreement. Corporate certificates, opinions of counsel, and schedules (of equipment, leases, cows(!), licenses, etc.) are examples. In addition, there is usually a separate promissory note and, in secured loan transactions, a security agreement and a financing statement.

Frequently, as chapters in this Part illustrate, security agreements are peculiar to the kind of collateral involved. Sometimes, a general security agreement will suffice. Document 12-4 is an example of a general security agreement.

In any security agreement, it is critical to identify the parties with care and to obtain the signature of the "debtor." The description of the collateral is also a matter for careful attention.

The financing statement, the document that the lender files in the public records as a notice to the world of its security interest, also calls for care. Courts are disposed to challenge the sufficiency of such documents if they do not identify the parties correctly or if the description of the collateral is in any way insufficient. The most common errors are in the designation of the "debtor." Lawyers and bankers should be aware that the law recognizes certain entities and does not recognize others. Individuals, corporations, partnerships, trusts, and estates have legal names. The lawyer or lender that fills out a financing statement without verifying the legal name of a borrower does so at its peril. Financing statement forms are prescribed by state variations of the Code and usually take the form of Document 12-5.

§12.7 POLICING

In any loan setting, the lender must take steps to protect itself from the consequences of the borrower's default. In asset-based loans, that policing often requires the lender to keep current on the status of the borrower's inventory or accounts and, in particular, on the value of such collateral — a difficult task.

Some working capital loans are secured; some are not. In the unsecured loan the lender relies primarily on the creditworthiness of its borrower. The borrower establishes that creditworthiness primarily through its credit history and through its financial statements. Lenders in these cases must know whether there are any material adverse changes in the financial posture of the borrower. In the best of all possible worlds, the lender perceives adverse trends before debilitating changes occur.

There are a number of steps that lenders take in monitoring the financial health of borrowers that do not give security. First, lenders will insist on periodic statements certified by independent **auditors**. The audits that generate audited financial statements are usually time-consuming and expensive for the borrower, who pays for them. They also arrive at the desk of the loan officer several months after the fact. An audit that covers a fiscal year ending on September 30, for example, might not be completed until the following February. The information in these audits is invaluable to the sophisticated loan officer, who may spot problems before the borrower's corporate officers are aware of them or at least before they are prepared to admit to their bank that they are aware of them.

In addition to the certified audit, it is customary for the lender to require the borrower to submit unaudited financial information on a periodic basis, probably monthly or quarterly. Loan officers might be particularly concerned with the age of accounts receivable and accounts payable and with inventory values. These financial records are generated internally by the borrower and are therefore less reliable than those prepared by independent certified public accounting firms. Internally prepared statements usually must be certified by a financial officer of the borrower, and the criminal sanctions that attend the false certification of information to a federally insured financial institution give them a measure of reliability.

Some credit-reporting agencies offer comparative reports that permit loan officers to evaluate a borrower's financial position. Thus, for example, Dun & Bradstreet, Inc. markets an Industry Norm Report that permits a loan officer to determine whether a hardware store borrower has too much inventory at a given time of year or whether a pipe wholesaler's payables are too high. Such comparisons can indicate that the borrower, though current in its payments, faces difficulty in coming months.

In addition to these statements and reports, loan officers rely on credit information agencies and legal newspapers that report on litigation, bankruptcies, name changes, and other activity that may spell financial difficulty for a borrower. Nothing, however, will substitute for a bank loan officer who consistently monitors industry activity. A loan officer with responsibility for agricultural lending is every bit as concerned about commodity prices and weather predictions as the farmers is.

$_____

19___

Pay to the order of _____   after date for value received _____   promise to

_____   Dollars

at _____

at _____ per cent per annum after _____   with interest

until paid

And to secure the payment of said amount _____ hereby authorize, irrevocably, any attorney of any Court of Record to appear for _____ in such Court, in term time or vacation, at any time hereafter, and confess a Judgment without process, in favor of the holder of this Note, for such amount as may appear to be unpaid thereon, together with costs and _____ dollars attorney's fees, and to waive and release all errors which may intervene in any such proceedings, and consent to immediate execution upon such judgment, hereby ratifying and confirming all that said attorney may do by virtue hereof.

SPECIMEN

No. _____

Due _____

W.L. Bond.

Document 12-2. Promissory Note

Michigan National Bank

PROMISSORY NOTE
(Line of Credit)

Note No. _____

$ _____

_____ , Michigan

Due Date: _____

Dated: _____

FOR VALUE RECEIVED, on the Due Date, the undersigned, jointly and severally, (the 'Borrower"), promise to pay to the order of Michigan National Bank, a national banking association (the "Bank"), at its office set forth below or at such other place as Bank may designate

in writing, the principal sum of _____ Dollars ($ _____) or such lesser sum as shall have been advanced by Bank to Borrower under the loan account hereinafter described, plus interest as herein after provided, all in lawful money of the United States of America. The unpaid principal balance of this promissory note ("Note") shall bear interest computed upon the basis of a year of 360 days for the actual number of days elapsed in a month, at a rate of interest (the "Effective Interest Rate") which is equal to:

(COMPLETE ONE:)

(1) _____ percent (_____ %) per annum.

(2) _____ percent (_____ %) per annum in excess of that rate of interest established by _____

_____ (the "Designee Bank") as its _____ rate (the "Index"), as such Index may vary from time to time. Borrower understands and agrees that the Effective Interest Rate payable to Bank under this Note shall be determined by reference to the Index and not by reference to the actual rate of interest charged by the Designee Bank to any particular borrower(s). If the Index shall be increased or decreased, the Effective Interest Rate under this Note shall be increased or decreased by the same amount, effective upon the day of each increase or decrease in the Index. If at any time, the Designee Bank shall abandon the rate of interest used as the Index for this Note, the Index shall be the Bank's own Prime Rate of interest.

Interest on all principal amounts advanced by Bank from time to time and unpaid by Borrower shall be paid on the _____ day of

_____ , 19 _____ , and on the _____ day of each _____ thereafter.

Advances of principal, repayment, and readvances may be made under this Note from time to time, but Bank, in its sole discretion, may refuse to make advances or readvances hereunder during any period(s) this Note is in default. All advances made hereunder shall be charged to a loan account in Borrower's name on Bank's books, and Bank shall debit to such account the amount of each advance made to, and credit to such account the amount of each repayment made by Borrower. From time to time, Bank shall furnish Borrower a statement of Borrower's loan account, which statement shall be deemed to be correct, accepted by, and binding upon Borrower, unless Bank receives a written statement of exceptions from Borrower within ten (10) days after such statement has been furnished.

This Note may be paid in full or in part at any time without payment of any prepayment fee. All payments received shall, at the option of the Bank, first be applied against accrued and unpaid interest and the balance against principal. Borrower expressly assumes all risks of loss or delay in the delivery of any payments made by mail, and no course of conduct or dealing shall affect Borrower's assumption of these risks. If Bank shall determine that the Effective Interest Rate under this Note is, or may be, usurious or otherwise limited by law, the unpaid balance of this Note, with accrued interest at the highest rate then permitted by law shall, at the option of the Bank, become immediately due and payable.

Unless this Note is due upon demand, in which case the provisions of this paragraph shall not apply, upon the occurrence of any of the following events of default, Bank, at its option and without notice to Borrower, may declare the entire unpaid principal balance of this Note and all accrued interest, together with all other indebtedness of Borrower to Bank, to be immediately due and payable: (a) Borrower's failure to pay any installment of principal or of interest when due; (b) any breach by Borrower of any warranty, representation, covenant, term or condition stated in any loan agreement, security agreement, mortgage, or other agreement executed in connection with this Note; (c) the death, dissolution, or termination of existence of Borrower; (d) if Borrower is generally not paying its debts as such debts become due; (e) the commencement of any proceedings under any bankruptcy or insolvency laws by or against Borrower; (f) if any other indebtedness of Borrower to the Bank or to any other creditor shall become due and remain unpaid after acceleration of the maturity or after the maturity stated; (g) if any writ of attachment, garnishment, execution, tax lien, or similar process shall be issued against any property of Borrower; (h) Borrower's business shall be sold to, or merged with, any other business, individual, or entity.

Upon the occurrence of any event of default, or upon non-payment of this Note after demand, the unpaid principal balance of this Note shall bear interest at a rate which is two percent (2%) greater than the Effective Interest Rate otherwise applicable. If any payment under this Notice is not paid within ten (10) days after the date due, at the option of the Bank a late charge of not more than five cents ($.05) for each dollar of the installment past due may be charged by Bank. In addition to any other security interest granted, Borrower hereby grants Bank a security interest in all of Borrower's bank deposits, instruments, negotiable documents, and chattel paper which at any time are in the possession or control of Bank, and after the occurrence of any event of default, Bank may apply its own indebtedness or liability to Borrower or any guarantor to any indebtedness due under this Note. Borrower agrees to pay all of the Bank's costs incurred in the collection of this Note, including reasonable attorney fees.

Acceptance by Bank of any payment in an amount less than the amount then due shall be deemed an acceptance on account only, and Bank's acceptance of any such partial payment shall not constitute a waiver of Bank's right to receive the entire amount due. Borrower and all guarantors of this Note do hereby jointly and severally waive presentment for payment, demand, notice of non-payment, notice of protest or protest of this Note, and Bank diligence in collection or bringing suit, and do hereby consent to any and all extensions of time, renewals, waivers, or modifications as may be granted by Bank with respect to payment or any other provisions of this Note, and to the release of any collateral or any part thereof, with or without substitution. The liability of the Borrower under this Note shall be absolute and unconditional, without regard to the liability of any other party. This Note shall be deemed to have been executed in Michigan, and all rights and obligations hereunder shall be governed by the laws of the State of Michigan. This Note is secured by:

☐ Security Agreement dated _____

☐ Loan Agreement dated _____

☐ Real Estate Mortgage dated _____

☐ Guaranty dated _____

☐ Other _____

Reference is hereby made to the document(s) and agreement(s) described above for additional terms and conditions relating to this Note.

Borrower Address

_____

_____

Bank Address

_____

_____

BORROWER

SPECIMEN

Tax ID or Social Security No.

10015 (11/91)

© 1991 Michigan National Corporation

WHITE-BANK ORIGINAL   YELLOW-BANK PROCESSING COPY   PINK-CUSTOMER COPY

BUSINESS LOAN AGREEMENT
(SHORT FORM)

The undersigned _____

SPECIMEN (NAME OF BORROWER)

a _____, with its chief executive offices located

at _____ (ADDRESS)

(the "Borrower") has requested from _____ (FULL PROPER BANK NAME)

of _____ , Michigan ("Bank") and Bank agrees to make, or has made, the loan(s) described below (the "Loans") under the terms and conditions set forth in this Business Loan Agreement ("Agreement").

I. LOANS:

The following Loan(s) and any amendments, extensions, renewals or refinancing thereof are subject to this Agreement:

	TYPE OF LOAN	INTEREST RATE	NOTE AMOUNT	NOTE MATURITY DATE	LOAN DATE
A.					
B.					

Purpose of Loan(s) listed above:

A. _____

B. _____

Unless otherwise specified, any previous Business Loan Agreements are superceded by this Agreement.

II. BORROWER'S REPRESENTATIONS AND WARRANTIES.

Borrower represents and warrants to Bank, all of which representations and warranties shall be continuing and shall survive the execution of this Agreement until all of the Indebtedness is fully paid to Bank and Borrower's obligations under this Agreement and the Related Documents are fully performed, as follows:

A. **Borrower's Existence and Authority.** Borrower is a _____ and the person
Sole proprietorship/partnership/corporation

or persons executing this Agreement have full power and complete authority to execute this Agreement and all Related Documents.

B. **Nature of Borrower's Business.** The nature of Borrower's business is: _____ .

C. **Financial Information.** All Financial Information provided to Bank has been prepared and will continue to be prepared in accordance with generally accepted accounting principles (GAAP), consistently applied, and fully and fairly present the financial condition of the Borrower, and there has been no material adverse change in Borrower's business, Property, or condition (financial or otherwise) since the date of the Borrower's latest Financial Statements.

D. **Title and Encumbrances.** Borrower owns and has good title to all of its Property, including the Collateral, and there are no liens or encumbrances on any of the Property, including the Collateral, except as have been disclosed to Bank in writing prior to the date of this Agreement and as are identified and listed in an attachment to this Agreement (the "Permitted Encumbrances"). Borrower agrees that Borrower shall not obtain further loans, leases, or extensions of credit from any of the parties identified in the said Permitted Encumbrances list without Bank's prior written consent.

E. **No Litigation/No Misrepresentations.** There are no pending suits or proceedings pending before any court, government agency, arbitration panel, or administrative tribunal, or, to Borrower's knowledge, threatened against Borrower, which may result in any material adverse change in the business, Property or financial condition of Borrower, and all representations and warranties in this Agreement and the Related Documents are true and correct and no material fact has been omitted.

F. **Environmental Compliance.** No part of the Property is classified or classifiable as hazardous waste under Federal and Michigan environmental laws and regulations, and Borrower (and all Obligors) agree to indemnify and hold Bank harmless from any and all violations by Borrower of any Federal or Michigan environmental laws and regulations.

III. AFFIRMATIVE COVENANTS.

As of the date of this Agreement and continuing until the Borrower's obligations under this Agreement and the Related Documents are fully performed and the Indebtedness is fully repaid to Bank, Borrower shall at all times:

A. **Financial Requirements.**
1. Requirements: _____

B. **Books and Reports.**
1. Furnish to Bank, in form acceptable to Bank: [ ] management prepared and certified [ ] certified public accountant prepared [ ] compiled [ ] reviewed [ ] audited Financial Statements within _____ days after the end of each [ ] month [ ] quarter [ ] six months [ ] fiscal year.

2. Furnish to Bank, in form satisfactory to Bank, within _____ days after the end of each Borrower's fiscal [ ] month [ ] quarter [ ] year [ ] compiled [ ] reviewed [ ] audited Financial Statements prepared by certified public accountants acceptable to Bank.

3. Promptly furnish to Bank such other information and reports concerning the Borrower's business, Property, and financial condition as are provided to Borrower's owners, or as Bank shall request, and permit Bank to inspect, confirm, and copy Borrower's books and records at any time during Borrower's normal business hours.

C. **Notice of Adverse Events.** Promptly notify Bank in writing of any litigation, governmental proceeding, default or any other occurrence which may have a material adverse effect on Borrower's business, Property or financial condition.

D. **Maintain Business Existence and Operations.** Do all things necessary to keep in full force and effect Borrower's corporate, partnership or proprietorship existence, as the case may be, and to continue its business described in Paragraph II B. as presently conducted, and maintain its present business status. Borrower shall not change its corporate, partnership or proprietorship existence, nor sell or merge Borrower's business, in whole or in part, without the prior written consent of Bank.

E. **Insurance.**
Maintain adequate fire and extended risk coverage, business interruption, workers compensation, public liability and such other insurance coverages as may be required by law or as may be required by Bank. All insurance policies shall be in such amounts, upon such terms, and be in form acceptable to Bank, and shall be carried with insurers acceptable to Bank. Borrower shall provide evidence satisfactory to Bank of all insurance coverages and that the policies are in full force and effect, and all insurance coverages upon any Property which is Collateral for any of Borrower's Indebtedness to Bank, shall name Bank as a loss payee and shall be endorsed to require thirty (30) days advance written notice to Bank of any cancellation of coverage. If Borrower fails to maintain insurance as provided in this Agreement, such failure shall be an Event of Default and Bank may obtain the insurance but shall have no obligation to do so; and all amounts so expended by Bank shall be added to the Indebtedness or shall be payable on demand, at Bank's option.

10027 (12/86)

Reprinted with the permission of Michigan National Corporation.

F. **Payment of Taxes.** Promptly pay all taxes, levies and assessments due all local, State and Federal agencies. Except to the extent that Borrower has established a cash reserve therefore and is actively pursuing a tax appeal, any failure by Borrower to promptly pay any taxes, levies and assessments due shall be an Event of Default.

G. **Use of Proceeds; Purpose of Loans.** Use the proceeds of the Loans only for Borrower's business described in Paragraph II B, and for those purposes stated in Paragraph I.

H. **Maintenance of Records; Change in Place of Business or Name.** Keep all of its books and records at the address set forth above in this Agreement, and shall give the Bank prompt written notice of any change in its principal place of business, in the location of Borrower's books and records, in Borrower's name, and any change in the location of the Collateral.

I. **Workers Compensation Insurance.** At all times during the term of this Agreement and until the Indebtedness shall have been fully repaid, maintain workers' compensation insurance as required by law unless Borrower is qualified and duly authorized by law to self-insure with respect to its workers' compensation liability and is not otherwise prohibited by this Agreement from doing so.

IV. NEGATIVE COVENANTS.

Until all of Borrower's obligations under this Agreement and the Related Documents are fully performed and the Indebtedness is fully repaid, Borrower shall not:

A. **Investment In Fixed Assets.** Invest in fixed assets in excess of $_____ in any 12 month period, without the prior written consent of Bank.

B. **No Borrowings, Guarantees, or Loans.** Borrow money or act as a guarantor of any loan or other obligation of others, or lend any money to any person. Any sale of Borrower's accounts receivable shall be deemed the borrowing of money.

C. **Liens and Encumbrances; Transfer of Assets.** Mortgage, assign, hypothecate, or encumber in any way any of its Property to any person except to Bank, nor sell, transfer, or assign any Property except in the ordinary course of Borrower's business.

D. **Salary Limitations.** During the term of this Agreement and until all Indebtedness is repaid to Bank, the annual total of all salaries, bonuses, fringe benefits, and all other monetary compensation paid by Borrower to the following officers, directors, or employees shall not exceed the following limitations:

Name	Limitation
_____	$ _____
_____	$ _____

V. EVENTS OF DEFAULT.

The occurrence of any of the following events shall constitute an Event of Default under this Agreement.

A. **Failure to Pay Amounts Due.** If any principal or interest on any Indebtedness to Bank is not paid when due.

B. **Misrepresentation; False Financial Information.** If any warranty or representation of the Borrower in connection with or contained in this Agreement, or if any Financial Statements now or hereafter furnished to the Bank by or on behalf of the Borrower, are false or misleading in any material respect.

C. **Noncompliance with Bank Agreements.** If the Borrower shall fail to perform any of its obligations and covenants under, or shall fail to comply with any of the provisions of this Agreement or any other agreement with the Bank, including but not limited to the Related Documents.

D. **Other Lender Default.** Any non-Bank indebtedness of Borrower matures or is declared to be due and payable prior to the stated maturity thereof.

E. **Judgments; Attachments; Garnishments; Tax Liens.** If there shall be entered against Borrower or any other Obligor, any judgment which materially affects Borrower's or the Obligor's business, Property or financial condition, or if any tax lien, levy, writ of attachment, garnishment, execution or similiar writ shall be issued against the Collateral or which materially affects Borrower's business, Property or financial condition, and which remains unpaid, unstayed on appeal, undischarged, unbonded, or undismissed for a period of thirty (30) days after the date thereof.

F. **Business Merger, Suspension, Bankruptcy.** If Borrower or any other Obligor shall sell or merge Borrower's business to or with any other business; shall voluntarily suspend transaction of its business; shall not generally pay debts as they mature; shall make a general assignment for the benefit of creditors; or shall file or have filed against Borrower any reorganization or liquidation under the Bankruptcy Code or under any other state or federal law for the relief of debtors which is not discharged within thirty (30) days after filing; or a receiver, trustee or custodian shall be appointed for the Borrower or any Obligor.

G. **Material Adverse Change.** Any material adverse change in the Borrower's business, Property or financial condition has occurred or is imminent; if the full performance of the obligations of any Obligor is materially impaired; or if the Collateral and its value or the Bank's rights with respect thereto are materially impaired in any way.

H. **Authority to Charge Interest Rate Adversely Affected.** If Bank shall determine that the Loan(s) interest rate is usurious, or is otherwise unlawful or limited in any way, including but not limited to Bank's right to periodically adjust the agreed upon rate of interest or the method of adjustment.

I. **Non-Compliance with Worker's Compensation Laws.** If Borrower fails to comply with any workers' compensation law, regulation, administrative rule, directive or requirement; has its workers' compensation insurance terminated or cancelled for any reason; or, if applicable, has its self-insurance certification revoked or should such certification lapse for any reason.

VI. REMEDIES ON DEFAULT.

A. **Acceleration/Set-off.** Upon the occurrence of any Event of Default, the Loan(s) and all Indebtedness to Bank may, at the option of Bank, be declared to be immediately due and payable, and Bank shall have the right to apply any or all of Borrower's or any Obligor's bank accounts or any other property held by Bank, against any Indebtedness of Borrower to Bank.

B. **Remedies; No Waiver.** The remedies provided for in this Agreement are cumulative and not exclusive, and Bank may exercise any remedies available to it at law or in equity and as are provided in the Related Documents or other agreement between Borrower and Bank. No delay or failure of Bank in exercising any right, remedy, power or privilege under this Agreement or the Related Documents shall affect that right, remedy, power or privilege, nor shall any single or partial exercise preclude the exercise of any other right, remedy, power or privilege. No delay or failure of Bank to demand strict adherence to the terms of this Agreement shall be deemed to constitute a course of conduct inconsistent with the Bank's right at any time, before or after any Event of Default, to demand strict adherence to the terms of this Agreement or the Related Documents.

VII. CROSS-COLLATERALIZATION/CROSS-DEFAULT.

Borrower agrees that all of the Collateral is security for the Loan(s) and for all other Indebtedness of Borrower to Bank, whether or not such Indebtedness is related by class or kind, and whether or not contemplated by the parties at the time of executing each evidence of Indebtedness. Any Borrower default under the terms of any Indebtedness to Bank shall constitute an Event of Default under this Agreement.

VIII. MISCELLANEOUS.

A. **Compliance with Bank Agreements.** Borrower acknowledges that Borrower has read and understands this Agreement, the Related Documents, and all other agreements between Borrower and Bank, and Borrower agrees to fully comply with all the agreements.

B. **Expenses.** Borrower agrees to pay all of Bank's expenses incidental for in this Agreement are incidental to perfecting Bank's security interests and liens, all insurance premiums, Uniform Commercial Code search fees, and all fees incurred by Bank for audits, inspection, and copying of Borrower's books and records. Borrower also agrees to pay all costs and expenses of Bank in connection with the enforcement of the Bank's rights and remedies under this Agreement, the Related Documents, and any other agreeement between Borrower and Bank, and in connection with the preparation of any amendments, modifications, waivers or consents with respect to this Agreement, including reasonable attorney fees.

C. **Further Action.** Borrower agrees, from time to time, upon request of Bank, to make, execute, acknowledge, and deliver to Bank such further and additional instruments, documents, and agreements, and to take such further action as may be required to carry out the intent and purpose of this Agreement and the repayment of the Loan(s).

D. **Governing Law/Partial Illegality** This Agreement and the Related Documents shall be interpreted, and the rights of the parties hereunder shall be determined under, the laws of the State of Michigan. Should any part, term, or provision of this Agreement be adjudged illegal or in conflict with any law of the United States or State of Michigan, the validity of the remaining portion or provisions of the Agreement shall not be affected.

E. **Writings Constitute Entire Agreement; Modifications Only in Writing.** This Agreement together with all other written agreements between Borrower and Bank, including but not limited to the Related Documents, constitute the entire agreement of the parties and shall be interpreted in harmony one with the others. None of the parties shall be bound by anything not expressed in writing, and this Agreement can not be modified except by a writing executed by Borrower and by the Bank. This Agreement shall inure to the benefit of and shall be binding upon all of the parties to this Agreement and their respective successors, estate representatives, and assigns, provided, however, that Borrower can not assign or transfer its rights or obligations under this Agreement without Bank's prior written consent.

F. **Headings.** All section and paragraph headings in this Agreement are included for reference only and do not constitute a part of this Agreement.

G. **Term of Agreement.** Unless superseded by a later Business Loan Agreement, this Agreement shall continue in full force and effect until all of Borrower's obligations to Bank are fully satisfied and the Loan(s) and Indebtedness are fully repaid.

IX. DEFINITIONS.

The following words shall have the following meanings in this Agreement:

A. **"Collateral"** shall mean that property which Borrower and any other Obligor has pledged, mortgaged, or granted Bank a security interest in, wherever located and whether now owned or hereafter acquired, together with all replacements, substitutions, proceeds and products thereof.

B. **"Base Rate" or "Prime Rate"** shall mean that variable rate of interest from time to time established by the Designee Bank as its prime commercial lending rate.

C. **"Event of Default"** shall mean any of the events described in Section V of this Agreement and in the Related Documents.

D. **"Financial Statements"** shall mean all balance sheets, earnings statements, and other financial information (whether of the Borrower, or an Obligor) which have been, are now, or are in the future furnished to Bank.

E. **"GAAP"** shall mean "generally accepted accounting principles" consistently applied as set forth from time to time in the Opinion of the Accounting Principles Board of the American Institute of Certified Public Accountants and the Financial Accounting Standards Board, or which have other substantial authoritative support.

F. **"Indebtedness"** shall mean all Loans and indebtedness of Borrower to the Bank, including but not limited to, Bank advances for payments of insurance, taxes, any amounts advanced by Bank to protect its interest in the Collateral, overdrafts in deposit accounts with Bank, and all other indebtedness, obligations and liabilities of Borrower to Bank, whether matured or unmatured, liquidated or unliquidated, direct or indirect, absolute or contingent, joint or several, due or to become due, now existing or hereafter arising.

G. **"Michigan National Bank Prime Rate"** shall mean that variable rate of interest so designated and from time to time established by Michigan National Corporation as the Michigan National Bank prime commercial lending rate.

H. **"Obligor"** shall mean any person having any obligation to Bank, whether for the payment of money or otherwise, under this Agreement or under the Related Documents, including but not limited to any guarantors of Borrower's Indebtedness.

I. **"Permitted Encumbrances"** shall mean that list of existing secured parties or mortgagee identified in a list attached to this Agreement.

J. **"Property"** shall mean all of Borrower's (or other Obligor's, as applicable) assets, whether tangible or intangible, real or personal.

K. **"Related Documents"** shall mean any and all documents, promissory notes, security agreements, leases, mortgages, guarantys, pledges, and any other documents or agreements executed in connection with this Agreement. The term shall include both documents existing at the time of execution of this Agreement and documents executed after this date of this Agreement.

X. ADDITIONAL PROVISIONS.

_____

_____

_____

IN WITNESS WHEREOF, the parties have executed this Agreement on this _____ day of _____ , 19____.

Witnesses: **BORROWER**

_____

_____

_____   **SPECIMEN**

_____   **BANK**

_____   By: _____

_____   Its: _____

AGREEMENT OF GUARANTORS

By executing this Agreement each Guarantor: (1) acknowledges and agrees that the Guarantor has completely read and understands this Agreement; (2) consents to all of the provisions of this Agreement relating to Borrower; (3) agrees to furnish such financial information to Bank concerning the Guarantor as Bank shall reasonably request; (4) agrees to all of those portions of this Agreement which apply to Guarantor; (5) acknowledges and agrees that this Agreement has been freely executed without duress and after an opportunity was provided to Guarantor for review of this Agreement and the guaranty agreement by legal counsel of Guarantor's choice; and (6) that the Bank has provided Guarantor with a copy of this Agreement, the Guaranty, and such other related documents as the Guarantor has requested.

Witnesses:

_____   _____

_____   _____
                                                                (ADDRESS)

_____   _____

_____   _____
                                                                (ADDRESS)

SECURITY AGREEMENT
(General)

I.   The parties to this agreement are as follows:

Debtor:_____

Secured Party:_____

II.   The Debtor for valuable consideration, receipt whereof is hereby acknowledged, hereby transfers to the Secured Party a security interest in the following property and any and all additions and accessions thereto:

SPECIMEN

III.   The Collateral has been acquired and is used by the Debtor (or will be acquired and will be used) primarily for the purpose checked below:

☐ Equipment used in business.   ☐ Consumer goods (personal, family or household goods).

If checked here ☐, the Collateral will be acquired with proceeds of loans from the Secured Party which may disburse the proceeds thereof directly to the Seller.

IV.   The Collateral will be kept at_____
(No. and Street)

_____

| (City or Town) | (County) | (State) |

and the record owner of said premises is_____

Debtor agrees to promptly notify Secured Party of any change in the location of the Collateral and that Debtor will not remove the Collateral from said State without the written consent of the Secured Party.

V.   The aforesaid security interest shall secure the obligations evidenced by notes described as follows:

Date_____Amount_____

and shall secure the payment of any and all indebtednesses and liabilities whatsoever of the Debtor to the Secured Party, whether now existing or hereafter arising, together with all costs and expenses of Secured Party in respect of or connected with any of the indebtedness or Collateral.

VI.   Debtor at its expense will keep and maintain in force such insurance in such amounts covering loss or damage to the Collateral, including extended coverage, as is usually and customarily carried by owners of like property or as may be requested by Secured Party, including loss payable clauses if demanded.

VII.   Debtor hereby warrants and covenants that except for the security interest granted hereby Debtor is, or to the extent that this agreement states that the Collateral is to be acquired after the date hereof, will be, the owner of the Collateral free from any adverse lien, security interest or encumbrance and that Debtor will defend the Collateral against all claims and demands of all persons at any time claiming the same or any interest therein.

VIII.   If any or all of the Collateral has been or is to be attached to real estate, Debtor on demand of Secured Party shall furnish the Secured Party with a disclaimer or disclaimers signed by all persons having an interest in the real estate (including landowners, mortgage holders, and lessees) disclaiming any interest in the Collateral prior to the interest of the Secured Party.

IX.   Debtor will pay on demand all costs and expenses of filing and recording, including the costs of any searches deemed necessary by Secured Party, to establish and determine the validity and the priority of the security interest of the Secured Party and also all other claims and charges which in the opinion of Secured Party might prejudice, imperil or otherwise affect the Collateral or its security interest therein. At its option, Secured Party may discharge taxes, liens or security interests or other encumbrances at any time levied or placed on the Collateral, may pay for insurance on the Collateral and may pay for the maintenance and preservation of the Collateral. Debtor agrees to reimburse Secured Party on demand for any payment made, or any expense incurred by Secured Party pursuant to the foregoing authorization.

X.   Debtor will keep the Collateral free from any adverse lien, security interest or encumbrance and in good order and repair and will not waste or destroy the Collateral or any part thereof. Debtor will not use the Collateral in violation of any statute or ordinance. Secured Party may examine and inspect the Collateral at any time, wherever located.

XI.   In the event the Debtor fails to pay when due any installment of interest or principal of any indebtedness secured by this Security Agreement, or in the event the Debtor violates any term of this Security Agreement, or in the event the Secured Party in good faith deems itself insecure either as to the payment of the obligations secured by this agreement, as to the Debtor's ability to perform this Security Agreement, or as to the sufficiency of the collateral securing the indebtedness, then the Debtor shall be in default of this Security Agreement and the Secured Party may proceed in accordance with law. In furtherance of and not in limitation of the foregoing, in the event of default, the Secured Party shall have the right to take immediate possession of the Collateral, and for that purpose may pursue the same wherever it may be found and may enter any of the Debtor's premises, with or without force or process of law, wherever said Collateral may be, or be supposed to be, and search for the same, and if found, may take possession of and remove and sell the Collateral or any part thereof at public or private sale. Unless the Collateral is perishable or threatens to decline speedily in value or is of a type customarily sold on a recognized market, the Secured Party will give the Debtor reasonable notice of the time and place of any public sale or of the time after which any other intended disposition is to be made. The requirement of reasonable notice shall be met if such notice is mailed, postage prepaid, to the Debtor at the address given herein or if none to any address in the Secured Party's files; at least five days before the time of sale or other disposition. Expenses of retaking, holding, preparing for sale, selling or the like shall include Secured Party's reasonable attorney's fees and legal expenses. Out of the money arising from such sale, Secured Party may retain all costs and charges for pursuing, searching for, retaking, removing, keeping, storing, advertising and selling such Collateral, together with the amount due and unpaid upon any notes held by it, accounting to the Debtor for any surplus.

XII.   No default shall be waived by Secured Party except in writing and no waiver of any default shall operate as a waiver of any other default or of the same default on a future occasion. All rights of Secured Party hereunder shall be cumulative and shall inure to the benefit of itself, its successors and assigns; and all obligations of Debtor shall bind legal representatives and successors. If there is more than one Debtor, all undertakings, warranties and covenants made by the Debtor and all rights, powers and authorities given to or conferred on the Secured Party shall be made or given jointly and severally.

Dated:_____, 19_____.   Signed:_____

_____   _____
Address   Debtor

Document 12-5.   Financing Statement

This FINANCING STATEMENT is presented for filing pursuant to the Michigan Uniform Commercial Code.	*(Please Type All Information)*		FOR FILING OFFICER (Date, Time, Number, and Filing Officer) DO NOT WRITE IN THIS SPACE

1. *Debtor(s) (Last Name First, If Individual) & Address(es)*

Soc. Security #/Tax ID #

Address

City	*State*	*Zip Code*

Debtor(s) (Last name First, If Individual & Address(es)

Address

City	*State*	*Zip Code*

2. *If Filing without debtor signature, item a, b, c, or d must be marked* [X].

a. [ ] Collateral was already subject to the security interest in another state when it was brought into Michigan, or when the Debtor's location changed to Michigan;

b. [ ] Collateral is proceeds of the original collateral in which a a security interest was perfected;

c. [ ] A previous filing covering the collateral has lapsed (Prev. Filing #   );

d. [ ] The filing covers collateral acquired after a change of name identity, or corporate structure of Debtor (MCLA 440.9402(2) & (7)) FROM: _____

(Prev. Filing #   ).

3. *Secured Party(ies) and Address(es)*

Secured Party #

4. MAIL ACKNOWLEDGEMENT COPY TO:

5. *No. of Add'l Sheets*

6. *State Account No.*

7. (Mark [X] if applicable):

[ ]   Products of collateral are also covered.

[ ]   The debtor is a transmitting utility as defined in MCLA 440.9105 (1)(o).

8. *Assignee(s) (If any) and Address(es)*

Secured Party #

9. This financing statement covers the following types (or items) of property:

X_____
Signature(s) of Debtor(s)

X_____
Signature(s) of Secured Party(ies) or Assignee(s) of Record

X_____
Signature(s) of Debtor(s)

X_____
Signature(s) of Secured Party(ies) or Assignee(s) of Record

IF YOU WISH THE ACKNOWLEDGEMENT COPY TO BE MAILED TO AN ADDRESS OTHER THAN THE SECURED PARTY SHOWN IN ITEM 3, PROVIDE COMPLETE MAILING INFORMATION IN ITEM 4.   UCC-1

SECRETARY OF STATE COPY.

119

13

The Financing Seller

§13.1 INTRODUCTION

Banks and finance companies are major participants in secured lending, and the secured transaction that involves them is customarily a three-party transaction, which Figure 13-1 illustrates.

There is, however, another category of secured lender that also plays a major role in secured lending. This secured lender is the seller of goods,

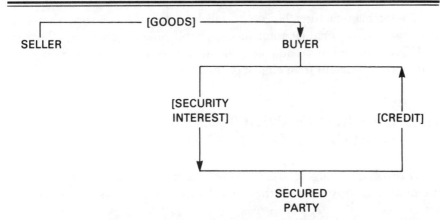

Figure 13-1. Three-Party Secured Transaction

Figure 13-2.   Two-Party Secured Transaction

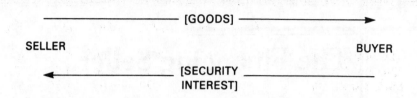

and in two significant ways the security interest of the secured seller differs from the security interest of the secured lender. First, the sales transaction is two-party, not three-party. Second, in the secured sales transaction, we normally think of the seller as "retaining" a security interest, while in the three-party secured transaction, the debtor "grants" the security interest to the **secured party**. In addition, in the sales secured transaction, the documentation is somewhat simpler. There is no need for a loan agreement here. This "loan" (or extension of credit) is discretely related to a single item or a designated group of items — the product or products that the seller is selling to the debtor on credit. The security agreement in these cases is usually part of the sales agreement, which itself contains the payment terms, there being no promissory note. Figure 13-2 illustrates the two-party nature of this secured transaction.

Retailers generate a great volume of secured seller transactions, and those sellers fall into one of two categories. The first is the credit plan seller that takes a security interest in all merchandise sold on credit under a "charge-account" arrangement. Traditionally, department stores and large national or regional retailers have engaged in this kind of consumer credit transaction. The second category involves credit granted in connection with a single purchase. These transactions usually arise out of big ticket sales, that is, sales of home appliances, automobiles, and the like.

There are other sellers, usually of business or manufacturing equipment, that finance the buyer's purchase, but some of them are really lenders. Equipment financing frequently takes the form of a finance lease that is in reality a security agreement. The lessor in those cases, may be the equipment manufacturer but often will be a finance company that is a subsidiary of the manufacturer or of a bank holding company. Section 13.4 discusses indirect equipment financing generally, and Chapter 18 deals with equipment financing at greater length.

§13.2 SECURED TRANSACTIONS AND CHARGE-ACCOUNT SALES

Many revolving charge accounts do not entail any security agreement. If the retailer is satisfied with the credit history of a customer, the retailer

Figure 13-3.   Revolving Credit-Account Balance

	FEB.	MAR.	APR.	MAY	JUN.	JUL.
JAN. SALE ($10)	5.00	3.33	2.50	1.66	0.83	-0-
FEB. SALE ($10)		6.67	5.00	3.34	1.67	-0-
MAR. SALE ($10)			7.50	5.00	2.50	-0-

ALLOCATION OF
$5 MONTHLY PAYMENT

	FEB.	MAR.	APR.	MAY	JUN.
JAN. SALE	5.00	1.67	0.83	0.84	0.83
FEB. SALE		3.33	1.67	1.66	1.67
MAR. SALE			2.50	2.50	2.50

accepts charges and bills periodically, usually with a service charge for bills that are not paid promptly. Although direct retailer secured lending is diminishing as a source of consumer credit relative to all sources, some retailers who are unwilling to extend credit on that basis at all or are unwilling to extend it to some customers grant credit to such customers only if they can do so on a secured basis.

Efforts by retailers to secure revolving credit accounts have fostered some controversy. Usually, the retailer uses a **cross collateralization** provision in the agreement whereby all goods purchased secure all of the debt. Retailers have given that provision expanded effect by providing that the buyer's periodic payments shall be allocated ratably among the principal balances due on each purchase. Assume, for purposes of illustration, that a consumer acquired a videocassette recorder in January and a refrigerator in June, and that the balance due in August was $500 on the VCR and $1,000 on the refrigerator. Under these revolving charge account provisions, the retailer allocates one-third of the August payment to the VCR balance and two-thirds of the payment to the refrigerator balance. The effect of the arrangement is to leave a small balance owing on an early purchase, thereby insuring that the security interest in that item will continue and that it will retain its purchase-money character.

Because of the Code's **perfection** rules and restrictions on the ability to use **consumer goods** as collateral, the purchase-money nature of the security interest is important to the retailer. Figure 13-3 illustrates this attempt to retain purchase-money status as to each item of collateral.

Consumer advocates and some courts have objected to these arrangements as unconscionable. It does not require a great deal of sophistication to realize quickly that retailers take security interests in these cases not because used consumer goods are valuable collateral that will fetch good prices in the used furniture market. Retailers use these security agreements for their ad terrorem effect.

It is a hot summer day; the unemployed parent of small children hears the doorbell. At the door are two burly gentlemen in green uniforms. "We come to get the fridge," one of them announces, and it occurs to the parent that perhaps the proceeds of the welfare check on the kitchen table should go to the department store instead of the grocer. In one case, a department store sought to repossess a used shower curtain and used children's toys among other items a welfare mother had acquired over a period of months.

Some have argued that the creditor practices in question are a concomitant of poverty and not the consequences of merchant greed. These commentators contend that if these agreements are not enforceable, poor people will not be able to obtain credit or will pay more for that credit. They also point out that security provisions make it easier for retailers to collect from those buyers who can afford to pay but who prefer to default and let the rest of the consuming public share the loss.

§13.3 CONSUMER PAPER

In secured transactions law, **consumer paper** is a far more important source of credit than revolving charge account agreements. Revolving charge account charges are often small purchases, and many consumers satisfy them monthly before interest charges accrue. Often, moreover, retailers do not retain a security interest in goods purchased under a revolving charge account.

Big ticket sales of consumer durables (home appliances and automobiles) involve substantial sums that many consumers finance over relatively long periods, from 12 to 60 months. These transactions yield considerable interest, and are attractive subjects for bank lending. In a typical transaction, an automobile dealer enters into a credit sale with a customer who grants the dealer a purchase-money security interest in the subject of the sale. Figure 13-4 illustrates this frequent consumer purchase transaction.

Figure 13-4.   Consumer Sale (Retail Installment Sales Contract)

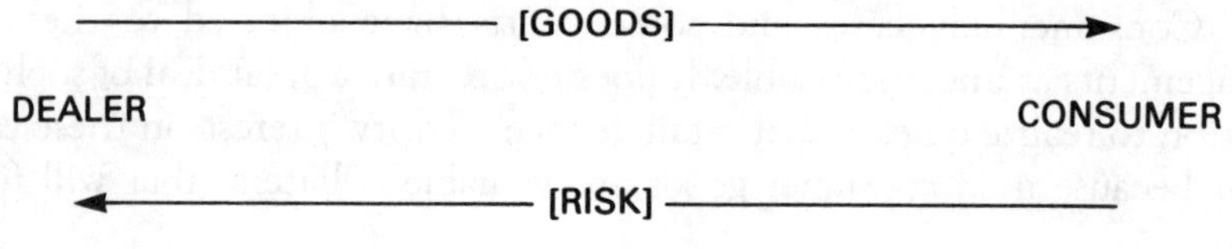

Automobile dealers are not financial institutions and cannot carry the volume of **chattel paper** that they generate. It would not be unusual for a dealer's volume of paper generated in a given year to exceed its assets by a factor of ten or more. Only a financial institution can afford to finance such paper, and automobile dealers, as well as other merchandisers that generate chattel paper, "sell" that paper to a bank or finance company or arrange the loan for the institutional lender by using loan documents supplied by the lender itself. Chapter 17 discusses chattel-paper financing. For now it suffices to compare the chattel-paper financing transaction, illustrated in Figure 13-5, with the simple sales transaction of Figure 13-4. The chattel-paper transaction involves three parties; the simple sale involves two. The chattel-paper transaction involves, at the outset, a secured transaction, the retention by the dealer of a security interest in the vehicle. Usually, the simple sale does not.

§13.4 EQUIPMENT FINANCING

Some manufacturers and dealers of industrial or farm equipment engage in the same kind of financing that automobile dealers and other retailers use. The equipment dealers sell on credit and retain a purchase-money security interest in the equipment they sell. That security agreement often appears in the form of a lease. They then discount the paper (the lease) to a financial institution. Other equipment sellers, especially some manufacturers, use leasing companies to finance equipment sales. These transactions take one of two forms. First, the manufacturer can lease the equipment directly to its customer. In this case, the manufacturer will then finance the lease by transferring it to a financial institution. In other cases, the buyer will approach a financial institution's leasing company subsidiary, ask the leasing company to buy the equipment, and lease it from the company.

In all of these lease transactions, the law distinguishes true leases from finance leases. The former are not secured transactions; the latter are.

§13.5 POLICING

Financing sellers tend to engage in minimal policing. While security agreements in this kind of financing traditionally contain clauses that make it an instance of default to "remove the collateral from the jurisdiction," most financing sellers will not learn that the goods are gone until the buyer defaults. In commercial equipment financing, sellers may take more sophisticated steps to ensure that the collateral is not moved, that it is properly maintained, and that it is insured adequately. In connection

Figure 13-5. Discounting the Risk

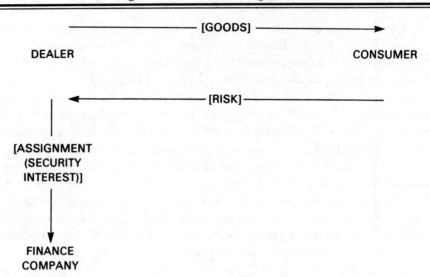

with this last concern, sellers may insist that the buyer provide evidence of insurance from the company providing it, sometimes with the requirement that the insurer notify the seller in advance of any policy termination.

In all events, of course, removal of the goods and failure to maintain and insure them must be instances of default, which give the seller the right to proceed against the collateral under the foreclosure provisions of the agreement and under Article 9.

14

Pledges (Especially of Securities)

§14.1 INTRODUCTION

Because we know something about ancient systems of collateral and because we see them re-created in the financial markets and on the schoolyard, we can guess with some assurance of accuracy that the pledge is the oldest security device. The Code of Hammurabi, the Roman legal system, and medieval practices testify to the effectiveness of using the pledge of valuable "property" (sometimes a slave or child) to secure performance of an obligation. To twentieth-century minds, it is curious that ancient legal systems did not always accept the notion that the pledgor had the right to redeem his property. Ancient minds, it seems, did not distinguish transfers for a limited purpose from outright transfers. Fortunately, commercial law has advanced since those days. Today, debtors cannot pledge their grandmothers to secure a debt, and the right to redeem whatever the debtor does pledge is secure.

Ancient as it may be, the pledge is still very much alive and is an important facility for certain secured transactions. In effect, the pledge serves two purposes: First, under the Uniform Commercial Code, it gives the secured party a perfected security interest; and second, it deprives the debtor of the ability to dispose of the collateral that is the subject of the pledge.

In ancient times a Celtic base client might desire to borrow a bull from a neighboring king. The king would agree to the loan for a fee, perhaps paid in advance, but was concerned that the base client might not return the bull. In order to secure the base client's promise, the parties would agree that the client's eldest son would stay with the king until the base client returned the bull. The son, in effect, was the collateral for the base client's promise, and the delivery of the son to the king was a pledge.

Note that in this secured transaction, the king is probably not interested in the son per se, though he might sell him as a slave in the event of the base client's default. The crucial feature of the transaction, however, is not the value of the son to the king, the lender. The crucial feature is the value of the son to the base client, the borrower, who would probably make heroic effort to return the bull rather than lose his first born into slavery.

That feature of the pledge, fear of losing the subject of the pledge, does not survive in most modern commercial transactions. Today, most collateral is fungible, but fear of losing the collateral is still inherent in the pledge transaction. In the case of a work of art or heirloom, moreover, fear of loss remains part of the pledge calculus, though works of art and heirlooms are not common in commercial pledges.

Some lenders are not above taking advantage of that fear. Although the law would not permit parties to pledge their children today, there are pledges involving collateral more valuable to the borrower than to the lender. Stock in a closely held company is usually more valuable to its owner than to the bank to which she pledges it. The owner of stock in a closely held company can parlay the ownership interest into an executive position in the corporation for herself. Banks are uninterested in that feature of a closely held stock's value, but they are willing to deprive the owner of the stock when she defaults on her loan and are willing to use the owner's loss as leverage to get the loan paid.

§14.2 POSSESSION

Depriving the borrower of possession is an essential requirement of the pledge. Generally, Article 9, the secured transactions article in the Uniform Commercial Code, renders the pledgee's security interest perfected and does away with the requirement of a written security agreement only so long as the pledgee remains in possession. That possession may be by an agent of the secured party, but the secured party, not the borrower, must control the agent for the pledge to work; and the borrower itself cannot act as that agent.

Frequently, merchants and brokers store goods with a commercial bailee. They store raw materials and agricultural commodities in warehouses, elevators, and tank farms. At other times owners of goods transport them, often in containers. Owners of petroleum derivatives transport them by pipeline and store them in large underground facilities.

During the time that products are stored, their owners may choose to borrow against them. The owners of whiskey aging in barrels for a period of years and the owner of a tanker of petrochemicals crossing the Atlantic need credit and use their goods as collateral. By notifying the bailee of the secured party's interest, the parties can create a pledge under Article 9, the notice serving to make the bailee the agent of the secured party rather than that of the owner-borrower. Part IV discusses transport and storage in more detail.

In the event the secured party loses possession of the goods, his security interest usually expires. Generally, the loss of possession renders him unperfected, if not unsecured. In those narrowly limited cases where Article 9 countenances surrender of possession, the secured transactions article protects third party purchasers of the collateral by giving them rights in the collateral superior to the secured party who surrendered possession to the borrower or its agent. Thus secured transactions law deprives the lender of its collateral when the lender permits the borrower to take possession of it.

Because by their nature **general intangibles** and accounts are intangible, Article 9 does not permit security interests in them to be created or perfected by possession. In these two instances, there is nothing for the lender to possess.

§14.3 COMMON PLEDGE TRANSACTIONS

Secured parties resort to the pledge rather than to the nonpossessory secured transaction usually because the lender is unwilling to let the borrower remain in possession of the collateral. These pledges may arise in commercially marginal situations but do not arise with much frequency. If Uncle Charlie is going to lend money to his profligate nephew and take a security interest in the nephew's gold watch, Charlie may be well advised to make his security interest possessory rather than to rely on a written security interest. Even though Article 9 generally protects the secured party's interest by stipulating that it follows the goods into the hands of purchasers, the problem of finding the collateral is often sufficient reason to insist that the secured party retain possession of it. Pawnbrokers are frequent users of the pledge. Security interests in art objects, coins, jewels, and precious metals often take the form of a pledge.

More commercially common is the situation where the borrower holds paper that moves in commerce from hand to hand without inquiry.

Certificated securities, negotiable instruments (promissory notes and drafts), chattel paper (leases and installment sales contracts), and documents of title (bills of lading and warehouse receipts) fall into this category and may be the subject of a pledge. Lenders often, however, will leave this valuable commercial collateral with the borrower (often a broker), even though the borrower's possession permits the broker to convey the collateral to innocent purchasers. Lenders, more frequently than not, trust their borrowers; and Article 9 rules permit such arrangements for brief periods that are sufficient for brokers to buy and sell their paper. Thus commercial practice and commercial law break with the ancient tradition that the pledgee must remain in possession. Figure 14-1 is a simple pledge transaction.

In some cases, a pledge is essential to the creation of a security interest. Generally, the Code does not permit security interests in money, certificated securities, or negotiable instruments except by pledge. The theory of the Code drafters was that such collateral is so readily accepted by transferring possession that it would be impossible to render a nonpossessory security interest effective. Curiously, some negotiable paper (negotiable documents of title) can be the subject of a nonpossessory security interest.

Under the Uniform Commercial Code, the beneficiary of a letter of credit can create a security interest in the proceeds of the credit, but the secured party will be perfected only if it takes possession of the credit instrument. Such "**assignments**," as they have traditionally been called, of letter of credit proceeds are not uncommon in import financing. Chapter 19 discusses the use of letters of credit to finance imports and exports.

Although the use of stock certificates has declined with the widespread adoption of **book entry securities**, one of the more common pledge transactions arises when an owner of valuable stock in the form of a certificate seeks to borrow for a short time. Stock certificates, because they are negotiable, are attractive collateral. Although banks and other lenders are constrained somewhat by federal regulations in the amount that they can lend against stock, the pledge of a stock certificate is a quick, easy way to secure a short-term personal loan or even a business loan.

Figure 14-1. Simple Pledge

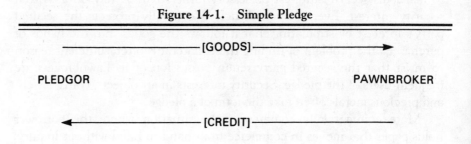

130

In the stock pledge, the parties assume that the borrower will repay the loan and that the lender will return the certificate to the borrower. For that reason, the borrower will not indorse the stock certificate. Were she to do that, upon payment of the loan and redelivery of the certificate to her, she would hold a certificate in "bearer" form — a dangerous way to hold securities. Bearer certificates can be negotiated by a thief. Document 14-1 is a copy of a stock certificate. Note the signature line provided on the reverse side for the registered owner's indorsement.

The pledgee, however, wants the stock in a form that will permit quick sale in the event of the borrower's default. An unindorsed stock certificate will not do the job. The corporation's registered agent will not issue a new certificate to the pledgee's buyer until there is an indorsement. Buyers are unwilling to pay for an unindorsed certificate.

The parties have worked out an arrangement under which the borrower grants the pledgee a power of attorney to indorse the certificate in the event of default. In fact, the power of attorney is usually executed in blank and without date, so that anybody can sign the back of the certificate; and in the event of a sale, the bank or its buyer will forward both the unindorsed certificate and the blank stock power to the registered agent when requesting a new certificate. Document 14-2 is a stock power form.

§14.4 BUYING SECURITIES ON MARGIN

The securities industry has fashioned a system of bailments that is consistent with the pledge rules and has avoided the nuisance and cost of transferring millions of stock certificates in the fast-paced securities industry. Under this system, a depository institution holds jumbo certificates covering, say, 100,000 shares of Microsoft common stock. A small investor that owns 100 shares of Microsoft common will not have possession of a certificate covering those shares, rather, his broker (ABC Co.) holds the depository institution's acknowledgment that of the 100,000-share jumbo certificate it holds, 100 shares belong to the broker, who, in turn, acknowledges that it holds the 100 shares for the investor. Figure 14-2 is an illustration of a sale of securities in this "book entry" setting.

In fact, notice of many securities sales never reach the depository. Since brokers make most securities trades for their customers, the securities industry effects considerable efficiencies by using a clearing corporation to net trades between broker members. When A sells 100 shares of Microsoft to B, then, A's broker and B's broker notify the clearing corporation of the sale; and the clearing corporation factors the transaction in with all other sales among customers of the two brokers when it nets the brokers' respective positions, charging and crediting their respective ac-

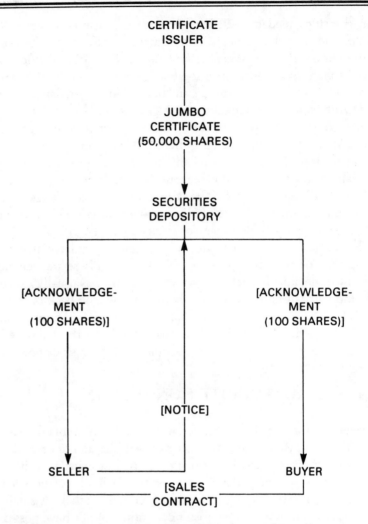

Figure 14-2. Sale of Securities (Theory)

CERTIFICATE
ISSUER

JUMBO
CERTIFICATE
(50,000 SHARES)

SECURITIES
DEPOSITORY

[ACKNOWLEDGE-
MENT
(100 SHARES)]

[ACKNOWLEDGE-
MENT
(100 SHARES)]

[NOTICE]

SELLER

BUYER

[SALES
CONTRACT]

counts, at the end of the trading day. Figure 14-3 illustrates the short-circuit reality of this typical trade.

This system fits neatly enough into the pledge concept as codified in the Code. Often the investor desires to buy stock on margin, that is, she wants to pay only 50 percent of the purchase price in cash and to borrow the balance under her customer agreement with the broker. Given the demands and traditions of the securities industry, the broker is willing to lend the unpaid balance to its customer, but only on the condition that it have adequate security. The broker, therefore, takes a security interest in the shares. Figure 14-4 illustrates the pledge in a margin purchase transaction.

With the 1994 revision of Article 8 of the Uniform Commercial Code, secured transactions involving securities took on a somewhat different hue. The drafters of the revised Article 8 characterize a securities account as the securities equivalent of a deposit account and have dubbed

Figure 14-3. Sale of Securities (Actual)

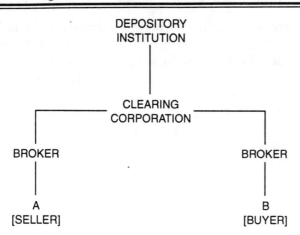

the interest of a securities owner who does not hold the security (whether certificated or not) as a securities entitlement. Thus when an investor permits his broker to hold the securities that the investor has purchased, the interest of the purchaser is a securities entitlement. The property interest of a person holding a certificated or uncertificated security remains, in the parlance of the new article, a security.

Figure 14-4. Pledge to Broker (Margin Purchase)

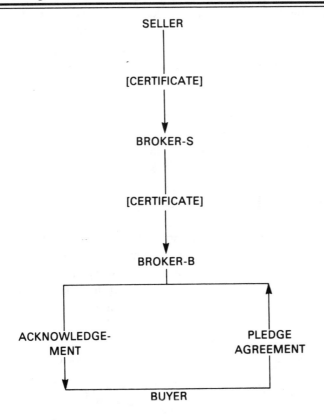

While there was great hope among the drafters of the old version of Article 8 of the Uniform Commercial Code that the uncertificated security would become the norm in the securities industry, most securities are in fact certificated; but trading in them is conducted by entries on the books of financial intermediaries as earlier discussion explains. In 1994, when the new version of Article 8 became effective, authorities estimated that individuals held from 20 to 40 percent of the shares of publicly traded companies in certificated form, while the balance was covered by the jumbo certificates described above.

§14.5 REPLEDGES

Brokers that finance their customers' purchases of securities on margin face significant credit needs and generally turn to commercial banks to satisfy them. At the end of each business day, a typical broker's bank determines the amount by which the broker's checks or wire transfers exceed the broker's deposits. Then, under a general loan agreement between the bank and the broker, the bank generates a loan to cover the deficit, if any. The bank, of course, prefers to take security to protect itself, and the obvious collateral is the investors' stock in which the broker itself has taken a security interest. Under the customer agreement between the broker and its client and under the Code, such practice is proper and efficient. The rights of the broker in the stock are limited, of course, by the amount of the customer's debt, and there may be a problem if the broker defaults on its loan with the bank and the bank takes the Microsoft stock to satisfy that debt. In some cases, that will be a risk investors who buy on margin take, but securities investor insurance, issued by an agency of the federal government, covers most such losses. As for losses not covered by such insurance, investors may be well advised to evaluate the financial strength of their brokers. Figure 14-5 illustrates the repledge transaction.

§14.6 REPURCHASE AGREEMENTS

In the securities and banking industries it is common to borrow on securities under a **repurchase agreement**. Under this agreement, referred to in the industry as a "**repo**," the owner of a security enters into a contract with a lender to "sell" the security at a given price and to "repurchase" it at another price, say, 30 days later. Its form notwithstanding, the arrangement is a secured transaction, and the difference between the two prices is the interest the "seller," i.e., the borrower, is paying the "buyer," i.e., the lender. Often, at the end of the loan period, the parties will ex-

Figure 14-5. Repledge

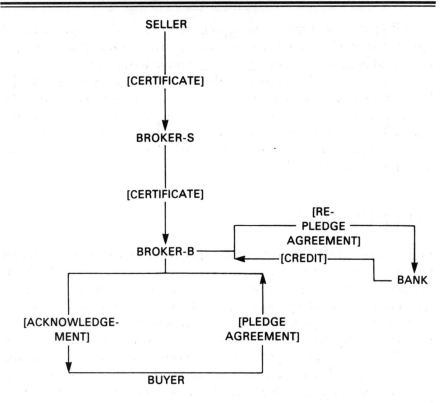

tend the term of the loan by agreeing to roll the repo over for another 30 or 60 days.

The buyer under a repo agreement may take physical possession of the security in order to effect its security interest, but it may also use the bailment or book entry system referred to above. Under that system, the buyer will ask the seller to provide notice of the transfer under the repo agreement to the depository institution bailee or to the clearing corporation. In a sophisticated transaction, the purchaser under the repo agreement may want to borrow on its interest under the agreement. This arrangement is a repledge. The transaction requires two notices to the bailee of the jumbo certificate. The repo transaction is illustrated in Figure 14-6.

§14.7 FIELD WAREHOUSING

Another traditional form of pledge by bailment is the **field warehouse**. Under this method of inventory financing, the secured party, through its field warehouse agent, holds the debtor's inventory. Although the primary purpose of the arrangement is to prevent an inventory borrower from

Figure 14-6. Repurchase Agreement

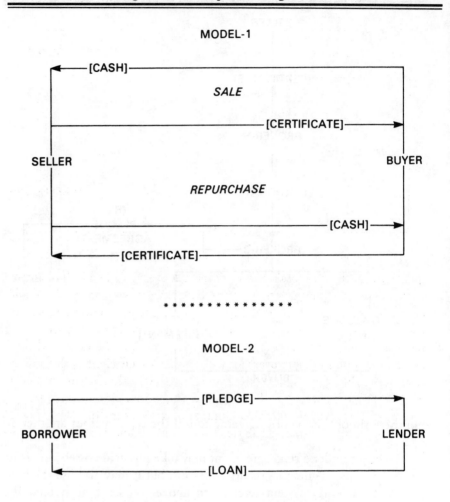

MODEL-1

SALE

REPURCHASE

SELLER — [CASH] / [CERTIFICATE] — BUYER — [CASH] / [CERTIFICATE]

* * * * * * * * * * * * * * *

MODEL-2

BORROWER — [PLEDGE] / [LOAN] — LENDER

selling collateral out from under the secured party, conceptually, the arrangement is a pledge.

In a classic instance of field warehousing, a manufacturer of automobile parts will sell to an automobile dealer's service operation on credit taking a security interest in the parts. Under the Code, customers of the dealer who purchase parts in the ordinary course of business take the parts free of the manufacturer's security interest. Unless the dealer is financially strong, the manufacturer faces the risk that it will not have any collateral to resort to in the event of the dealer's failure to pay the manufacturer: The dealer may have sold all the parts.

The field warehouse provides a policing mechanism that reduces the manufacturer's exposure. Under the arrangement, the dealer "leases" a portion of its premises to a field warehouse company. The field warehouse may have an office in San Francisco but no warehousing facilities other than the premises it leases in the field from dealers such as the one in

136

Figure 14-7. Field Warehouse

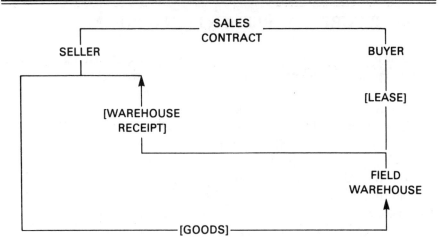

question. Under the lease, the warehouse may pay only a dollar a year in rent. When the manufacturer ships parts in satisfaction of the dealer's purchase orders, it directs the shipment to the field warehouse representative, a bonded employee of the field warehouse (and probably the dealer's parts manager) with instructions that the goods not be delivered to the dealer without manufacturer authorization. An efficient operation uses non-negotiable documents of title to effect that authorization, as Section 33.4 explains. Figure 14-7 illustrates the field warehouse transaction.

Field warehousing suffered a number of reverses in the 1980s. Lenders were successful at holding the field warehouse liable when the borrower circumvented the warehouse's security and sold or otherwise removed the collateral. At least one national field warehouse entered bankruptcy as a consequence of adverse judgments in such circumstances. Some experienced field warehousing personnel prefer to offer inventory control services that do not involve taking possession of the collateral.

Some observers concluded that field warehousing was largely a thing of the past. Commercial practices, however, have a tendency to reappear at the very time academics pronounce them finished. The idea remains a good one. Perhaps in an era when courts and juries are less inclined to find everyone liable to everyone for everything, the field warehouse will reappear in U.S. commerce. One law teacher (me again) who pronounced the field warehouse a commercial anachronism learned from a former student that his client, a commercial bank, was field warehousing in Helsinki Mercedes Benz automobiles being sold by dealers in St. Petersburg. Given the unstable commercial climate in Russia, the bank preferred to maintain possession of its collateral (the cars) through a field warehouse in stable Finland, until the dealers' customers paid for the vehicles and remitted sufficient proceeds to the bank to satisfy the inventory loan. When that happened, the bank authorized its agent, the warehouse, to deliver the vehicles to the dealers for redelivery to the buyers.

§14.8 SECURITY AGREEMENTS IN GENERAL

Although Article 9 does not require a written security agreement for secured transactions created by pledging collateral, the well-advised secured
party will insist on a security agreement. In some cases, there may be a
dispute over the nature of the lender's possession. If the nephew in the
example mentioned above defaults on his repayment obligation, he may
dispute the right of Charlie to sell the watch. At that point, Charlie will
have to prove that he held the watch as security and not for some other
reason. In addition, security agreements can spell out the rights of the
parties that are not delineated in the Code and can alter the Code's allocation of rights and responsibilities. Document 12-4 is a general form security agreement that can be used to cover pledged collateral.

§14.9 NOTICE TO BAILEE

In many pledge situations, the parties will effectuate the change of possession by notice to a bailee that is holding the goods. A dealer or manufacturer may have inventory stored with an independent bailee, such as a
terminal warehouse. A vegetable oil refinery may have grain stored in
elevators located on the midwestern prairie or may have processed oil
stored in tank farms next to rail facilities. If the operators of the elevators
or the tank farms have not issued negotiable documents of title, notice to
them of a lender's security interest will perfect that interest. The theory of
the arrangement is that the notice serves to change the status of the
bailee from agent of the vegetable oil company to agent of the lender and
to transfer possession of the grain or the oil to the lender.

Similarly, a second secured party will use notice to effect a transfer of
possession. If an owner of a security has pledged the security with First
National Bank and if the owner wants to grant a second security interest
to Second National Bank, there is no convenient way for both secured
parties to hold the security. The Code permits the second secured party to
notify the first secured party of the second security interest. That notice is
supposed to render the first secured party a bailee for the second secured
party. Figure 14-8 illustrates the transaction.

Under the old version of the letter of credit article, still in force in
many jurisdictions, the same kind of arrangement is used in import
financing involving letters of credit, whereby second secured parties will
use notice to the holder of the credit to effect their vicarious possession.
Chapter 19 discusses import and export financing.

The law in this area is not altogether clear. Some commentators have
cast doubt on the efficacy of these notices to first secured parties and

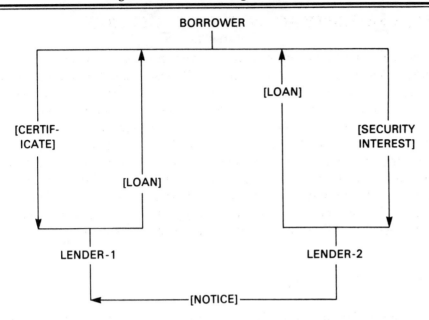

Figure 14-8.   Two Pledges, One Bailee

question whether the first secured party cannot release the collateral to the debtor despite the notice. Out of concern that the courts might accept those arguments, some second secured parties have obtained acknowledgments from the first secured party that it holds the collateral for the second secured party.

§14.10 UNCERTIFICATED SECURITIES

Just as the securities dealers invented the concept of the jumbo certificate and the securities depository in order to do away with the transfer of paper in their industry, so corporate and government borrowers saw the advantage of recording the ownership of equity and debt securities by book entry rather than by the issuance of certificates or **bonds**. Many corporations now offer owners of common stock the option of having the stock issued to the owner or of having the ownership recorded on the books of the issuing corporation, with a notice to the owner. The federal government has created a similar system of recording the ownership of U.S. Treasury securities, which are no longer issued in paper form. There is no method of transferring possession of such intangible interests, and the practice of notifying the issuer is the method the Code fashions for effecting a security interest in such certificateless securities. Significantly, the Code refers to this notice as an instruction to register a "pledge" of the intangible. Figure 14-9 illustrates the transaction.

Figure 14-9. Book-Entry Security Interest

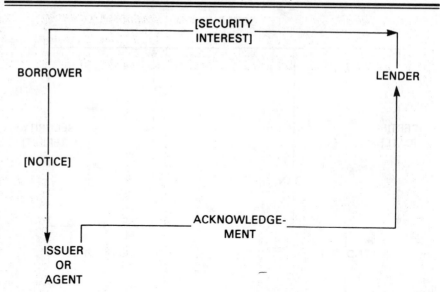

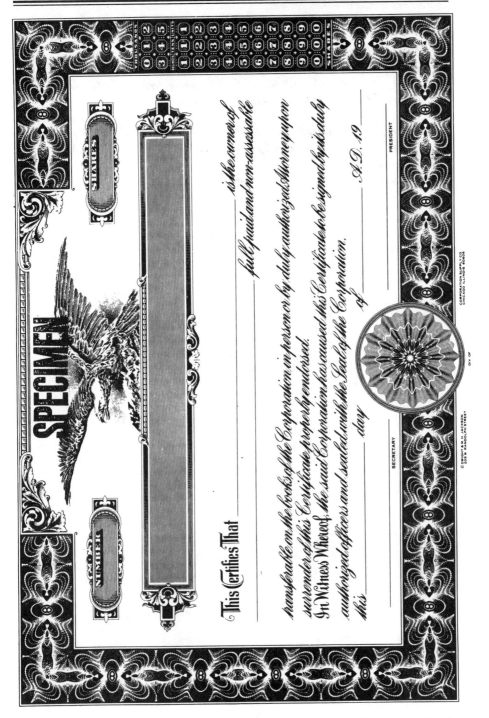

Printed with the permission of Dwight & M.H. Jackson, a Division of Corporation Supply Co.

For Value Received, _____ hereby sell, assign and transfer unto _____

_____ Shares represented by the within Certificate, and do hereby irrevocably constitute and appoint

_____ Attorney to transfer the said Shares on the books of the within named Corporation with full power of substitution in the premises.

Dated _____ 19 _____

In presence of

_____   _____

THIS SPACE IS NOT TO BE
COVERED IN ANY WAY

Roney & Co.

Irrevocable Stock/Bond Power

For value received, The undersigned does (do) hereby sell assign and transfer to

_____

_____

_____

If STOCK

complete

this portion

_____ shares of the _____ stock of _____

represented by certificate(s) No.(s) _____

standing in the name of the undersigned on the books of said company.

If BONDS

complete

this portion

_____ bonds of _____

in the principal amount of $_____ No.(s) _____

standing in the name of the undersigned on the books of said company.

The undersigned does (do) hereby irrevocably constitute and appoint

_____

attorney to transfer the said stock or bond(s) as the case may be on the book of said company with full power of substitution in the premises.

SIGN BELOW:

X _____ SPECIMEN _____

X _____ X _____

Please PRINT last name

Account Number

IMPORTANT: The signature(s) to this power must correspond with the name(s) that appear on the face of the stock certificate(s) or bond(s) and must be guaranteed by a member of a Medallion Signature Guarantee Program.

Reprinted with the permission of Roney & Co.

RONEY & CO.   Stock/Bond Power Request

Dear Client:

To effect the transfer of the unsigned or incorrectly signed securities which we are presently holding in your name, kindly sign your name exactly as it appears below.

Simply sign on the reverse side where indicated by the "X". If securities are jointly registered, all signatures are required.

Please return this power promptly in the enclosed self-addressed, postage paid envelope.

Sincerely,

RONEY & CO.

(Rev 9/96)

15

Financing Accounts (Including Factoring)

§15.1 INTRODUCTION

Most sales in the commercial sector of the economy, that is, nonconsumer sales, are on open account. Under that kind of sale, which Chapter 3 discusses in some detail, the commercial seller holds the obligation of an account debtor, the buyer to whom it sold on open account. For a period of from 30 to 60 or 90 days, depending on the industry and the relative bargaining strengths of the parties, the seller has sold the goods but has no cash to show for it. It has depleted its inventory, reduced the value of the collateral securing its inventory loan, but has no money to pay its suppliers, employees, and other creditors.

Yet, the seller has something of significant value. Because cautious sellers make their open account sales only after checking the credit records of their buyers and because those credit records are reliable, virtually all open account buyers pay, and most of them pay on time. There are exceptions. Some sellers are less risk averse than others, and some sell in markets that are problematic. Lenders can familiarize themselves with a seller's industry and practices and are willing to make a judgment about the predictability that a seller's accounts will become cash within a short period of time. These lenders take accounts as security and are the source of a significant part of the commercial credit necessary for the efficient open account sale, a staple of the U.S. economy.

Similarly, a business that seeks a **working capital loan** may confront a request from its bank for as much collateral as the borrower can provide. Since accounts are frequently one of the biggest assets that a borrower will own, perhaps its single largest asset, working capital lenders often insist that the borrower grant them a security interest in that property. These institutional lenders are engaging in account financing.

Generally, account lenders fall into three categories. First are those lenders that are particularly interested in accounts. These lenders, usually finance companies, utilize considerable expertise and familiarity with an industry in the course of their lending operations and often exercise tight control over the activity of the borrower. It is not unusual, for example, for a finance company lending against accounts to keep daily records of the payments received by the borrower from the account debtors or to maintain a lock box — a device under which payments from account debtors find their way into the finance company's bank account.

The second lender, usually a commercial bank, is interested in the accounts only incidentally. It takes a security interest in the accounts because it is the best security to protect the loan. A working capital lender lends to undercapitalized businesses, enterprises that cannot function without secured borrowing. The lender makes the loan because it is secured by an interest in the most valuable asset of the enterprise, the accounts. These accounts are often more valuable than all the rest of the enterprise's assets combined. They are, furthermore, self-liquidating, that is, it is usually not necessary to look for purchasers of them, they generate funds in the normal course. Finally, accounts are almost always short term and, therefore, match the life of the loan of the commercial lender, who is a short-term lender.

This second kind of account lender will often have nothing to do with the accounts unless the borrower defaults, while the finance company may be intimately involved in the evaluation of the account debtors' creditworthiness and in the collection of the accounts.

The third kind of account lender is the factor. In this transaction, which the law treats as a loan secured by the accounts, the parties think of the transaction as a sale of the accounts by the commercial seller to the factor. Factors are intimately involved in evaluating the credit strength of the account debtors whose obligations they purchase. Often the factor gives the commercial seller preapproved credit limits for accounts and reserves the right to reject new accounts from account debtors who have defaulted. Factors, moreover, typically purchase accounts **without recourse**, that is, the factor agrees to pay for the account even though the account debtor fails to pay the factor. The first two account lenders described above usually take the accounts **with recourse**, that is, on the understanding that if the account debtor does not pay, the commercial seller will take the account back from the lender and suffer the loss.

§15.2 THE TRANSACTION

Account receivable financing is essentially a three-party transaction that begins with the borrower's sale of goods or services on credit to a buyer whom commercial law calls the *account debtor*. When the seller decides to become a borrower and to use the accounts as security for its loan, it must transfer the accounts to the lender. Traditionally, secured transactions law has called that transfer an assignment and has designated the borrower as the **assignor** and the lender as the **assignee**. Figure 15-1 illustrates the transaction.

§15.3 REVOLVING ACCOUNTS

While it is possible for a seller to borrow against or sell accounts separately or in a specified bulk, many account lenders take a security interest in accounts that revolve. As a seller sells more product or services and collects sums due on outstanding accounts, it creates new accounts and extinguishes old ones. Under a revolving account loan agreement, the

Figure 15-1.   Account Financing

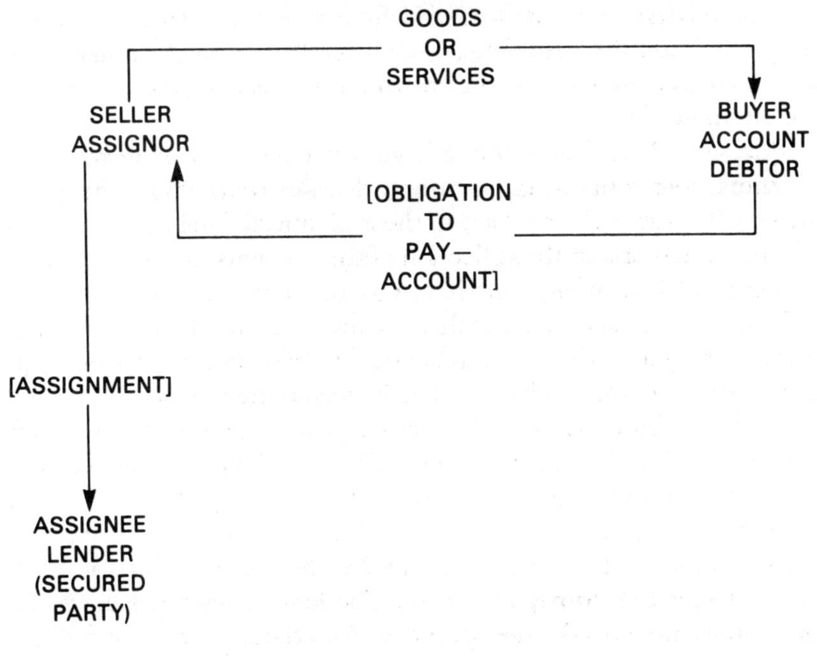

collateral changes daily, and the body of accounts that are due the seller at any given moment in time secure the loan debt. Document 15-1 is a security agreement used in connection with revolving account financing. In Figure 15-1, the batch of accounts changes constantly and may turn over completely in a 30- or 60-day period.

§15.4 DISCRETE ACCOUNT FINANCING

Some borrowers will borrow against a specific batch of accounts or against a single account. This kind of borrowing may occur if the seller is not ordinarily in the practice of financing its accounts. There are costs in borrowing, and many businesses conclude that they can evaluate credit and collect accounts with their internal credit and collections departments at less cost than having a factor perform those processes for them. Yet, these businesses may find themselves, from time to time, with cash-flow problems and may use their accounts to secure short-term borrowing.

§15.5 FACTORING

The factor, the third of the account lenders described in Section 15.1 above, is more prevalent in some industries than in others. In those industries, notably the garment industry, manufacturers are often small and yet are faced with the problem of selling to numerous buyers located, perhaps, all over the country. The cost of maintaining credit information on a national industry as widespread and full of recent entries as the retail clothing industry would impose a serious burden on small garment manufacturers. It is economically efficient and, therefore, not surprising that in such an industry certain account financers undertake to evaluate and collect a seller's accounts. Factors, the name these industries have given to the finance company that performs these functions, traditionally "buy" accounts from their customers, notify the account debtors (the buyers from the manufacturers), and collect the accounts by instructing the account debtors to make payment directly to the factor.

Factors, given their size and their access to credit information, are in a position to evaluate the accounts they purchase, which they usually purchase on a without recourse basis. By evaluating the credit strength of the various buyers, the factor determines the value to it of a given manufacturer's accounts and will price them accordingly. Some manufacturers may sell their accounts at a small discount; others may have to pay a larger discount.

Note that these transactions involve discrete accounts and differ somewhat from the revolving account arrangement described above. That is not to say that the factoring industry is unwilling to engage in revolving account financing. It is, but the traditional factoring arrangement involves the transfer of discrete accounts.

It is worth mentioning that in the nineteenth century and the early years of the twentieth, sales representatives of manufacturers that sold merchandise on behalf of the manufacturer often called themselves "factors." The term survives to some extent in commercial literature and even in some legislation, but the "old" factor and the "new" factor described here perform distinctly different commercial functions. For a number of reasons, "new" factors, though still important and profitable in some industries, are declining in number. "Old" factors have disappeared from the commercial scene.

§15.6   SALE OR SECURED TRANSACTION

Secured transactions law, as the Uniform Commercial Code delimits it, does not distinguish between accounts that the factor or other lender buys and accounts it lends against. In a fashion similar to that which the Uniform Commercial Code accords transfers of chattel paper, discussed in Chapter 17, Article 9 defines a security interest to include generally all sales of accounts. It does not matter that the parties think of the transfer as a sale, or that they intend it to be a sale, or that the transfer is with or without recourse. Article 9 applies in all these events, and the lender will have to satisfy the requirements of the article in order to create and perfect a security interest.

§15.7   POLICING

The pitfalls of account lending arise in two ways. First, the lender runs the risk that the seller has fraudulently created the accounts. Accounts are, by definition, intangible. The lender cannot see them and must rely first on the borrower's sales records and on the **warranty** that is traditionally part of the security agreement. That warranty is a representation that the accounts exist and that there are no defenses to the account debtor's obligation to pay. Cautious lenders will insist on periodic, certified audits of the borrower's records and will conduct unannounced audits of their own from time to time. Those audits consist of independent verification of the existence and the amount of outstanding accounts and are effected by asking the various accounts, by mail or telephone, to acknowledge such facts.

By virtue of the fact that secured lending law permits borrowers to finance their accounts without notifying the account debtor, there is always a risk that the debtor will make payments to the borrower-seller after the lender has acquired the accounts. Sometimes, those payments cause no problems. If the lender and the borrower agree that the borrower is to collect the accounts and remit the proceeds to the lender, payments by the account debtor to its seller will be consistent with the parties' understanding.

Sometimes, if the lender is unsure of the borrower's financial integrity and is unwilling to let the borrower collect the accounts, the lender chooses to collect the accounts itself. At other times, the borrower is not equipped to collect the accounts, and the factor is selling its collection services when it acquires an interest in the accounts. In these cases, the lender (or factor) will not want the account debtors to pay the borrower-seller. Secured transactions law protects all parties concerned by putting the risks in these cases on the lender until it notifies the account debtor. Prior to that notice, the account debtor's payments to the borrower-seller will discharge the account debtor pro tanto. After notice to the account debtor of the assignment of the account, payments to the borrower-seller will not discharge the account debtor.

If the borrower is reluctant to let its customers know that it is financing its accounts, it may be able to negotiate an agreement under which the lender does not notify the account debtors until there is a default by the borrower. There will not be any notice to the account debtors in the event the lender does not want to collect the accounts. Working capital lenders often take a security interest in the borrower's accounts but have no interest in collecting them. In these cases of non-notice borrowing, lenders will reserve the right to notify the account debtors in the event of default by the borrower. After such notice, the account debtors must make their payments directly to the lender.

§15.8 DEALER RESERVE

It is not uncommon in the financing of any third-party obligations, such as account and chattel-paper financing, for the lender to insist on a reserve account, commonly referred to as a dealer's reserve account. The terms of the arrangement can be negotiated to fit the needs of the parties. Usually, the arrangement calls for the lender to collect the accounts and to reserve a portion of the collections in the reserve account. The amounts allocated to the account are charged against the borrower's portion of the collections. If, for example, the arrangement between the borrower and the lender calls for the lender to pay the borrower 95 percent of the face amount of each account, the **dealer reserve** provision may stipulate that 1 percent of that 95 percent will not be paid to the borrower but will be credited to the dealer reserve until the reserve account has accumulated to an agreed-upon figure. After that accumulation, the lender will remit the full 95 percent to the borrower. In the event of default on an account, the lender will debit the reserve account by an amount equal to the lender's loss and will then recommence the practice of crediting the account with 1 percent of future collections until the reserve balance is restored to the specified figure.

§15.9 INVOICE STANDBY LETTER OF CREDIT

Remember that accounts are an asset of the borrower that it wants to make attractive to the lender. To the extent that the lender views the accounts as valuable, it will take them more readily. There are ways in which the dealer can enhance the attractiveness of its accounts. In earlier times, it would take a negotiable instrument from the buyer and negotiate it to the bank or finance company, which took free of claims and defenses under the holder-in-due-course doctrine. To some extent, the dealer could achieve the same effect with chattel paper and the rules that the law fashioned for chattel-paper financing. (Section 17.1 discusses these efforts to enhance the attractiveness of the dealer's customer obligations.)

In the international setting, parties have used trade acceptances and banker's acceptances to achieve much the same effect. These acceptances are negotiable instruments, and, if they are the obligations of creditworthy enterprises, they generally find a ready buyer in the money markets. Chapter 4 and Chapter 19 explain trade and banker's acceptances in this setting, and Chapter 20 discusses banker's acceptances as a medium of financing goods in general.

Accounts are not so easily marketed. First, by law, they are not free from defenses in the underlying sales transaction. Generally, under the Uniform Commercial Code, the account debtor may assert against the assignee of an account all of the defenses it has against the assignor, unless the account debtor expressly agrees otherwise — an unusual commercial arrangement. In addition, factors or other assignees of accounts must assume that a certain number of them are due from parties that will encounter financial difficulties, with the consequences of those difficulties: late payment or bankruptcy (i.e., no payment). Dealers have some incentive, therefore, to reduce the number of and potential for defaults and thereby make their accounts more attractive.

One device that dealers use is the invoice **standby letter of credit.** Under this device, a seller will insist that all of its accounts or select accounts (those with poorer credit ratings) may not purchase on open account unless they post a standby letter of credit securing their open account obligations. Such buyers must obtain from their banks or other financial institutions a standby letter of credit that is payable against the

Figure 15-2.   Invoice Standby to Distributor

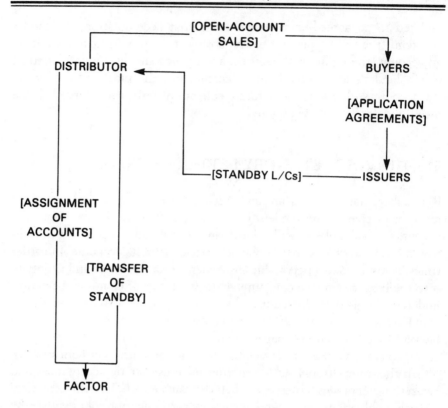

seller's draft accompanied by the invoice and the seller's certification that it has not been paid.

A pipe and pipe fittings distributor may sell to contractors on 60-day open account terms, that is, under terms that permit the contractor to take delivery of the pipe and pay for it 60 days after the date of the invoice. The distributor will need to finance the accounts with his factor, bank, or finance company, but the financer may not like the accounts. Contractors have serious cash-flow problems. If work on a project is delayed by bad weather, labor difficulties, or the like, payments tend to be late. The finance company, therefore, may subject the accounts to heavy discount.

The distributor can enhance the accounts with the standby device. First, the distributor will ask his open-account buyers to have their banks issue the standby credits. The credits may be issued directly to the distributor with the right to transfer them to the finance company or they may be issued to the finance company in the first instance. Figure 15-2 illustrates the former case, Figure 15-3 the latter.

Once the pipe distributor's buyers cause the credits to issue, the distributor will proceed to sell them on open account, and the factor will take the accounts at an attractive discount rate. In the event of default by one of the buyers, the beneficiary of the credit (either the distributor or

Figure 15-3. Invoice Standby to Factor

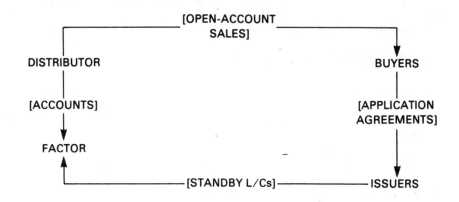

the finance company) will draw a draft on the issuer of the credit and present it to the issuer with the overdue invoice and the appropriate certification. Upon that presentation, the issuer will pay the draft, thereby making the account good.

Parties have fashioned a variation of the invoice standby under which buyers themselves initiate use of the device. In the garment industry, an industry with many sellers and many buyers, it is traditional for garment manufacturers to sell on open account and to factor those accounts, as Section 15.5 explains. There are times, however, when the factor will refuse to accept certain accounts. If Ace Clothiers, Inc. is a poor credit risk in the eyes of the factor, garment manufacturers will not want to sell to Ace because the factor will not take an account arising from sales to Ace.

In these circumstances, Ace might approach its bank and ask the bank to issue a standby letter of credit in favor of the factor, payable against the factor's draft and its certificate that it holds accounts from Ace's suppliers that Ace has not paid according to the industry's open account terms. Ace can then assure the factor that its obligation to pay is secure and can avail itself of the garment manufacturers' open account credit.

Note that in both of these invoice-standby situations, the standby letter of credit may never be drawn on. If the account debtors (the contractors who purchase the pipe in the first example and Ace Clothiers in the second) pay their open account obligations, there will be no need for the assignee of the accounts to draw. The standby is itself a form of collateral that enhances the value of the accounts. Note also that the standby in these cases is an efficient device because it puts the bank issuer (a party that knows the creditworthiness of the account debtor and that has taken collateral or guaranties to secure its obligation under the standby) at risk in the place of the assignee (factor), who is uneasy about the account debtor and is not in a position easily to obtain collateral or guaranties from the account debtor or its principles.

Document 15-1. Security Agreement (Revolving Accouts)

SECURITY AGREEMENT

Michigan National Bank

THIS SECURITY AGREEMENT ("Agreement") made and entered into on this _____ day of _____, 19 ____,
by and between Michigan National Bank, a national banking association, of _____, Michigan (the "Bank"), and
_____, a _____ with chief executive offices located at
_____, _____ ("the Borrower").

WHEREAS Borrower has obtained or may from time to time obtain loans from Bank or be otherwise obligated to Bank and has agreed to secure its Obligations (as defined in Paragraph 1. below) to Bank by granting Bank security interests in that personal property described in this Agreement, and

NOW THEREFORE Borrower and Bank AGREE AS FOLLOWS:

1. GRANT OF SECURITY INTEREST. Borrower hereby grants Bank a continuing security interest in the collateral described in Paragraph 2. below (all of the personal property described in Paragraph 2. is individually and collectively referred to in this Agreement as the "Collateral"), to secure the repayment of all loans (including all renewals, extensions, modifications or refinancing thereof) from Bank to Borrower, together with any and all other obligations now or in the future owing from Borrower to Bank (including future advances), however incurred or evidenced, whether primary, secondary, contingent or otherwise, whether arising under this Agreement, under other security agreements, promissory notes, guarantys, mortgages, leases, instruments, documents, or under any other contractual obligation now or hereafter arising (hereinafter collectively called the "Obligations") together with all costs, expenses and reasonable attorneys' fees incurred by Bank in the disbursement, administration and collection of the Obligations or in the protection, maintenance, and liquidation of the Collateral. Borrower agrees not to sell the Collateral except in the ordinary course of Borrower's business and will not assign, transfer, pledge, grant a security interest in, or otherwise dispose of or encumber the Collateral without Bank's prior written consent.

2. COLLATERAL. The Collateral covered by this Agreement is all of Borrower's property described below where an "X" or check mark has been placed in the box applicable thereto, which Borrower now owns or shall hereafter acquire or create, immediately upon acquisition or creation, and includes, but is not limited to, any items listed on any schedule or list attached to this Agreement:

☒ **A. Accounts.** All accounts, documents, chattel paper, instruments, and general intangibles, including any rights to any tax refunds from any governmental authority (all of which are hereinafter individually and collectively referred to as "Accounts");

☐ **B. Inventory.** All inventory and goods including, but not limited to, raw materials, work in process, finished goods, tangible property, stock in trade, wares and merchandise used in, sold by, or stopped in transit by Borrower;

☐ **C. Equipment.** All equipment and fixtures, including all machinery, furniture, furnishings and vehicles, together with all accessions, parts, attachments, accessories, tools and dies, or appurtenances thereto, attached, kept, used, or intended for use in connection therewith, and all substitutions, improvements, replacements and additions thereto;

☐ **D. All Assets.** All of Borrower's personal property described in Paragraph 2.A. through 2.C. above, inclusively;

☐ **E. Specific.** The following specific property and all related rights:

If none of the above boxes are checked, it is understood and agreed that Borrower grants Bank a security interest in all of Borrower's assets as if the box adjacent to Paragraph 2.D. had been checked.

For each and every type of Collateral described above, the proceeds of the Collateral and the proceeds of all insurance, eminent domain, condemnation awards, and all products of and accessions to the Collateral are also part of the Collateral. In addition, any and all bank deposits and bank accounts or other sums at any time credited or due from Bank to Borrower and any and all instruments, documents, policies, certificates of insurance, securities, goods, accounts, chattel paper, cash, property and the proceeds thereof which Borrower owns or in which Borrower has an interest and which are at any time in the possession or control of Bank or any third party acting on Bank's behalf, shall also be considered Collateral.

3. PERFECTION OF SECURITY INTEREST. Borrower agrees to promptly execute and deliver to Bank, concurrently with execution of this Agreement and at any time or times hereafter at the request of Bank, all financing statements, assignments, certificates of title, applications for motor vehicle or watercraft titles, affidavits, reports, notices, schedules of Accounts, designations of Inventory, letters of authority and any and all other documents and agreements as Bank may request, in form satisacatory to Bank, to perfect and to at all times maintain perfected Bank's security interests in the Collateral. Borrower also agrees to make appropriate entries on its books and records disclosing Bank's security interests in the Collateral.

4. WARRANTIES. Borrower agrees and warrants to Bank, that: (a) Borrower has or forthwith will acquire full legal title to the Collateral and is the lawful owner of all of the Collateral with an unqualified right to subject the Collateral to the security interest here granted to Bank; (b) except as specifically stated in any attachment to this Agreement, Bank's security interest in the Collateral is a first priority security interest, there are no financing statements covering any of the Collateral in any public office, and Borrower will defend and indemnify the Bank against the claims and demands of all other persons claiming an interest in the Collateral; (c) all of the Collateral is located in the State of Michigan at the address specified above or as specified in Paragraph 10. of this Agreement or is in the possession of the Bank, and Borrower agrees not to remove the Collateral outside the State of Michigan without Bank's prior written consent, nor use or permit the Collateral to be used for any unlawful purpose; (d) Borrower shall not conduct Borrower's business under any other name than that given above, nor change or reorganize the business entity under which it does business, except upon the prior written approval of Bank and, if such approval is granted, Borrower agrees that all documents, instruments, and agreements requested by Bank shall be prepared, filed and recorded at Borrower's expense, before such change occurs; (e) Borrower agrees not to remove any records concerning the Collateral from the address specified above nor keep any of its records at any other address unless written notice thereof is given to Bank at least ten (10) days prior to the creation of any new address for the keeping of such records; (f) Borrower agrees to at all times maintain the Collateral in good condition and repair; (g) Borrower has full authority, complete power, and is duly authorized to enter into this Agreement with Bank, and the execution of this Agreement does not constitute a breach of any provision contained in any other agreement or instrument to which Borrower is or may become a party or by which Borrower is or may be bound or affected; (h) all financial statements and information delivered and to be delivered by Borrower to Bank are true and correct and have been prepared in accordance with generally accepted accounting principles and there has been no material adverse change in the financial condition of Borrower since the last submission of such financial information to Bank; (i) there are no actions or proceedings either threatened or pending against Borrower which might result in any material adverse change in Borrower's financial condition or which might materially affect any of Borrower's assets; (j) Borrower has filed all Federal, State and local governmental tax returns which Borrower is required by law to file and all such taxes required to be paid have been paid in full; (k) no part of the Collateral is classified or classifiable as hazardous waste under Federal or Michigan environmental laws and regulations, Borrower is in full compliance with all Federal and Michigan environmental laws and regulations, and Borrower hereby indemnifies Bank against any and all expenses and costs, including reasonable attorney fees, arising from or related to any breach of these warranties. All of Borrower's warranties in this Paragraph 4. shall be deemed to be continuing warranties until Borrower shall have no Obligations to Bank.

5. TAXES, INSURANCE. Borrower agrees to: (a) promptly pay all taxes, levies, assessments, judgments, and charges of any kind upon or relating to the Collateral, to Borrower's business, and to Borrower's ownership or use of any of its assets, income, or gross receipts; (b) at its own expense, keep all of the Collateral fully insured against loss or damage by fire, theft, explosion and other risks, in such amounts, with such companies, under such policies, and in such form as shall be satisfactory to Bank, a copy of which policies shall be delivered to Bank with evidence of premium payment and which policies shall be endorsed to provide Bank a standard loss payable clause with not less than 30 days notice of cancellation or of any change in coverage (CF 12181185) and the Bank shall have a security interest in the proceeds of all such insurance and may apply any such proceeds received by it toward payment of Borrower's Obligations, whether or not due, in such order of application as Bank may determine; (c) maintain at its own expense public liability and property damage insurance in such amounts, with such companies, under such policies, and in such form as shall be satisfactory to Bank, and shall furnish Bank with a copy of such policies and evidence of payment of premiums thereon. If Borrower at any time fails to obtain or maintain any of the policies required above or pay any premium relating thereto, or shall fail to pay any tax, assessment, levy or charge, or discharge any such lien, or encumbrance, then Bank, without waiving or releasing any obligation or default of Borrower hereunder, may at any time (without obligation to do so) make such payment, obtain such discharge, or obtain and maintain such policies of insurance, pay such premiums, and take such action with respect thereto as Bank deems advisable. All sums so disbursed by Bank, including reasonable attorney fees, court costs, expenses, and other charges relating thereto, shall be part of the Obligations secured hereby, shall be payable on demand, and shall bear interest until paid to Bank at Three (3%) percent over Bank's Prime Rate of interest.

10054 (11/92)

© 1992 Michigan National Corporation

Document 15-1. (continued)

6. COLLECTION OF ACCOUNTS. A. If Paragraph 2A. or 2D. above are checked, Bank hereby conditionally authorizes Borrower to collect Accounts from Borrower's Account debtors provided, however, this privilege may be terminated by Bank at any time upon written notice from Bank and, upon mailing such notice, Bank shall be entitled to and shall have all of Borrower's rights, title, and interest in and to all of Borrower's Accounts. After notice as aforesaid or upon Default (as subsequently defined), Bank may notify any Account debtor(s) of Bank's security interest in Borrower's Accounts and shall be entitled to collect same and Borrower will thereafter receive all Accounts payments as the agent of and as trustee for Bank, transmitting to Bank on the day of Borrower's receipt, all original checks, cash, drafts, acceptances, notes and other payments received on Accounts and, until delivery of same to Bank, Borrower shall not use or commingle any Accounts payments and shall at all times keep all such remittances separate and apart from Borrower's own funds, capable of identification as the property of Bank. After any Default, Borrower agrees to open all mail only in the presence of a representative of Bank, who may take therefrom any Account remittance(s). Bank and its' representatives are hereby authorized to endorse in Borrower's name, payments on or other proceeds of any of the Collateral, and may sign Borrower's name upon all Accounts, invoices, assignments, financing statements, notices to debtors, bills of lading, storage receipts, or other instruments or documents in respect to the Accounts, the proceeds therefrom, or property related thereto. Borrower agrees to promptly give Bank copies of all Accounts statements and records, accompanied by such information and by such documents or copies thereof as Bank may request. Borrower shall maintain all records with respect to the Accounts and with respect to the general conduct and operation of Borrower's business, including balance sheets, operating statements and other financial information, in accordance with generally accepted accounting principles and as Bank may request.

B. If Paragraph 2B. or 2C. above are checked, until such time as the Bank shall notify Borrower of the revocation of such power and authority, Borrower: (i) may, in the ordinary course of its business only, at Borrower's expense, sell, lease, or furnish under contracts of service any of the Inventory normally held by Borrower for such purpose; (ii) may use and consume any raw materials, work in process or materials, the use and consumption of which is necessary in order to carry on Borrower's business; and (iii) shall, at its own expense, endeavor to collect, as and when due, all amounts due with respect to any of the Collateral, including the taking of such action with respect to such collection as the Bank may reasonably request or, in the absence of such request, as Borrower may deem advisable. A sale in the ordinary course of business does not include a transfer in partial or total satisfaction of any debt of Borrower.

7. INFORMATION. Borrower agrees to permit Bank or Bank's agents to have access to and to inspect the Collateral and from time to time inspect and verify Accounts, Inventory, and Equipment and check, make copies of or extracts from the books, records and files of Borrower, and Borrower will make same available at any time for such purposes. Bank is hereby authorized to conduct from time to time such investigation of Borrower's continuing creditworthiness as Bank shall deem appropriate including, without limitation, Bank contact with Borrower's accountants or other third parties, and Bank is also authorized to respond to any credit inquiries received from trade creditors or other credit granting institutions. Borrower agrees to promptly supply Bank with such financial and other information concerning its financial and business affairs, assets and liabilities as Bank may from time to time request, and Borrower agrees that Bank or its agents may from time to time verify Borrower's continuing compliance with any of Borrower's warranties made in Paragraph 4. above, at Borrower's cost and expense.

8. DEFAULT. The occurrence of any of the following events shall constitute a Default (as such term is used herein): (a) the non-payment, when due, of any amount payable on any of the Obligations or any extension or renewal thereof; (b) failure to perform any agreement of Borrower contained herein or in any related agreement; (c) any statement, representation, or warranty of Borrower made herein, in any other agreement with Bank, or in any other writing at any time furnished by the Borrower to the Bank, is untrue in any respect as of the date made; (d) any Obligor (which term, as used herein, shall mean the Borrower and each other party primarily or secondarily liable on any of the Obligations) becomes insolvent or unable to pay their debts as they mature, makes an assignment for the benefit of creditors, conveys, substantially all of their assets, any proceedings are instituted by or against any Obligor alleging that such Obligor is insolvent or unable to pay debts as they mature or a petition of any kind is filed under the Federal Bankruptcy Code by or against such Obligor; (e) entry of any judgment against any Obligor or any order of attachment, execution, garnishment, forfeiture, sequestration, or other writ or order is levied on the Collateral; (f) the death of any Obligor who is a natural person or of any partner of any Obligor which is a partnership; (g) the dissolution, merger, consolidation or transfer of a substantial part of the property of any Obligor; (h) Borrower fails to pay the full amount of any tax, fee, or assessment due and owing to any Federal, State or local government authority; or (i) any criminal proceeding is initiated against any Obligor.

B. Whenever a Default shall exist, the Obligations may, at the option of the Bank and without demand or notice of any kind, be declared, and thereupon shall immediately become, due and payable, and the Bank may exercise from time to time all rights and remedies, including the right to immediate possession of the Collateral, available to it under applicable law. Bank shall have the right to hold any property then in or upon the Collateral at time of repossession not covered by this Agreement until return is demanded in writing by the Borrower. Borrower agrees, upon Default, to assemble all the Collateral at a convenient place acceptable to the Bank and to pay all costs of collection of the Obligations, and enforcement of Bank's rights, including reasonable attorney fees and legal expenses, (including bankruptcy proceedings), and all expenses in locating the Collateral and all expenses for any repairs to any realty or other property to which any of the Collateral may be affixed. Any notification of intended disposition of any of the Collateral required by law shall be deemed reasonably and properly given if sent at least (7) seven calendar days before such disposition, postage prepaid, addressed to Borrower either at the address shown on the reverse side of this Agreement or at any other address of Borrower appearing on the records of the Bank.

9. GENERAL. Except as otherwise defined in this Agreement, all terms in this Agreement shall have the meanings provided by the Michigan Uniform Commercial Code as amended from time to time. Any Bank delay in exercising any power, privilege or right hereunder, or under any other instrument or agreement executed by Borrower in connection herewith shall not operate as a waiver thereof, and no single or partial exercise shall preclude other or further exercise thereof, or the exercise of any other power, privilege, or right. The waiver by Bank of any Default by Borrower shall not constitute a waiver of any subsequent Default, but shall be restricted only to the Default waived. All rights, remedies and powers of Bank hereunder are irrevocable and cumulative and not alternative or exclusive, and shall be in addition to all rights, remedies, and powers given in any other instrument or agreement or by the Michigan Uniform Commercial Code. This Agreement cannot be modified except by a writing signed by Borrower and by the Bank.

This Agreement has been delivered in Michigan, and shall be construed in accordance with the laws of the State of Michigan. Whenever possible, each provision of this Agreement shall be interpreted to be effective and valid under applicable law, but if any provision of this Agreement is prohibited by or invalid under applicable law, such provision shall be ineffective only to the extent of such prohibition or invalidity without invalidating the remainder of such provision or the remaining provisions of this Agreement. The rights and privileges of the Bank hereunder shall inure to the benefit of its successors and assigns, and this Agreement shall be binding on all heirs, executors, administrators, and successors of Borrower. If more than one Borrower has signed this Agreement their obligations shall be joint and several.

10. SPECIAL PROVISIONS/ADDITIONAL AGREEMENTS. (If Collateral includes Fixtures, describe the real estate here and in Form UCC-1A.)

IN WITNESS WHEREOF Borrower and Bank have executed this Security Agreement on the above-referenced date.

Borrower's Address	Borrower
_____	By: _____
_____	Its: _____
Borrower's Tax I.D.	By: _____
_____	Its: _____
Address of Bank	Bank
_____	By: _____
_____	Its: _____

SPECIMEN

Inventory Lending (Including Automobile Dealer Financing)

§16.1   INTRODUCTION

Inventory, the stuff that the commercial seller sells in the ordinary course of its business, is an important asset but one that is illiquid. Concrete sellers may have large supplies of gravel next to barge terminals they replenish during the winter months when the road-building industry is quiet. During February, the owner of that gravel cannot pay suppliers, employees, and other creditors with gravel, though the gravel is valuable and will be a reliable source of income to the gravel company when the spring thaw permits its customers to resume their profitable activity.

Sometimes, a business enterprise will hold assets that are more valuable in the hands of another. A manufacturer's accounts, for example, may be more valuable to a factor that can collect them efficiently than to the manufacturer who cannot use the accounts to pay bills. Inventory, however, is almost always more valuable to the borrower than to its secured creditor. Farina in the hands of a pasta manufacturer is more valuable than farina in the hands of a banker; newborn hogs are more valuable in the hands of a farmer than in the hands of a finance company. Pasta companies know how to make pasta; bankers do not. Farmers can feed young hogs and bring them to market; finance company executives cannot imagine themselves engaging in such activity (in a three-piece suit?). Bankers have to hire strangers to load and unload gravel. The gravel company owner probably can run an augur or a front-end loader herself.

This illiquid feature of inventory renders it problematic collateral, and lenders must discount it when they lend against it, that is, they must establish a significant margin to protect themselves against the eventuality of having to liquidate this illiquid asset. It is not unusual for a lender to fashion significant margins in inventory lending transactions, margins that are considerably higher than the 95 percent that a banker might pay for accounts or the 5 percent premium the banker might pay for chattel paper.

A second problem with inventory collateral is that it is difficult to value. Gravel close to the site of heavy road building activity next summer is far more valuable than the same gravel situated far from that activity. Hauling gravel is expensive. Parts for the automotive industry lose their value when automobile manufacturers change dimensions on original equipment or change design so that the parts no longer have any use. This latter valuation problem is the obsolescence feature that can cause an inventory's value to vanish overnight.

There is a third problem with inventory collateral: For various reasons set out in more detail in Section 7.10, borrowers do not have as much collateral as they use to and what they have they tend to use up quickly. Just-in-time and quick-response inventory practices have diminished the amount of inventory that a borrower holds and have enabled the borrower to turn the inventory over more rapidly than in the past. This diminution in the volume of inventory collateral should be reflected on a borrower's financial statements, but the quick-turnover phenomenon may trap the unwary lender that finds a high volume of inventory on one day and relatively little inventory a few days later. Generally, the law protects buyers out of inventory from the security interest of the inventory lender, and if the borrower is not replenishing inventory on a regular basis, just-in-time and quick-response inventory practices may prompt the lender's collateral to disappear with alarming celerity.

For these reasons, inventory financing poses a challenge to the inventory financer. It must value the inventory carefully and evaluate the competence of the borrower to transform inventory into dollars. This is not an easy task, and one consequence of it is that borrowers do not enjoy much **leverage** when they are borrowing against inventory. The cautious lender may limit the amount of an inventory loan to 50 percent of the value an independent audit accords inventory.

The inventory financer assumes many disguises. Sellers who retain security interests in goods they sell on credit constitutes a significant part of the inventory financing picture. Working capital lenders who take a security interest in all or a substantial part of a firm's assets often hold a security interest in inventory and often contribute cash for inventory ac-

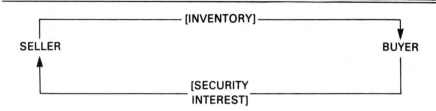

Figure 16-1. Secured Seller

quisition. This chapter deals with these secured lenders only peripherally and concentrates instead on the lender that makes enabling loans to an enterprise that will use the proceeds to acquire inventory. Some industries, especially the automobile industry, call these lenders "floor planners," since they traditionally loaned against inventory that was on the showroom floor. Figures 16-1 and 16-2 illustrate these inventory-loan transactions.

§16.2 INVENTORY DEFINITION

The Code defines the term *inventory* broadly. In a manufacturing operation the term encompasses raw materials, work in process, and finished goods. In a wholesale or retail operation, it includes stock in trade, supplies used by the business, and goods held for lease. Curiously, the Code does not include a farming operation's inventory in the definition, such inventory falling within a separate Code classification: **farm products**. In this chapter, we will include farm products as part of the "inventory" category.

§16.3 BORROWER SPECIFIC

In any secured transaction, the lender must learn about its borrower's business in order to evaluate the chattel paper, equipment, accounts, and general intangibles that it is taking as security for the repayment of its loan advances. Generally, however, no category of collateral challenges the loan officer as much as inventory financing does in confronting the valuation problem. Wire rods have a market value, but the ability of a steel fabricator to resell wire rods that it cannot use because of falling demand for steel fabrication can be easy and inexpensive or difficult and costly depending on location, market conditions, and other factors. Finished goods inventory is a notoriously difficult category of inventory to evaluate. A manufacturer may have obsolete finished goods and vendor parts that retain only salvage value.

Inventory control is another problem that loan officers must confront. Even though a lender takes large amounts of collateral as security, the

Figure 16-2.   Inventory Lender

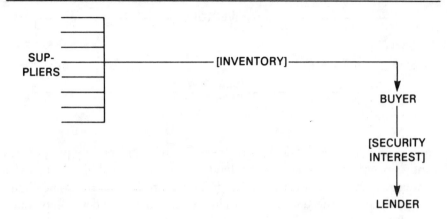

health of the loan and the prospects of repayment correlate directly with the health of the borrower's business. Large inventories may reflect the health of a going concern. They may also reflect the ill-advised purchase of too much inventory or the consequences of falling sales. The value of inventory in the hands of a going concern drops precipitously if that concern suddenly finds itself in the bankruptcy court. At distress sales, inventory of the highest quality often yields pitiful prices.

In any commercial loan transaction, but particularly in inventory loan transactions, loan officers must be in a position to know the borrower's industry and business practices in order to determine the quality of the collateral and the status of the loan.

§16.4   AUTOMOBILE DEALER FINANCING

Automobile manufacturers, both domestic and foreign, enjoy a measure of bargaining strength in relation to the dealers that constitute their network of buyers. The manufacturers have exploited their market and financial strength to exact from dealers a cash-sale arrangement whereby dealers must pay in cash for all goods shipped to the dealer. Automobile manufacturers, then, have been able to avoid the cost of the open account sale that is the subject of Chapter 3 and that is common in most merchant-to-merchant sales.

Typically, the automobile manufacturer/dealer relationship calls for a bank local to the dealer to finance the dealer's inventory. Sometimes, however, a manufacturer-owned finance company may play the bank role. The inventory lender issues to the manufacturer a standby letter of credit. Under the credit, which often goes by other names, such as "standby payment authorization," the manufacturer ships vehicles to the dealer and immediately forwards invoices, shipping documents, and certificates of origin to the dealer's bank. Under the standby credit, if the documents are

160

Figure 16-3. Floor Planning with Standby

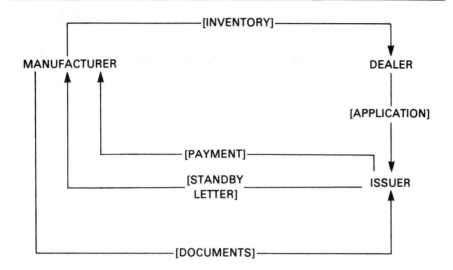

in order, the bank must pay the invoices promptly and does so, often, before the vehicles arrive at the dealer's showroom.

The dealer's bank is willing to issue the standby only if the dealer's obligation to reimburse the bank is clear and is secured. In virtually all cases, the vehicles themselves will comprise the bank's security, and the application agreement between the bank and the dealer when it applies for the letter of credit will spell out the dealer's reimbursement obligation. Contemporaneously, the dealer will enter into a floor plan agreement, which grants a security interest in the vehicles to the bank.

In short, the manufacturer sells, i.e., transfers title to, the vehicles to the dealer. Simultaneously, the dealer grants a security interest to the bank. The bank pays for the vehicles, thereby generating the loan that the security interest secures. Figure 16-3 illustrates the transaction.

§16.5 PROCEEDS

Frequently, especially in floor planned loans, borrowers satisfy the inventory loan out of the proceeds they receive upon the sale of the inventory. Floor planning is the financing of big-ticket items of inventory. To a large extent, it is discrete financing, that is, the lender expects the borrower to pay off that portion of the loan balance that was generated when the dealer purchased the item of inventory. If a bank pays $15,000 to an automobile manufacturer when the manufacturer ships the vehicle to the dealer, the bank will expect the dealer to pay off that $15,000 loan when the dealer sells that vehicle.

That is not to suggest that floor plans are devoid of cross-collateralization provisions. In fact, floor plan agreements typically provide that all

Figure 16-4. Chattel Paper to Floor Planner

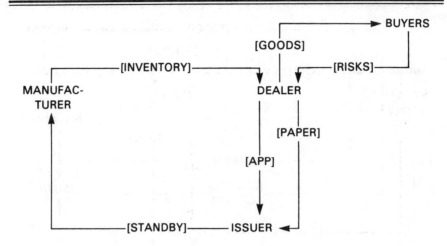

collateral secures all advances. Nonetheless, the bank and the dealer understand, and the floor plan agreement provides, that the dealer will pay the bank upon sale of the vehicle.

For dealers that sell for cash, those payments are not difficult, but many dealers of big-ticket items such as automobiles or large home appliances will not receive cash from their customers upon the sale of inventory. Sometimes, the dealer will sell for cash, either when the customer is a cash buyer or when the customer obtains credit from his own financial institution. Many buyers finance their motor vehicle purchases directly through their own credit union or bank and use the proceeds of the loan from financial institutions to pay the dealer cash. In those cases, the dealer will pay the bank the amount the bank advanced to purchase the vehicle from the manufacturer plus **finance charges** and will retain the rest.

Often, however, automobile dealers do not receive much cash upon the sale of a vehicle. They may only receive proceeds in the form of either a small cash down payment or a trade-in vehicle (or both) covering 10 percent of the cost of the new vehicle and a **retail installment sales contract** for the balance. In these cases, the dealer does not have sufficient cash on the sale of the new car to repay the bank's loan against that car and must use the retail installment sales contract (chattel paper) to generate cash to pay the bank. The dealer can generate that cash by transferring the chattel paper to a second financial institution or to the bank itself. That transfer is itself a secured transaction, since the Code makes all transfers of chattel paper secured transactions whether they are outright sales of the paper or merely the transfer of the paper for the purpose of securing an advance.

Generally, Chapter 17 discusses chattel-paper financing. Figure 16-4 illustrates the transaction when the floor planner takes the paper.

Figure 16-5.   Chattel Paper to Third Party

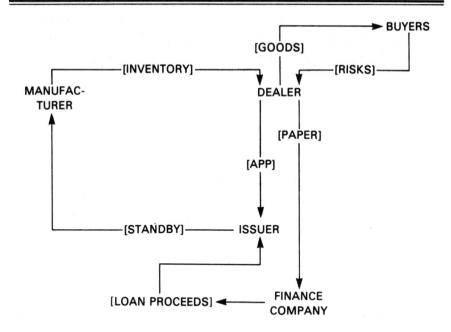

If the dealer transfers the chattel paper to a third party, say a finance company, the finance company makes an advance to the dealer who pays off the bank's loan. Figure 16-5 illustrates this transaction.

Significantly, the Code gives the floor planner an automatic security interest in the proceeds received by the dealer (and by any other borrower that grants the bank a security interest in inventory) upon the sale, exchange, or other disposition of the inventory. It is quite easy, however, for third parties to cut off the bank's security interest in those proceeds. The finance company in Figure 16-5, for example, that takes chattel paper from the dealer and makes an advance to the dealer will probably defeat the bank's interest. Floor planners must take some precautions to prevent the dealer who faces financial exigencies from depriving them of their collateral or its proceeds — a process that is strikingly easy for the less-than-honest dealer. If such a dealer sells inventory to a customer for cash, he can pocket the proceeds. If he sells to a customer under a retail installment sales contract, he can discount the paper with the finance company and pocket the proceeds of the transfer. Eventually, of course, the floor planner will catch up with this rogue, but by that time he may have sold a million dollars' worth of collateral and be sunning himself on an island somewhere.

Some inventory lenders, such as those that finance manufacturing concerns and some farming operations, will confront collateral that changes. Raw materials become work in process, which becomes finished goods. Heifers in a cattle feedlot operation become mature, and dairy cows give milk and have offspring. The carefully drafted security agreement anticipates these collateral changes and defines the collateral in such a way that the security agreement extends to original collateral as modified by accessions or manufacturing processes and to the products and natural increase of livestock.

§16.6 POLICING

Floor planners and other inventory lenders face unique problems in policing their collateral. Under the Uniform Commercial Code, most buyers out of inventory will take the goods free of the inventory lender's security interest. The floor planner that has a security interest in 100 motor vehicles on a dealer's lot may be surprised the day after the George Washington's Birthday sale to find that there are only 25 vehicles on the lot and no proceeds in the dealer's office. Floor planners typically make unannounced visits to the dealer's showroom to make spot or complete checks of inventory. By comparing serial numbers and counting vehicles or home freezers, a loan officer's checkers can determine quickly whether the dealer is "out of trust," that is, whether the dealer has sold inventory without accounting to the lender for the proceeds. In the event a dealer is in default under the loan agreement or the security agreement, the floor planner may have an officer on the dealer's premises to witness the opening of mail (in order to take the checks) and to sit in on **closings** with the dealer's customers (in order to take the down payments and the retail installment sales contracts). Floor plan security agreements traditionally spell out the floor planner's rights to take such action.

Often, lenders do not rely solely on the floor plan agreement but also take a "trust receipt" from the dealer at the time the manufacturer delivers merchandise to the dealer. The trust receipt has the advantage of listing the items of merchandise separately and facilitates the lender's policing of the transaction. Note that it is in fact a security agreement. It takes its name from the old Uniform Trust Receipts Act, which Article 9 of the Code replaced.

As discussion at the beginning of this chapter explains, in any inventory loan transaction, the lender must review inventory values periodically to ensure that the value of the inventory is sufficient to secure repayment of the loan. Most loan agreements require the borrower to submit financial statements periodically that include inventory evaluations. Loan officers must be able to determine whether those statements are reliable. In the case of audited statements, certified public accountants will explain their evaluation of the inventory. Such auditors make spot checks to determine whether inventory is obsolete, whether the market for it has fallen, and whether it is in fact there. In creating the audited statement, auditors climb up into the warehouse and inspect the dusty bins to make sure the borrower is not claiming to own inventory that it has already sold.

Computer information systems have aided inventory control and auditing to a considerable extent by permitting sellers to record sales as they are made and to generate computer printouts that auditors can review and verify. The auditing process is not perfect, and the inventory loan officer will have to know a good deal about the borrower's business and its integrity before he can sleep without worrying that his inventory collateral is insufficient.

Some secured lenders hire their own auditors. A dealer may be tempted, when cash is short, to sell one of its cars "out of trust," that is, to sell the car and not remit the proceeds to the floor planner. When the lender's auditors arrive and start checking the serial number of every vehicle on the dealer's floor and lot, that sale out of trust will become a matter of concern to the lender. It may prompt the lender to ask the dealer for the keys to the dealership, that is, a sale out of trust may prompt the lender to **accelerate** the dealer's note and close the dealer down.

In the past, some inventory lenders policed collateral by using the fiction of a pledge. A lender against automobile parts to an automobile dealer, for example, delivered the collateral to a professional warehouse (usually represented by the borrower's former parts manager). The warehouse would hold the parts as security for the loan. The transaction was the "field warehouse" transaction described in Section 14.7. As that section explains, the field warehouse has, for the present at least, pretty much disappeared from the commercial scene. Yet, a new entity has taken on some of its functions — the inventory verification service. Inventory verification is conducted by persons familiar with the borrower's business, who audit the inventory collateral from time to time on an unannounced schedule. Dealers that sell inventory without accounting to their lenders, therefore, run the risk of being caught "out of trust." Because some lenders, more it would seem than formerly, are distant from their inventory borrowers, the inventory verification service makes it easier and safer for the lender and frees up credit for the honest dealer.

17

Chattel-Paper Financing (Including Automobile Paper Financing)

§17.1 Introduction
§17.2 Relationship to Inventory
§17.3 The Collateral
§17.4 Policing
§17.5 Defenses

§17.1 INTRODUCTION

Secured lending is a direct function of the value of a business's assets. Borrowers with no assets have a hard time getting any credit and, by definition, cannot get secured credit, not having any collateral to serve as security. One of the challenges that faces secured lenders and borrowers is to render the borrowers' assets something that the "market" will accept. A borrower with valuable Etruscan art objects may have a more difficult time obtaining credit than someone with Microsoft stock of the same value. Exotic assets have a market, but lending institutions are not familiar with that market and are disinclined to take such assets as collateral. The value of an asset often depends on the manner in which parties liquidate it. Garments imported from the Pacific rim by a national retail chain are more valuable than the same garments held by a bank in Kansas that took them from a defaulting customer. The retail chain will sell the garments at top dollar; the Kansas bank will probably have to sell at distress prices. Real estate sold at auction often fetches a lower price than real estate held for weeks or months while brokers attempt to locate a buyer, and financial institutions that are not equipped to liquidate real estate in the slower manner are ill advised to take real estate as collateral.

In effect, the secured loan is a device for making an illiquid asset liquid. A firm cannot pay taxes and payroll with its accounts or equipment, but it can pay them with the loan proceeds that these assets generate in a secured-loan transaction. The liquidity of the asset, that is, the ease of realizing the value of the asset, often determines whether institutional lenders are willing to accept it as collateral for a loan.

In a medium-sized or small business, one of the single biggest assets of the enterprise will be the sums owed to the business by its customers. Various customary industry practices and distinctions fashioned by the Uniform Commercial Code as a consequence of those practices have distinguished those sums owed to the company into a number of classes. The broadest might be called "accounts receivable." These are the sums due from sales on open account. Chapter 15 deals with the financing of accounts.

The second category of sums due covers sums reflected in pieces of paper that are recognized in financial markets. In the past, sellers often took promissory notes from their credit buyers and "discounted" the notes with a financial intermediary (usually the local bank), which marketed them to other banks. That practice has largely fallen into disuse, except in forfaiting, a practice used in export financing. Chapter 22 discusses promissory notes.

There is another kind of paper that embodies a buyer's obligation to pay a seller, however, that has survived in modern commercial law. That paper consist of two features: (1) the buyer's obligation to pay the purchase price and (2) the buyer's grant to the seller of a security interest in the goods that are the subject of the sale. Commercial law calls this paper *chattel paper*, the first word in the term reflecting the property interest feature of the device, the second word being an ancient commercial-law term referring to an obligation to pay money embodied in a piece of paper.

Chattel paper is readily accepted in institutional financial markets. Banks and finance companies consider it an attractive medium of investment. Traditionally, it has paid relatively high rates of interest. In fact, at times financial institutions will pay sellers a premium for their chattel paper, that is, they will pay the seller more than the face amount of the paper.

When a bank takes chattel paper from a dealer, it makes a loan secured by obligations payable by multiple debtors. The bank that finances an appliance store's chattel paper, looks to many debtors (the appliance store's buyers), not to a single debtor (the appliance store), for repayment of the advance. (If the sale of the chattel paper is without recourse, the bank may not look to the store at all.) The effect of taking chattel paper is to spread the loan repayment risk. This spreading of the risk joined with the American ethic of paying one's bills and with the fact that chattel paper includes an interest in the goods sold has kept losses at an attractive level. Recently, banks and finance companies have been able to package the chattel paper they take from borrowers as security for bonds, which they sell in the financial markets. The predictability of default rates and their generally low level make such bonds attractive investment products.

In short, chattel paper is a rich source for secured borrowing, and the dealer that generates it usually has little trouble finding a financial institution that will take it.

There are two kinds of chattel paper that are important collateral in the economy: retail installment sales contracts and leases.

The retail installment sales contract usually arises out of the consumer purchase of a big-ticket item: snow blower, washing machine, automobile. Because the consumer prefers to pay for the item over a period of time, the retailer provides credit but retains a purchase-money security interest in the sold goods.

Automobile retail installment sales contracts constitute a significant portion of the chattel paper in the economy. They arise out of the dealer's sale of an item with a significant price. Most buyers under these contracts are consumers or small businesses.

The equipment leasing industry is the source of most chattel paper in lease form. Some of these leases are **lease purchase** arrangements, that is, they are disguised security agreements. Here, the parties create a lease for various business reasons, but the law regards the transaction as a sale with the "lessor" as a secured party and the "lessee" as the buyer-owner of the goods. Others leases are true leases, that is, the law regards the lessee as one with a leasehold interest but no more.

Whatever their nature (true lease or disguised security agreement) all leases are chattel paper for purposes of the financing that this chapter describes. Chapter 9 describes leasing.

Taken together, leases and retail installment sales contracts constitute an enormous amount of consumer and commercial borrowing that requires a significant allocation of credit. Figure 17-1 illustrates chattel-paper financing in which an automobile dealer is marketing its product under true, short-term leases and under retail installment sales contracts.

§17.2 RELATIONSHIP TO INVENTORY

The sale or lease of inventory is the event that gives rise to chattel paper. Selling inventory is the business of the borrower, a dealer, or other retailer. When the dealer sells inventory, it receives proceeds. In some industries, notably the automotive and appliance industries, retailers do not sell for cash. They sell on credit under arrangements whereby the buyers give the dealer paper. That paper, usually retail installment sales contracts or leases, is the most common type of chattel paper that is the subject of this chapter.

Figure 17-1. Chattel-Paper Financing

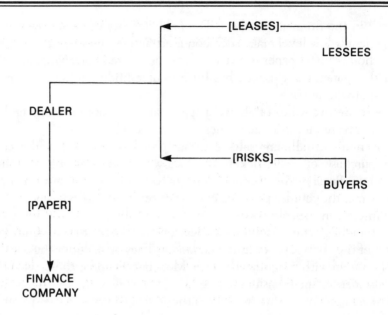

In the hands of the retailer, the sale of inventory acts as a process of substituting inventory assets (e.g., automobiles) into paper assets (chattel paper), and the inventory lender may confront the paper lender in a contest over the collateral, which the inventory lender claims as proceeds from the sale of its collateral and the paper lender claims as security for a loan it made against the paper. The Code has a definite set of rules for determining the priorities between the two lenders.

The relationship between inventory lenders and paper lenders has another important dimension. An enterprise engaged in retail sales usually turns its inventory over quickly. In fact, quick inventory turnover is usually a chief feature of a dealer's business strategy. Traditionally, chattel paper runs for terms longer than the period it takes the retailer to exhaust a supply of inventory, perhaps 10 or 20 times as long. The dollar amount of chattel paper that a retailer generates, then, is usually considerably more than the dollar amount of the retailer's inventory.

For institutional lenders, loans are income-producing assets, and lenders that are interested in increasing their loans and their income will be more inclined to engage in chattel-paper lending than in inventory lending. The relatively high rate of interest on chattel paper and the remarkably low rate of default by the widely dispersed obligors on such paper enhance that inclination. Often, the lure of chattel-paper profits drives lenders to finance the retailer's inventory, sometimes at quite competitive inventory lending rates, and the bank that makes a retailer an inventory secured loan often insists that the retailer offer its chattel paper to the bank. At other times, the retailer may be able to shop for a chattel-paper financer accepting the best bid from competing lenders.

In short, chattel paper in the form of retail installment contracts and leases constitute a significant source of collateral for retailers and equipment manufacturers.

§17.3 THE COLLATERAL

It is a peculiarity of secured transactions law that chattel paper is collateral (1) when the dealer, as we call the retailer, borrows against it and (2) when the dealer sells it outright to a bank or finance company. The law cannot distinguish these transactions easily and, therefore, treats them both as secured transactions, the intent of the parties and the form of the transaction notwithstanding. Sometimes, dealers transfer their paper to banks or finance companies without recourse. In those cases, if the account debtor, the obligor on the paper, i.e., the buyer or lessee, defaults, the finance company takes the loss and has no recourse against the dealer. In other cases, the transfer is "with recourse." In those cases, the dealer must repurchase from the finance company those contracts or leases on which the account debtor defaults.

Under the Code, it does not matter whether the chattel paper transferee takes the paper with or without recourse. In both cases, the transfer is a secured transaction subject to the rules of Article 9. Chattel paper in the hands of the institutional lender is always collateral.

It is not the only collateral, however. In the original chattel paper transaction, that between the dealer and its customer, if the transaction is a sale, the customer grants an explicit security interest to the dealer. That security interest is in the retail installment sales contract language. The security interest is implicit in the lease/sale transaction where the lease is a disguised security agreement. In that transaction, the lease document recites that title remains in the lessor, but the law recognizes in that retention of title only a security interest. The security interest created by these security agreements (the installment sales agreement or the lease/sale lease) is in the equipment or other goods that are the subject of the installment sale or the lease.

In brief, chattel-paper financing involves two kinds of collateral. One is paper collateral — the chattel paper, a valuable obligation of the account debtor to make the payments he has promised to make. The history of chattel-paper financing evidences the value of that obligation, which traditionally bears relatively high rates of interest and experiences low default rates. The second kind of collateral is durable — the automobile or refrigerator or industrial equipment that is the subject of the sale or lease. This collateral is also valuable, though often less so than the account debtor's obligation to pay the full purchase price. In the event of default, however, the value of the account debtor's obligation becomes question-

Figure 17-2. The Collateral in Dealer-Paper Financing

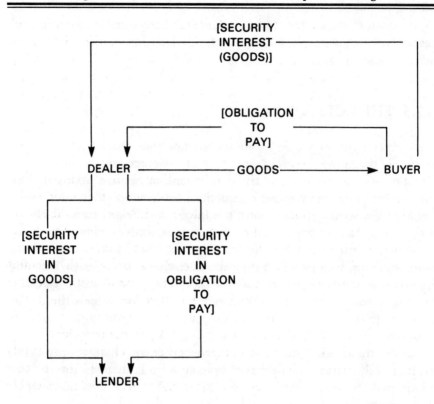

able, and the holder of the chattel paper will resort to a used automobile or a used metal stamping machine that may retain sufficient value to satisfy part or all of the balance due on the finance company's investment in the paper.

All of this assumes that the transfer of the paper from the dealer to the institutional lender is without recourse. In the with recourse transaction, the institutional lender will put the paper back on the dealer. If the default of the account debtor, the buyer, reflects the buyer's insolvency or other inability to pay, the dealer who will have resort to the equipment, his only collateral.

Figure 17-2 illustrates the various collateral involved in the chattel-paper transaction.

§17.4 POLICING

It does not take the imagination of a great swindler or a dealer with pressing cash needs to conclude that he can obtain that cash with a little creativity. Normally, a dealer takes paper to its lender periodically, perhaps in the morning of each business day, and asks the lender to credit the dealer's account in the face amount of the paper delivered or in the face amount, less a discount or plus a premium, as the general relationship between the parties requires. Although the dealer's assignment form on the chattel paper and the agreement governing the dealer-lender relationship usually includes an express warranty by the dealer that the chattel paper is genuine, such warranties do not always deter business people that are facing financial ruin.

Hope springs eternal in the human breast and never more so than in the breast of the dealer who thinks that he can turn the corner next week and repay the money he is planning to steal this week.

Lenders must be aware of the danger in chattel-paper financing that the dealer is in a position to create chattel paper when there are no sales or leases to back the paper. The cautious lender will make periodic checks of account debtors, especially in non-notice situations, where the dealer collects from the account debtor and remits to the lender. Even in notice financing situations, where the lender undertakes to notify the account debtors that their obligations have been assigned and to make payments directly to the lender, there is the possibility that the dealer can practice fraud for a brief period of time. Ultimately, the fraud will unravel, but the time it takes to do so may be sufficient to cost the lender considerably.

These fraud risks prompt lenders who take chattel paper from thinly capitalized operations or dealers that have a poor credit history to take additional collateral or personal guaranties and to maintain considerable dealer reserve accounts.

§17.5 DEFENSES

Remember that the reason the dealer takes chattel paper from its customers is to enhance the attractiveness of the obligation in the financial market. The dealer could sell on open account, but the fact is that banks and finance companies are much less inclined to buy an automobile dealer's accounts when they consist of significant consumer obligations that are not secured by the property the consumer purchased. When the obligation is secured by the snow blower or automobile, however, financial institutions are more interested and will pay the dealer more money for the obligation, that is, they will lend more for the paper.

Long ago, dealers learned that if they could abstract the buyer's obligation from the sales transaction, financial institutions were even more interested in the paper. To abstract an obligation is to render it independent of the transaction out of which it arises. The promissory note that was a common device for financing receivables up until 80 years ago was a negotiable instrument. Under the law, most purchasers of that paper, i.e., the banks that bought it from the dealer, were holders in due course who held the paper free from claims and defenses arising out of the sales transaction.

To a significant extent, the law created similar treatment for holders of chattel paper. In fact, the earliest kind of chattel paper, which has now largely disappeared, was a promissory note and a security agreement together. When the dealers put the two documents into a single document (the retail installment sales contract), the paper lost its negotiability, but the legislatures fashioned an abstraction rule that put the holder of the chattel paper in much the same position that the holder in due course had occupied. The holder of the paper took free of the defenses.

Unfortunately, this legal abstraction concept, which, one might argue, made credit more readily available to the consumer, was often the subject of abuse. Chattel-paper history bears witness to fraudulent practices. Fly-by-night retailers, many of them door-to-door, high-pressure sales organizations, took retail installment sales contracts or negotiable instruments from consumers in return for overpriced or shoddy merchandise. In a manner that took full advantage of the commercial doctrines of good-faith purchase and holder in due course, these retailers then discounted their paper with finance companies or bank installment loan departments. The effect of the two commercial doctrines was to render the holder of the paper free of any defenses that the consumer had under the contract with the unconscionable retailer. All too often, the aluminum siding started to fall off, the vacuum sweeper failed after two months of use, or the consumer suddenly realized that he had entered into subscriptions to purchase $100 per month worth of magazines or dancing lessons for life. At that point, the holder of the paper was able to say that the consumer's only remedy was against the retailer, who by then was in the next county if not the next state.

By virtue of a combination of judge-made doctrines, state consumer-protection rules, and Federal Trade Commission regulations, the law has eliminated most of those unethical and socially harmful practices by preventing assignees of consumer paper from cutting off the consumer's defenses. Today, when a consumer buys shoddy merchandise from a dealer, he can assert his right of recoupment in the transaction with the dealer against the finance company that buys the paper from the dealer. There is still room in commercial law, however, for some purchasers of paper to raise the argument that they take free of defenses. Outside the consumer setting, a rule abstracting the paper from the underlying transaction makes sense, and much financing of industrial equipment purchases benefits from these rules that raised so many problems in the consumer context. Chapter 22 discusses this history of consumer protection from commercial doctrine in the promissory note setting.

18

Equipment Financing

§18.1 UNIQUE FEATURES OF EQUIPMENT LENDING

Generally, equipment financing differs from inventory and account financing in two respects. First, it is uncommon for an equipment financer to rely heavily on **after-acquired property**, though equipment financers may take a security interest in such property.

The equipment loan, however, is often discrete. It relates to a single piece of equipment or a number of pieces acquired at the same time in connection with plant expansion or improvements. Thus, if a manufacturer needs $4 million to purchase equipment in order to increase capacity, it may borrow that sum under an arrangement whereby the lender takes a security interest in that new equipment alone and receives payment over a prescribed schedule for a definite period. At the end of the period, the loan balance will be zero, and the lender will release its security interest. Such a loan is discretely related to the collateral and is quite different from the revolving loans that are common in account and inventory financing described in Chapters 15 and 16, respectively. Equipment security interests are much less likely to revolve than security interests in inventory and accounts. By virtue of the discrete nature of the equipment loan, the debtor tends to reduce it to zero and not to take it back up. Later advances are less frequent than in inventory and account financing.

That is not to say that working capital lenders do not take security interests in equipment. They do, but their loans are not primarily equipment loans. The equipment stands as supplemental security. The working capital lender usually takes a security interest in the borrower's equipment, but the security interest in the equipment is secondary to that in the inventory and accounts. Working capital lenders may want security interests in a borrower's equipment, so that in the event of default, the lender may sell the business as a going concern, rather than piecemeal.

By virtue of its discrete nature and the lack of after-advance and after-acquired property features, the equipment loan usually forbids the debtor to sell the collateral; and the parties, unlike the parties to the farm loan, take the prohibition seriously. Chapter 21 explains the traditional prohibition of sale in the farm-loan transaction and the general tendency of both borrower and lender to ignore it.

The second major difference between the revolving inventory and account loans and the equipment loan is that equipment financing usually involves an enabling loan, that is, the loan most often relates to the acquisition of equipment. Consequently, equipment financers are quite often purchase-money secured parties.

Equipment secured parties include sellers and their subsidiaries as well as financial institutions and subsidiaries of financial institutions. Some equipment security agreements are more general than others. In a transaction involving large sums, the security agreement may be transaction specific, that is, drafted for that single transaction. At other times, industries will fashion security agreements for one kind of collateral or another.

§18.2 LEASE FINANCING

For a variety of reasons, many equipment lenders style themselves lessors of the equipment. In fact, there is considerable confusion in the law over the demarcation between a true lease, which is not a secured transaction, and a finance lease, which is.

Sometimes an enterprise with a capital asset will find it attractive for tax or **liquidity** purposes to sell the asset to a bank or other financial institution or investor and lease it back. Under this sale and leaseback the seller, who is about to become a lessee, sells the asset, say, a metal stamping machine, to a bank leasing subsidiary. The payment the seller receives under the sale provides the seller with cash, that is, with liquidity. By virtue of the sale, the seller has transformed an illiquid asset, a machine, into a liquid asset, cash, that it can use to meet payroll, tax, insurance, and other obligations. Also, the seller is now a lessee, and generally it can deduct on its income tax return the payments it makes to the bank leasing subsidiary under the lease.

In effect, the sale-leaseback transaction is a financing arrangement under which a company uses its equipment as collateral for a loan. The

Uniform Commercial Code treats most parties that buy and leaseback equipment as secured parties under Article 9.

Sometimes the driving consideration in the sale-leaseback transaction is not the seller/lessor's need for cash but the buyer/lessee's need for an investment. The sole shareholder of a company, for example, may buy equipment in order to arrange for an attractive rate of investment return. If the lease payments (return of capital plus interest) are sufficiently generous, the shareholder may have effected an investment more attractive than anything available elsewhere. Similarly, an insider may use a sale-leaseback transaction to get money out of a profitable corporation without the corporation's having to pay income tax on the profits. Since the lease payments are deductible to the corporation while corporate dividends are not, a shareholder that can take profits out of the firm in the form of lease payments will avoid corporate income taxes.

In short, there are incentives in the structure of corporations and in the tax laws for the shareholder to use a sale-leaseback when it may not be in the best interest of the corporation to do so. The law of fraudulent conveyances and the rules of income taxation do not permit shareholders to avail themselves of these options willy-nilly, however; and if there are insufficient corporate reasons for the sale-leaseback, creditors of the corporation, courts, or the Internal Revenue Service may object with justification and may be able to set the transaction aside or tax the parties as if it had not occurred.

There are considerations other than income tax consequences that motivate users of equipment to lease it. Sometimes, in a fast-changing industry, users are concerned that manufacturers will develop new products quickly and render recently purchased equipment obsolete. Short-term leases protect such users.

Other equipment users are concerned that purchases of expensive equipment will distort their financial reports. A company that acquires $200 million dollars worth of new equipment in one fiscal year can be quite healthy financially, but its earnings ratios for that year could well be anemic. If the company's stock is traded publicly, its price may fall. That fall would not be good news for senior management, the value of whose stock options would also fall.

Frequently, bank loan "facilities," that is, complex loan arrangements usually between large industrial borrowers and large banks, contain covenants that the borrower maintain certain financial ratios. A sophisticated loan arrangement might require the borrower to limit its debt to a percentage of its capital. If that borrower buys equipment and borrows from the equipment manufacturer's leasing subsidiary, the borrower must record the debt on its financial statements and may, if the loan is large, breach its covenant. If the equipment user leases the equipment, however, it need not include the lease obligations in the computation of its debt and will not violate the covenant.

Similarly, under securities laws, companies that offer securities must disclose borrowings as debt in a prospectus but need not include lease obligations in the debt calculation. The securities of companies with large debt may be less attractive to investors than companies with less debt.

All of this may sound to the uninitiated and to those schooled in the traditions of realism and of substance over form that many equipment leases are charades. That conclusion is not without some merit, but it would be a mistake to assume that the securities laws and providers of loan facilities always accept the parties' characterization of a transaction as a lease. They don't, just as the Internal Revenue Service and Article 9 don't always accept it. In the securities industry, independent certified public accountants must follow rules promulgated by the Financial Accounting Standards Board (FASB) and refuse to accept as leases transactions that are clearly secured transactions.

The lines are frequently finely drawn, however; and the current situation is not without its critics, especially in the securities law domain. Sophisticated bank loan officers are not often fooled, but the investing public may be.

§18.3 CLOSED-END AND OPEN-END LEASES

Equipment lessors may be concerned about the value of the equipment they are leasing at the end of the lease term. One would think that the finance lessor is less concerned than the true lessor; but, in fact, both the true lessor and the lender disguised as a lessor may be concerned about residual value, unless, of course, there will be no residual value.

This concern has given rise to the industry's distinction between closed-end and open-end leases. The closed-end lease is one under which the lease payments are sufficient to compensate the lessor for all of its acquisition costs and interest charges. The lessor under this type of lease is not concerned with residual value. Open-end leases are those in which the lease payments are insufficient to satisfy the lessor's costs and charges. In the open-end lease, then, the lessor is concerned about residual value, because the lessor will have to look to that residual value as a source for satisfying unrecovered costs.

In order to protect the residual value of leased equipment, lessors sometimes incorporate a terminal rental adjustment clause (TRAC) into the open-end lease. Under that clause, the parties estimate the residual value of the equipment at the termination of the lease. If the actual value of the equipment at the end of the lease exceeds that value, the lessee will receive the difference; if the actual value is less than the estimated value, the lessee is required by the lease to pay the lessor that difference. Thus, the lessee that cares for equipment can sometimes receive a premium upon the termination of the lease, while the lessor whose equipment declines in value to a point below the termination value estimated in the lease may have to make additional payments to the lessor.

§18.4 FIXTURES

Equipment lenders face knotty problems when non-Code law renders the equipment a fixture. Under real estate law, fixtures pass with the real estate, so that a sale, mortgage, or other encumbrance of the real estate affects the secured party's interest in the equipment. Equipment lenders often take warranties from their borrowers to the effect that the equipment will not become a fixture, but that warranty gives the lender only a cause of action if the borrower breaches. The lender would rather have its equipment without having to litigate with the mortgagee or some mechanic's lien holder. To some extent, the Code gives the secured party a method of protecting itself by making a fixture filing in the office where real estate transactions are recorded. That relief is somewhat illusory, however, since the fixture filing rules require the secured party to search the real estate records for a description (somewhat abbreviated) of the real estate and sometimes for the identity of the record owner. The credit seller of a $4 million printing press is willing to bear the cost of those searches, but the finance lessor of a copy machine is not. To some extent Article 9 fashions exceptions to protect lenders or sellers with a security interest in equipment, but the fixture possibilities bear watching.

19

Financing Imports and Exports

§19.1 IMPORT TRANSACTIONS

For a long time, a few major banks in New York dominated the import business. They issued up to 90 percent of the commercial letters of credit in the United States, had a lock on international banking, and formed an efficient little group of competitors. All that has changed.

Although New York continues to be an important center of international trade and banking, the import business is now dispersed throughout the country, so that money-center banks in other parts of the country and many regional banks are significant players in export and import trade.

Some importers specialize in imports. A fabricator in Kansas City may need a quantity of specialty steel manufactured in Italy. The fabricator often finds it cost-effective to approach a metals importer that has contacts with Italian suppliers. The fabricator places an order through the importer, who arranges the transaction with the foreign supplier.

A small chain of souvenir shops is interested in obtaining merchandise from abroad. An importer of manufactured goods from the Pacific Rim is able to present the chain with new lines of merchandise at attractive prices. This importer, unlike the metals importer in the earlier example, may arrange to import some goods before it has found buyers for them.

Figure 19-1.   Importing Specialty Steel

In both cases, the importers need to turn the goods around quickly, for the importers are buying the goods or financing them, in effect, with their customers' money, as the following sections explain. Figures 19-1 and 19-2 illustrate these import transactions.

Other importers import for themselves. Automobile manufacturers import parts; computer hardware manufacturers import chips; large chain retailers import garments. In each of these cases, the importer buys from foreign vendors for its own account and resells directly in the domestic market, often with considerable delay. Figure 19-3 illustrates this kind of import transaction.

The importer for its own account generally is able to hold the goods it imports, perhaps in a warehouse or in its sales outlets. Unlike the first group of small, thinly capitalized importers the automobile manufacturer and the retail chain are not forced to turn the goods over in a short time, though there is always an incentive to move inventory quickly. The small import operation often deals in large quantities of valuable merchandise and commodities, and it faces a critical need for financing. The larger importer, acting for its own account, may arrange import financing as part of its overall inventory borrowing.

§19.2 EXPORT TRANSACTIONS

We can differentiate exporters in much the same way we differentiated importers, that is, those that export for themselves and those that export for others. Automobile manufacturers, oil refiners, and grain companies often export their own product to buyers that they locate in foreign markets. Smaller manufacturers, coal producers, and some farming operations will rely on brokers who find customers in foreign countries and handle the export arrangements.

Figure 19-2.   Importing for Wholesale

FOREIGN SELLERS → IMPORTER → DOMESTIC BUYERS

Figure 19-3. Chain Importer

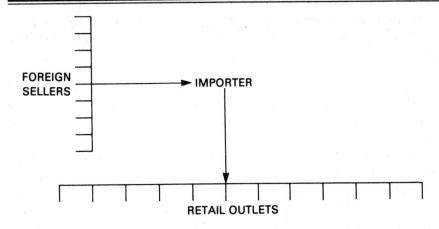

FOREIGN
SELLERS

IMPORTER

RETAIL OUTLETS

Sometimes the exporter will purchase the commodity or goods from the domestic seller; sometimes it serves as a broker bringing the parties together. To the extent that an automobile manufacturer buys parts from domestic vendors, incorporates them into a finished product, and exports that product, it serves as an exporter of the vendor's goods. Most export financing occurs in cases where the exporter buys the product from the domestic producer, finds a foreign buyer, and arranges for the financing and transport of the goods overseas. Figure 19-4 illustrates this transaction.

§19.3 THE COMMERCIAL LETTER OF CREDIT IN THE IMPORT TRANSACTION

In the past, the vast majority of import transactions into the United States were supported by a commercial letter of credit. That day and the

Figure 19-4. Exporting

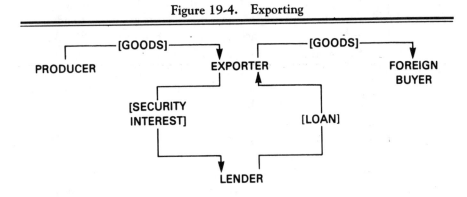

critical role for the commercial letter of credit in international trade has passed. Today, telecommunications, information systems, and up-to-date credit histories on U.S. buyers render the open account sale, which formerly was confined to domestic transactions, a major factor in import trade. Nonetheless, the commercial letter of credit retains an important role in import transactions. Foreign sellers are not always satisfied with the credit histories of U.S. buyers, and some foreign sellers are reluctant to sell on credit and face the possibility of having to sue a defaulting buyer in a U.S. court. For these sellers and many others, the commercial letter of credit transaction remains a staple of international trading practices.

In the commercial letter of credit import transaction, a credit issuer, usually the buyer's commercial bank, issues a letter of credit on behalf of the U.S. buyer in favor of the foreign seller. The credit obliges the issuing bank to honor the seller's drafts if they are accompanied by certain documents. Usually, commercial credits call for a commercial invoice, a document of title (most often a negotiable bill of lading), and various certificates of origin, insurance, and inspection. When the foreign seller ships its goods, it obtains the necessary documents, forwards them to the paying bank, which may be the issuer or its foreign correspondent, and receives payment while the goods are still en route.

The arrangement facilitates the import transaction in a number of ways. First, the foreign seller gets its money before it surrenders control of the goods, since as long as it holds the bill of lading, it controls the goods. Thus, unlike the open account sale, the commercial letter of credit transaction retains cash sale features. It is a sale for cash against documents.

Second, under the commercial letter of credit transaction, the buyer, through its bank, the issuer, does not pay for the goods until it gets control of them (through transfer of the bill of lading) and until it is satisfied (through the certificates) that the goods conform.

If an Atlanta buyer needs petrochemicals it may ask a New York importer to find the product and arrange for its shipment to Atlanta. The importer will enter into a contract of sale with, say, a Dutch refinery and will have a New York bank issue its credit in favor of the refinery. Probably, the New York bank will ask its Amsterdam correspondent to advise or confirm the credit. Under the arrangement, the refinery will take the documents to the Amsterdam bank and receive payment promptly, usually within three days. If the Amsterdam bank determines that the documents are not in order, it must return them immediately to the refinery. In most cases, the documents will be acceptable, and the bank will pay. The Amsterdam bank will then seek reimbursement from the New York bank, which will debit the importer's account.

Figure 19-5 illustrates this import transaction with the correspondent bank. Document 19-1 is a typical import letter of credit issued by a domestic bank. Chapter 5 provides further discussion of the commercial

Figure 19-5. Import Letter of Credit

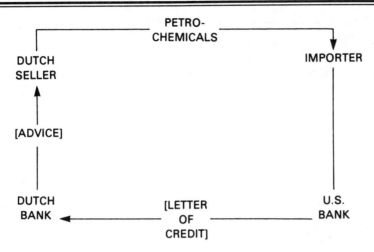

letter of credit and illustrations of the various documents in the transaction. Chapter 35 discusses the use of the bill of lading in the import transaction.

§19.4 THE COMMERCIAL LETTER OF CREDIT IN THE EXPORT TRANSACTION

Export transactions were also formerly the virtual exclusive domain of the commercial letter of credit. Traditionally, U.S. exporters did not have credit information on their foreign buyers and were reluctant to rely on foreign courts or foreign law to enforce breach of contract claims. In short, they would not sell overseas on open account. In many foreign markets, that reluctance has diminished. As western European countries rationalized their economies and generated reliable credit data, the open account sale became a reality in north Atlantic trade. Similarly, today U.S. exporters will sell on open account to established enterprises in the Pacific rim and other regions.

There remain, however, foreign buyers of U.S. goods and services that do not merit, at least in the eyes of U.S. exporters, the trust on which the open account sale rests. Shipments of used tires to buyers in the former republics of the Soviet Union or of telephone equipment to new enterprises in the mixed markets of China remain the province of the commercial letter of credit export transaction.

In the export transaction the domestic bank's role is that of correspondent of a foreign issuer. When a U.S. grain producer exports to Bangladesh through a Chicago grain broker, the broker is the beneficiary of a credit issued by a bank in Dacca. The broker insists that the Dacca bank's credit be advised or, more probably, confirmed by a Chicago bank.

185

Figure 19-6.   Export Transaction

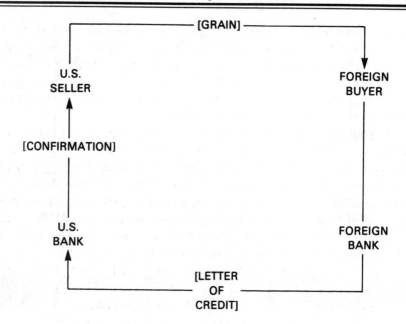

When the grain is loaded on a vessel in Chicago, the carrier issues the bill of lading to the broker, who assembles the other documents and presents them to the Chicago bank for payment. Figure 19-6 illustrates the transaction.

§19.5 NEED FOR FINANCING (IMPORTS)

The common need for financing imports occurs when the importer is a broker. A metals broker, for example, may import 100 tons of chrome from Africa for a number of small manufacturers in the home appliance, automobile parts, and kitchenware industries. Although the broker may have purchasers for all of the chrome at favorable prices, the broker must pay the African seller of the chrome before it arrives in, say, Seattle. Under the letter of credit that the Seattle bank issues in favor of the African seller, the bank's correspondent in Italy or Switzerland, where many African sellers do their banking, must pay the seller as soon as it presents the documents.

If the goods are loaded on board an ocean going vessel on May 1, the African seller may have its documents at the Zurich counter of the paying bank by May 4. The goods are still on the vessel and may not arrive in Seattle until May 14. In the meantime, the Seattle bank has paid the Swiss bank and seeks to debit the metal broker's account, but the account does not contain enough to cover the charges. It would be extraordinary and inefficient for a metals broker, a middleman, to have the kind of capital necessary to import not only this chrome, but also the bauxite from Venezuela it is buying for an aluminum foundry, the tin ore from Ecuador for its smelter client, and the copper from southeast Asia for its specialty manufacturer's account. Rather, the broker and the Seattle bank fashion an arrangement whereby the resale transactions and the commodities themselves finance the import transaction.

Under this arrangement, the issuing bank, that is, the Seattle bank that issues the letter of credit, takes a security interest in the metals. It effects that interest, usually, through the bill of lading. As long as the bill is negotiable, the issuer's possession of it, under the Code, makes it the party with first crack at the goods. By insisting in the letter of credit that it will not pay the seller unless the seller presents negotiable bills of lading indorsed in blank or to the order of the issuing bank, the issuer knows that once it pays, it will hold the goods through the negotiable bill.

Sometimes, the parties do not use a negotiable bill of lading. If, for example, the goods are shipped by air and arrive at the broker's city before the mail can get the bill of lading to the issuer, it makes no sense to use a negotiable bill. (Carriers will not release goods subject to a negotiable bill without surrender of the bill.) In the case of air shipments, therefore, the parties use a non-negotiable air bill. In the case of shipment by non-negotiable bills or in circumstances where there are no bills of lading, the issuing bank must insist that the broker grant the bank a security interest in the goods. The agreement between the issuer and the broker, the application agreement, normally contains the grant of a security interest.

In either of these arrangements, the bank is secure and will make an advance, i.e., a loan, when it reimburses the foreign bank that paid the seller. Instead of debiting the buyer's checking account for the amount reimbursed, the issuer generates a loan and increases the broker's principal loan balance.

Often the bank takes a security interest both ways. It insists on negotiable bills, and it takes a security agreement in the application agreement. If the broker enters into these transactions on a frequent basis, as it probably would, the bank takes a **blanket security interest**.

Despite all of its efforts to use the subject matter of the sale as security for its advances, the bank faces a hiatus in its security when the broker ships the goods to its customer. Generally, the Code protects these customers, so that once they pay for the goods or take negotiable documents of title covering them, they cut off the bank's security interest. The bank cannot rely on negotiable bills once it surrenders them to the broker, as it must when the goods arrive in Seattle. The broker needs the bills in order to take delivery from the ocean carrier and to arrange shipment on a domestic carrier to the ultimate buyer. Once the bank surrenders the bills, it puts the broker in position to resell them to a good-faith purchaser or to take delivery from the ocean carrier and resell the goods to the customer without accounting to the bank for the proceeds. In either event, an honest buyer will defeat the bank's security interest.

Banks are generally willing to take the risk inherent in delivery of the bills to the broker and in letting the broker have possession of the goods. First, the bank knows the broker and trusts him. Second, the bank is financing other imports and can look to other commodity shipments in the event the broker defaults on one transaction. The security agreements generally provide that each shipment secures all advances the bank makes, whether for the shipment in question or other shipments. In the event the broker's credit is weak, the bank can take steps to arrange shipment of the goods to the ultimate purchaser itself and thereby guard against misappropriation of the proceeds, or the bank can insist on a commercial letter of credit from the buyer in a back-to-back letter of credit transaction.

It is not necessary, of course, that the letter of credit issuer finance the transaction or finance all of it. In at least one case, an importer of women's apparel used its factor to finance the purchase of the goods. The importer's bank issued the credit; but the factor, a finance company, satisfied the bank's reimbursement claim after the bank paid the foreign manufacturer and took a security interest in the accounts generated by the importer when it resold the imported goods to retailers throughout the country.

§19.6 NEED FOR FINANCING (EXPORTS)

Export financing can assume a number of forms, but all of them are essentially account financing. In the classic case, the exporter sells its goods under a foreign bank's commercial letter of credit that calls for time drafts. Under this arrangement, the foreign buyer has exacted credit terms from the domestic seller. If the exporter and the foreign buyer agree, for example, on 90-days' credit, the seller's drafts will be payable 90 days after the date of the acceptance, or after the date of the shipment, or after some other ascertainable date. When the exporter presents its drafts to the paying bank, that bank will accept them, that is, will sign them and thereby undertake to pay them when they come due. The acceptor returns these banker's acceptances to the exporter who now holds valuable paper that it can discount in the money market. Often the paying bank itself will discount the acceptances for the exporter.

Acceptances that are eligible under Federal Reserve Board regulations are called "eligible acceptances" and are a prime medium of investment. Most acceptances that (1) arise under export transactions involving commodities and (2) have a life of not more than 180 days will be eligible. They provide the exporter with readily marketable paper that attracts investors at a small discount. Chapter 20 discusses those acceptances in general.

§19.7 FORFAITING AND SIMILAR ARRANGEMENTS

Just as most law professors had decided that the negotiable promissory note had outlived its usefulness, international sellers and their banks devised a new practice to which the negotiable note is indispensable. The practice is called *forfaiting,* and its purpose is to enhance the attractiveness of a foreign buyer's obligation to pay the exporter. The reason for that enhancement, of course, is to make the obligation more attractive in the financial markets so that the exporter may provide credit to the foreign buyer and yet obtain funds promptly.

In a forfaiting transaction, an exporter of 12 shipments of beef to Germany over the next 12 months, for example, might want to make 90-day credit terms available to her buyer. She could, of course, resort to the commercial letter of credit transaction described in Section 19.4 and use a 90-day time draft that will result in a 90-day banker's acceptance — a medium of investment that is highly attractive in the financial markets. That method entails expenses that the buyer may be unwilling to incur, however. If the buyer is strong enough, he will insist on the 90-day credit terms and refuse to obtain the letter of credit.

In that case, the seller might be able to arrange a forfait with a bank. The seller will ship the beef against the buyer's promissory notes for the purchase price of each shipment. After each shipment, the seller will hold a negotiable instrument executed by the buyer payable to the seller's order. The seller will indorse the note to the forfaiting bank, which will take it at a discount and enforce it against the buyer when it comes due.

The beauty of the arrangement for the seller is that under a forfait, the bank will permit the seller to indorse "without recourse." That indorsement means that the seller does not guarantee payment of the note in the event the buyer defaults.

The first bank to take the notes under the forfait may not hold them until maturity but has the option of negotiating them to subsequent holders. In some transactions, notes arising from a forfait will change hands many times before maturity when the holder presents them to the buyer through the banking chain for payment.

Often, the first bank maintains a relationship with the foreign buyer. In the example of the German buyer of beef, it may be the German buyer that initiates the forfaiting arrangement. The buyer will arrange to have its bank, or a U.S. branch of its bank, agree to take the notes without recourse. If the bank agrees, then, to advance $5 million to the German buyer, it may make those advances when it forfaits the notes the seller takes from the buyer.

Forfaiting is becoming common in sales to less-developed countries and sometimes involves the use of an *aval*, which is a device, common to civil law systems, that is similar to a guaranty. A buyer in the less developed country will cause its bank to issue an aval that the bank will place directly on the note using the French words "par aval" followed by a signature. When the note comes due, the holder presents it directly to the bank and receives payment.

Forfaiting can also be used with drafts. Under this arrangement, the seller draws a time draft on the buyer, who accepts the draft and whose bank guarantees it using the same aval arrangement. When the draft comes due, the holder presents it directly to the bank which pays it.

The forfait is attractive to sellers because it permits them to discount their notes with the forfaiter without recourse. In the event of dishonor by the buyer or the buyer's bank, the forfaiter may not seek recourse against the seller because the indorsement is without recourse.

Paper generated by forfaiting moves readily in the money market. Forfaiters, then, can spread the risk of a foreign bank's default among a number of investors or other banks.

The resemblance between the forfait and the commercial letter of credit transaction is obvious. The advantages are also obvious. Under the forfait, the forfaiter needs to present only the promissory note or the acceptance. Documentation typical in a letter of credit transaction (invoice, inspection certificate, customs documents, insurance documents, and transport documents) are absent.

In the forfait transaction, the holders of the notes may look only to the buyer and indorsers subsequent to the seller for payment. Usually, therefore, the buyer is a concern of sound financial repute. Significantly, of course, the holders are holders in due course and are unconcerned about the underlying transaction. If the beef turns out to have too many hormones to satisfy German customs inspectors, the buyer may not want it and may have a defense to payment in the underlying transaction of sale with the seller. That defense, however, is unavailable to the buyer when the holder sues him on the notes. Thus the negotiable nature of the note renders it attractive to the financial institutions and other investors who take it and who provide the credit for the export transaction.

There are a number of variations to the financing of foreign obligations arising from exports. Under one of them, the seller ships on open account and finances its accounts with a bank. The bank is willing to take the accounts because the accounts are insured. That insurance may extend to commercial risk (i.e., the risk that the buyer will not pay) or political risk (i.e., the risk of war, political upheaval, or exchange-control problems in the importing country). These subsidized arrangements have the same effect on the marketability of the seller's receivables that negotiable promissory notes have — they enhance the attractiveness of the obligation.

Bank of America

PAGE: 1

DATE: OCTOBER 25, 1996

IRREVOCABLE DOCUMENTARY CREDIT NUMBER:

ADVISING BANK

SELLER"S BANK

BENEFICIARY

SELLER'S NAME AND ADDRESS

APPLICANT

BUYER'S NAME AND ADDRESS

AMOUNT

EXPIRATION
, 1997 IN

WE HEREBY ISSUE THIS IRREVOCABLE DOCUMENTARY CREDIT AVAILABLE WITH
ANY BANK IN CHILE BY NEGOTIATION AGAINST PRESENTATION OF THE ORIGINAL
OF THIS LETTER OF CREDIT AND BENEFICIARY'S DRAFTS AT SIGHT DRAWN ON
BANK OF AMERICA, LOS ANGELES, CA FOR 100 PERCENT OF INVOICE VALUE,
BEARING THE CLAUSE "DRAWN UNDER BANK OF AMERICA NT & SA, LETTER OF
CREDIT NUMBER   , AND ACCOMPANIED BY THE DOCUMENTS DETAILED
BELOW:

+ ORIGINAL AND 3 COPIES OF COMMERCIAL INVOICE
COVERING:

+ CERTIFICATE OF ORIGIN

+ PACKING LIST

+ VETERINARY CERTIFICATE

+ QUALITY CERTIFICATE

+ PACKING MATERIAL AND COMPONENT CERTIFICATE.
+ INSURANCE POLICY OR CERTIFICATE IN DUPLICATE
FOR 110 PERCENT OF INVOICE VALUE IN NEGOTIABLE FORM COVERING
INSTITUTE CARGO CLAUSES AND ALL RISKS.

+ SOLE ORIGINAL AND 2 COPIES OF CLEAN ON BOARD VESSEL MARINE BILL OF
LADING CONSIGNED TO ORDER OF SHIPPER, BLANK ENDORSED, MARKED: FREIGHT
PREPAID, NOTITY
     , EVIDENCING SHIPMENT FROM   FOR TRANSPORTATION
TO   NOT LATER THAN .

PARTIAL SHIPMENTS NOT ALLOWED
TRANSHIPMENTS NOT ALLOWED

ORIGINAL

Bank of America NT&SA Trade Operations Center 5655
333 South Beaudry Avenue, 19th Flr., Los Angeles, CA 90017
CABLE ADDRESS: Telex MCI 67652 BANKAMER SFO • SWIFT ADDRESS BOFAUS6S

Recycled Paper
(Reprint 3-96)   CORR-1041A 10-95

Reprinted with the permission of Bank of America NT&SA.

B **Bank of America**

PAGE: 2

THIS IS AN INTEGRAL PART OF LETTER OF CREDIT NUMBER: ᵔᵔ⁻ ᵔ

ALL BANK CHARGES, OTHER THAN THOSE OF THE ISSUING BANK, ARE FOR THE
ACCOUNT OF THE BENEFICIARY.

DOCUMENTS MUST BE PRESENTED AT PLACE OF EXPIRY WITHIN 21 DAYS OF
ISSUE DATE OF TRANSPORT DOCUMENT AND WITHIN VALIDITY OF CREDIT.

DOCUMENTS MUST BE FORWARDED TO BANK OF AMERICA TRADE OPERATIONS
CENTER, 19TH FLOOR 333 SOUTH BEAUDRY AVENUE LOS ANGELES, CA 90017 IN
ONE LOT.

THE AMOUNT OF EACH DRAFT MUST BE ENDORSED ON THE REVERSE OF THIS
DOCUMENTARY CREDIT BY THE NEGOTIATING BANK.

THIS LETTER OF CREDIT IS SUBJECT TO THE UNIFORM CUSTOMS AND PRACTICE
FOR DOCUMENTARY CREDITS (1993 REVISION), INTERNATIONAL CHAMBER OF
COMMERCE PUBLICATION NO. 500 AND ENGAGES US PURSUANT TO THE TERMS
THEREIN.

AN ADDITIONAL HANDLING FEE OF USD 60.00 WILL BE DEDUCTED FROM
PROCEEDS FOR DOCUMENTS PRESENTED WITH DISCREPANCIES.

SHOULD PAYMENT BE EFFECTED BY WIRE TRANSFER OR CHECK, A USD 35.00
HANDLING FEE WILL BE DEDUCTED FROM PROCEEDS.

IF YOU REQUIRE ANY ASSISTANCE OR HAVE ANY QUESTIONS REGARDING THIS
TRANSACTION, PLEASE CALL 213-345-6616.

BANK OF AMERICA NT & SA

SPECIMEN

------------------------   --------------------------
AUTHORIZED SIGNATURE   AUTHORIZED SIGNATURE

THIS DOCUMENT CONSISTS OF 2 PAGE(S).

ORIGINAL

Bank of America NT&SA   Trade Operations Center 5655
333 South Beaudry Avenue, 19th Flr., Los Angeles, CA 90017
CABLE ADDRESS: Telex MCI 67652 BANKAMER SFO • SWIFT ADDRESS BOFAUS6S   (Reprint 3-96)   CORR-1041A 10-95

♻ Recycled Paper

20

Banker's Acceptances

§20.1 UNDERSTANDING THE DEVICE

The banker's acceptance is a commercial bank product or "facility," as they say, that arises in a number of transactions. In many ways the product is unique, and its unique features make it difficult to position the device in the commercial law curriculum.

The banker's acceptance is a negotiable instrument, yet it is not altogether clear what kind of instrument it is. The acceptance begins life as a draft, when a drawer creates (or "utters") it. It may travel through the hands of a number of parties in that form until ultimately the drawee, a bank, accepts it. That acceptance transforms the item from an instrument with no one promising to pay it into an instrument on which a bank (often one of a few strong banks that are involved in the acceptance market) has signaled its undertaking to pay the instrument. At that point, the item is much more akin to a promissory note or certificate of deposit than it is to a draft.

Once transformed into a banker's acceptance, the item usually becomes a prime medium for investment in the money market. There are about 400 banks involved in banker's acceptances and a small number of dealers who buy and sell these acceptances. Thus, unlike most negotiable instruments today, which usually serve as media of payment, the banker's acceptance becomes a medium of investment, something in the nature of a security.

Notwithstanding its nature as a payment mechanism and as an investment product, the description of the device is in the secured lending section of this book. The decision to place it here rests on the fact that today the banker's acceptance grows primarily out of the financing of goods. From a pedagogical standpoint, it is best to think of the device in terms of a financing device. That said, it is important to bear in mind that the beauty of the device is that although banks use it to get funds to their borrowers, they do not have to use any of their own funds. Because the device is so attractive in the money market, the bank can obtain funds from third parties contemporaneously with the creation of the acceptance. Thus the banker's acceptance is a classic facility for intermediation. Banks create the acceptance, give credit to their borrowing customers, and contemporaneously draw credit from the investing public.

The procedure is not only quick; it is also inexpensive. Traditionally, only banks of good credit repute have engaged in the creation of banker's acceptances, and investment brokers have been able to rely on the acceptances and to represent them to their customers as sound investments.

Much of the literature confines itself to discussion of the regulations that govern banker's acceptances and ignores the important fact that they often arise out of a transaction in goods.

§20.2 EXPORT TRANSACTIONS

Chapters 5 and 19 explain in some detail the way in which parties may use a letter of credit in the export of goods. This chapter concentrates on the draft in that transaction, the way that draft becomes a banker's acceptance, and the way the exported goods or commodities become security for the bank's obligation on the acceptance.

Recall that in the time letter of credit transaction, the exporter agrees to sell goods to a foreign buyer on credit terms. An exporter of U.S. citrus concentrate to Japan, for example, might agree with its Japanese buyer that payment will be due 90 days after the issuance of the bill of lading covering the shipment of the concentrate to Japan. The exporter will agree to that arrangement only if the buyer causes its bank to issue a time letter of credit in favor of the exporter. Under the terms of the sales contract, moreover, the exporter will insist that the credit be confirmed by a Los Angeles bank.

The confirmation will require the exporter to obtain a negotiable ocean bill of lading covering the concentrate and to present it (and probably other documents) to the confirming bank in Los Angeles with a time draft payable 90 days after the date of the bill.

Once it has the confirmation in hand, the exporter arranges for the shipment of the goods, obtains the bill of lading, and takes the bill and the draft to the Los Angeles bank. Document 4-3 is a time draft such as the one the exporter would prepare.

When the exporter presents the documents to the bank, its document examiner determines whether they are in order. If they are, the bank signs the draft on its face and thereby "accepts" it, transforming the draft into a banker's acceptance.

At that point, the parties must decide what to do with the acceptance. It is, at that time, the property of the exporter, but the exporter probably does not want it. It wants money to pay the growers who sold it the concentrate and to pay other creditors. A likely customer for the acceptance is the acceptor itself. The Los Angeles bank may have funds it wants to invest in an acceptance, knowing that the acceptance is liquid, that is, that it is readily marketable. The bank will be satisfied that it can sell the acceptance quickly if there is a need for funds. In case the bank wants the acceptance, it will take it from the exporter at a discount. The bank computes the discount by applying the current interest rate to the face amount of the acceptance for 90 days.

Sometimes the bank takes the acceptance only momentarily and immediately rediscounts it in the money market through one of a small number of banker's acceptance dealers who broker acceptances among other financial institutions and investors.

Ultimately, the acceptance may pass through a number of parties' hands before it comes due on the ninetieth day. On that day, the holder will present the acceptance to the Los Angeles bank, which honors it by payment.

Note that the Los Angeles bank is on the hook for a considerable period of time here, and as you might suspect, it will want some security for its undertaking. Admittedly, the bank expects to be reimbursed by the Tokyo bank, the Japanese buyer's bank that opened the credit that the Los Angeles bank confirmed. The U.S. exporter got its money, less the interest charges, when the bank discounted the acceptance; but during the 90 days, the Japanese seller is sitting on its money, as it has the right to do under the sales contract, which gave it 90-day terms and under the reimbursement agreement that it negotiated with its bank when it asked it to open the letter of credit. If all goes according to plan, of course, the Los Angeles bank pays the holder of the acceptance on maturity, the Tokyo bank reimburses the Los Angeles bank, and the Japanese buyer reimburses the Tokyo bank. During the 90-day interim, however, the Los Angeles bank has created a liability for itself, and under sound banking practices, it must have security for the undertaking.

The citrus concentrate is the security. As long as the bank holds the negotiable bill of lading, the bank knows that it will be able to resort to the concentrate if it is not reimbursed. In the unlikely event, then, that the Tokyo bank does not reimburse, the Los Angeles bank will cause its

Tokyo agent to surrender the bill of lading to the ocean carrier or to a warehouse at the dock in Yokohama where it has been stored since the ship docked, take delivery of the concentrate, sell it, and forward the proceeds to Los Angeles. If the Tokyo bank does reimburse, the Los Angeles bank will deliver the document to the Tokyo bank, which will hold it until the Japanese buyer reimburses it. Upon that reimbursement, the Tokyo bank will deliver the bill to the Japanese buyer, who will then be in a position to take delivery of the merchandise.

There are variations in the transaction. If the Japanese buyer wants the concentrate before the 90 days have expired, he can put his own bank in funds or can grant his own bank a security interest in the concentrate or in other collateral. In those events, the Japanese bank will be able to buy the bill of lading from the Los Angeles bank and deliver it to the buyer, who will then be able to take delivery of the goods.

§20.3 IMPORT TRANSACTIONS

The banker's acceptance in the import transaction is similarly secured by the goods that are being imported. In the import situation, a New York importer might arrange to buy polypropylene granules from a Frankfurt, Germany seller. Under the sales agreement, the importer has obtained 180-day credit terms but has agreed to pay by letter of credit. Importer causes its New York bank to issue the credit in favor of the German seller, payable against the seller's 180-day time draft. The draft is payable 180 days after the New York bank accepts it.

The seller prepares the documents required by the letter of credit, including a negotiable bill of lading covering the granules. When the New York bank's document examiner determines that the documents are in order, it accepts the draft and creates the banker's acceptance.

The New York bank holds the bill as security for its obligation on the acceptance. When the 180 days have passed, the holder of the acceptance presents it for payment, and the New York bank pays. By that time, however, the importer probably has resold the granules and has something of value to give the bank either in reimbursement for its payment to the holder of the acceptance or as replacement security for the bank's advance.

In order to effect that resale, it may be necessary for the importer to obtain delivery of the bill of lading or the granules. In that case, the New York bank might be willing to surrender the bill, but usually it does so only if it has other collateral from the importer. In any event, in the short term, the imported goods serve as collateral for the bank's undertaking on the acceptance.

§20.4 STORED COMMODITIES

There may be times when a broker holds commodities (sugar, for example) that she does not want to sell and that she desires to use as collateral for a loan. The broker may need the sugar to fill a contract in a month, but she needs cash now. The broker could simply grant a lender a security interest in the commodity and take a simple inventory loan, as Chapter 16 describes. There may be times, however, when acceptance financing yields more attractive interest charges. In this case, the borrower draws a time draft, say, one payable 30 days after sight. She presents the draft to the bank for acceptance accompanied by a negotiable warehouse receipt covering the sugar. Document 33-1 is an example of a negotiable warehouse receipt. The bank knows that the warehouse will not deliver the sugar to anyone who does not surrender the receipt. In effect, then, the bank's possession of the receipt is possession of the sugar. Under the Uniform Commercial Code, the bank has a perfected security interest in the sugar.

Once the bank accepts the time draft, the broker has an attractive investment medium that investors who know nothing about the sugar market are willing to buy. When the 30 days elapse, the holder of the acceptance presents it to the bank and receives payment. If the broker does not reimburse the bank for its payment, the bank sells the receipt to someone who wants the sugar or takes the receipt to the warehouse, receives the sugar, and resells it or uses it for lemonade at the next board meeting.

21

Financing the Farmer

§21.1 INTRODUCTION

The United States has had a curious romance with the farm producer. Americans are fond of the American Gothic image of the proud and proper farm couple standing with a pitchfork before the white frame dwelling. The myth of the sturdy yeoman farmer working the fields from dawn to dusk dies hard. American politicians and the American media never tire of advancing the cause of the family farm, and the popular myths enhance their efforts.

   In fact, of course, the American farmer is a business person. Producers of most agricultural commodities in this country are university-trained people, sophisticated in the sciences of agronomy, animal husbandry, and irrigation technology. Farmers sell under futures contracts and other complicated marketing arrangements that they monitor on their computer terminals or those of their brokers. They finance their operations with the help of a vast private and government-subsidized credit industry. Many of them test their soil scientifically and irrigate with computer-devised equipment and programs. Others raise and breed hogs in antiseptic environments. In short, agriculture is a big, complicated business. The people who engage in it are not hayseeds. Their investment in land and equipment matches or exceeds that of many medium-sized urban commercial enterprises. Agricultural production is a business much like any other business.

History, the large number of marginal farms, and the American romance with the farm myth leave a different impression, however, and different practices, different financing institutions, and even different legal rules distinguishes farm lending from much of the rest of the lending sector.

§21.2 GOVERNMENT ROLE

There is perhaps one significant difference between the small agricultural enterprise and the small or medium-sized commercial establishment. When the farm economy is in trouble, the government and the public perceive it as a national problem that the government must address. However efficient it may be from an economic standpoint, the political price of letting many family farms be sold at bankruptcy auction is one the U.S. government is unwilling to pay.

In the lean years that inevitably confront the cyclical agricultural sector, the federal government has responded with a wide array of special legislation that includes significant efforts to provide credit to agriculture. Among the legislative creatures that these efforts have spawned are the **Farm Credit System** and the **Farm Service Agency**. The former is a **government-sponsored enterprise (GSE)** that raises funds in the money markets and acting through the Cooperative Bank makes those funds available to **production credit associations (PCAs)** and **agricultural credit associations (ACAs)** that make short term loans to farmers, fisherman, and the timber industry. The latter, the Farm Service Agency, makes credit available to farmers but more often guarantees loans to farmers.

§21.3 FARM INVENTORY

Under the Uniform Commercial Code, farmers do not have inventory. They have farm products, and the inventory **priority** and purchase-money rules do not apply to them. Purchasers from farmers, moreover, do not enjoy the full protection that buyers in ordinary course normally enjoy under the Code, though federal law has changed that rule somewhat. Farm lenders are aware of these anomalies in the Code treatment of agricultural activity and take advantage of them. Security agreements covering crops and livestock, for example, almost always forbid the farmer to sell collateral without the prior approval of the lender. Document 21-1 is such a security agreement. Such prohibition is the exception in nonfarm sectors of the economy. In actual practice, the farm lender almost never objects if the farmer sells the collateral and accounts for the proceeds. Only when the proceeds disappear does the lender argue that the sale was unauthorized and that, under the rules of the Code, the buyer or, in some cases, the auctioneer, is liable in conversion.

§21.4 FARM BUYERS

In the usual course of business, farmers market their grain and livestock either through the federal government or, in private markets, through brokers and large buyers: grain companies, slaughterhouses, and elevators. Although the farmer is clearly a business person, his operation, even with significant investments in real estate and equipment, is relatively small, especially in relation to the larger operations to whom he sells his product. This picture (small sellers, big buyers) is a reversal of the paradigmatic sales transaction (big sellers, small buyers) in other sectors of the economy and that the Code drafters confessed was the model they had in mind when they drafted the sales article, Article 2. The effect of the disparity in size is a disparity in bargaining strength, and farm sellers are usually not in a position to bargain with their buyers over sales terms, which may be fixed by distant exchanges.

The result in many grain and livestock transactions is to leave the farm seller unprotected. Livestock sellers normally cannot sell for cash, since the price of the livestock cannot be computed until the animals are slaughtered, dressed, and graded. The rancher, then, must wait one or more days after delivery of his cattle for a check. He has, in effect, made a credit sale, and he has done so without retaining any security interest in the goods: He is an **unsecured creditor**. The Packers and Stockyards Act and similar legislation in many states provide, however, that the livestock seller and sometimes the grain seller as well have a super **lien** that defeats the rights of the buyer and the buyer's creditors, if the seller is not paid.

Creditors of buyers from farm sellers must take these super liens into account. The inventory lender of a slaughterhouse cannot rely on the slaughterhouse's inventory of beef or hogs without considering that much of the inventory is not paid for and, therefore, subject to the statutory seller's super lien. Figure 21-1 illustrates the super-lien setting.

§21.5 FARM LENDERS

Three enterprises play significant roles in short-term, personal property farm lending: (1) commercial banks, (2) production credit associations and agricultural credit associations, and (3) the Farm Service Agency.

The role of commercial banks in farm lending is not, on the surface, altogether different from that role in nonfarm lending. The banks take loan applications, subject the loan to their credit-review process, and

Figure 21-1.   A Super Lien

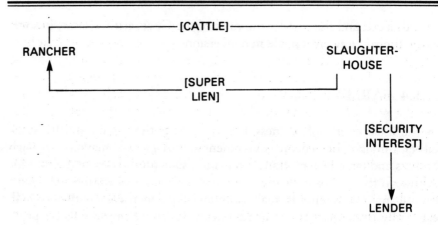

document the transaction with a promissory note, security agreement, and financing statement. The chief difference is that the farm lender's security agreement generally contains a prohibition against sale.

A significant feature of farm lending is that often the commercial lender can avail itself of the benefits of the farm credit system — a vast array of federally supported and subsidized loans and guarantees implemented by a number of government agencies. In a typical case, the agency is the Farm Service Agency, and the service it performs is one of guaranteeing the farmer's loan for an amount equal to a percentage (90 percent) of the loan balance.

Under the agreement, if the farmer defaults, the bank that made the loan assigns all of its interest in it and in the security interest that secures it to the agency, which then pays the bank 90 percent of the loan balance. Figure 21-2 illustrates the Farm Service Agency loan-guaranty arrangement.

Figure 21-2.   Loan Guaranty

```
                                          FARMER

                                            |
                                            |
                                      [SECURITY
                                       INTEREST]
                                            |
                                            ▼
     FARM SERVICE                         LENDER
       AGENCY                               ▲
          |_____|
                    [GUARANTY]
```

204

Production credit associations and agricultural credit associations are in the nature of mutual organizations, that is, they are owned by their borrowers. Traditionally, the board of a PCA or ACA consists of the leading farmers in the farm community. The Cooperative Bank and the Federal Intermediate Credit Banks provide the associations with the funds. The association lends the funds directly to the farmer and often takes a security interest to secure the loan. (ACAs, but not PCAs, make long-term loans that they secure with real estate mortgages.) Association loan documentation does not differ from the typical loan documentation of a commercial bank that is acting as a secured lender. The associations know the rules of agricultural lending. They nearly always provide in their security agreement that the farmer may not sell his crops or livestock without the association's prior written approval, but in practice the associations rarely enforce the provision before the fact.

The Commodity Credit Corporation (CCC) also makes agricultural loans. Under the CCC program, a farmer may store grain with an elevator, receive the government-designated price for the crop from the CCC in the form of a nine-month loan, and hold the commodity until the price improves or until the farmer decides to sell. Upon the sale, the CCC receives the proceeds first, to the extent of its loan, and the farmer receives the balance, if any. If the market price never exceeds the support price (used in funding the loan) and if the loan is a **without-recourse** loan, the CCC takes the crop in satisfaction of the loan debt and has no recourse against the farmer.

Rather than storing the product in its own facility, the CCC may take and perfect a security interest in one of two ways. First, it can take a negotiable warehouse receipt from an elevator, cotton gin, or other bailee and hold the document until the farmer finds a buyer. At that point, the CCC must release the document to the farmer or to the buyer in order to permit the sale to close. Figure 21-3 illustrates the entire transaction.

Alternatively, the CCC either can ask the farmer to have the bailee issue non-negotiable receipts directly to the CCC or can notify the bailee of the CCC's security interest. Either method constitutes perfection under the Code.

Figure 21-3. Commodity Credit Corporation Loan

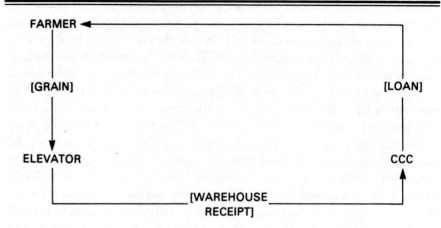

PRODUCTION CREDIT ASSOCIATION SECURITY AGREEMENT

1. CREATION OF SECURITY INTEREST.

For value received, the undersigned Debtor grants to Production Credit Association of _____ (Secured Party hereinafter referred to as "PCA") a security interest in the property described opposite the box(es) checked in Section 2 and in Debtor's PCA stock and participation certificates ("Collateral"), to secure the payment and performance by Debtor of all Debtor's obligations. "Obligations" shall mean (a) all loans, advances, liabilities, and amounts owing by Debtor to PCA at any time, whether representing existing or future credit granted by PCA to Debtor, to Debtor and another, or to another guaranteed or endorsed by Debtor; and (b) to the extent not prohibited by law, all costs and expenses, including attorneys' fees and legal expenses, incurred or paid by PCA in the preservation or enforcement of its rights under this Agreement.

2. DESCRIPTION OF COLLATERAL.

Except as otherwise stated herein, the Collateral includes the following designated property, whether now owned or hereafter acquired, and all proceeds of such property. All Collateral (except any covered under Section 2.4) is covered regardless of whether it is classified under the Uniform Commercial Code as equipment, farm products or inventory and regardless of whether or not such classification changes.

☐ 2.1 All equipment, motor vehicles and fixtures, all accessions thereto, and all spare parts and special tools for such equipment.
☐ 2.2 All livestock and poultry and the young of such livestock and poultry.
☐ 2.3 The following products of livestock and poultry: _____
☐ 2.4 All accounts arising from the sale, lease, or other disposition of other Collateral (but Debtor is authorized to sell, lease, or dispose of Collateral only to the extent stated in Section 3 hereof).
☐ 2.5 All crops growing or to be grown by Debtor, and the products of all such crops, on real estate described as:

☐ 2.6 All: harvested and processed crops not covered under other sections of this Agreement (whether or not produced by Debtor); feed; seed; fertilizer, insecticides, herbicides and other agricultural chemicals; and other supplies.
☐ 2.7 Property specifically described here and on any Addendum hereto.

3. RESTRICTIONS ON DISPOSITION OF COLLATERAL BY DEBTOR.

3.1 **GENERAL RESTRICTION.** DEBTOR MAY NOT SELL, LEASE OR OTHERWISE DISPOSE OF ANY COLLATERAL UNLESS SPECIFICALLY AUTHORIZED IN SECTION 3.2 OR IN A SEPARATE WRITING SIGNED BY PCA, OR IN AN ADDENDUM HERETO.

3.2 **Collateral Which May be Sold, Leased or Expended.** Subject to any conditions stated in Sections 3.3 and 3.4 and to PCA's continuing security interest in all proceeds and accounts arising from permitted disposition of Collateral, Debtor, before default, may in a commercially reasonable manner, (a) market milk, (b) market eggs, (c) use feed and crops or products thereof as feed for Debtor's livestock and poultry, and (d) sell or lease any other Collateral listed here:

_____
_____

3.3 **Required Livestock Herd Size.** ☐ If checked here, then, notwithstanding any rights given Debtor herein to dispose of livestock, such disposition shall not reduce the size of Debtor's livestock herds below the following specified number of head. [Debtor represents that such herd(s) is/are presently maintained]:

Type	Breed	Number	Age	Other

3.4 **Conditions for Disposition.** Debtor's right to dispose of Collateral listed in Section 3.2 is further conditioned upon the following restrictions, if any:

_____
_____
_____
_____
_____

3.5 **Termination of Debtor's Right to Dispose of Collateral.** PCA reserves the right, in its sole discretion, to revoke or modify any permission granted herein to Debtor to dispose of Collateral.

4. WARRANTIES AND AGREEMENTS. Debtor warrants and agrees that:

4.1 **Ownership.** Debtor is the owner of Collateral free of all liens, encumbrances and security interests, except PCA's security interest and the following exceptions, if any:

4.2 **Records.** Debtor shall keep and maintain permanent records of all material information relating to the acquisition, maintenance, identification and disposition of all Collateral, in a form acceptable to PCA. PCA shall have the right to examine and copy such records at any reasonable time and place. Debtor's records are kept at Debtor's residence. Debtor shall not remove any of the Collateral or Debtor's records of accounts from the state of Debtor's present residence.

4.3 **Address and Location.** Debtor's residence (registered or main office if Debtor is a corporation or partnership) is at the address to the left of Debtor's signature. If all Collateral is not at such address, its location is:

4.4 **Change of Address.** Debtor shall immediately advise PCA in writing of any change in Debtor's address, the location of Collateral, and of any changes in the location of Debtor's records described in Section 4.2 of this Agreement.

THIS AGREEMENT INCLUDES ALL THE PROVISIONS ON THE REVERSE SIDE. DEBTOR ACKNOWLEDGES RECEIPT OF AN EXACT COPY OF THIS AGREEMENT.

Dated: _____ 19___

Address: _____
[See Section 4.3]

County: _____

_____
(Debtor)

_____
(Debtor)

*Type or Print Name Signed Above

PCA 449 Revised 11/78   **ORIGINAL PCA COPY**

207

5. COLLECTIONS

5.1 Verification and Notification. PCA may verify accounts constituting Collateral in any manner and Debtor shall assist PCA in so doing. PCA may at any time and Debtor shall, upon request of PCA, notify the account debtors to make payment directly to PCA and PCA may enforce collection of, settle, compromise, extend or renew the indebtedness of such account debtors. Unless account debtors are otherwise notified, Debtor, as agent of PCA, shall make collections on the accounts.

5.2 Deposit with PCA. When required by PCA, all proceeds of Collateral received by Debtor shall be held by Debtor upon an express trust for PCA, shall not be commingled with any other funds or property of Debtor and shall be turned over to PCA in precisely the form received (but endorsed by Debtor, if necessary for collection) not later than the third business day following the date of receipt. All proceeds of Collateral received by PCA directly or from Debtor shall be applied against the Obligations in such order and at such time as PCA shall determine.

6. ADDITIONAL PROVISIONS.

6.1 Maintenance of Collateral. Debtor shall: care for the Collateral and not permit its value to be impaired; keep it free from all liens, encumbrances and security interests (other than those created or expressly permitted by this Agreement); defend it against all claims and legal proceedings by persons other than PCA; pay and discharge when due all taxes, license fees, levies and other charges upon it; not permit it to become a fixture or an accession to other goods except as specifically authorized by PCA; and not permit it to be used in violation of any applicable law, regulation or policy of insurance. Loss of or damage to the Collateral shall not release Debtor from any of the Obligations.

6.2 Insurance. Debtor shall keep the Collateral and PCA's interest in it insured under policies with such provisions, for such coverages, in such amounts and by such insurers as shall be satisfactory to PCA fom time to time, and shall furnish evidence of such insurance satisfactory to PCA and at the request of PCA shall have PCA specifically named in an appropriate loss payable clause endorsed on such insurance policy. Debtor assigns (and directs any insurer to pay) to PCA the proceeds of all such insurance and any premium refund and authorizes PCA to endorse in the name of Debtor any instrument for such proceeds or refunds and, at the option of PCA, to apply such proceeds and refunds to any unpaid balance of the Obligations, whether or not due, and/or to restoration of the Collateral, returning any excess to Debtor. PCA is authorized, in the name of Debtor or otherwise, to make, adjust and settle claims under any credit insurance financed by PCA or any insurance on the Collateral, or cancel the same after the occurrence of an event of default.

6.3 Inspection of Collateral. PCA is authorized to examine the Collateral wherever located at any reasonable time or times; and Debtor shall assist PCA in making any such inspection.

6.4 Maintenance of Security Interest. To the extent permitted by law, Debtor shall pay all expenses and, upon request, take any action reasonably deemed advisable by PCA to preserve the Collateral or to establish, determine priority of, perfect, continue perfected, terminate or enforce PCA's interest in it or rights under this Agreement.

6.5 Authority of PCA to Perform for Debtor. If Debtor fails to perform any of Debtor's duties set forth in this Agreement or in any evidence of or document relating to the Obligations, PCA is authorized, in Debtor's name or otherwise, to take any such action including without limitation signing Debtor's name or paying any amount so required (including the payment of any insurance premium, tax, lien, or other charge or cost for the protection or preservation of the Collateral) and the cost shall be one of the Obligations secured by this Agreement and shall be payable by Debtor upon demand with interest at the current loan rate of PCA from the date of payment by PCA.

6.6 Default. The occurrence of any of the following events shall constitute a default by Debtor:

A. Nonperformance. If Debtor fails to pay when due the principal or interest due on any of the Obligations, or if Debtor fails to perform, or rectify the breach of any warranty or other undertaking by Debtor in this Agreement or in any evidence of or other document relating to the Obligations;

B. Unauthorized Disposition of Collateral. If Debtor disposes of Collateral and such disposition is not expressly permitted by PCA under this Agreement;

C. Inability to Perform. If Debtor or a surety for any of the Obligations dies or ceases to exist; or if the Debtor shall admit in writing the inability to pay its debts, or shall have made a general assignment for the benefit of creditors, or shall have been adjudicated bankrupt, or shall have filed a voluntary petition in bankruptcy or for reorganization or to effect a plan or other arrangement with creditors, or shall have filed an answer to creditor's petition or other petition filed against it (admitting the material allegations thereof) for an adjudication of bankruptcy or for reorganization; or if a petition in bankruptcy or for reorganization or to effect a plan or other arrangement with creditors shall be instituted against the Debtor and the petition shall remain undismissed for a period of sixty (60) days; or if Debtor shall have applied for or consented to the appointment of a receiver, or trustee, or custodian for any of its property or assets, or such a receiver or trustee or custodian or similar officer shall be appointed without the application or consent of Debtor and such appointment shall continue undischarged for a period of sixty (60) days;

D. Misrepresentation. If any warranty or representation made to induce PCA to extend credit to Debtor, under this Agreement or otherwise, is false in any material respect when made;
or

E. Insecurity. If any other event occurs which causes PCA, in good faith, to deem itself insecure.

6.7 PCA's Rights and Remedies Upon Default. If default occurs, then all of the Obligations of Debtor shall, at the option of PCA and without any notice or demand, become immediately payable and PCA shall have all rights and remedies for default provided by the Uniform Commercial Code, as well as any other applicable law and as provided in any evidence of or other document relating to the Obligations. With respect to such rights and remedies on default the following shall apply when permitted by applicable law:

A. Repossession. PCA may take possession of the Collateral without notice or hearing, which Debtor waives;

B. Assembling Collateral. PCA may require Debtor to assemble the Collateral and to make it available to PCA at any convenient place designated by PCA;

C. Notice of Disposition. Written notice, when required by law, sent to any address of Debtor shown on the first page of this Agreement or to any new address given by Debtor to PCA as required herein, at least 10 calendar days (counting the day of sending) before the date of a proposed disposition of the Collateral is reasonable notice;

D. Expenses and Application of Proceeds. Debtor shall reimburse PCA for any expense incurred by PCA in protecting or enforcing its rights under this Agreement, including, to the extent not prohibited by law, reasonable attorneys' fees and legal expenses and all expenses of taking possession, holding, preparing for disposition, and disposing of the Collateral. After deduction of such expenses, PCA may apply the proceeds of disposition to the Obligations in such order and amounts as it elects; and

E. Application. PCA may apply the proceeds of Debtor's PCA stock and participation certificates to the Obligations in such order and at such times as PCA shall determine.

PCA may waive any default without waiving any other subsequent or prior default by Debtor.

6.8 Non-Liability of PCA. PCA has no duty to protect, insure or realize upon the Collateral. Debtor releases PCA from any liability for any act or omission relating to the Obligations, the Collateral or this Agreement, except PCA's willful misconduct.

6.9 PCA Stock. Debtor shall acquire and maintain PCA stock or participation certificates in the amount required by the Farm Credit Act of 1971 and the PCA By-Laws from time to time.

6.10 Wisconsin Performance Deposit. If Debtor has a right to redeem any Collateral under Section 425.208, Wisconsin Statutes, and Debtor exercises that right, the performance deposit tendered by Debtor shall not bear interest while held by PCA.

6.11 Persons Bound. The Obligations hereunder of all Debtors under this Agreement are joint and several. This Agreement benefits PCA, its successors and assigns, and binds the Debtor(s) and their respective heirs, personal representatives, successors and assigns.

6.12 Agency. Unless and until PCA is prospectively notified in writing by Debtor to the contrary, PCA may rely upon the following:

A. In the event Debtors are two or more individuals, the act or signature of any one of them shall bind all hereunder.

B. In the event Debtor is a partnership, each partner is fully authorized to act for the partnership in all matters governed by this Agreement.

C. In the event Debtor is a corporation, each officer is fully authorized individually to act for and bind the corporation in all matters governed by this Agreement.

6.13 Interpretation. The validity, construction and enforcement of this Agreement are governed by the laws of the state in which Debtor has its principal business. All terms not otherwise defined have the meanings assigned to them by the Uniform Commercial Code.

Promissory Notes

§22.1 HISTORY

The promissory note, one of the three common negotiable instruments—the draft and the check being the others—achieved a measure of prominence in domestic commerce during the nineteenth century. Prior to the advent of open account sales, many merchant sellers accommodated their buyers' need for credit with a time draft in the documentary draft transaction that is the subject of Chapter 4. The buyer's acceptance of the draft gave the seller a negotiable instrument, which the seller could negotiate to a bank or other lender as security for a loan, often at a discounted price. The negotiability feature of the draft made it attractive to the lender since the instrument was abstract from the underlying transaction, that is, it was free of that transaction's equities. If the goods that the seller sold the buyer were not merchantable, short, or otherwise noncomplying, the buyer, as acceptor of the draft, could not raise those objections against the holder when the draft came due.

The documentary draft transaction entailed more detail and cost than the merchants were willing to bear. First, the transaction required the seller to obtain a document of title; and there were times when it was otherwise unnecessary for the parties to use a document. Second, merchants designed the draft for presentation through the banking system twice: first for acceptance and second for payment.

If the seller and the buyer did not use a document of title, as they apparently did not on many occasions, and if they wanted to avoid the need to present the negotiable instrument for acceptance and, in fact, wanted the buyer's signature on a negotiable instrument before they shipped the goods, the promissory note was the preferred instrument.

Eastern seaboard sellers would take a promissory note from their customers in the midwest and ship goods via the sellers' factors from time to time until the amount of the note was exhausted. The note, being negotiable, was designed for discount, having the same attractive abstraction feature that characterized the draft.

Although not all of the reasons for the growth of the note are clear, we know that it gained a measure of prominence in the nineteenth century, for it appeared in the banking system with considerable frequency and reflected large volumes of commerce.

The twentieth century witnessed the note's comparative demise, as it also witnessed the demise of the documentary draft in domestic commerce. As reliable credit reporting made open account selling an attractive alternative to both the promissory note transaction and the documentary draft transaction, the two negotiable instruments largely disappeared from domestic commercial sales, though they have both survived in other transactions and in some international sales.

§22.2 THE CONSUMER DEBACLE

In the twentieth century, a dramatic change in consumer buying practices brought the note back into commerce in a role for which, it is now clear, the note was ill suited. That change was the advent of consumer credit.

In more than one way, Henry Ford's manufacturing, employment, and marketing practices have changed the face and commerce of America. For our purposes, an important change arose when he made automobiles available to the mass market. That event, especially when it combined with the prosperity that followed the First World War, made it necessary for consumers to obtain credit. Similarly, after the Second World War, the increase in automobile sales and the rise of consumer durable sales (washing machines, refrigerators, and the like) increased that need exponentially.

Understandably, the merchants that sold automobiles and consumer durables resorted to the negotiable promissory note. They were familiar with the note, and they understood the advantage of presenting an abstracted obligation to the financial intermediaries that were ultimately the financers of these consumer purchases.

The merchant buyer who signed the note understood its implications, especially its negotiability feature that rendered the merchant buyer's defenses unavailable against the holder. The consumer buyer, however, was unaware of those implications; and when the consumer's refrigerator failed to keep the ice cream frozen, he could not understand why the law forced him to pay for the refrigerator. Thus, a rule of law surprised a party; it worked a result contrary to that party's reasonable expectations. Law that effects that kind of surprise is a prime candidate for change.

The consumer credit transaction suffered from another disability. It lent itself too readily to fraud or other sharp practices. Unscrupulous, often fly-by-night dealers employed the note in a way that shocked the legal and commercial communities. Such dealers would sell shabby services or merchandise to unsuspecting consumer buyers on credit, take a promissory note from the consumers, discount the notes at a local lending institution, and then move on to the next county. When the consumer learned that the services or goods were not as warranted, the dealer was gone; and the finance company was asserting its holder-in-due-course right to cut off the consumer's fraud or breach-of-warranty defense.

Consumers were and remain less sophisticated buyers than their merchant counterparts. Unscrupulous sellers to merchant buyers were never able to use the note with the success that attended its use in the consumer setting.

Courts, legislatures, and regulators ultimately responded to the situation but not until considerable time had elapsed and until the practices gave impetus to a consumer movement that is still with us. The result was twofold. First, the law extirpated the negotiable note from the consumer transaction. Second, there arose a measure of odium in the minds of many toward the note, the effect of which has been a lingering suspicion that it is not an honest, efficient, commercial device, but a trap laid by unscrupulous sellers and lenders for unwary buyers or borrowers.

§22.3 THE DEMAND NOTE AND LENDER LIABILITY

One of the current uses of the promissory note is in connection with commercial borrowing. When a firm borrows, the lender frequently requires the borrower to execute a demand note, that is, a note payable on demand. If the borrower fails to meet an interest payment or if the lender deems itself insecure, the lender "calls" the note by demanding payment. Traditionally, however, the instrument does not detail the instances that permit the lender to call the note, and one can easily conjure up scenarios in which the lender calls the note for reasons that third parties, especially third parties unfamiliar with commercial lending, consider less than dainty. A lender that calls a note when market interest charges exceed those of the note may strike some judges and jurors as a greedy sort. The same lender might strike bank regulators, insurers of deposits, and stockholders as a conscientious banker. By not delimiting the power of the lender to call the demand note, the drafters of it apparently intended the lender to be able to call the loan for reasons satisfactory to the lender. Presumably, commercial borrowers are aware not only that their notes are subject to call but that they are subject to call for the lender's selfishly inspired reasons.

There arose in the 1980s something of a tradition of second-guessing lenders when they made these decisions. Prompted by cases involving decisions that struck even other commercial bankers as ungracious, a new area of liability began to evolve, that of lender liability for calling loans under circumstances that did not strike courts as fair.

It was not difficult to predict that judges and juries faced with the choice of allocating losses between the deep-pocketed bank and the struggling enterprise would more often than might be appropriate rule that the bank should shoulder the loss for consequential damages sustained by the borrower when the bank called the loan.

Lawyers who specialized in deep-pocket searches may have enjoyed too much success, for the awards in these cases were sometimes staggering. Generally, the law inhibits the award of consequential damages against financial institutions. If a bank is indeed liable for consequential damages when it calls a debtor's loan, those damages are usually quite large, for the calling of the loan often coincides with the borrower's insolvency. In this instance, moreover, the large jury awards coincided with the widespread strain that the third world debt crisis, the recession of the late 1980s, and disintermediation combined to impose on the banking system. The resulting wave of bank failures may have prompted courts to take a second look.

At this writing, lender liability seems to be losing its allure. Recent decisions indicate that courts are reluctant to impose a good faith standard or a reasonableness standard on banks when they call their demand loans. That reluctance may not reflect the courts' view that banks should be able to behave in bad faith or without reasonable care but may reflect fear that forcing banks to defend their conduct in court may impose too great a cost on the system and may result in too many unjustified awards against lenders.

It may be significant, however, that this episode with the demand note, which, by the way, often is not in negotiable form, is a second instance in which commercial parties appeared, at least at first blush, to be using the note as an instrument to take advantage of an unsuspecting party, the negotiable note in the consumer setting being the first.

§22.4 CURRENT CHALLENGES TO THE NOTE

Although the promissory note has survived the consumer debacle and the lender liability threat and still plays a central role in a number of commercial transactions, as the following section illustrates, there remains one challenge to the note, at least as a negotiable instrument. That challenge is a frontal assault on the concept of negotiability itself. In the view of some academics, commerce no longer needs negotiability, which is essentially a sneaky device merchants and bankers have borrowed from the bad old days to keep pure and simple folk poor.

It is true that in many areas the negotiable feature of instruments, documents, and securities is less necessary today than formerly or is not necessary at all. The book-entry system that the securities industry has adopted for trading in government and corporate paper has made the negotiable security of marginal importance. Sometimes goods reach buyers before the documents make their way through the banking system. Often sellers rely on credit reports and ship on open account domestically and, now, in some international sales. In these cases, negotiable documents of title are not only unnecessary, they are costly.

Yet, sophisticated commercial parties, sophisticated buyers, sophisticated sellers, sophisticated lenders, and sophisticated borrowers still use negotiable instruments and documents. That fact by itself should be sufficient to convince my colleagues in academe that the law should protect the negotiability feature. As the following section illustrates, moreover, the negotiability feature affords efficiencies that those sophisticated parties need in their commercial transactions.

§22.5 CURRENT USES

There are two transactions that occur frequently in commerce that involve the promissory note and a third that appears infrequently but may be growing:

- *Borrowing.* Most financial institutions take promissory notes, often negotiable in form, from their customer. While those notes may be negotiated to third parties, often they are not; the note simply rests in the lender's vault. Many lenders, however, pool their loans and sell them through the securities markets. This practice of asset securitization, discussed briefly in Section 11.6, involves the transfer of the loan, including the note representing it, to a special purpose vehicle, usually a trustee. The trustee issues securities and sells them in the capital markets after a rating agency issues a rating for them. Presumably, the agencies will rate the loans higher if they are represented by negotiable promissory notes rather than non-negotiable ones, that is, if the special purpose vehicle holds the notes free of defenses rather than subject to defenses arising in the transaction between the borrower and the original lender.

- *Limited Partnership Syndications.*   Sometimes borrowers, because their ventures are risky, cannot borrow from financial institutions and must generate venture capital from small investors willing to engage in high stakes enterprises. Commonly, these borrowers raise capital by syndicating interests in a limited partnership. The syndicators enhance the attractiveness of the transaction by requiring the investors to contribute only a portion of the limited partnership price in cash and the balance with a negotiable promissory note.

  If an enterprise plans to buy a $300 million aircraft for lease to a charter company, the enterprise will sell limited partnership interests at, say, $200,000 per interest but will require the investor to pay only $40,000 in cash and the balance in the form of a promissory note. The syndicator uses the note, often secured by a standby letter of credit issued by the investor's bank, as collateral for a loan from a financial institution or a consortium of such institutions. These institutional lenders regard the loan as attractive for a number of reasons. One of them is that the loan is secured by promissory notes that are free of any defenses (fraud or securities law violations) in the underlying transaction.

- *Forfaiting.*   As Section 19.7 explains, some exporters take negotiable promissory notes from their foreign buyers to whom they sell goods or services on open account. The sellers then negotiate the notes without recourse to a bank that collects the notes when they come due. The practice is common in some foreign banking markets, notably London, and may be gaining a foothold in the United States. Forfaiting is attractive to the lending banks in part by virtue of the fact that the notes are negotiable and that the banks, therefore, take the notes free of the equities in the underlying sales transaction.

PART III

PAYMENTS SYSTEMS

23

Introduction to Payments Systems

§23.1 MOVING MONEY

Payment is the transfer of money, often in execution of a contract for the sale of goods, investment securities, or services. In order to study the payments system it is necessary to have some understanding of what the commercial sector regards as money.

In general, money is any medium that people are willing to accept for the goods, securities, or services that they sell. Sellers accept this medium because they know that they can use it when they are buyers who want to **purchase** goods, securities, and services from other sellers, that is, they know that other sellers will accept the medium. Coins and federal reserve notes, the greenbacks we carry with us, are obviously such a medium. Less obvious is the fact that **bank** deposits are also money. They are money for the same reason that a dime is money: Sellers accept bank deposits as payment.

In-primitive commercial societies buyers and sellers barter, that is, they pay for goods and services with commodities. In colonial times, states printed paper money payable in agricultural commodities, so that you could pay for your haircut with a sheaf of tobacco. Today, imaginative merchants and bankers have devised a new exchange that permits traders in securities and currencies to pay each other in shares of a mutual fund that invests in government securities. Because Fedwire, the Federal Reserve's wire payments system, does not operate 24 hours each day, these traders devised a mutual fund in which they all own shares. They then pay each other for transactions during the period that Fedwire is closed by having the Global Settlement Fund, as they call the clearing agent, debit and credit corresponding accounts. The innovation is so simple it makes one wonder that no one thought of it earlier. Barterers, of course, did.

Bank deposits are, in the legal metaphor, debts of **depository institutions** and credits of the depositor. When a bank's customer takes cash or a **check** to the bank for deposit, the bank accepts the deposit and becomes the customer's debtor. The customer has loaned the bank the amount of the deposit, usually at interest. The account balance, then, is the amount due from the bank to the customer. When a buyer pays a seller with a check drawn on the buyer's account, the buyer is transferring to the seller a portion of his bank's debt due him.

Checks are only one way of transferring money. That method and other various methods that buyers and sellers use to transfer the money described above comprise the payments system, the subject of Part III of this book.

§23.2 THE NEED FOR PAYMENTS SYSTEMS

In early commercial times, there was little need for a payments system. In the barter transaction, payment occurred through the exchange of goods. As soon, however, as merchants began using cash, a payments system became necessary. Cash attracts brigands and thieves and can become lost or destroyed. A medieval Italian merchant who purchased tapestries in Belgium was no more inclined than his modern counterpart to carry specie from his bank in Florence to a fair in Bruge.

Medieval bankers responded to the situation by developing a rather sophisticated system that made that dangerous and potentially expensive exercise unnecessary: They developed a payments system. Payments systems are as old as money.

Even in today's "cash" sale, such a system is necessary, since many cash sales are by check, and checks require a system for collecting the check proceeds. **Credit sales**, of course, may be satisfied by the payment of cash, but increasingly, cash plays a diminished role in all commercial activity, both "cash" and credit. Today the lines at the utility company payments window and the insurance and rent collector have largely disappeared. They are images from a bygone era.

Today, tenants, insureds, buyers on open account, and other debtors generally pay their creditors not with goods or cash but with deposit credit. The transfer of that credit from the one to the other occurs through the banking system. Although the debtor's credit may be with someone other than a commercial bank — mutual fund, **thrift**, **credit union**, broker, investment banker, or insurance company — unless the

item is "on us," the transfer of the credit to the account of the creditor in satisfaction of the debtor's obligation will, in the vast majority of cases, involve the banking system. Nonbank depository institutions usually avail themselves of the banking system when they transfer funds.

§23.3 CREATING MONEY TO MOVE

The deposits that are subject to transfer in this fast-paced system of payments are **demand deposits**, that is, they are funds available to the depositor on demand. The depositor need not wait a period of time after demand, as it sometimes must when it desires to withdraw funds on time-deposit. Demand deposits are those that function as cash. They are the equivalent of money. These are the deposits economists include in their computation of the nation's money supply, and they satisfy the definition of money this chapter uses to describe the payments system. They are money; sellers accept them as payment.

Banks, since they create deposits (with a bookkeeping or computer entry), create money. They do so subject to constraints imposed by the **Federal Reserve Board**, the nation's central bank, and by market forces. When a farmer asks his local commercial bank for a loan, the bank will grant that loan request only if it decides, after proper credit evaluation, that the farmer can repay the loan. If the farmer is creditworthy, the bank assumes a liability by "creating" a deposit in favor of the farmer. That liability arises by virtue of the bank's undertaking to honor the farmer's checks or withdrawal requests up to the amount of the deposit. At the same time, the bank adds the farmer's note to the asset side of its ledger, the note being his liability to satisfy the loan obligation. Most of the time, the farmer's duty to repay the loan is secured by collateral, e.g., crops, equipment, or livestock. In all events, the effect of the transaction is to increase the money supply, for the farmer will quickly begin to "use" his deposit by writing checks against it or otherwise transferring portions of it to pay taxing authorities, suppliers, feed companies, and other creditors.

The farmer example illustrates the quainter features of the economy's payment activity. In addition to the 50 billion small collections and payments the system handles each year, there are large-dollar payments generated by the securities and banking industries, by the government, and by large corporate **payors**. The 50 billion checks **cleared** in the United States annually constitute a small fraction of the dollar transfers that are now effected by wire. **Wire transfers** in the United States exceed $1 trillion per day, the average transfer being in excess of $2 million. Many of these transfers have nothing to do with domestic sales of goods, securities, or services but are the concluding step in acquisitions, international lending, or commercial activity that originates in foreign jurisdictions.

When a German bank purchases eurobonds from a French securities dealer, the parties may effect payment by transferring dollars between accounts at New York **correspondent** banks. **CHIPS**, a wire transfer system fashioned by money-center banks in New York, is designed to facilitate such transfers.

This Part deals with the various payments systems. It begins with the simplest transaction involving a check drawn by a customer on her account at one bank to pay a creditor who maintains an account at the same bank and ends with the international payments that might arise in the securities example between two European parties. In all cases, the problems are similar and the goals are the same — to provide quick, cheap, safe, reliable transfers of funds. The process is at times complicated, is always challenging to the operations people involved, and is moderately fascinating to the nonbanker who watches machines and the human imagination make commercial life easier and safer in a fast-paced payments world.

24

Check Collections

§24.1 IN GENERAL

Although the growth in the use of checks is slowing from about 6 percent per year in the early 1990s to about 2 percent per year now, the check-collection system in the United States currently handles roughly 60 billion checks per year. Some of those checks clear through a single bank, some through local **clearinghouses**, and some through the national check-collection system maintained by the **Federal Reserve Banks**. In addition, there are private systems for clearing. This chapter discusses the single-bank collection of the "on-us" item, direct presentment, the local clearinghouse, and the federal reserve check-collection system.

Check clearing was originally a manual process, whereby a bank's clerks manually sorted checks drawn "on us" from those that were drawn on clearinghouse members and those that were **transit items**, i.e., checks that had to be mailed or otherwise forwarded to banks in distant communities. Today, **magnetic ink character recognition (MICR)** symbols permit reader-sorter machines to do that sorting and to read the amount of the check and the number of the account on which the check is drawn. Financial institutions preprint checks containing routing information, checking account number, and check number. Thus, when a bank customer receives his checks from the check printer, they are ready for the collection system except for the amount of the check, which amount the customer must enter when he writes the check. When a payee deposits a check, the depositary bank's data-entry clerks read the amount entered by the customer and encode it in MICR (pronounced "micker") symbols on the item before they send it through the reader-sorter machines.

Document 24-2 is a typical check with a preprinted MICR line at the bottom. The first nine MICR symbols are routing and transit digits. The first two of those designate the **Federal Reserve District** in which the **drawee**-payor bank is located. The third digit indicates the proper place within the designated Federal Reserve District. A "1" for the third digit indicates the main office of the Federal Reserve Bank in that district. Any numeral other than a "1" indicates the federal reserve branch that serves the drawee bank. The fourth digit indicates the city (if a main office or branch is indicated) or **regional check processing center** to which the check should be routed. Digits five through eight are unique to the drawee-payor bank. The ninth is an algorithm that the system uses to check the digit regime and guard against counterfeit MICR symbols designed to misroute checks and delay notice of dishonor. Checks constitute roughly 25 percent of the volume of payments through the bank collection system, and 20 percent of the value.

Encoding the amount of the check is one of the more labor-intensive and costly features of check collections. Banks are now beginning to automate this process using equipment that captures the image of the deposited check and "reads" the handwritten amount. If the equipment cannot read the amount, the machinery sorts the check for manual encoding. At present, equipment is able to read less than half of deposited checks, but that rate is successful enough for banks to invest in the equipment. This innovation first found acceptance by money-center banks with large volumes of checks to encode. Now, even small community banks find the programs efficient.

Note that Document 24-2 contains a fractional designation in the upper right-hand corner. The number in the numerator identifies the branch and bank of the customer. In the denominator, the figures indicate the proper federal reserve destination, i.e., whether main office or a branch of a Federal Reserve Bank or a federal reserve regional check processing center. The fractional figures are not machine readable. They are a safety net to permit manual handling of those checks whose MICR lines are accidentally mutilated or otherwise rendered unreadable.

Figure 24-1. The On-Us Item

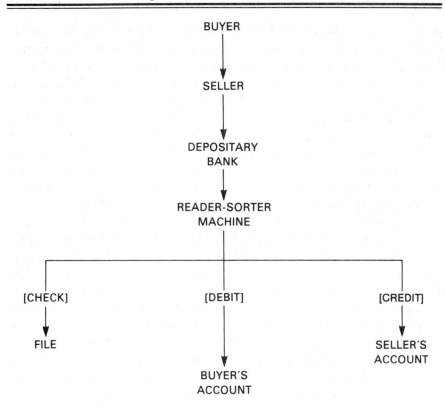

§24.2 THE ON-US TRANSACTION

In the simplest payments system, a debtor seeks to transfer funds held at a depositary institution to a creditor who maintains an account at the same institution. If Smith owes Greengrocer $44, and if Smith and Greengrocer maintain accounts at First National Bank, Smith's payment to Greengrocer is uncomplicated.

First, Smith writes a check in favor of and delivers it to Greengrocer. Second, Greengrocer deposits the check at First National Bank. Immediately, the teller gives a provisional credit to Greengrocer's account, that credit will become fixed unless the check bounces. Next, First National's clerk encodes the check with MICR symbols in the amount specified by Smith, in this case $44, and runs the check through First National's reader sorter machines.

The machines, having the capability of "reading" the MICR symbols, determine that the account to be charged is that of Smith and that the amount to be charged is $44. The machines then feed that information to First National's computer, which determines whether there are sufficient funds on deposit in Smith's account, and, if so, debits the account. Then the machines route the check to a holding file, where it resides until it is time to forward it to Smith with her periodic statement. Figure 24-1 illustrates the transaction.

§24.3 THE CLEARINGHOUSE

Only about 20 percent of checks written in the United States are on-us items. Most of the time, Greengrocer, the seller-creditor, will not maintain an account at the bank where Smith, his buyer-debtor, maintains an account. In that event, Smith's payment of Greengrocer becomes more complicated.

In a city with two banks, Smith's bank, First National, and Greengrocer's bank, Second National, might maintain a correspondent relationship, that is, each bank might hold a deposit account of the other. such corresponding balances would permit them to effect payment of Smith's check in a three-step payment process. When Greengrocer deposits his check at Second National, where he maintains his account, (1) Second will give him a provisional credit, that is, enter a credit of $44 to Greengrocer's account; (2) Second will then debit First's correspondent account in the same amount and will forward the check to First; (3) First will determine that the check is properly payable and will debit Smith's account.

Each day, there will be many checks deposited at First that are drawn on accounts at Second and many checks deposited at Second that are drawn on First. If at the end of the day the corresponding balances are in a state of **net** imbalance one bank will be overdrawn and will have to forward funds to the other or accept a loan from the other. Although there are not many communities with only two banks, there are collections that proceed in this fashion. In international transactions, for example, a foreign bank, say, an English bank, may maintain a dollar-denominated account with a domestic bank. The domestic bank may maintain a pound sterling account with the English bank. Each of these banks, as a depositor, may nominate the other to honor **drafts** to satisfy the depositor's debts. If a customer of the English bank owes dollars to an American concern, for example, he may pay that concern by asking the English bank to draw on its U.S. bank account or to authorize the American concern to draw on that account. In the same way, the U.S. bank may pay pound sterling obligations of its customer through the English bank. Periodically, the banks must settle between themselves.

Similarly, the 12 Federal Reserve Banks, which play a critical role in the **Federal Reserve System's** check-collection service, must settle among themselves. At the end of any given day, one Federal Reserve Bank may be "overdrawn" with respect to another. The Federal Reserve Banks use the interdistrict settlement fund to settle at the end of each

Figure 24-2.   Local Presentation

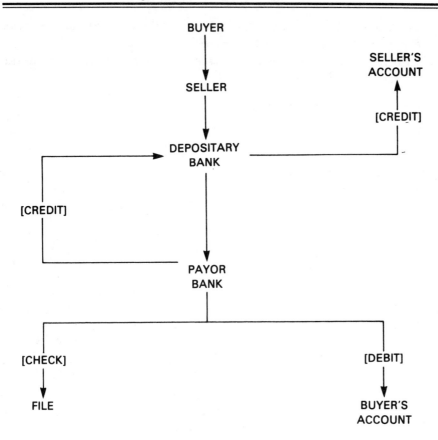

day. Section 24.4 discusses the federal reserve check-clearing system. Figure 24-2 illustrates the typical two-bank transaction.

In fact, most people do not live in a community with only two banks, and most local checks, that is, checks drawn on and deposited in banks located in the same community, are paid through an arrangement that dates from the early days of banking called the *clearinghouse*. A clearinghouse is an association of banks that maintain premises for the purpose of getting together to exchange checks or other items drawn on each other. In the classic clearinghouse arrangement, each participant prepares a batch of checks drawn on each other participant and presents the batch with a **cash letter** at the designated meeting time at the clearinghouse premises. Second National will include the Smith check deposited by Greengrocer in the batch Second prepares for the clearinghouse. The cash letter is a summary of the items presented, and the payor banks are concerned, at this point, primarily with totals. When the banks submit those cash letters, the clearinghouse can net out all letters from all banks as against all banks, simply by **netting** each bank's position against the clearinghouse. The process yields a net position for each bank. If the net amount of draws on a bank exceeds the net amount of credits in favor of the bank, the bank owes the clearinghouse. If the net draws are less than the net credits, the clearinghouse owes the bank. The bank and the clearinghouse settle through the bank's clearing account, which the clearinghouse will credit or debit, as the case may be.

Members of the clearinghouse could maintain corresponding balances with one another. Under such an arrangement, each pair of banks would settle by making corresponding debits and credits to these mutual accounts. In a community with 20 banks, however, that arrangement would be complicated and expensive, since banks prefer to invest their money in relatively high-interest-earning loans or other investments rather than in corresponding balances that earn little or no interest. It is more efficient for the clearinghouse members to use the balances they are required to maintain by law at the local Federal Reserve Bank or federal reserve branch to effect settlements. In fact, the clearinghouse will probably be located on the premises of the Reserve Bank. At the end of the day, the Federal Reserve Bank will debit a net debtor bank's account and credit the accounts of its corresponding creditor banks. If, for example, at the end of the day, the cash letter amount that Second presented to First exceeds the cash letter amount First presented to Second, the Federal Reserve Bank will debit First's account and credit Second's in an amount equal to the difference. Under this arrangement, each clearinghouse member need maintain only a single account, that at the Federal Reserve Bank, an account, incidentally, that is available for short-term (usually overnight) loans to the extent that its balance exceeds the bank's reserve requirements. To the extent that a bank's reserves do not suffice to cover the bank's check-clearing volume, the Federal Reserve Bank will require the bank to deposit additional funds into a clearing account. Figure 24-3 illustrates the clearinghouse transaction.

Federally mandated funds availability schedules have created an incentive for clearinghouses to hasten the clearing process. Because funds must become available in a relatively short time, fraudulent customers have resorted to drawing checks on insufficient funds at one institution, depositing the checks at a second, and withdrawing the funds before the depository bank learns that the check is dishonored. This is a form of check "kiting." One method to combat this fraud is electronic clearing. Under this innovation, the clearinghouse transmits data captured from the checks' MICR lines in advance of transmitting the paper checks themselves. Because it is quicker to transmit such data than to transport the paper checks, payor banks can discover checks drawn on insufficient funds or closed accounts earlier and can give notice of dishonor before the funds become available at the depository bank. Business corporations have entered or are about to enter this field by offering their own electronic clearing facilities, thereby competing directly with the Federal Reserve's clearinghouses and clearinghouses operated by banks. Thus both

Figure 24-3. The Clearinghouse

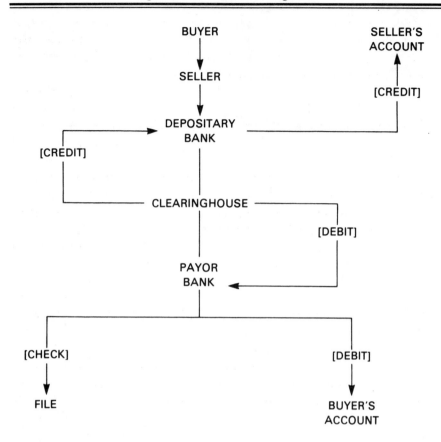

private and public clearinghouses are experimenting with electronic clearing.

§24.4 THE FEDERAL RESERVE
CHECK-CLEARING SYSTEM

Since 1914, the Federal Reserve has provided check-clearing services, first to members of the Federal Reserve and now to all depositary institutions, that is, all institutions, including credit unions and savings institutions, that maintain deposits at the Federal Reserve Banks. The system operates, in some respects, like a large clearinghouse, with the Federal Reserve Banks serving as members of the clearinghouse and their depositors playing the role of payors and payees. Access to the system must be through a "depositary institution," i.e., an institution maintaining a clearing account. Individuals cannot route checks directly to a Federal Reserve Bank or branch but must first deposit the check with a depositary institution or with a broker or other institution that maintains a correspondent relationship with a depositary institution.

Figure 24-4. Through the Federal Reserve

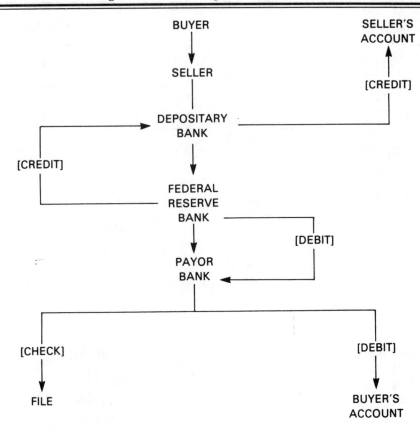

Since 1972, the Federal Reserve System has had two components. The first involves clearing through the Federal Reserve Banks and their branches. There are 12 Federal Reserve Banks and 25 branches. Usually, a depositary institution will route checks to its local Federal Reserve Bank or branch. That bank or branch follows one of two courses. In the simpler case, the check is drawn on an institution that maintains an account at the same bank or branch. The bank or branch can clear that check by crediting the account of the **presenting bank** and debiting the account of the payor bank. In a typical case, Smith will maintain an account at First National Bank and Greengrocer at Second National Bank, both banks being in the same Federal Reserve District and both being depositary institutions. Figure 24-4 illustrates the collection of the Smith check in such a transaction.

If one or both of the parties to a payment transaction maintains an account at an institution that does not maintain deposits at a Federal Reserve Bank, the transaction requires an additional step. Figure 24-5 illustrates the collection of the Smith check when Smith writes checks on a money-market account with a brokerage firm or other nondepositary institution.

228

Figure 24-5. The Fed and Depositary Institutions

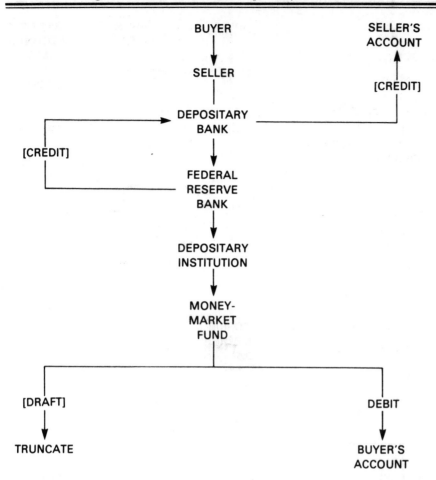

In the more complicated case, the check is drawn on a depositary institution that is in the district of a different branch or bank. In that case, the Federal Reserve Bank or branch that first receives the check must forward it to the other branch or bank. The two Federal Reserve Banks or branches then must settle between themselves. Figure 24-6 illustrates the clearing procedure when First National Bank and Second National Bank are in different districts.

Collection through the Federal Reserve Banks creates the phenomenon of **federal reserve float**. When the Federal Reserve Bank receives an item from the depositary bank, it credits that bank's account according to a federal reserve **funds availability** schedule. The Reserve Bank does not immediately charge the account of the drawee bank but delays that debit until the checks are delivered to the drawee bank. Because the funds availability schedule sometimes provides for credit to the account of the depositary bank prior to the time that the Federal Reserve Bank debits the account of the drawee-payor bank, there may be a period of time during which the accounts of both banks reflect the amount of a check. That

Figure 24-6. Interdistrict Settlement

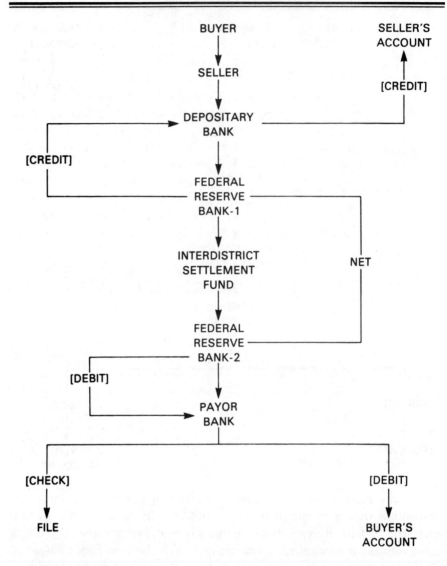

phenomenon is federal reserve float. Until the Federal Reserve Board reformed the system, federal reserve float could aggregate as much as $4 billion in a given day—a significant windfall for the nation's private banks. The reforms have reduced federal reserve float by about 75 percent.

Traditionally, banks have done all of their check processing on the bank's premises or in a remote location dedicated to check processing. Some banks use independent data processors, and at least one independent processor has encouraged banks to process their checks jointly thereby increasing volume and reducing costs.

Check fraud is an expensive problem for banks and is made worse by laser printing techniques that make the printing of counterfeit checks rather easy. Estimates of fraud losses from such checks range from $800 million to billions of dollars per year. Checks bearing a digitized image of the depositor or entailing backgrounds that disappear when the check is photocopied are two efforts the industry has fashioned in response to the problem. Some banks take information electronically from their corporate customers regarding the dates and amounts of checks that the customer has written. Counterfeit checks can be screened quickly against the data provided by the customer. Software programs that use imaging technology permit corporate customers to see their checks at any time during the month, so that internal corporate auditors can spot-check fraud in the early stages. Another scheme to combat check fraud involves transmission by the corporate customer of daily check information to the bank that can be compared against incoming checks. Some banks are also resorting to manual review of large-dollar checks to spot fraud.

§24.5 REGIONAL CHECK-PROCESSING CENTERS

The second component of the federal reserve clearing system involves regional check-processing centers. Regional offices receive from banks in any district checks drawn on banks in the region served by the center. A bank in Sacramento that wants to hasten the collection of a check drawn on a New Jersey bank can avoid the step of depositing the check in the San Francisco Fed by forwarding the check directly to a regional check-processing center. That center will give the Sacramento bank, which is a depositary institution, credit to its account at the San Francisco Fed. The processing center then collects the check's proceeds and does so more quickly than the San Francisco Fed would do.

§24.6 INTERDISTRICT SETTLEMENTS AND TRANSPORTATION

Transactions that cross Federal Reserve District lines are not so simple as the interbank transactions that occur once a day at the clearinghouse. The volume of interdistrict transactions among the banks includes many of the millions of checks that the system clears each day and the thousands of wire transfers that are effected on the average day by the more than 8,000 depositary institutions that use **Fedwire**, the Federal Reserve System's **electronic funds transfer** service. In order to deal with that volume, Federal Reserve Banks utilize an interdistrict settlement fund. That fund is essentially a computerized bookkeeping system that tracks interdistrict transactions and nets them out periodically. The Federal Reserve Banks then settle among themselves by wiring funds over Fedwire, which is explained in Chapter 26.

Interdistrict transportation of checks and drafts is not a problem with wire transfers, which consist of signals transported over telecommunications facilities linking the computers of the various Federal Reserve Banks and branches. Transfer of the more than 16 billion pieces of paper that clear through the Federal Reserve System each year involves considerable transport. The Federal Reserve System has developed an interdistrict transportation system (I.T.S.), which is a hub-and-spoke system. Presently, there are five hubs, one each in Atlanta, Chicago, Cleveland, Dallas, and New York. The system operates to consolidate transportation at the various hubs with collection and distribution along the "spokes," that is, in and out of the hubs to banks in a hub's region. "Inter-region" transport is limited to that between hubs.

§24.7 DIRECT PRESENTMENT

As the previous discussion explains, most of the time, when a depository bank receives an item drawn on a payor that is not a member of the clearinghouse, the bank will resort to the Federal Reserve System's check-collection apparatus. That decision rests in large measure on economics. The Federal Reserve's System is quick and inexpensive. There are times, however, when it makes economic sense for the depository bank to avoid the Federal Reserve's System and, in effect, to create an ad hoc system of its own. If a New York bank periodically receives large-dollar checks drawn on a Los Angeles bank, it may make sense to present the items directly to the Los Angeles bank. The New York bank will arrange to open an account or may already have an account at the Los Angeles bank. When it receives a million dollar check, the New York bank will present the item directly, usually on the day of deposit, by transmitting the item by private messenger service to the counters of the Los Angeles bank prior to the cutoff time for that day under the Los Angeles bank's funds availability schedule. The Los Angeles bank will debit the **drawer's** account and credit the New York bank's account immediately. Thus, the account of the New York bank is augmented by the million dollars on that day.

This crediting of the New York bank's account is not the end of the matter, however. At this point, the New York bank has the funds in Los Angeles, but it cannot use them easily and cannot make them available to its customer, the depositor, whose interests drive the collection efforts in this example. The New York bank, therefore, knowing the Los Angeles bank's cutoff time and knowing that its account with the Los Angeles bank will be credited that day, simultaneous with the presentment in Los Angeles of the check, will order the Los Angeles bank to transfer the funds to New York by Fedwire. That transfer will be effected without delay by the Los Angeles bank, and the net effect of the entire process will

Figure 24-7. Long-Distance Direct Presentation

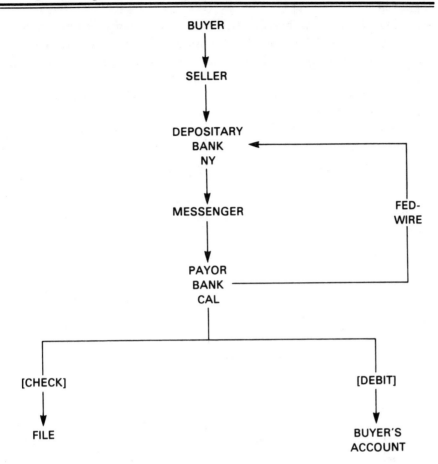

be to credit the depositor's account at the New York bank much more quickly than would have been possible if the New York bank had resorted to the Federal Reserve's system. Figure 24-7 illustrates the direct presentment arrangement.

§24.8 CASHIER'S CHECKS, CERTIFIED CHECKS, AND OTHER PAYMENT INSTRUMENTS

Checks and drafts are "pull" orders, that is, the party that introduces them into the collection system utilizes them to pull funds from the drawer's account into his own account. The nature of **pull orders** is such that a payee holding one does not know whether the order is good. The drawer may stop payment, the account may be closed, or there may be insufficient funds in the account to pay the item. By virtue of the relatively slow process by which checks clear, furthermore, even though a check does clear, the payees do not always know when it clears, that is, at what point payment has occurred. Even though federal law requires depository institutions to make funds available to a customer within specified time periods, if ultimately the check does not clear, the payee depositor must return the funds to his bank.

These problems with the check-collection system are not serious in most commercial transactions. In many cases, the payee extends credit to his customer, and the check arrives after the seller has delivered the merchandise or provided the services. In some cases, however, sellers are reluctant to part with merchandise or valuable documents without cash or its equivalent.

A seller of real estate, for example, will not deliver a warranty deed, the recording of which will permit the buyer to sell the property to a good-faith purchaser free of the original seller's interest, unless the seller receives cash at a closing. It would be folly for a homeowner to give a buyer a warranty deed in return for a check. The buyer could record the deed, sell the property to an innocent purchaser, and stop payment on the check. The original seller would not have his money, and the innocent purchaser would have the real estate. Similarly, a seller of negotiable securities is not inclined to accept a check in payment for them, because the buyer can take the securities and resell them to a good-faith purchaser who will take them free of the original seller's rights. The purchaser ends up with the securities, while the seller holds a checked stamped "NSF" or "Payment Stopped."

Sellers are well advised to guard against these eventualities. They are not interested in a claim against the dishonest buyer. He may be insolvent or may have disappeared with the money. Even if he is next door, the prospect of incurring the costs and suffering the headaches of suing him and collecting a judgment is not a happy one.

The **cashier's check** and the **certified check** provide significant protection for any seller that is parting with something of value at a closing. First, the obligor on each of these checks is a bank. Solvent bank's do not dishonor their own cashier's checks or certified checks for insufficient funds. If a financial institution becomes insolvent between the time it issues a cashier's check or the time it certifies a check, the federal agencies that insure deposits cover the check up to the insurance limit. Generally, moreover, the law does not permit stop orders against cashier's checks and certified checks.

Document 24-1 is a cashier's check. Note that it is really a two-party instrument, the payee being the first, and the bank being the second in its dual role as drawer and drawee. There is, of course, a third party in the transaction, though it is not a party to the instrument. The person who provides the funds to the bank for the check is the **remitter**, and her name usually appears at the bottom of the check or on the check stub.

Document 24-2 is a certified check. It is a typical check drawn by the bank's customer on his own account, payable to the payee. The certifying bank is the designated drawee, and by certifying the check, the drawee signals its undertaking to pay the check when it is presented. Certification is the equivalent of **acceptance**. When a bank **accepts** a draft, we call it a **banker's acceptance**; when it accepts a check, we call it certification. The certification on Document 24-3 is the stamp on the face of the check containing a date, authorized signature, and certification number.

Although there is some sentiment among politicians and consumer advocates for a law or regulation requiring banks to offer checking accounts to poor people, such a mandated government program of "lifeline" banking is not the law at the present time, and there remain some consumers that do not maintain checking accounts. For these people to transfer funds by "check" it is necessary to purchase items that can be collected through the bank-collection system.

Bank or postal money orders are instruments that a consumer may purchase and make payable to himself or his creditor. Personal and postal money orders, an example of which appears as Document 24-3, differ from bank money orders in that the customer, not the bank, signs the money order. When the postal service or a bank issues a personal money order, the drawer's signature line and the drawee's signature line are blank. A thief of a personal money order that the remitter has not signed can sign his own name to it, and subsequent parties will have a difficult time arguing that the signature is a forgery.

Most authorities seem to agree that a personal money order is analogous to a personal check and that the "owner" of it, that is, the remitter, may stop payment on it. The issue arises when the remitter loses the item before signing it. There is some risk, of course, in signing the instrument in blank, because a thief or finder can fill in his name as payee. Sometimes, however, the remitter will not know the exact name of the payee and cannot complete the instrument at the teller's window.

Traveler's checks are available to a party who may travel in a foreign country or in a part of his own country where checks drawn on his bank will not be readily acceptable. Travelers checks are drawn on the company that issues them and require two signatures of the remitter — one at the time the check issues, and the second at the time the remitter uses the check to purchase goods or services.

§24.9 LOCK BOXES

Firms that sell products or services in many states face a problem in consolidating the funds they must collect from their customers. A mail-order business in Massachusetts does not want its California customers to mail checks drawn on California banks to the house in Massachusetts. Since most California buyers would draw checks on California banks, checks received in Massachusetts would have to be collected by depositing them in the house's Massachusetts bank, which would forward them through the banking chain back to California for collection. The mail-order house prefers to have its California customers' checks collected at a bank, say, in California. That bank recovers the checks from a California postal box (the **lock box**) and collects the checks for the mail-order house by indorsing them and sending them to the payor banks. When the payor banks honor the checks, the lock-box bank forwards the proceeds to Massachusetts or notifies the Massachusetts mail-order house that the funds are available. The lock-box system accelerates the collection and thus saves the seller interest charges.

While formerly a nationwide system of lock boxes required 12 separate lock boxes, the standardization of availability schedules and mail deliveries have produced sufficient efficiencies to reduce that number to six or seven. The Internal Revenue Service maintains about 40 lock boxes nationally to collect tax payments quickly.

Wire-transfer technology permits further savings and speed in the collection of checks from widely scattered regions. Banks can use their access to **automated clearinghouses (ACHs)** (*see* Section 27.5) when they collect items they have gathered from a lock box. One company may operate a system of lock boxes that takes advantage of preprinted payment envelopes and a zip-code program offered by the postal service. Under the program, a seller will include with the invoice to its customers a preprinted envelope that bears a zip code the postal service has reserved for **truncation**. Instead of delivering the mail at the written address, the postal service's sorting machines route the envelope to a processing bank that opens it, takes the customer's check for deposit, and wires funds through the ACH to an account at the payee's bank.

Image processing is a technological innovation that may increase the use of lock boxes. Image processing permits the lock-box bank to capture information from the checks, destroy them, and transmit the information to the various payor banks and to the payee inexpensively by wire.

Lock boxes may be either retail lock boxes or wholesale lock boxes. Retail lock boxes are of the type described above in the catalogue sales illustration. Collection of insurance company premiums is another classic example of a retail lock box operation. Wholesale lock box operations involve larger and less frequent payments, such as those a manufacturer receives from its dealers or wholesalers.

§24.10 RETURNS

While most checks are paid on the first **presentation**, the drawee-payor bank dishonors some for insufficient funds, stop-payment order, uncollected funds, account closed, and the like. Under federal and state law, the drawee that honors a check is under no duty to give notice of that fact, and the silence that accompanies payment ultimately signals the fact that the depositor's funds are good. When the drawee dishonors, however, it must give notice promptly of that fact, so that the depositary bank will know that the funds are not good.

Under revised check return rules, each **collecting bank** debits the account of the bank to which it sends the check during the forward collection process, and the presenting bank debits the account of the payor bank. Those entries are final, even though the payor bank may ultimately dishonor the check. In the event of dishonor, the payor recoups the money that the presenting bank debited from its account by returning the check to the depositary bank under a system similar to the forward collection process, that is, in the return of the check, each bank debits the account of the bank to which it sends the check, so that ultimately, a returned check is debited to the account of the depositary bank, where it comes to rest. The routing may vary. The banks in the return of the check may not be the banks involved with the forward collection. Sometimes, the payor bank returns the item directly to the depositary bank. In any case, the payor recoups its debit not by reversing the forward collection entries, as in the past, but by recollecting the amount of the check through the return process, which treats the depositary bank as if it were the payor.

Thus, the process of dishonor includes the return of the dishonored item. Absent instructions to the contrary from the owner of the item, the banks are entitled to assume that the owner wants the item back in order to hold secondary parties or to make other collection efforts. Until recently, the return process was largely manual and much slower than the forward progress of the check from the depositary bank to the drawee bank. With the advent of Federal Reserve Board Regulation CC, however, which mandates the availability of deposited funds against short deadlines, the banking system made adjustments to hasten the return process. The payor bank encodes the dishonored check or places it in an encoded envelope as if it were a check drawn on the depositary bank. The Federal Reserve System's reader-sorter equipment handles such returns as it handles forward collections. Some money-center banks offer return services in competition with the Federal Reserve Banks, just as they compete with the Federal Reserve in the forward collection arena; and in some cases the private systems are outperforming the Federal Reserve Banks.

Thus, a payor bank that dishonors an item must take steps to see to its prompt return. First, the dishonoring bank will encode the item itself or an envelope containing the item for return, that is, it will have its data entry clerks encode the MICR symbols of the depositary bank. Next, the dishonoring bank must decide whether to initiate the return by sending the item to the local Federal Reserve Bank or branch or by sending it to a large bank that offers wholesale banking services, including the return of items. The final step in the process occurs when the Federal Reserve Bank or the wholesale bank runs the item through its reader-sorter equipment and effects the automated return of the dishonored item to the bank of first deposit.

While the Federal Reserve and, to a lesser extent, wholesale banks are the key players in check collections and returns, the advent of wire transfer technology has brought independent data processors into the check collection picture. When a bank engages in check collections today, it must consider the savings available through check truncation, image processing, and wire presentment, all of which are modifications of the old paper system. Chapter 26 discusses these features of wire transfers, which have been used to some extent by banks in connection with wire payments; and Chapter 30 discusses wire transfers in connection with credit card collections.

Some banks conclude that independent data processors can better provide data processing services, especially in the credit card collection area; and those banks farm out their data processing business to these independent nonbank enterprises. One such national enterprise is establishing regional centers and promises a nationwide network for check collections and will invite banks as joint venturers to submit their checks to it instead of to the Federal Reserve. Regional telephone companies have made similar overtures to the banking industry.

Undoubtedly, these new ventures will use check truncation and image processing to reduce the volume of paper and speed the collection and return of items. Imaging is still in its infancy, but it augurs well for those who feel that competition in bank collections will benefit banks and their customers.

"Outsourcing," as the practice of engaging independent data processors to handle a bank's operations is called, may have peaked already, however. Recent reports suggest that the savings are not as great as some banks had hoped. Nonetheless, independent processors are having their effect on check collections, and the private automated clearing house is now very much involved in check collections. The automated clearinghouse (ACH), which is explained in more detail in Section 27.5, traditionally handled electronic payments. Now, however, it is handling checks. In order to hasten the collection of checks, some bankers are using the ACH to collect data from the encoded paper and forward it to the payor bank. If the check is drawn on insufficient funds, the payor can dishonor it much more quickly than if it has to wait for the delivery of the paper. The Federal Reserve's ACHs are also experimenting with electronic clearing, but this development, along with others in the 1980s and early 1990s, indicates that the volume of interbank clearing done by the Federal Reserve will continue to diminish.

Electronic clearing in this fashion not only speeds up the availability of funds, it reduces the fraud losses that have arisen since Congress adopted legislation mandating the early availability of deposited funds.

Electronic innovations have also assisted banks in check truncation and processing. Imaging, the process of storing check images in computer memory, permits banks to truncate checks at the bank of first deposit and forward the check's image electronically, both to the payor bank and, after collection, back to the customer. Some banks process their checks after transforming them into computer images and are experimenting with character and signature recognition equipment in the hope of reducing the high cost of encoding checks and of verifying the customer's signature.

§24.11 CHECK-GUARANTY PROGRAMS

Virtually anyone may open a checking account for a small deposit, and the cost of a few printed checks is relatively small. Thus, it is rather easy for unscrupulous individuals to write checks on accounts that are closed or that have insufficient funds to cover the checks that are written. Many check writers issue checks, moreover, and then stop payment on them, either because they are dissatisfied with their purchase or because they never intended to pay for the product or services in the first place. These dishonest or ambivalent individuals arise commonly enough in retail trade to make many retailers reluctant to accept payment by check.

Banks, to which checking accounts serve as a source of deposits, are aware of that retailer reluctance and, anxious to make the checking account attractive to creditworthy customers, have fashioned a facility to deal with the suspicions of the retailer. That facility is the check-guaranty program.

Under a typical check-guaranty program, the bank that accepts checking-account deposits will enter into a contract with retailers under which the retailer may rely on the bank's promise that the checks are good. Banks provide verification of their guaranty by computer or telephone or by virtue of the issuance of a plastic card similar to a credit card. Some bank credit-card issuers, in fact, make checks available to card-holders for maximum preauthorized amounts.

As Section 24.8 mentioned, some politicians and consumer advocates argue that the banking system should provide low-cost or free banking services in a limited way to the poor. Banks have generally contended that the facility is not necessary. Governmental agencies resort often to wire transfers of social security and other benefits, and recipients without checking accounts or other depository accounts cannot avail themselves of the speed and safety of these wire transfer innovations; at the same time, the agencies cannot avail themselves of the savings inherent in wire transfers. In recent years there has been a proliferation of what one economist refers to as "check cashing outlets" in the United States. Studies show that the poor, those who customarily avail themselves of currency exchanges and the like, pay considerably more than users of bank services. One academic has argued that there should be revision in the banking laws to permit grocery store chains to provide check cashing services. This writer reasons that if the law imposes lifeline banking on commercial banks, they will lose money and close branches in less affluent neighborhoods, while supermarket chains are already located in poorer neighborhoods and would be able to offer the service without sustaining a loss. He notes, moreover, that many supermarket chains currently maintain ATMs on their premises and, therefore, are already a quasi-branch bank.

In fact, growth of branch banks in supermarkets is strong. In 1994 there were over 2,000 such branches, and one study predicted that by the end of the century there would be more than 5,000. Those figures are all the more remarkable in light of the fact that as of 1989 there were only 675 branches in supermarkets and that branch consolidation and branch closings has been a significant feature of the banking industry during this decade.

At least one state (New Jersey) now requires banks and other financial institutions to make low-cost checking accounts available. Under the law of that state, accounts used for personal or household purposes cannot require more than a $50 initial balance followed by a balance as low as $1. The account must allow for eight free checks and a charge no higher than $.50 for additional checks.

§24.12 THE DEPOSITOR AGREEMENT

The array of bank products offered by today's retail bank operation is extensive. Banks now regularly provide **overdraft** protection to their customers, offer them charge cards, **debit cards**, telephone banking, interest bearing accounts, and transfer of funds between accounts.

The depositor agreement, which a few short years ago was set forth on a "signature card" small enough to fit into the depositor's wallet, is now a lengthy agreement. To some extent that length is dictated by federal and state disclosure laws. In the past, the depositor agreement often incorporated terms and provisions of the institution's bylaws by reference.

Document 24-1. Cashier's Check

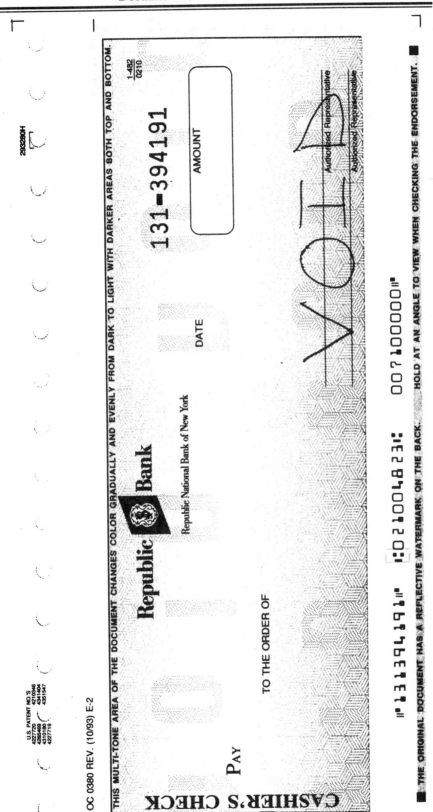

241

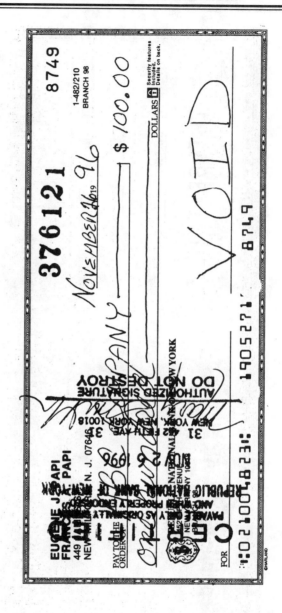

Reprinted with the permission of Republic National Bank of New York.

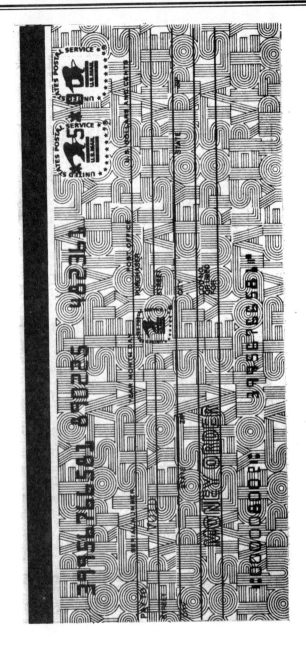

25

Collecting Drafts

§25.1 NONCASH ITEMS

The check-collection system is a highly mechanized program that collects about 50 billion **cash items** a year and does so in a curious way. A check "clears" or is "paid" usually when time passes or when the drawee-payor bank affirmatively decides to pay it. Significantly, however, when the payor decides to pay or when the time limit is reached and the check is paid as a matter of law, the parties that have taken the check do not learn about it. Silence signals payment. Notice occurs only when there is dishonor.

A depositary bank that takes a check for deposit from the payee of the item permits the depositor to use the funds according to a "funds availability schedule." Presumably, the check-collection system is efficient enough that the depositary bank will learn about nonpayment in time to prevent the uncreditworthy customer from withdrawing the uncollected funds.

Some items that pass into the banking system are not cash items and are not subject to the payments apparatus the banking industry has developed for checks. Most noncheck drafts are **noncash items.** A check is a draft drawn on a bank payable on demand. It is the classic cash item. In this chapter and in the parlance of most people familiar with the banking industry, the term *draft* refers to negotiable orders to pay but does not include the check.

Significantly, when the final bank in the chain receives a draft, its obligations are different from the obligations that bank faces when it receives a check. In the check case, the bank must dishonor a check before a deadline (usually midnight of the banking day following the day of receipt) or it becomes responsible for the amount of the check, that is, failure to dishonor by the deadline constitutes payment of the check. When the bank receives a draft, however, its obligations are determined by a number of factors, including the nature of the draft and whether it is drawn on the bank or a third party. "On arrival" drafts, "time" or "usance" drafts, and drafts drawn under letters of credit are subject to payment rules different from those for cash items. Generally, banks handling noncash items must act with due care and diligence and have a reasonable period of time within which to act and a longer period than the law allows for cash items.

§25.2 DEMAND AND TIME DRAFTS

"Demand" or "sight" drafts are payable by the drawee upon presentation. If the bank receives a **sight draft** drawn on Buyer Corp., the bank will notify Buyer of the arrival of the draft and ask Buyer to put the bank in funds. If Buyer fails to do so within the time limits provided, Buyer has dishonored, and the bank must give notice to the prior party in the collection chain. Figure 4-1 illustrates the transaction.

Time drafts differ from demand or sight drafts. The time draft is not payable upon presentation but at a period after a specified date or a period after sight or on a specified date. It is not unusual for a time draft to be payable 90 days after date, that is, after the date of the draft itself. It is also quite common for drafts to be payable a given number of days after sight (e.g., "at 90 days' sight"), that is, after presentation. Document 4-3 is an example of a time draft.

When the last collecting bank in the bank collection chain receives the time draft, it asks the drawee, the person to whom the order to pay is directed, to "accept" the draft by signing it on its face. The bank then holds the draft or returns it to the drawer or the drawer's agent until it becomes due. When the acceptance is due, the holder will present it again, probably through the banking system, to the drawee, this time for payment.

§25.3 USING THE DRAFT

The draft arises in a number of transactions. Cotton producers have used drafts drawn on their broker buyers with samples of the cotton attached. If the buyer likes the cotton, it accepts the draft. In the **documentary draft** transaction, sellers of commodities draw drafts on their buyers and attach a document of title (usually a negotiable warehouse receipt or negotiable bill of lading) to the draft. When the buyer honors the draft, it receives the document of title from the bank.

In the international sale of goods, exporters draw drafts on banks that issue letters of credit supporting the sale. Drafts are quite common in the standby letter of credit transaction. The following transactions illustrate, in the first, the use of a sight draft and, in the second, the use of a time draft.

Automobile dealers take many used vehicles "in trade" that they cannot sell themselves. By virtue of a dealer's location or the nature of its clientele, it cannot sell or prefers not to sell the used vehicles at retail. Such dealers frequently sell their trade-in vehicles to wholesalers who conduct auctions. Buyers at the auctions (used car dealers) may travel considerable distances to attend. When a buyer bids successfully for vehicles, the wholesaler will frequently extend him credit by permitting him to take the vehicles at the conclusion of the auction. The wholesaler effects collection by using a sight draft drawn on the buyer accompanied by the title certificates for the vehicles. After drawing the draft, an illustration of which appears as Document 4-2, the wholesaler attaches the certificates and "deposits" the draft with its bank for collection. The depositary bank, which may or may not give the wholesaler available credit, forwards the draft and certificates through the bank collection system to the buyer's bank. The buyer's bank then notifies the buyer that the draft and certificates have arrived. The buyer goes to his bank, examines the certificates, and honors the draft by putting the bank in funds. At that point, the bank delivers the certificates to the buyer.

In a typical time-draft transaction, an importer of garments will grant 90-day credit terms to his domestic buyer. The terms of the sales contract require the buyer to create **trade acceptances,** which the seller can use to finance his own purchase from the foreign supplier. Under the contract, the importer will cause the goods to be shipped to the buyer and will obtain evidence of that shipment, probably a non-negotiable truck bill of lading. The importer will then draw a draft on the buyer in the amount of the purchase price payable 90 days after date, being the date of the bill of lading. The importer will then "deposit" the draft at his bank, which will forward it through the collection chain to the buyer's bank. The buyer's bank will notify the buyer that the draft is available for acceptance. The buyer will then sign the draft on its face. At that point the draft becomes a trade acceptance, which the buyer's bank or some other bank may purchase from the importer.

The acceptance's attractiveness as an investment will depend in part on the financial reputation of the buyer (the **acceptor**) and also of the importer, who is the drawer and who will indorse the acceptance to any investor. Because the acceptance is a negotiable instrument free from the equities of the underlying contract between the importer and the buyer, it may be an attractive medium of investment in the money market. Investors may not be interested in acceptances indorsed by Joe Smith Importers, but they are interested in acceptances accepted by Joe's national retail chain customers (e.g., Banana Republic). By virtue of this marketability of the acceptances, Joe can get his cash early, before the 90-day term expires; the national retail chain gets 90 days of credit; and some investor (often a bank or a mutual fund) finances the transaction.

The net effect of the arrangement is to give the buyer credit while allowing the importer to be paid. In effect, banks or other financial intermediaries, by purchasing the acceptance, provide the credit. The parties' obligations as drawer, acceptor, and indorser of the acceptance serve as the collateral.

§25.4 PAYABLE-THROUGH DRAFTS

There are occasions when a payor authorizes parties to draw but wants to retain control of payment. In self-administered insurance programs, an insurance company authorizes its insured, an employer providing self-administered health benefits coverage to employees, to draw payable-through drafts on the insurance company. It would be risky for the company to let its many insureds write checks on its account without some control on the part of the company over payment.

The insurance company can achieve that control with the payable-through draft. The employer obtains copies of the employee's medical bills, satisfies itself that there is coverage, and draws a payable-through draft on the insurance company. When the draft arrives at the bank through which it is payable, the bank refers the draft to the insurance company, whose clerks re-determine that the claim is payable and, if so, authorize the bank to make payment and charge the insurance company's account.

Credit unions and money-market funds have also used payable-through drafts in lieu of checks. In the money-market fund transaction, an investor purchases shares in the fund, which may consist of short-term, highly liquid securities that yield reasonable interest income. When the investor desires to transfer a portion of her investment, she draws a payable-through draft on the money-market fund's account at a commercial bank. The bank honors the draft if the fund approves it. Document 25-1 is a payable-through draft.

There is some evidence that insurance companies are resorting to the direct-pay letter of credit in lieu of the payable-through draft. Under the direct-pay standby, the authorized party draws on a designated standby, and the standby issuer pays. The insurance company retains a measure of control over the authorized drawer by limiting the amount of draws in a given period or the maximum amount of a single draw.

The federal government uses the direct-pay standby in similar fashion. When a federal agency grants funds to a municipality, it may authorize the municipality to draw on a standby at the Treasury. The standby will limit the amount of the draws in a way similar to that used by insurance companies in the prior example.

Document 25-1. Payable-Through Draft

Reprinted with the permission of CUNA Service Group, Inc.

26

Wholesale Electronic Funds Transfer

§26.1 SCOPE

This chapter deals with "wholesale" electronic funds transfer (EFT). By the term *wholesale* in EFT law, we generally mean nonconsumer EFT transactions. This chapter does not deal with debit and credit cards, automated teller machines, and **point-of-sale terminals,** all of which have important EFT features. Those subjects generally fall under the "consumer" rubric, and Chapter 27 deals with consumer EFT. Electronic transfers initiated by banks, corporations, governmental agencies, and large enterprises are the main concern of this chapter.

This distinction between wholesale and consumer wire transfers parallels the distinction that has evolved in EFT regulation. Generally, the federal government, through the Truth-in-Lending Law and its concomitant, Regulation Z, and the Electronic Fund Transfers Act and its concomitant, Part 205 of Regulation E, deals with *consumer* EFT transactions. On the other hand, under the sponsorship of the American Law Institute and the National Conference of Commissioners on Uniform State Laws, Article 4A of the Uniform Commercial Code is confined in scope to "commercial" or "wholesale" wire transfers.

Figure 26-1. Wire Transfer

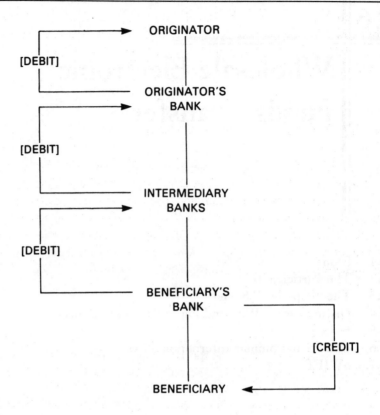

§26.2 THE PARTICIPANTS

EFT innovations introduce a new lexicon into payments law, and it is worth pausing a bit here to consider the names EFT systems and statutes have given to the parties involved in an electronic payment transaction.

Most wire transfer systems are accessible only to banks. If a nonbank initiates a wire payment or transfer, it must issue a transfer order to a bank participant in the system. This nonbank is the **originator** of the wire transfer "payment order." The bank to which the originator directs the wire transfer order becomes a **sender** when it carries out the originator's order by issuing a new order or transferring the originator's order to a second bank. The first bank, the initial contact in the payments system, is sometimes referred to as the **originator's bank.** The second bank becomes a **receiving bank** upon receipt of the order and, if it passes the order to another bank, becomes a "sender." Ultimately, the order arrives at the bank, the "beneficiary's bank," where the "payee" or **beneficiary** of the transfer order maintains an account. Receipt by that bank of the transfer order prompts the bank to credit the account of the beneficiary and notify it of the credit. Sometimes, banks initiate transfers and receive transfers for their own accounts. In those cases, there is no nonbank originator or beneficiary. Figure 26-1 illustrates the parties to a wire transfer that involves a nonbank initiator and a nonbank payee.

§26.3 THE "PAPERLESS" SOCIETY

With the advent of the computer, reader-sorter machines, image processors, and other technological advances, some have been predicting the demise of the paper-based payments system and its replacement by electronic funds transfer. The object of these changes would be a system that does not eliminate paper itself from the collection and payments systems but eliminates paper as the medium of payment and replaces it with electronic impulses and computer memory. Wire payments are now a significant part of the payments system. Cash and checks still comprise 90 percent of all payments transactions, but 90 percent of the value of payments made in a given day are by wire.

Even wire transfers generate paper. Banks that permit consumer customers to deposit and withdraw funds through terminals at home or in shopping centers must provide paper records of those "paperless" transactions. Similarly, banks that wire funds for their large corporate customers provide access to computer-stored information that is available in "hardcopy" form. In these wire transfers, however, there is no piece of paper that serves as the operative instrument. In that important sense, the wire transfer is paperless.

To some extent, we have had wire transfers for a long time. Payments initiated by telephone, **telex,** or telegraph are wire transfers, since there is no piece of paper that embodies the payment order or obligation. For many years bankers accommodated their customers' instructions by telephone. The vacationer who called his banker and asked him to transfer funds from a savings account to a checking account was effecting a transfer of funds by wire.

For many years, moreover, international payments have been effected by telex. A New York importer could ask its bank to transfer pounds sterling to a British exporter. The New York bank would telex instructions to its London correspondent directing the correspondent to debit the New York bank's pound sterling account and credit the account of the exporter. Since there was no "instrument" in the transaction, though there would have been paper records of the importer's directions to its bank and the New York bank's instructions to its London correspondent (the telex printout), the payment was a true wire transfer.

It was not until the 1960s, however, that the silicon chip and rapid and reliable means of communication made high volume and rapid pace for such transactions practicable. It was the exponential growth of such transfers and the vast variation in systems that developed to effect them that gave rise to important distinctions between this payment activity and paper-based systems. Not surprisingly, the law fashioned by the judges of King's Bench in the seventeenth and eighteenth centuries did not always fit these innovations.

§26.4 DISTINGUISHING WIRE AND PAPER PAYMENTS CONCEPTS

Under a paperless system, a debtor uses electronic messages instead of paper to effect payment. An automobile manufacturer in Detroit can "wire" funds to its suppliers and achieve quick and relatively inexpensive payment. Under such a payments scheme, the manufacturer's computer operator instructs the manufacturer's bank to credit, through an interbank wire system such as Fedwire, the accounts of its suppliers at various banks throughout the country. The arrangement is quicker than payment by check. Transfers occur instantaneously, by the end of the day, or at the beginning of the next day, depending on the interbank settlement arrangements of the wire system. The paperless system is usually considerably less expensive than a paper system, since the manufacturer avoids check preparation and mailing costs and can use stored computer information to generate and record payment for more than one purpose. It is true that the manufacturer may lose **float** by virtue of having reduced the check-collection system's delays, but the manufacturer can time its wire transfer in such a way that payment occurs no sooner than it would under the check-collection system. In short, in this setting, substitution of wire transfers for paper payment makes economic and commercial sense.

In other settings, however, that substitution does not make sense. In the paper-based system, paper, i.e., checks, drafts, notes, and other items, functions not simply as a record of payment or a record of an underlying obligation but becomes an obligation in and of itself. The King's courts long resisted this peculiar merchant innovation. In particular, the judges of King's Bench feared an avalanche of litigation if someone other than the original obligee (the seller of goods, for example) could sue on the obligation (promissory note or acceptance) that the buyer gave the seller. After considerable effort, the English courts of the seventeenth century accepted the idea that a piece of paper can embody an obligation and that that obligation can be independent of the underlying commercial transaction. American courts have accepted the notion from the start.

These ideas are central to the paper-based system, which treats the paper as an obligation of the signatories to it and which gives the holder of the paper, provided he takes in the ordinary course, rights quite apart from the equities of the transaction out of which the paper arises.

This appreciation for the differences between negotiable paper and non-negotiable wire transfers explains the survival of paper as a means of payment. In fact, the number of paper payments by check and the volume of payments by wire have enjoyed lusty growth in the last two decades, and while the use of drafts and notes has declined, there is evidence that their use continues and that, in the case of notes, is growing again. Some of paper's resilience is, no doubt, a function of its relatively low cost in comparison to wire transactions, but some of it is a function of commercial parties' desire for an obligation that is abstract from the underlying transaction.

Forfaiting, a recent export innovation, involves loans against receivables. In order to make those receivables more attractive in the financial markets, the exporters' lenders have asked the exporter to obtain a negotiable promissory note from the exporter's customer. That note is more marketable than the buyer's naked obligation to pay. The note is negotiable, the obligation to pay arising out of the underlying transaction is not. By using the note, the parties have abstracted the payment obligation from the underlying transaction and rendered the obligation valuable to investors who know nothing about the transaction and do not want to invest in the obligation if it is subject to defenses arising out of the underlying contract. This abstraction feature is also present in the trade-acceptance example discussed in Section 25.2.

The abstraction of the payment obligation, a unique and critical feature of commercial law, enhances the value of the obligation and benefits all parties. Credit becomes more readily available at lower cost. The obligor, of course, loses its contract defenses, but it can protect itself in the contract by providing for security against contract breach (e.g., an escrow arrangement, bond, or letter of credit) or can require an inspection certificate from an independent party. In the alternative, it can save transaction costs and take the risk.

Some commercial parties used the negotiable features of promissory notes unfairly against consumers. In response, there arose a concerted effort by legislators, judges, and many law teachers to limit the use of such instruments. Generally, however, those limitations have confined themselves to the consumer setting. It is nonetheless fashionable among law teachers to view the abstraction principle with disdain. Indeed, there is something of a campaign among law school faculties these days against the whole notion of negotiability. Academic literature sometimes argues against this commercial evil. In the consumer context, those arguments are well taken; in the commercial context, they are not. For further discussion of the abuse of the negotiability concept in the consumer setting, *see* Chapter 22.

A few years ago the federal government paid farmers for not planting crops under a commodity certificate arrangement. Under this system, a farmer in a rural Iowa county could agree with representatives of the Department of Agriculture not to plant acreage on which he customarily cultivated corn. The government's payment for that agreement consisted of a piece of paper, a commodity certificate, that was denominated in dollars and was redeemable at a specified date.

It makes sense, however, that some holders of certificates would want to convert them into cash early. A certificate issued in May 1989 and redeemable in January 1990 will not pay a June feed bill, a September college tuition statement, or airline expenses for that November trip to Disneyland. The federal government knew, therefore, that the certificates would be more attractive to the farmers they wanted to attract to the program if the certificates were readily transferable. Not surprisingly, the certificates that the government fashioned were negotiable, though not fully. Under the terms of the certificates and the regulations governing them, transfer was effected by restrictive indorsement, and the Commodity Credit Corporation honored them when a holder with a certificate with a proper chain of indorsements presented the certificate. Significantly, the form of certificate adopted by the government provided in blanks on the reverse side for as many as 14 transfers.

Negotiable paper has its raison d'être. Parties will resort to it when it suits their commercial purpose. Wire transfers have their raison d'être as well, and commercial parties will resort to wire transfers when they suit the transaction.

One might argue that the two ideas, (1) that a piece of paper can embody an obligation and (2) that the obligation exists independently of the transaction out of which the paper arises, are the key elements of "commercial" law that have provided certainty for that field and differentiated it from the ill-defined and litigation-ridden swamp of "contract" law.

A paperless system loses the commercial attributes. Some may see that loss as a threat to the very features of the payments system that render it uniquely fitted for commerce. Others see those features as anachronisms that the system can discard. Arguably, both of those views are erroneous. The first ignores the advantages electronic funds transfers provide to commerce, and the latter ignores the continuing need for a system that provides quick movement of abstracted obligations in the form of paper.

There are a number of systems fashioned to provide for paperless payments. The balance of this chapter discusses some of them. Readers should bear in mind that this area of commercial activity, perhaps more than any other, is subject to rapid change. Many of these systems are in their infancy. Participants are revising them frequently, creating new systems that compete with them, and discarding some of them altogether.

§26.5 FEDWIRE

Since 1970 when it was first introduced as an electronic payments system and 1982 when it achieved its present form, the Federal Reserve System has operated a wire transfer system. Under the arrangement, more than 8,000 depository institutions transfer payments by wire among the Federal Reserve Banks and their branches. In addition to the private depository institution participants, the system serves the federal government, the Federal Reserve Banks themselves, the Federal Reserve Board, and the Treasury. The system serves more than 100,000 private customers of depository institutions.

Under Fedwire, a debtor-payor (originator) instructs its bank to transmit funds. The bank, in turn, advises its Federal Reserve Bank or branch to wire the funds to the account of a payee-beneficiary. Daily Fedwire transactions are in the hundreds of thousands, and annual transfers aggregate more than $100 trillion. Fedwire transfers generally involve large-dollar amounts. The average Fedwire transaction is $2 million. The average check is about $600.

Assuming that the originator and the payee-beneficiary maintain accounts at depository institutions, that is, banks that maintain accounts with Federal Reserve Banks, the transaction is relatively simple. The originator, whose terminal is often connected directly to the office of its bank, the depository institution, signals the bank to transfer funds to the payee-beneficiary's designated account at the receiving depository institution, the beneficiary's bank.

The message in the Fedwire system actuates the payment, that is, Fedwire is not simply a message system, as **SWIFT** is, discussed in Section 26.7. Fedwire is a payments system as well. When the receiving Federal Reserve Bank receives the message, it effects payment by debiting and crediting accounts according to its instructions. If both the originator's bank and the payee-beneficiary's bank maintain deposits at the Federal Reserve Bank, the Federal Reserve Bank debits the account of the originator's bank and credits the account of the payee-beneficiary's bank. Figure 26-1 above illustrates the payment.

Only a depository institution, that is, a financial institution that maintains an account with a Federal Reserve Bank may send funds via Fedwire. If either or both the payor and payee do not maintain deposits at depository institutions, there must be an additional layer of participants. Assuming that both maintain their accounts at non-depository institutions, money-market funds, for example, the payor's fund must forward the signal to a depository institution, and the payee's fund must receive the transfer message from a depository institution. In both cases, the funds must maintain accounts at the transmitting and receiving depository institutions or must have other arrangements for reimbursement. Again, if the depositary institutions maintain accounts at the same Federal Reserve Bank, the Federal Reserve Bank debits that of the sending depositary bank and credits that of the receiving depositary bank. The depositary banks must also make corresponding debits and credits to the accounts of their customers, the funds with which the payor and the payee maintain accounts. When the depositary institutions maintain accounts at different Federal Reserve Banks there must be an additional step in the process, that whereby the Federal Reserve Banks settle between themselves.

§26.6 CHIPS AND SIMILAR INTERNATIONAL SYSTEMS

The New York Clearinghouse Association, an organization of money-center banks located in New York City, operates the Clearinghouse Interbank Payments System (CHIPS). The system facilitates international dollar-denominated payments. There are two kinds of CHIPS participants: those that have access to the CHIPS system and those that have access and are settling participants. The former may initiate transfers through the system but must settle through one of the latter.

A French investor agrees to purchase securities from a German seller for a price denominated in dollars. The investor may want to effect payment by transferring funds between accounts at the parties' U.S. banks, where they maintain their dollar accounts. If the investor maintains an account at one CHIPS settling participant, First Bank, and the German seller maintains an account at another CHIPS settling participant, Second Bank, the investor will notify First Bank, probably through SWIFT, to make the transfer. First Bank will enter the transaction into the CHIPS computer by designating the account at Second Bank to be credited and the amount of the transaction. Under the rules fashioned by CHIPS participants, the CHIPS computer stores the information until First Bank sends a second signal verifying the stored information. At that point, the transaction occurs under CHIPS rules, and the CHIPS computer will make the corresponding debit and credit entries. Second Bank will notify its customer, the German seller of the credit.

Although CHIPS rules consider the transaction to be final and **unwindable** at the time First Bank verifies its original message, settlement between First and Second Bank does not occur until the end of the day. When the CHIPS day ends, currently at 4:30 P.M. New York time, the CHIPS computer advises CHIPS settling participants of their net positions with respect to all other CHIPS settling participants. At that point, the CHIPS participants must effect settlement among themselves through the New York Federal Reserve Bank. Nonsettling participants must arrange to settle separately with their settling participant correspondents.

Figure 26-2. CHIPS Transfer

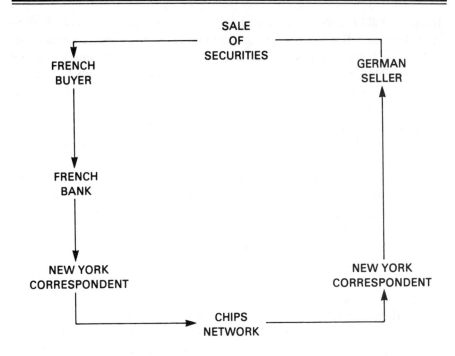

Figure 26-2 assumes that only settling participants are involved and illustrates the payment in the French investor's purchase of securities from the German seller.

Nonparticipants in CHIPS may use the system but cannot access it without going through a CHIPS participant. If the French investor in the foregoing example did not maintain its dollar account with a CHIPS participant bank, he would have to instruct the bank at which he did maintain an account to arrange for the transaction through a CHIPS participant. The CHIPS participant will be responsible for the transaction under CHIPS rules and will debit an account that the nonparticipant bank maintains at the CHIPS participant bank or otherwise arrange for reimbursement from the investor or his bank. Similarly, if the payee, the German seller, does not maintain an account with a CHIPS participant institution, payment to the seller of the securities requires an additional layer of parties, with the CHIPS receiving bank transferring the funds to the nonparticipant bank where the seller maintains its account. The CHIPS system does not concern itself with transfers outside the system, which are normally made by debiting and crediting correspondent accounts.

The CHIPS system replaces the rather slow process of using **bank drafts,** i.e., checks drawn by one bank on an account it maintains at another bank. Under that system, the French investor would "purchase" a bank draft from a French bank that maintains a U.S. dollar account at a bank, probably in New York. The investor would then send the draft to the German seller, who would deposit it in another bank, probably in New York, where the German seller or its bank maintained a dollar account. That mode of effecting international payments survives, but it is slower and costlier than using the CHIPS system. Chapter 28 discusses bank drafts and international collections in more detail.

Also surviving is the system of correspondent accounts. Under this arrangement, banks that serve international activity maintain a network of correspondent relationships whereby a domestic correspondent maintains a **nostro account** (in, for example, French francs) at its foreign correspondent and holds a U.S. dollar **vostro account** covering the correspondent's deposit with the domestic bank. Correspondent relationships provide quick and efficient payment. A French bank may telex its U.S. correspondent and instruct it to transfer dollars to the German bank's dollar account with its U.S. correspondent. The practice of maintaining correspondent balances, however, is generally more costly and slower than using the CHIPS network.

CHIPS currently clears as many as 40,000 transfers each day among 140 bank participants. Those daily transfers total about $660 million on an average day. They occur on the day they are initiated, are remarkably free from error, and do not entail the transportation risks that inhere in the mailing of bank drafts. On the first day of the week following a three-day weekend, CHIPS may handle transfers totalling more than $1 trillion.

CHIPS began operation in 1970. In 1981, its participants substantially revised its operations. In the same year, the Federal Reserve Bank of Chicago began operating the Clearinghouse Electronic Settlement System (CHESS), which utilized **BankWire** — a private competitor of the Federal Reserve System's Fedwire. When BankWire suspended operations in 1986, CHESS suspended operations also.

FXnet is a London-based limited partnership that provides foreign **exchange** settlements to participating banks. Under the FXnet wire system, two banks can net out their respective positions arising out of foreign exchange transactions. The settlement procedure avoids certain risks and reduces the number of settlements per day between the two banks to one.

English banks have developed their own wire transfer system, Clearing House Automated Payments System (CHAPS), Australian banks their system, Bank Interchange and Transfer System (BITS), and banks of other countries comparable wire-transfer systems.

In short, there are a number of existing electronic systems for transferring funds between and among banks on behalf of their customers. By all indications, the industry is still somewhat in a state of disequilibrium as it evolves into an efficient transfer network.

§26.7 SWIFT

In 1973, more than 200 banks in a number of countries established the **Society for Worldwide Interbank Financial Telecommunications (SWIFT)**, a not-for-profit cooperative established under Belgian law. Currently, SWIFT, with more than 1,500 banks now participating in its ownership, is a message, not a payments, system; that is, it facilitates interbank transfer of information but presupposes a separate system for effecting the payments that a given message may indicate. In the CHIPS transaction described in the preceding section, the French investor instructed his New York CHIPS participant by SWIFT, and the New York bank effected the payment through CHIPS.

SWIFT participants transmit messages quickly and inexpensively by using signals that computers encode and decode. An English sender of a message to a New York bank must contact a SWIFT participant, usually a bank, that maintains a SWIFT terminal on its premises. The participant enters the encoded message via telecommunications equipment dedicated to SWIFT usage. The message passes to one of a SWIFT system control centers that permit SWIFT to handle up to 1.4 million transactions daily. In an average day, there are slightly more than 1.2 million messages transferred on SWIFT. Among operations SWIFT envisions are use of SWIFT as a data base, for electronic data interchange, and for the handling of recurring payments in a fashion similar to those made through automated clearinghouses.

27

Retail Electronic Funds Transfer

§27.1 SCOPE

This chapter deals with those features of electronic funds transfer that involve the bank customer and, importantly, the consumer. By *consumer*, we mean here the customer that uses the bank's system for personal, family, or household purposes. Many of the rules for these transactions will affect business enterprises. Commercial parties use point of sale terminals and automated teller machines, and the largest corporation will maintain a checking account with a bank that uses the automated clearinghouse and check truncation. Yet, in these areas, unlike the **wholesale wire transfer** area, the consumer is a major concern of the law, and the rules are fashioned largely with the consumer in mind. The distinction is an important one, and while there is considerable overlap, differentiating the two kinds of transfers along lines that reflect their importance to the two kinds of parties involved (consumers on the one hand and commercial parties on the other) is appropriate.

§27.2 AUTOMATED TELLER MACHINES (ATMs)

By using a plastic access card and a **personal identification number** (PIN), bank customers may conduct some of their banking without having to deal with long lines in front of the teller window or with early bank closing hours. They can also avoid the $1 to $3 charge that some banks are now assessing customers that use tellers instead of automated teller machines. The ATM, which may be located in a vestibule outside the bank, in a shopping center, or elsewhere, normally permits the customer to make deposits of any kind and to make limited cash withdrawals. By sharing terminals, a consortium of financial institutions can make ATM banking available to their customers in a wide area at a large number of terminals.

The PIN is a computer-generated number given to the customer to be used with the card and memorized or stored in a place away from the card. The mathematical probabilities of a thief's guessing a person's PIN are too low for him to use a stolen card without knowing the number.

ATMs are not without their detractors. Many bank customers avoid them as impersonal and sometimes as unsafe. Enduring the long lines in a cozy bank lobby is often preferable to waiting outdoors on a blustery Minnesota mid-winter day. Criminals are more inclined to essay their fraudulent practices or their thuggery against the young and the elderly at desolate ATM locations than inside a bank, and while they are rare under the watchful eye of bank security personnel, muggings are not uncommon at some ATM sites. Inevitably, many consumers will keep their PIN on pieces of paper in their wallets, where a pick-pocket or thief finds it and the access card.

The evidence suggests that there is a measure of customer fraud and of bank fraud in connection with ATMs. Some customers claim that their transaction statements reflect withdrawals they never made or fail to reflect deposits they did make. Bankers, on the other hand, claim that no one has access to the customer's PIN, without which it is not possible to activate the account and that security measures (usually, two-employee verification of cash-deposit envelopes) make bank fraud unlikely. While industry observers report that some banks are lax in enforcing security measures, other data support the position that some customers make withdrawals and either forget about them or falsely claim that they did not make them. Fraud losses suffered by banks from ATMs have been large but manageable. The industry estimates that 10 percent of such losses have been from customer fraud and the balance from bank employee fraud.

More sophisticated ATMs may resolve some of the problems. However, the cost of a camera to record withdrawals and deposits, of a thumb-print recognition apparatus, or of a retina scanner to deter thieves are expensive modifications to a system that has not lived up to early predictions of significant cost savings. Some banks, however, charge customers that use ATMs a fee, this for a service that the banks encouraged their customers to use in the hope that such use would reduce personnel costs and save the bank money. Some banks, however, charge fees for teller use that exceed the charges for ATM use.

The industry estimates that ATMs handle roughly 50.2 billion transactions a year, 76 percent of which are cash withdrawals. Financial institutions estimate that they have issued approximately 135 million ATM cards, which are a kind of debit card.

When the ATM is dedicated to a single bank's ranks of customers, it is on-line to the bank's computer. Transactions at the terminal are recorded immediately to the customer's account, though deposits are held a sufficient time for verification. When a single terminal serves a number of banks and when one bank's terminals are available to customers of other banks, the communication of deposit and withdrawal data becomes more complicated. First Bank must charge to Second Bank's account cash withdrawals made at First Bank's terminal by a Second Bank customer. Periodically, Second Bank must thereafter charge its customers' accounts. Deposits at a multi-bank ATM of necessity require longer availability time than deposits at a terminal dedicated to one bank's customers.

While the terms of the relationship between a card issuer and its customer are to some extent governed by law, most of the rules and regulations are spelled out in the bank/customer agreement.

New uses for ATMs include electronic benefits transfers — the transfer of food stamps, welfare payments, and other government benefits — to persons who do not have bank accounts. Commentators estimate that 50 percent of all households earning less than $10,000 per year do not have a bank account, and yet these parties typically are the recipients of periodic government payments. While the automated clearinghouse discussed in Section 27.5 makes it possible for the government to transfer funds quickly and cheaply to persons having bank accounts, there is no efficient wire transfer system for those without bank accounts. Under the proposed electronic benefits transfer system, recipients will have an ATM card that they can use to access the ATM terminal, receiving the food stamps or other benefits in cash. The system is potentially less expensive than mailing payments to recipients, is arguably safer, and benefits banks through increased use of their ATM facilities.

At least one bank makes account statements available at its ATMs, and other banks are fashioning ATM capabilities that permit the customer to access account and product information at the ATM with access to a live teller, who appears on screen at the push of a button. The same bank also makes payrolls available at its ATMs. Corporate customers of the bank can pay employees via the bank's ATM network even if the employee does not maintain an account at the bank. In a manner similar to that used by ACHs to credit payroll accounts, the employer telecommunicates payroll information to the bank, which then makes net salary available to the employee at the ATMs.

ATMs are expensive to install and operate, and in some locations the traffic is not sufficient to make the ATM profitable. At least one regional ACH is now offering equipment to retailers that permits the customer to access his bank for authorization in script form for the retailer to advance cash to the customer. This innovation avoids the necessity of servicing the ATM to see that it is adequately stocked with cash to serve customers and avails the bank of the merchant's stock of cash.

At first, banks found customer resistance to ATMs, but usage appears to be growing. Monthly usage is increasing from year to year. To some extent ATM equipment is replacing branch banks. Current projections estimate that 20 percent of all branches will be closed by the end of the century, in part as a consequence of increased acceptance by customers of ATMs as substitutes for branches. Increasingly, customer transactions are conducted outside the branch or main office of a bank. One study estimates that already more than 50 percent of customer transactions are so conducted.

As public acceptance of ATMs becomes more pronounced, banks are now planning to use ATM equipment to market mutual funds. At least two banks are already marketing their mutual funds through ATMs. It is their experience that many of the customers who use ATMs are younger professionals, the type of people who are also interested in mutual funds both as an investment and as a source of transactions accounts. Thus banks are capturing some of their lost accounts through the medium of the ATM.

Most ATM networks are owned by a bank or a consortium of banks, but at least one data processor plans to maintain what would be the largest network of machines in the country. Each machine would take all national ATM cards. The data processor would make its profit by charging the banks for each transaction.

§27.3 DEBIT CARDS, SMART CARDS, AND THE POINT-OF-SALE (POS) TERMINAL

While many think of credit cards, which are discussed in Chapter 30, as plastic money, they are, in fact, plastic credit, since the credit-card sale is a credit transaction. Debit cards, on the other hand, are the equivalent of money, or, at least they could be, if the law lets them be.

The debit card looks much like a credit card. In fact, many credit cards may serve as debit cards. It is the function of the two cards that differs, not so much their appearance or attributes.

Debit cards come in three types depending on the technology the card issuer uses. Some debit cards are on-line, others off-line, and others pre-paid. Most debit cards are used with the first type of technology and permit instant or virtually instant debiting of the card user's account with the card issuer. Most retailers use telecommunications to relay purchase information to the card issuer. Off-line cards require the issuer to capture the information periodically from the terminals that accept the card for debiting of the customer's accounts. Prepaid cards, sometimes referred to as cash or stored value cards, require the customer to pay for the card at the time of issuance, if it is a throw-away card, or to pay to credit the card's memory for a programmed amount when the card's previously credited balance is exhausted. The first of the prepaid cards, the throw-away variety, is sometimes referred to as a "special purpose card." Parking garages, mass transit systems, and telephone companies are common issuers of such cards, which usually can be purchased from a machine that takes the customers' cash and dispenses the cards. One credit card company is now offering a travel card that permits its holders to withdraw from a prepaid account at any ATM terminal bearing the card's logo. Another company offers a card that it fancies as a world card or smart wallet, which can store cash in more than one currency. Smart debit cards have a memory that can be accessed by retailers who debit them for the amount of a purchase and by ATM machines that replenish their credit.

While special purpose cards have found acceptance in the U.S. market and are growing in use, smart cards have not been successful in a major way in the United States, except to the extent that the ATM access card is in reality a debit card. The use of debit cards is growing, however. The debit card has had more success in Europe where technology is more compatible and consumer acceptance is higher. With the U.S. Postal Service's acceptance of debit and credit cards in post offices, some see greater domestic use of the debit card. As long as U.S. consumers have ready access to credit cards with their float benefits, however, the debit card may have trouble finding its niche in the U.S. plastic money industry.

The **smart card** replaces the credit card's magnetic stripe with a silicon chip. While smart cards are relatively more expensive to manufacture than credit cards, the smart card can contain significant amounts of data. That data, moreover, may be accessed and altered by terminals at a merchant's establishment. The smart card, then, does not require the on-line capabilities of the system designed for the cards presently in use. For the most part in the United States, because of the industry's investment in technology that serves present cards, use of smart cards has not proceeded as quickly as some had hoped. Nevertheless, in many transactions, especially the point-of-sale (POS) transaction, the smart card can achieve efficiencies.

The POS terminal permits the customer to pay the retailer by inserting the debit card into the terminal, activating the terminal with a PIN, and then approving the amount of the purchase price. If the card is a traditional debit card with a magnetic stripe, the terminal may be on-line with the bank's central computer, which receives the information, debits the customer's account, and credits that of the merchant. If the terminal is not on-line, the bank must gather the information periodically and make the corresponding debit and credit entries. Under some systems, the bank or other data processor captures the information periodically (usually daily) by telephone line or electronic transmission. Thus, there is under these systems some delay in effecting the transfers and in updating the cardholder's and the merchant's balances. In these cases, the debit card takes on some of the attributes of a credit card and loses some of its advantages as a separate product.

The absence of on-line capabilities also creates problems for credit authorization and verification. Some systems, however, transmit that information daily, usually at off-peak hours. These off-line or "short-term, on-line" systems reduce credit risk but do not eliminate it. During any given day, a merchant will not have up-to-date information on overdrawn accounts or reports of lost or stolen cards that arose during that day. These systems have the advantage, however, of reducing cost. They involve considerably less computer time and less merchant time spent on verification and authorization requests. At the present, systems offering the off-line, smart card POS are marketing their product with low-dollar retailers such as fast-food merchants. The systems, however, are still pretty much in their infancy.

With a smart card and its embedded silicon chip, the on-line capability of the POS is not necessary. Smart cards can be used with equipment that is off-line but that has the capacity to alter the information on the card. For example, a consumer with a smart card can go to the bank and have the card encoded for a given amount of credit. Armed with the card, the consumer can proceed to make purchases. At each merchant establishment, the POS terminal reads the smart card to determine that there is sufficient credit available and deducts the amount of the immediate purchase. When the consumer has exhausted the card's credit, she must return to the bank or to an ATM machine to replenish the smart card credit by withdrawing funds from an account or otherwise purchasing the additional credit.

A merchant using such smart card equipment must deliver data from its machines to the bank periodically so that the bank can credit its account.

§27.4 CHECK TRUNCATION

In the best of all possible payments worlds, the account information of all payors and all payees would be recorded in a single computer to which all parties would have access. When a payor wanted to transfer credit to a payee, the payor would simply signal the computer to make the corresponding entries.

That world does not now and may never exist. To some extent, all wire transfer systems are partial efforts at achieving the most efficient system. Those efforts include the notion of hybrid paper/wire transfer systems that fall into the general category of "check truncation."

The simplest check truncation system involves the payor bank's interruption of the normal transport of the check. Under the check-collection system, a buyer's check normally travels from the buyer to the seller, who deposits it in the banking system. The check-collection system ultimately delivers the check to the buyer's bank, and the bank pays it and returns the check to the buyer with his monthly statement. In the simplest check-truncation system, the bank does not include the check with the buyer's statement but includes details of the transaction in the statement and destroys the paper. The system saves on mailing and handling costs.

Most banks that have introduced this simple check-truncation system adapt their preprinted checks to the system by providing a carbonless copy arrangement whereby the customer can keep the copy, if he chooses to do so. The carbon copy may not be sufficient evidence of payment for a court or for the Internal Revenue Service, but the payor bank photocopies the check before destroying it and makes the copy available to the customer for a fee. Presumably, bank customers do not need copies of their checks, the information recorded by the customer in the check register and the information in the periodic bank statement being sufficient.

In a somewhat more radical check-truncation program, financial institutions have used a combination of the payable-through draft and check truncation. Because credit unions did not have their own system for collecting cash items, when they began offering the **share draft** to their customers, they needed entry to the commercial banking system's check-collection machinery. They achieved that entry via payable-through drafts.

The credit union share draft is a demand item payable through a commercial bank or other financial institution with sophisticated collection facilities. Under the arrangement, the credit union maintains an account with a large financial entity, often a money-center bank. When a credit union member draws a share draft, the draft is on the credit union account at the money-center bank and is payable through the money-center bank. The MICR routing symbols on the share draft permit the payee to route the draft through the commercial bank check-collection system.

When the draft arrives at the money-center bank, the bank pays it and debits the credit union's account. The bank does not route the share draft to the credit union but supplies the debit information to the credit union by wire and truncates the share draft, that is, photocopies and destroys it.

There are projects involving more radical check truncation. Under one of them, checks are truncated at the clearinghouse, under another at the Federal Reserve Bank or regional check-processing center. Image processing is an innovation that increases the possibility of check truncation. An image-processing system captures the check's image in a fashion that permits the storage and retrieval of the image electronically. The system has two clear advantages over the traditional microfilming method of storing images. First, image processing permits high-speed and high-volume transmission of the images. Second, the system permits users to manipulate the stored information. For example, if a depositary bank has full image-processing capabilities, it can program its computer to transmit images of checks according to routing direction on the checks. It can also cull out checks in excess of a threshold amount and forward them while only forwarding data from, but not the image of, the smaller checks. Thus, payor banks could see images of large-dollar checks and verify their signatures but avoid the cost and time of such verification for small-dollar items.

Drawee payor banks are also using image-processing technology to truncate checks at the drawee payor bank. These banks are not returning checks to their customers but are sending images of the front of the check only and in reduced size. The advantage for customers is that they receive copies of their checks in a form that makes it easy to store the checks. The disadvantage is that the reverse of the check is not available, so that the customer cannot inspect indorsements. Most banks offering the service also allow customers to elect to receive the check itself but may charge more for that service than they charge for check images.

Advanced imaging systems will either use "power encoders" that encode the amount of the check in MICR symbols or other technology that permits reader sorter machines to read the amount of the check without having that information encoded onto the check by keypunch operators. Banks using the technology expect huge labor savings from the innovation.

Image processing providers claim that ultimately the technology will permit payor banks to compare signatures electronically and thereby avoid forged check losses. The ultimate effect of the full image-processing capabilities will be to do away with a significant amount of data entry, reader-sorter equipment at depositary and payor banks, and transportation of paper.

Check truncation yields considerable savings, and the earlier the system can replace the paper with an electronic impulse, the greater those savings will be. To date, the costs of implementing radical check truncation have exceeded the benefits, but the system is beginning to overcome the technological obstacles. Of the estimated 50 billion checks collected in the United States yearly, significantly less than half are truncated, and few of them are truncated at the bank of first deposit.

§27.5 THE AUTOMATED CLEARINGHOUSE (ACH)

In a sense, the automated clearinghouse (ACH) is misnamed. That name conjures up images of automation substituting for the manual processes currently conducted at the clearinghouse. Section 24.3 discusses the clearinghouse. In fact, there are efforts to render the clearinghouse process amenable to electronic procedures under which members of the clearinghouse would hold or truncate checks at the **depositary bank** and forward them electronically to the drawee or clear them through a central computer to which each clearinghouse member is connected. Those efforts are not included in the phrase "automated clearinghouse."

Essentially, the ACH of today is not so much a facility for clearing checks among local banks as it is a mechanism for handling recurring debits and credits that do not involve checks at all. The similarity between the clearinghouse and the ACH lies in the fact that the ACH substitutes computerized information for the cash letters that member institutions exchange at the clearinghouse.

There are as many as 30 ACHs in the United States, which are connected by an interregional network linking 16,000 depositary institutions. Often the ACH conducts its transactions through a Federal Reserve Bank. However, one of the largest ACHs, the New York Automated Clearinghouse, is a private clearinghouse, and the Hawaii and Arizona automated clearinghouses are private. Visa's automated clearinghouse in California handles ACH transactions for commercial banks.

The National Automated Clearing House Association (NACHA) establishes rules for the local ACH associations that are among its members. The local association enters into a contract with the Federal Reserve Bank or other processor, and, in the case of a Federal Reserve Bank, the processor issues a circular to further regulate the ACH. Debits and credits through the nation's ACHs exceed $900 million annually, a little less than half of which are federal payments such as social security, veteran's benefits, and federal employee salary payments. According to recent estimates, only about 10 to 12 percent of all insurance premium payments and 6 to 8 percent of all payroll payments are made through the ACH. There is considerable room, then, for growth in this efficient payments system. In fact, use of ACHs is expanding dramatically, having increased by 22 percent in a single year, though the ACH industry remains convinced that future growth rates will exceed current rates. In the last few years, ACHs have altered their systems so that virtually all customers are now transmitting data to the ACH by telecommunication, the old process of delivering tapes or even paper having been phased out.

Traditionally, ACHs have handled recurring payments and debits, not checks. Recently, a few Federal Reserve ACHs and at least one private ACH have initiated check processing and returns for commercial banks. Under the arrangements, banks will lift data from the magnetic ink character recognition symbols on the checks and deliver the data electronically to the ACH that then sorts the data and routes it to the destination bank, either a drawee or bank of first deposit. Current plans are for the paper to follow the data by one day, but some participants hope that eventually the checks can be truncated at the bank of first deposit.

Imaging capabilities will play a role in this new electronic check collection setting. If the paper arrives at the drawee bank and the bank decides to dishonor, it may be able to return the item electronically through image processing. In the alternative, some advocate the use of imaging to forward checks to the drawee. Under these proposals, the drawee or the system would determine which checks should be forwarded.

In a typical ACH transaction, a payor initiates the transaction by instructing its bank, a member of the ACH, to forward the computerized information to the ACH, which acts on the information in the fashion described above. If the sending customer's bank is not a member of the clearinghouse, that bank must forward the information to a bank that is a member. Banks usually settle among themselves through the Federal Reserve Banks.

When an employer offers to make direct deposit of payroll, it probably uses an ACH. The employer prepares the payroll information to include the names and checking account numbers of the employees and transfers that information by telecommunications or by delivering a computer tape to the ACH member, which then forwards it, often in the same form (tape or transmitted computer signal) to the ACH. At the present time, there are efforts on the part of the ACH industry to require all communication with the ACH to be electronic, thereby eliminating computer tapes or paper from the system. The ACH, through its own computer, debits the account of the employer at one ACH member institution, notifies member institutions of the transfers to their depositors (the employees), and credits the account of the member institutions for the aggregate amount transferred to all accounts at that institution. Each member institution, in turn, must credit the account of the designated employee-payee. The depositary institution sends its depositor/customer a notice of the deposit and, usually, payroll information similar to that which would otherwise be included on the stub of the payroll check this wire-transfer arrangement replaces. Generally, ACH payments are made in next-day funds, that is, the funds are transferred to the payee on the banking day after the ACH receives the transfer order.

Figure 27-1. ACH Payroll

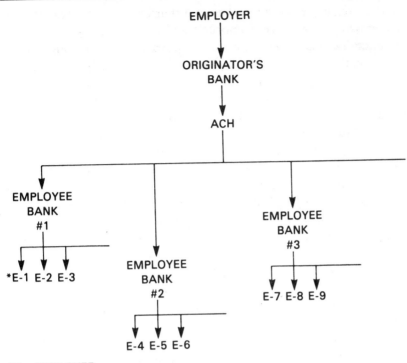

EMPLOYER

ORIGINATOR'S
BANK

ACH

EMPLOYEE
BANK
#1

*E-1 E-2 E-3

EMPLOYEE
BANK
#2

E-4 E-5 E-6

EMPLOYEE
BANK
#3

E-7 E-8 E-9

*E = EMPLOYEE

The ACH facility is quick and less expensive to both employer and employee than issuing and collecting a check for each employee and obviates postal delays and the loss of checks, which inevitably occur. The ACH is also far safer than the check collection system, since the ACH avoids the check fraud that has plagued the check-collection process. Figure 27-1 illustrates ACH transfer of payroll when employees maintain their accounts at banks that are all members of one ACH.

Recurring debits also lend themselves to collection through the ACH. Insurance company premiums, mortgage payments, and utility payments can be effected efficiently through the ACH in much the same way that the ACH serves payroll payments. In the insurance premium case, for example, the insurance company first obtains the insureds' debit authorizations for the recurring payments. Next, the company periodically instructs its bank to send the computerized information to the ACH, which then acts to collect the funds. The member institution credits the account of the insurance company. The ACH credits the account of the member bank and debits the accounts of member banks whose depositors have **preauthorized debits**. When the ACH notifies the member banks of the debits, the member banks debit the accounts of the various preauthorizing depositors.

The efficiency of these arrangements is enhanced by the fact that the same computer input serves to notify the ACH and the member institutions, since the ACH computers and member institution computers read the information supplied by the insurance company's member bank. There is no need to keypunch the information into the system more than once. Usually, the original data is entered on the insurance company's terminal and is transmitted by telecommunications to the member bank or delivered to the member bank by tape.

When bankers and commercial parties invented the ACH, they did not anticipate its use as a vehicle for **funds consolidation,** but, in fact, use of the ACH system for that purpose has accelerated. Funds consolidation is the process of bringing a firm's cash to a single point or several points quickly, so that the firm's financial officers can use it. Delay in funds consolidation is expensive, since it forces the firm to borrow or causes it lost investment opportunities. An enterprise with its financial offices in Chicago and retail outlets throughout the country must bring under the control of the Chicago office cash items received at the retail locations. The ACH lends itself readily to that process.

Periodically, perhaps daily, the Chicago office prepares computerized information instructing the Chicago ACH to debit the bank accounts of the retail outlets. Each afternoon, the retail financial managers signal the Chicago office the amount that will be available for the next morning's debit. The Chicago office then prepares the tape or other computer input, and the following morning, the ACH collects the funds by debiting the accounts of the various banks.

Note that funds consolidation is not a consumer wire transfer, yet it uses the ACH, which was originally designed for and thought of as a retail wire-transfer network. Because the funds consolidation operation traditionally involves sums greater than those involved in retail wire transfers, the chances of excessive daylight overdrafts might be a problem without rules limiting such overdrafts. Even with considerable use of the ACH system for funds consolidation the average ACH transfer is only about $4,000, substantially less than the wholesale wire transfer average over Fedwire and CHIPS, which approximates $2 million.

Some credit-card or debit-card systems are using the ACH to collect charges from their customers. Under these arrangements, the system collects transactional data and, at the end of a day, forwards it to the ACH for collection from the various customers' accounts.

The National Automated Clearing House Association (NACHA), the national umbrella organization for all automated clearinghouse associations, has developed a system to permit corporations to use the ACH to submit invoices and price information to customers. Under this electronic data interchange (EDI) system, merchants that do business with each other on a regular basis may provide each other with up-to-date information on prices, **discounts,** and other credit terms and may substitute electronic communication for such paper transfers as submission of purchase orders, order acknowledgments, and invoices. By combining this feature of the ACH with its debit facility, parties can accelerate the formation of the contract of sale and the invoicing and collection of trade debt.

§27.6 ELECTRONIC CLEARING

At the present time, at least one Federal Reserve Bank is experimenting with electronic clearing — the process of presenting items to the drawee electronically in the first instance.

There are two parts to the program. Under the first, participant payor banks in a designated region agree to accept electronic impulses from the Federal Reserve Bank and to make the determination whether to pay or dishonor before the paper arrives. When checks drawn on such an institution arrive at the Federal Reserve Bank, that bank's reader-sorter equipment reads the MICR line on the item and transmits the information to the payor bank. While the payor determines whether to pay or dishonor the item, the Federal Reserve Bank holds the paper under a schedule that permits it to return dishonored items to the bank of first deposit without ever presenting them to the payor. If the payor dishonors, the Federal Reserve Bank returns the item to the bank of first deposit. If the time for dishonor expires, the Federal Reserve Bank forwards the check to the payor for return to its customer with the periodic checking account statement.

Under the second phase of the program, when both the bank of first deposit and the payor bank are participants, the reader-sorter equipment of the depositary bank reads the MICR line of the item. That bank holds the check and forwards the information by "electronic cash letter" to the Federal Reserve Bank. The Federal Reserve Bank then forwards the information to payor participants, who have already agreed to act on it without receiving the paper.

Neither feature of the program involves truncation, since the paper ultimately follows the electronic impulse to the payor. In the case of returns, however, the programs save time — a full day in some cases. Because the Federal Reserve Bank in the first phase of the program and the depositary bank in the second treat the paper on a hold-and-forward basis. Paper that is ultimately dishonored travels less than under traditional check-clearing systems.

In another innovation, a money-center bank assembles checks for its smaller correspondents and presents them along with a cash letter to the local Federal Reserve bank. Under the traditional procedure, the money-center bank must read and sort each check through its machines several times. The Federal Reserve, in turn, has to run the checks through its machines several times. But under the electronic scheme, the money-center bank captures the check information electronically by reading and sorting the checks only twice and forwards the information to the Federal Reserve in an "electronic cash letter." At the present time, the money-center bank is delivering the checks to the Federal Reserve along with the electronic data, so that the Federal Reserve can verify that data. In the future, however, the money-center bank could hold the checks and avoid the paper transport and storage costs that the current system entails. Note that this system also uses wire transfer technology in the check-collection process, an adaptation of the traditional check-collection mechanism that appears with increasing frequency and that lends itself to image processing capabilities. For more discussion of imaging processing and check truncation, *see* Section 27.4.

§27.7 HOME BANKING AND TELEPHONE BILL PAYING

Some banks have marketed a home-banking system that uses a combination of telephone technology, cables, home computers, and terminals of various kinds. Under these arrangements, a consumer or a small business can obtain access to its account by telephone or cable. Under most of the programs, the customer can transfer funds among his accounts, pay some bills, stop payments, and obtain account balance information.

Home-banking programs suffer from their inability to permit customers to make deposits and withdrawals, and there has been more customer resistance to the innovation than some banks and computer technology experts originally anticipated. The number of banks offering home-banking programs showed little inclination to grow until recently, when major banks reinvigorated their efforts to market the home-banking facility. Some banks combine home-banking programs with brokerage services, data bases (e.g., news and current entertainment schedules), and the purchase of tickets for public events.

Home banking has made further strides, as banks continue to search for new products, and it may be that the home-banking service has survived the worst and is reversing the trend of the last ten years or so. A number of larger banks have reinstituted home-banking programs. Some use minimally complicated hardware such as an enhanced telephone, while others take advantage of computer technology. One bank is marketing a program that uses hardware that will permit customers to use their debit cards at home. The two giant credit card companies, VISA and Mastercard, have announced their intention to enter the home-banking field. At least one bank is entering the home-banking market with plans to use a smart card with telephone equipment.

Banks that offer home banking combine the home-banking facility with home bill paying. Bill-paying programs permit a customer to designate payees that are not necessarily recurring. While the ACH has for a long time permitted customers to designate recurring payments to, say, utilities, insurance companies, credit card issuers, and mortgagees, the ACH does not lend itself to the odd bill, say, the florist, the Bar Association, or the tree surgeon. Home bill-paying programs permit the customer to enter data at home that allows the bank to make payments electronically to the accounts of the designated payees.

Telephone bill paying predates home banking and achieved a higher level of acceptance. Telephone bill-paying programs vary, but generally they permit a customer of a bank or of a thrift to use the telephone to order the depository institution to pay creditors. Some systems permit the customer to use a touch-tone or rotary dial telephone to indicate the creditor, the amount of the payment, and the account to be charged. Other systems rely on voice transmission. In a sophisticated system, the institution may permit payments to creditors through the automated clearinghouse. Other systems confine payments to creditors in a smaller geographic area who are depositors at a limited number of institutions. Telephone bill-paying systems have lost some of their allure in recent years. Large banks were never much interested in offering them, but savings and loans and some brokerage firms offering money-market accounts still market telephone bill-paying systems. Usually, the bank ATM card agreement, which itself is part of the bank-depositor agreement, governs the home-banking and telephone-banking relationships.

Both home-banking programs and telephone bill-paying programs permit institutions to market other bank products. When a customer accesses a bank's computer to pay bills by telephone or by a personal computer, the bank program can offer advertising and loan and deposit account information. Some programs permit the customer to compute payment schedules for various loan amounts and various maturities. These programs, which are menu-driven, that is, which provide directions to the customer user, sometimes allow customers to apply for loans, reorder checks, verify that deposits have cleared or that checks have been paid, and indicate the location of the nearest ATM. Banks provide security for these programs by limiting customer access to the facility through use of the customer's bank card number and PIN.

§27.8 CONSUMER MONEY TRANSFERS

One of the earliest wire-transfer systems was that of telegraphing funds. The system is rather simple. A customer, usually a consumer with a relative in a distant location who needs funds, accesses the system at an office by paying cash to the system operator. The operator wires an office in the locale of the relative, and that office then advances the funds. Recent innovations by new competitors in the industry involve the use of independent entities at both ends of the transfer. Thus instead of wiring funds from and to offices maintained by the system, new operators make use of drug stores, food markets, and bus stations as they compete for the $3 billion market. Under this new variant, the system itself collects the funds from the sending participant and reimburses the participant that advances the funds.

If a parent in Boston wants to send $100 to her child in San Francisco, the parent pays the $100 plus a fee to a Boston drug store that participates in the system. The drug store notifies a participant in San Francisco, say a bus station, to advance the $100 to the child. The Boston drug store pays the $100 to the system, which reimburses the San Francisco bus station.

Collection of International Payments

§28.1 THE NEED

International trade, investment, and travel are the commercial and private activities that drive international payments. When a French tourist in Morocco uses a VISA card, a U.S. investor acquires eurobonds, or a Dutch refinery buys Nigerian crude oil, the transaction usually cannot proceed to conclusion without the international transfer of **bank credits.**

There are a number of obstacles to these international transfers. Sometimes the transfers confront exchange problems. If an Afghan merchant wants to buy trucks, he will find that most of the world's sellers of motor vehicles do not accept payment in afghanis, the Afghan currency. Sellers usually accept only "hard" currencies, that is, currencies that are exchanged freely in international trade and investment.

Other international transactions confront the problem of exchange control laws and regulations. A Venezuelan buyer may have an adequate supply of funds to his credit at a Caracas bank to purchase the steam-generating facility an American seller wants to sell him, but the buyer may not be able to obtain the necessary government permission to transfer dollars from the Venezuelan central bank or may not be able to obtain the dollars in time to satisfy the American seller.

International traders and investors have devised a number of responses to these problems. **Countertrade,** a form of international barter, and joint ventures are two common responses. Both of them, however, as well as the other arrangements adopted in order to overcome the problems of exchange controls and "soft" currencies are less efficient than the quick transfer of bank credits that this chapter describes.

Countertrade is probably the least efficient. It leaves the seller with goods that it usually must resell before it has cash or bank credit to use in its business. Only infrequently will a seller who takes goods in countertrade be in a position to use those goods himself. In theory, a seller of computer parts to a Soviet buyer might be able to take Soviet mining vehicles in countertrade and be able to use them in its business, but more often it will have to resell the mining vehicles and often in markets with which it may not be familiar.

Similarly, sales into countries with stiff exchange control laws or regulations are often encumbered by the need to obtain the importing country's approval of the transaction. In such cases, the seller may have to obtain a government functionary's stamp and countersignature on shipping documents or invoices before the buyer's bank will honor a draft drawn under a letter of credit. Obtaining such approval is time-consuming and in some countries creates opportunities for government officials to insist on graft — a practice that is common enough in some regions to be a trade requirement.

The lesson is plain enough: Efficient movement of goods must abide free transfer of international payments. Those who restrict those payments in order to protect domestic industry, to placate political critics, or for whatever other reason are restricting international trade and investment and are reaping the heavy economic burdens of that policy — a lessening of competition with the higher prices, product deficiencies, and other "taxes" that protected industries inevitably exact.

§28.2 THE INTERNATIONAL BANK DRAFT

The international bank draft utilizes a domestic bank's deposits denominated in foreign currencies and held in foreign banks.

A Miami purchaser of automotive parts may agree to pay a Milan seller in lire. The buyer will ask its Miami bank to draw a draft on its correspondent bank in Milan for the purchase price of the parts. The Miami bank will "sell" the draft to its customer, the buyer, who forwards it to the seller by mail or messenger. The seller then deposits the draft at its own bank for collection from the Miami bank's correspondent. Figure 28-1 illustrates the transaction.

Figure 28-1.   International Bank Draft

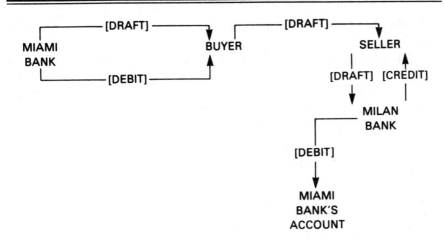

§28.3 PAYMENT BY CORRESPONDENT

The international bank draft is somewhat slow and poses a security problem to the extent that the draft might be lost in transit. Banks that maintain accounts with foreign correspondents can reduce some of the delay and most of the security risk by removing the draft from the transaction. The draft is a negotiable order to pay, and there may be situations in which the buyer properly wants to use such a device.

Most sellers will not be interested in negotiable drafts, however, and the parties can save the time and the risks of the draft by having the Miami bank wire its Milan correspondent to disburse the funds to the seller. This arrangement is a wire transfer and may be effected by cable, telex, or SWIFT. (For general discussion of wire transfers, see Chapter 26.)

§28.4 PAYMENT BY WIRE

It is inefficient for banks to maintain many correspondent accounts, so banks engaging in international activity have consolidated their foreign currency accounts in a relatively few banks. They then effect international payments by transferring funds among those few banks. Certain cities in countries with hard currencies such as New York, London, and Hong Kong have emerged as centers for international banking. Large foreign banks with international departments nearly always maintain a dollar-denominated account with one of the New York money-center banks. When the customer of one of those foreign banks wants to transfer dollars to a seller, his bank will initiate payment through the money-center bank network.

When a Dutch buyer of crude oil agrees to pay U.S. dollars to a seller in Dubai, the buyer and seller can agree to use CHIPS, the New York money-center banks' network for international payments. Under the arrangement, the buyer will ask its Dutch bank, First National Bank of Rotterdam, to transfer dollars to the seller's dollar-denominated account in a New York bank, Second Bank of New York. The Dutch Bank will debit the buyer's account and instruct its New York correspondent to make the payment. The New York correspondent will debit the Dutch Bank's account and will credit Second Bank of New York's account. Second Bank will then credit the seller's account.

If the seller does not maintain an account in New York, as it well might not, it becomes necessary to introduce another bank into the transaction. If the seller maintains an account at Third Bank of Dubai, First Bank of Rotterdam's New York correspondent will transfer the funds to the account of Third Bank of Dubai's New York correspondent. Figure 26-2 illustrates a CHIPS transaction.

The volume of these dollar-denominated payments is considerable. On the average day the New York Clearinghouse system for clearing these international transfers handles 60,000 orders, and on a busy day may transfer more than $1 trillion. In order to effect those transfers quickly and without error, the New York Clearinghouse has established CHIPS, a computer system that manages to clear the transfers by wire. Under CHIPS, banks make intraday transfers and net them out at the end of the day. They then settle through the Federal Reserve Bank of New York. For further discussion of CHIPS, see Section 26.6.

§28.5 PAYMENT BY LETTER OF CREDIT

Buyers and sellers under international sales agreements frequently pay by letter of credit. Under an international letter of credit, the seller must present its draft and certain other documents specified in the credit to the nominated bank, that is, the bank designated in the credit as the party that will pay the draft. Sometimes, the issuer of the credit will be the payor bank, but often the credit nominates another bank to make the payment. Frequently, moreover, the seller will want to have a bank local to it confirm the credit, that is, undertake to pay the credit just as the issuer does.

In the oil transaction described in the preceding section, the buyer's bank, the First National Bank of Rotterdam, causes a letter of credit to issue in favor of the Dubai seller. The Rotterdam bank might nominate a Dubai bank to confirm the credit and to pay the Dubai seller.

At other times, the buyer and the seller agree to payment in a currency that the issuer does not have on hand. In that case, the issuer nominates a correspondent that does have the required currency. Thus, if the Dubai seller wants to be paid in U.S. dollars, the Rotterdam bank might nominate a New York bank as the payor under the credit and might ask the New York bank to confirm the credit. The Dubai seller, if it is an international oil trader or supplier, probably maintains an account in another New York bank.

If the Dubai seller presents its documents in time and if the documents comply with the terms of the letter of credit, the confirming bank or other nominated bank will pay. The paying bank must then seek reimbursement from the issuer of the credit. Usually, the credit recites the arrangement for reimbursement.

When a Dutch buyer agrees to pay a Dubai seller in dollars, First Bank, the Rotterdam letter-of-credit issuer, might direct the Dubai buyer to draw on Bank of Miami and then instruct Bank of Miami to obtain reimbursement from the Rotterdam bank's New York correspondent where the Rotterdam bank maintains a dollar-denominated account. Figures 5-1 and 5-2 illustrate the letter-of-credit transaction. Chapter 5 discusses the letter-of-credit sale in more detail.

§28.6 COLLECTING THE SELLER'S DRAFT

Often, international sellers vary the letter-of-credit transaction described in the foregoing section. Letters of credit entail bank charges that buyers and sellers want to avoid. The parties may, nonetheless, still want bank assistance in collecting the seller's draft on the buyer. The seller may be willing to ship the goods without a letter of credit from the buyer's bank, but the seller may not want to surrender possession of the goods without payment or without the buyer's acceptance of a time draft.

In those cases, the seller prepares its documents and introduces them into the bank collection system with instructions on the steps the banks should take in collecting the draft. Chapter 4 discusses the documentary draft transaction in greater detail.

§28.7 INTRABANK NETWORK

One money-center bank, with branches and foreign subsidiaries scattered throughout the world's commercial centers, markets an international payments system that permits merchants to access the bank's own network. Under the program, an Atlanta buyer of goods from a Tokyo seller can arrange to credit the seller's Tokyo yen account from a terminal in the buyer's office. Because the bank takes daily positions in hard currencies, it can sell yen to the Atlanta buyer; and because it has its own trading and payments network, the bank can wire the funds to Tokyo. Under the program, which anticipates periodic transactions between the parties, the bank makes software available to the buyer. The buyer's payments officer can then purchase yen from the bank's trader and direct the payment to the seller in Tokyo via the buyer's own computer terminal.

The program is attractive in part because it speeds payments and combines the payments process and the currency exchange process into one communication. It is also attractive to buyers since the bank does a credit analysis of the buyer. If the buyer satisfies the bank's credit standards, the bank does not require the buyer to maintain an account with the bank. The buyer reimburses the bank by putting funds in the bank the day following payment. Figure 28-2 illustrates this quick, simple, and imaginative payment mechanism.

At least one foreign EFT network is entering the United States wire transfer market in order to facilitate international wire transfers. Under the arrangement, parties may wire funds between domestic banks and foreign banks. The cost of this system is sufficiently low that small enterprises and tourists may avail themselves of it to transfer small amounts overseas by wire. One advantage of the system is that it permits travelers to use the European network while they are abroad.

Figure 28-2.   International Payments through Intrabank Network

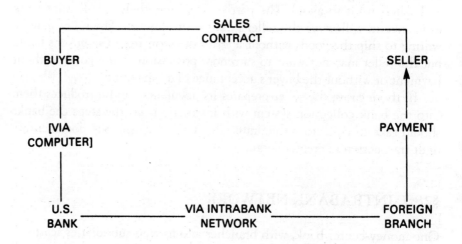

29

Giro Accounts

§29.1 PULL ORDERS AND PUSH ORDERS

Drafts and checks, with which most lawyers in the Anglo-American system of law are familiar, are pull orders. They pull funds from an account maintained by the drawer — the person who gives the order. The drawer of a check mails it to the payee, who deposits it in the collection system in order to pull the funds into his account. Similarly, the seller using a draft draws the draft payable to himself or his agent and deposits the draft in order to pull the funds into his account.

Continental countries generally have not used the check as commonly as the United States and British Commonwealth countries. In Continental Europe and elsewhere, the **giro** is more common. The giro is a **push order**. It pushes funds from the account of the drawer to the account of the payee.

In a giro system, a buyer or other debtor draws an order, the giro, on his own account and delivers or mails it either to the bank where he maintains that account or another bank that acts as a forwarding agent for his bank. The order specifies the amount to be transferred and the bank account number of the payee. The buyer's bank then debits the account of the buyer and credits the account of the payee's bank and forwards the giro to that bank, so that it can credit the payee's account.

Figure 29-1. Giro

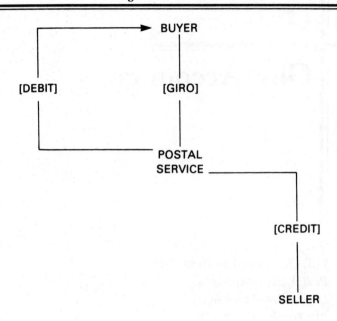

Under the system, when a plumber sells services to a buyer, the plumber's invoice specifies her giro account number. The buyer draws a giro credit directing a commercial bank to forward the funds to the plumber's account. Under some giro systems, a copy of the buyer's order accompanies the fund transfer, but under others, the plumber does not see the giro credit but receives a periodic statement on which the transfer is noted. Figure 29-1 illustrates the giro payment in this simple transaction.

Note that in the giro system, the funds move more quickly than in the check system. Checks are debit instruments, and depository institutions delay the availability of funds for a period to allow for their collection. There is always the possibility in the check-collection system that the check will arrive at the drawee bank when there are insufficient funds available to pay the check or after the drawer has issued a stop payment order. Although more than 95 percent of all checks clear in the United States, depository institutions do not know which checks will clear and which checks will not. Depository institutions also do not know when a check clears. Even though the payor bank decides to pay a check, the depository bank does not receive notice of the payment. Silence, the absence of notice of dishonor, is the signal that a check is paid.

In the giro system, however, the giro credit moves in the same direction as the funds, as it pushes the funds into the account of the payee. The payee's institution does not have to wait for the giro to clear. When the giro arrives, the funds, in effect, arrive with it.

§29.2 POSTAL GIRO ACCOUNTS

In many countries, the postal service or another nationalized agency operates a giro system. Every person in the country who wishes to participate may establish an account. The postal service's central computer tracks all accounts and makes payments simple and inexpensive. When the plumber in the foregoing example submits her invoice, in place of a bank giro number, she will designate her postal giro number. The homeowner will then prepare a giro payable to the plumber. The homeowner delivers the giro to the postal service that then debits the homeowner's account and credits the plumber's account.

§29.3 BANK GIRO ACCOUNTS

In a bank giro system, the customer who desires to transfer funds is the payor. His bank is the transferring bank, and the bank of the payee is the recipient bank.

When banks operate giro systems along side that of the postal service, they and the postal service arrange for intersystem payments. Banks, because they are independent entities and do not share a single central computer that tracks all accounts and payments, must arrange in the bank giro system to settle periodically among themselves. Similarly, in a market economy, there will be more than one bank, and interbank giro payments require a collection apparatus similar to that employed in a check collection system. Document 29-1 is a bank giro.

§29.4 ELECTRONIC GIRO SYSTEMS

Because the giro system involves push orders, some commentators consider a preauthorized debit system as an electronic giro. Under these systems, debtors preauthorize the payment of insurance premiums, utility bills, mortgage payments, and similar recurring charges. Section 27.5 discusses the automated clearinghouse, an electronic giro system. In a sense, point of sale terminals give rise to electronic giros since they involve the pushing of funds from the account of the buyer who activates the terminal and directs his financial institution to debit his account and credit the account of his creditor. Section 27.3 discusses the point of sale terminal. Similarly, telephone bill-paying programs and some features of home banking are a form of electronic giro.

Technological advances sometimes prompt reinvention of the wheel. One vendor is attempting to sell banks a payment by facsimile machine program that is merely a new kind of giro account. Under the proposed program, banks provide their customers with "facsimile payment slips," which the customers use to transfer funds from their own accounts to the account of the payee. The program calls for the customers to fill in the amount of the payment and the payee's account number and then to fax the "slip" to the bank, which would complete the transfer. The slips, of course, are giros. Only the technology, the fax machine, is new.

Document 29-1.   Bank Giro

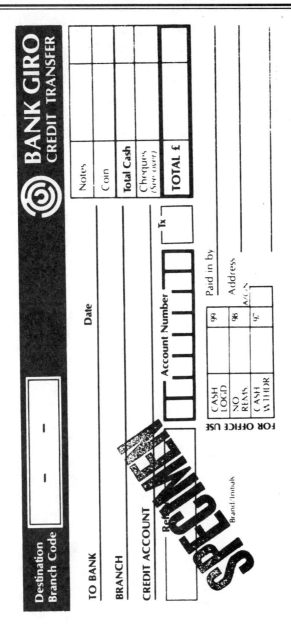

30

Credit Cards

§30.1 INTRODUCTION

This chapter deals primarily with bank credit cards but includes discussion of **travel and entertainment cards** and single-seller charge cards. Chapter 27 discusses debit cards. Credit cards have grown enormously in volume and importance in the retail sector of the economy, replacing many single-seller cards and displacing somewhat the significance of travel and entertainment cards, which predate bank credit cards. Today, roughly 16 percent of all retail purchases are by credit card.

Although the bank card system is efficient once it begins operating, the start-up costs are considerable. Such systems involve several contracts, association bylaws, and an elaborate collection network. Recent figures indicate that annually there are in excess of 3 billion bank charge card transactions.

§30.2 BANK CREDIT-CARD SYSTEMS

While a few banks continue to offer their own credit cards, there are two national bank credit-card systems: Visa and Mastercard. Both systems operate a national network of bank members or affiliates and an independent payments system. At the present time, however, the two systems are engaging in some cross-processing, whereby merchants authorized to accept cards for one system may accept the other system's cards and use the same processing arrangements for both.

There are five basic features of a successful national bank credit-card system. First, it must have a national network of banks that issue cards; second, it must solicit a significant number of merchants to participate in the program by accepting the card from customers; third, it needs to provide a verification service to the merchants; fourth, there must be a network of processors to take the charge slips from the merchants; and fifth, it must provide a quick, inexpensive, and reliable interchange system for collecting the charges from the issuer and transmitting them to the merchants' banks.

In the national system, then, banks play two critical roles. The **issuing bank** is the bank that issues a card to its customer and enters into a revolving credit arrangement with the customer. The **merchant bank** or "acquiring bank" is the bank that enters into a contract with a retailer and engages to purchase credit-card **sales slips** from the retailer and to collect them through the system.

Both banks are members of the system and are bound by its bylaws. The bylaws oblige the issuer to honor sales slips when they are "presented" through the system for payment. The bylaws also govern the collection of the sums due under the slips and the rules for charging back disputed amounts and generally displace the common law rules that evolved in the check-collection system.

Sometimes banks play a third role in the system by handling the data-processing function, though increasingly banks are referring that business to nonbank data processors.

§30.3 THE CARDHOLDER AND HIS BANK

When the issuing bank issues a card to a customer, the customer enters into a credit-card agreement. Under the agreement, the issuer obligates itself to provide the customer with a revolving line of credit up to a designated amount. The cardholder, in turn, agrees to pay for charges incurred and to pay interest on outstanding balances, which result if the cardholder elects the credit option and defers payment of the full periodic balance.

Usually, bank credit card issuers extend unsecured credit to their customers. This practice has the effect of leaving many individuals without credit cards, however, since to the extent that an individual is not credit-worthy, banks will not issue the individual a card. Some banks issue what they internally call a secured credit card. This card is no different in appearance from the regular credit card, but the card issuer has taken collateral from the cardholder, has a guaranty from someone whose credit rating is strong, or has otherwise collateralized the cardholder's obligation to reimburse the issuer for advances it makes to merchants that honor the card. That security generally consists of a deposit the customer makes with the credit issuer and on which the issuer pays interest. During a period of low interest rates on money-market investments, some cardholders found the rate of return on those deposits better than the rate in the money market. Thus some wealthy individuals, rather than the poorer credit risks for whom the secured card was designed, resorted to the secured card rather than the unsecured credit card that is more common.

The secured credit card's growth remains in that part of the market that cannot obtain a regular credit card: persons without credit histories (young people, immigrants, and widows) and those with poor credit histories. The unsecured credit card market is by now pretty much saturated. At least one bank card issuer, however, has used the secured card as a leader for the unsecured card. By offering to transform the secured card into a regular card if the holder obtains a cosigner with a good credit rating, that issuer is able to increase its regular card numbers.

Some business enterprises use purchasing cards. A purchasing card is a typical credit card issued to a corporation for use by the corporation's employees who purchase goods or services for the corporation. Instead of having the employees use their own cards, obtain petty cash, write corporate checks, or forward invoices to an authorized check writing employee, the purchasing-card program allows the employee to pay for goods or services immediately with a credit card that is issued to the corporation. The card issuer then bills the corporate employer rather than the employee for the card charges.

One of the advantages to the purchasing card is that it can have limits on the amount of the purchase. An employer that does not authorize an employee to make purchases in excess of $250, for example, can cause the card issuer to limit the employee's card to purchases not exceeding that amount.

§30.4 THE MERCHANT AND HIS BANK

Merchants who want to avail themselves of the ability to make credit-card sales must gain entry to the system through a merchant bank. The agreement between the merchant and the merchant bank, a member of the bank-card system, governs matters relating to the bank's purchase or discount of the merchant's paper or, in instances where the parties do not use paper, the merchant's accounts.

In the past, and to some extent today, the merchant periodically delivered her paper to the bank. The paper is the credit-card sales slip. Often at the end of a business day, the merchant delivered the sales slips to the merchant bank in a batch with an aggregate total. The bank then granted the merchant either immediate or delayed credit for that total, less a percentage. The percentage, which may range from 1 to 7 percent, is the discount. It is not altogether clear conceptually whether the bank is buying the merchant's sales slips or granting a loan against them, though the parties think of the transaction as a sale of the slips. They acknowledge, however, that the sale is with recourse, that is, that the merchant must repurchase any slip that is not honored. The transaction, in that particular then, resembles a loan that must be repaid if the third party (the cardholder) does not pay it.

With more modern technology, many merchants and their banks have avoided the need to transmit sales slips. The merchant bank and the merchant are in electronic communication, so that every time a customer purchases goods or services from the merchant, the merchants terminal notifies the bank of the purchase, and the bank credits the merchant's account.

In either case, paper or telecommunications, it is not clear whether the discount the merchant pays the merchant bank is a charge for the bank's services or, in the case of immediately available credit, the payment of interest for the merchant's use of the funds until the issuing banks pay the cardholders' obligations as evidenced by the slips.

After it has solicited its stable of merchants, the merchant bank's functions are essentially confined to data processing. Some merchant banks have assigned these functions to their data-processing subsidiaries or have contracted the services out to a nonbank data processor.

§30.5 PAYMENT

The broad credit-card transaction involves all four of the parties described in the preceding sections as well as one or more intermediaries.

In a typical sale, the cardholder makes a credit-card purchase of goods from a retailer. The retailer prepares the credit-card slip, sometimes called a **sales draft,** by imprinting it with the credit-card information, filling in the amount of the purchase and a description of the merchandise, and obtaining the cardholder's signature. The clerk is also supposed to compare the signature on the reverse side of the card with that on the sales slip, though, in practice, many clerks fail to perform that operation.

If the amount of the sale exceeds the **floor release limit,** before completing the sale, usually before the cardholder signs the slip, the retailer will run an inquiry through the card system. The purpose of the inquiry is to determine that the card is still valid, i.e., that it has not been reported lost by the cardholder or canceled by the issuer, and that the cardholder has not exceeded his credit limit. That information is available to the merchant through on-line computer access where the information is stored or through operators who check for the information. In both cases, the merchant receives an authorization number that he records on the sales slip as evidence that he has received authorization from the system.

Significantly, the process of obtaining authorization permits the card system to capture sales information. When the merchant provides that information to the system, the system's computer reduces the amount of credit available to the cardholder.

By virtue of an agreement between Mastercard and Visa, merchants can engage in cross-processing. Merchants that have an agreement with a merchant bank that is a member of one of the associations has access to information from both associations and, therefore, can honor both cards. The bank-card systems also make cross-processing agreements with non-bank systems.

The merchant bank collects its advances by forwarding the credit-card slips or the data it receives from its merchants in computer form to a clearing agent that may be a bank subsidiary, a captive of a regional association of banks, or an independent data-processing entity. Banks that use a given clearing agent can maintain clearing accounts, and the clearing agent may handle charges against those banks directly by debiting their accounts and crediting the account of the merchant bank.

The bylaws of the system and federal and state law provide for charge backs in certain instances. In the event of a charge back, the issuer must give notice to the merchant bank. The agreement between the merchant bank and the merchant generally provides that the merchant is responsible for all charge backs.

§30.6 TWO-PARTY CHARGE CARDS

Long before the advent of the bank credit card, many sellers — oil companies and department stores, for example — maintained their own charge accounts, and these sellers often gave their customers charge cards. Those cards and traditional telephone charge cards, which are similar, differ from the bank credit card in that they do not involve sophisticated national collection systems. Essentially, they are two-party cards, while bank cards are multi-party.

When a customer uses a department store's charge card, the arrangement calls for the store to grant credit to the customer. Although the store may well finance its accounts with a bank or finance company, the customer generally makes his payments directly to the store and does not deal with any financial institution. Until recently, it was unusual that the card issued by one entity could be used at any other entity.

Oil company credit cards are more complex than the customary two-party card, since they frequently involve a service station operator that is independent of the oil company and may include operators of competing brand outlets. In these cases, there is an additional party in the transaction, but the service station operator does not take his charge slips to his bank. He forwards them to the oil company, which acts as the clearinghouse.

A Marathon dealer forwards his sales slips periodically to the oil company's credit-card headquarters. In oil company credit-card operations, traditionally, the service station merchant used a small hand-operated, mechanical device to imprint the cardholder's account number, the dealer's number, and the amount of the sale on the sales slip in machine-readable form. When the oil company received the slips, its machines read them and provided batch verification for the company, that is, the machines verified the totals that the dealer submitted to the company with his slips. The company then credited the dealer's account in the amount of the slips or sent him a check.

The oil company collects the charges from the cardholders by billing them. Because the information has been captured by machines, the company can generate a cardholder's monthly statement from the computer that stored the sales slip information.

Many oil company credit cards are used at service stations other than those of the card issuer. If, for example, the Marathon card is available at an Exxon service station, there must be an arrangement for the Exxon dealer to collect his charges. The oil companies effect that collection by crediting the accounts of their own dealers for charges made on other oil company cards. The oil companies then settle among themselves, treating each other, in effect, as they do a dealer that has generated a significant number of sales slips.

Some nonbanks market a charge card, such as the Dean Witter Discover card, that the customer can use much as she uses a bank credit card. The Discover card clearly competes directly with bank cards. Charges under these cards find their way into the bank-card collection system when a credit-card bank issues the card and retailers enter into contracts with banks to collect the charges. At first, the national bank-card associations objected to the practice; which they saw as an attempt by retailers sponsoring competing cards to avail themselves of the costly collection system fashioned by the associations for their own cards. To date, those objections notwithstanding, commercial banks are using the national bank-card system to collect charges generated by cards issued by national retailers, and the indications are that the national bank-card associations are accommodating themselves to the fact that nonbank credit cards are a permanent part of the payments system.

§30.7 TRAVEL AND ENTERTAINMENT CARDS

As early as 1950, Diners Club began to market a travel and entertainment (T&E) card. It has since been joined by a number of competing cards. While growth of the T&E cards has slowed and been displaced somewhat by bank credit cards, the T&E industry still handles considerable business. There are approximately 20 million T&E cardholders charging in excess of $60 billion per year for services.

T&E cards allow holders to charge meals, hotel accommodations, and the like and to pay for them periodically, usually monthly. Most of the time, T&E cards have no credit limit. T&E cardholders tend to use the card, therefore, for higher-priced items such as airline travel and hotel accommodations, and the airline and hotel industries have been more inclined to pay the T&E card company discounts that are generally higher than those charged by banks that collect sales charges generated by merchants that accept bank cards. Retailers, whose sales are relatively small in dollar terms, however, have been reluctant to accept the T&E card with its higher discount. T&E cards also differ from bank credit cards in that usually the cardholder must pay his account in full upon receipt of the periodic statement. There is no credit term beyond the delay between the time of the purchase and the time the T&E company submits its statement. Finally, T&E cards differ from bank credit cards in that the periodic statement from the T&E company usually includes the signed receipts, while bank credit-card issuers truncate the receipts early in the collection process and provide only a printout of purchase made during the billing period.

Recently the lines between bank credit cards and T&E cards have blurred somewhat. At least one T&E card issuer, the subsidiary of a money-center bank, will now extend credit and charge interest on an unpaid principal balance, much as bank credit card issuers do. Bank credit card issuers, furthermore, have been aggressively marketing "gold" or "platinum" cards, which have sufficiently high credit limits that they are useful for travel and entertainment charging. One bank card issuer developed procedures for easy override of the credit limit for travel and entertainment purchases.

§30.8 PREPAID CARDS

The advent of smart cards (cards with an embedded silicon chip) or even cards with a magnetic stripe makes it possible for card companies to market prepaid cards or stored-value cards. These cards can be used at terminals that "charge" the customer for the amount of the purchase by reducing the balance of credit available on the card. Telephone companies are marketing these cards for use with pay telephones, and one card company sold such cards to participants in the 1994 Winter Olympics, equipped with credit in the Norwegian krone. Such cards are also available for use with electronic benefits transfer (EBT) programs under which benefit recipients of food stamps, say, can access their benefits at ATM machines periodically and replenish the credit in their cards. Such cards could also serve as traditional ATM cards.

Prepaid cards are not as "smart" as the smart card that has found some success in foreign markets and are now entering domestic markets. Prepaid cards may have an important effect, however, in small ticket purchases; that is, they may replace the small change purchase that some merchants find undesirable for credit cards. One bank has targeted the taxicab market in New York for prepaid cards. Parking decks and subway systems are experimenting with such cards. Other card companies are pursuing prepaid cards for use in fast-food and service stations.

Prepaid cards can be sold in denominations of $2 or $5 and can be discarded when their credit is exhausted. They serve, then, as a substitute for cash. They are only a partial substitute, however. While merchants benefit from this "cashless" product, unless the card entails the use of a PIN, the consumer does not benefit from its cashless feature. A thief who steals a prepaid card that does not require a PIN for its use will be able to use the card, and the original owner will have sustained a loss. Merchants, of course, benefit from prepaid cards whatever their PIN aspect.

PART IV

TRANSPORT AND STORAGE

31

Introduction to Bailments

§31.1 Introduction
§31.2 Scope

§31.1 INTRODUCTION

There is among law teachers and probably not a few lawyers the notion that **bailments** are a rather quaint subject. The older bailment cases and some old treatises treat bailments as largely uncommercial. These feature cases between restaurant patrons who leave a valuable package in a coat pocket and find it missing when they retrieve the coat from the clothes tree or who lose a hat from the hat rack. Others involve claims by a railroad passenger against the railroad when the parties cannot find baggage checked at the depot. These disputes arose in bucolic settings of the late-nineteenth and early-twentieth centuries. They reflect the pastoral era of the nation's history — the era of the railroad and the time when people actually wore hats, as those faded photographs of your grandfather and his friends as boys testify.

In the commercial arena, as opposed to the classroom, however, bailments are anything but quaint. They are an indispensable part of commerce in goods, comprise a vigorous and growing industry, yield enormous efficiencies, and are the subject of rapid and revolutionary technological innovation. The annual volume of international trade in goods is in the trillions of dollars, and most of it involves bailments. Domestic buyers and sellers transport commodities and manufactured goods largely by truck and rail operated by independent carriers. Energy companies transport oil, natural gas, and their derivatives via a network of pipelines that involve a curious blend of storage and transport of those fungible commodities. In short, the quaint old subject of bailments is in fact a giant segment of commercial practice.

§31.2 SCOPE

Part IV deals with some of the merchant and banking practices that relate to that modern giant. Bailments are so essential to commercial practices, however, that carving out a discrete niche for them in this study is a difficult exercise. The fact is that good portions of Part I on Sales and Part II on Secured Lending deal with bailments, for bailments play a crucial role in the marketing and financing of goods. Part III on Payments Systems deals with the collection of drafts that are often accompanied by documents of title, paper that **bailees** issue.

This Part rehearses some of those marketing and financing features of bailments but excludes others. Specifically, this Part will not deal with the documentary draft transaction, which Chapter 4 discusses, the documentary letter of credit transaction, which Chapter 5 discusses, and leasing, which Chapter 9 discusses. The documentary draft and letter of credit transactions arise out of bailments and the **bill of lading** that evidences them, and the lease is itself a bailment.

32

The Documents of Title

§32.1 Kinds of Documents of Title
§32.2 The Contract Function of the Document of Title
§32.3 The Marketing Function of the Document of Title
§32.4 The Financing Function of the Document of Title
§32.5 Bonds and Regulators: Protecting the Public
§32.6 Reification

§32.1 KINDS OF DOCUMENTS OF TITLE

A **document of title** is a piece of paper that a trade or industry treats as evidence of the bailment of goods. That treatment takes different forms. One industry treats possession of the document as the equivalent of possession of the goods. Another treats a document as only evidence that the party holding the document is entitled to delivery of the goods from the bailee who issued the document. Other industries use documents only as presumptive evidence that goods have been shipped.

Documents of title are bound to arise whenever commerce advances beyond the subsistence stage. As producers, manufacturers, and traders generate quantities of goods or produce greater than they can carry with them, they find the need to deposit their goods with third parties. Eventually, the owner's mother gets tired of having all of those carpets in the living room and tells her trader offspring to get that stuff out of the house. Reluctantly, unless he can find a willing friend or another relative with a big house, the trader turns to a commercial bailee, that is, someone who stores the goods for a charge.

In the arms-length bailment, the trader, who is a **bailor,** worries that the bailee may not redeliver the rugs to the trader when he is ready to sell them. Knowing that commercial bailees are not half so reliable as mothers, the cautious trader insists at the time of the bailment that the bailee provide him with a receipt. The receipt, which we now call a **warehouse receipt,** is a document of title.

Traders that transport merchandise themselves do not need to worry about documents of title. Sometimes, however, the trader decides to stay in Kerman and let his nephew in Damascus sell the carpets to those French nobles who want to keep their bare aristocratic feet off the castle's damp stone floors. The Kerman trader, therefore, will entrust the carpets to a friend, perhaps another relative, who will take them on the next caravan to Damascus. Although entrustment to a relative was often safe and perhaps the only safe means of marketing goods through third parties until the advent of modern communications at the end of the nineteenth century, eventually the trader found it efficient to entrust to a stranger who had some extra room on his dromedary and who enjoyed a good reputation. That reputation rested on reliability in (1) safekeeping goods from bandits while the goods were in transit and (2) delivering the goods at the caravan's destination. The cautious trader insisted, however, that the stranger (the carrier) issue a receipt for the carpets. After all, the bandits might not get the carpets or the camel but might get the stranger, and who is to say which carpets were the stranger's and which the Kerman merchant's? This receipt is a bill of lading. Document 32-1 is a non-negotiable truck bill of lading. Document 32-2 is a negotiable truck bill of lading.

In the late middle ages, as commerce grew in importance and volume and gradually replaced agriculture and land ownership as the source of wealth, merchants became frequent travelers. A London merchant might spend as much time in Bristol buying goods as they arrived from Ireland or the American colonies as he did in London arranging for credit from his banker or for sales to his customers. Sooner or later, the merchant would find himself in Bristol when his goods were in London or in London when his goods were in Bristol at a time when he wanted the goods delivered to someone. The goods might be in the hands of a partner, probably a brother, son, or other relative, or they might be in the hands of that stranger bailee.

In all events, the merchant, finding himself in the wrong city, sooner or later would simply issue an order to his bailee to deliver or ship the cotton or the cambric handkerchiefs to a third party, a buyer. The merchant could send the order directly to the bailee or could entrust the order to the buyer. Because merchants knew that the bailee would honor the order, which they came to call a **delivery order,** the buyer was often willing to pay the merchant against surrender of the order. Some American merchants seem to have forgotten the delivery order, though it does appear from time to time in U.S. commerce, recently in connection with electronic cotton warehouse receipts and, traditionally, in the pipeline industry. Document 32-3 is a delivery order used in the transport of imported goods.

There are other kinds of documents of title. Dock warrants or receipts are, as their names suggest, evidence of delivery to a bailee who holds merchandise until it is loaded on a ship. Carriers that accept goods before they are loaded issue **received-for-shipment bills of lading** and **on-board bills of lading** for goods that are on board at the time of issue.

No glossary of document-of-title nomenclature will be complete for long. Merchants are out in the busy world of commerce inventing new documents and discarding others. The delivery order has largely disappeared from the American merchant's consciousness, but the bean industry invented "drafts" for the delivery of beans. No doubt, at this moment, a group of merchants is inventing new uses for old documents and new names for old ones.

There are those who predict that the bill of lading as we now know it is destined for the commercial dustbin. Electronic data interchange (EDI), discussed in more detail in Section 3.6, makes it possible for carriers and their agents to issue electronic bills of lading that may replace the paper bills, which have been a central feature of transport arrangements. Whether the disappearance of the paper bill is imminent or not, the advent of the electronic bill is upon us, as international organizations adopt standards for the new EDI product.

Similarly, successful efforts by the cotton warehouse industry to introduce electronic warehouse receipts may signal the demise of paper warehouse receipts. Until 1995, federal law required warehouse receipts issued by federally licensed cotton warehouses to be in paper form. Those rules have been changed, however, to allow the use of electronically issued receipts, which entail a central filing system that reflects the interest of cotton owners.

Under the system, which is supervised by the United States Department of Agriculture (USDA), a cotton producer may bail his ginned and baled cotton with a warehouse that has qualified under standards set by the USDA and is a licensed participant in the system. The warehouse causes the electronic receipt to issue. The electronic receipt records all the information that would be included in a paper receipt, including the all-important weight of the bale and the tag number issued by the weigh master.

The electronic receipt is issued electronically through the system provider, a computer center that maintains hardware and telecommunications for the system. Once the provider records the issuance of a receipt to the first holder, the first holder transfers the cotton by notifying the provider, who then issues a new receipt electronically to the transferee.

The system allows various parties active in the industry to access it. Thus producers, merchants, governmental agencies, banks, ginners, mills, and of course warehouses may participate as long as they have the necessary computer hardware and software to access the system and, in the case of warehouses, as long as they satisfy USDA requirements.

The system entails security measures. All warehouses that participate must carry fraud and dishonesty insurance as well as errors and omissions policies. Transfer of an electronic receipt from one holder (e.g., the farm producer) to a second holder (e.g., a merchant) involves the use of keys or coded messages from the first holder to the provider. Those keys or codes protect against access to the system by interlopers.

When a holder of the receipt is ready to ship the bales of cotton covered by the receipt to a distant buyer, the holder commands the provider to transfer the receipt back to the warehouse. The holder also sends the warehouse a delivery or shipment order, and the warehouse arranges to deliver the cotton to a common carrier or to the holder's truck, car, barge, or vessel. Upon receipt of the delivery order, the warehouse cancels the receipt.

It is worth mentioning here that the *certificate* of title, which is a creature of modern legislation and which is a piece of paper that is issued by a state official indicating the identity of the owner of goods, such as a motor vehicle, yacht, or aircraft, is not a *document* of title. Certificates of title differ from documents of title in two ways. First, they are not inventions of merchants. They do not serve a private, commercial function. They result from the state's exercise of the police power and serve a public function — identifying the owner of goods for purposes of reducing theft and facilitating licensing and registration. Second, they do not involve any bailment. A document of title, by definition, is issued by a bailee indicating receipt of the goods or is addressed to the bailee directing their delivery.

The function of the certificate of title is to permit the buyer to reregister the vehicle and to obtain a new certificate in the name of his subbuyer. While there has been some confusion over the function of the certificate of title, the courts have generally recognized that the certificate does not stand for the goods, as a negotiable document of title does, and that the delivery of the certificate to the buyer at a used-car auction is a matter of facilitating issuance of the new certificate; it is not a substitute for delivery of the vehicle. Usually, state authorities will not issue a new certificate without surrender of the old one.

§32.2 THE CONTRACT FUNCTION OF THE DOCUMENT OF TITLE

The document of title serves three discrete functions. First, it is similar in nature to a contract, which allocates responsibilities and liabilities between bailor and bailee. A warehouse receipt usually sets out the terms of the warehouse's obligation to store the goods, the charges for that storage, limits on any liability for loss of the goods, and the warehouse's duty to redeliver the goods upon the owner's request and payment of charges. The bill of lading designates the duty of the carrier to transport the goods to a designated destination and specifies, in one form or another, the party to whom the goods are to be delivered at that destination and the party that the carrier is to notify that the goods have arrived.

Bills of lading almost always include disclaimers of liability, so that, for example, a carrier is not liable if the bailor (the **shipper**) does not fill the cartons with the goods it declares are in them. Usually, carriers do not give a warranty as to the content of packages. Carriers transport merchandise not knowing much about the constellation of merchandise and produce they carry — they are not industry inspectors. Other parties, who have industry expertise, perform that function for a fee; and if the buyer wants an inspection certificate, usually it will have to pay for it separately. Formerly, bills of lading usually incorporated charges under a schedule of charges, called a **tariff,** that the carrier filed publicly. With the advent of deregulation in the transport industry, tariffs have become less important.

§32.3 THE MARKETING FUNCTION OF THE DOCUMENT OF TITLE

Warehouse receipts, bills of lading, and delivery orders play an important role in the marketing of goods and commodities. As Chapter 4 explains, the negotiable bill of lading makes the documentary draft transaction work. Because the buyer of goods from a distant seller that the buyer does not trust can rely on the bill as evidence that the goods have been shipped and on accompanying papers as evidence that the goods conform, and because he can rely on the carrier to deliver the goods to the holder of the document, the buyer may safely pay for the goods before they arrive and before he has seen them. The bill reduces risks. Reducing risks reduces costs, to the benefit of all.

The warehouse receipt has in some industries, especially those that involve storage of agricultural or other fungible commodities, also served as a substitute for the goods themselves. Formerly, cotton growers marketed their cotton by storing it with the gin that processed the cotton. The gin would issue a warehouse receipt for each bale of cotton with a sample from the bale stapled to the receipt. The producer or broker that owned the cotton could then take the receipt to market and sell it, often for cash. The buyer would be able to examine a sample of the cotton before paying for it and would be able to take delivery from the gin after paying for it.

Grain producers and brokers use warehouse receipts issued by elevators to market grain. At harvest time, shortages of rolling stock make it expensive and otherwise inconvenient to transport grain commodities to grain consumers (feed lots, chemical companies, distilleries, etc.). The consumers usually do not have sufficient warehouse space to store all of the grain they will need until the next harvest and could not take delivery even if there were sufficient carrier capacity to get it to them. On the grand scale, then, it is best that agricultural commodities are stored and shipped periodically rather than all at once. Thus, farmers often store their grain in a local elevator located alongside a railroad spur.

In the meantime, the owner of the grain, if he feels the price is right and if he needs cash, will want to sell it. Finding a broker, grain merchant, or speculator who wants the grain, the owner can effect the sale by "negotiating" the receipt to the buyer. The seller, a farmer in Iowa with a suntanned visage (from the brow down), and the buyer, a Mercedes owner in Chicago, can consummate the transaction through brokers and can leave the grain at the rail siding on the prairie until the buyer or the grain company or the foreign trading company the buyer resells the grain to wants to take delivery some months later.

Delivery orders are also an effective device for marketing products, though there is evidence that American, as opposed to British, merchants have forgotten about it. The delivery order may be issued by anyone, but usually the buyer or the seller will issue it. The delivery order is similar to a check. Unlike a check, which is an order to pay money drawn on a financial institution, a delivery order is payable in a commodity and is drawn on a bailee of goods.

A dealer in agricultural commodities may have title to 50,000 bushels of potatoes stored in a warehouse in Pocatello, Idaho. If the broker is selling to a soup cannery in Sacramento, he may want to be in a position to sell some of the potatoes promptly. The cannery may be willing to buy but only if it has some assurances that it will receive the potatoes and that the potatoes do indeed exist. If the cannery and the broker strike a deal, either one of them may draw a delivery order on the warehouse. That draw creates the document of title, but the cannery is still concerned that there may not be any potatoes or that the warehouse will not deliver them. The cannery will not be certain that it has avoided those risks until the warehouse "accepts" the delivery order. Upon acceptance, the delivery order is the equivalent of a warehouse receipt. Of course, if the dealer and the cannery have been dealing with each other over a long period of time, the cannery may be willing to pay the dealer against his issuance to the cannery of an unaccepted delivery order.

The warehouse will normally check with the dealer when it receives the delivery order if it is drawn by the cannery. The parties may not use the delivery order as a substitute for delivery of the goods but merely as a method of causing the warehouse to ship the goods to the cannery, in which case, of course, the warehouse will want a delivery order from the dealer or assurances the delivery is authorized.

Note that in the delivery order transaction, there may be several documents of title involved. First, the warehouse will probably issue a non-negotiable warehouse receipt to the dealer. Because the parties anticipate the use of delivery orders, the receipt must be non-negotiable in this case. The warehouse will not deliver potatoes covered by a negotiable receipt unless the holder surrenders the receipt, so negotiable receipts do not work in this transaction. (For discussion of the negotiable document of title and the ways it differs from the non-negotiable document, see Section 32.6.) The second document of title is the delivery order, which may or may not be accepted by the warehouse. There will probably be a third document of title, a truck or a railroad bill of lading that a carrier will issue when the warehouse ships the potatoes to the buyer. Chapter 34 discusses the use of delivery orders in more detail.

The use of electronic bills of lading and electronic warehouse receipts is only partially consistent with the marketing function of the document. Under rules established for the electronically generated documents, a substitute for the traditional paper documents, bailees or their agents may identify the party entitled to obtain the goods from the bailee by virtue of a system of codes or keys. Under the system, the initial holder of the document has a key that is used to notify the issuer of a transfer. Upon such notice, the issuer retires the first holder's key, transfers the electronic document to the new holder, and issues a new key to the new holder. Thus many buyers, who currently take non-negotiable documents, will be able to rely on the issuance of electronic documents when they pay for goods, just as they rely today on the non-negotiable ones. With the electronic document, every transfer is registered with the issuer, who then issues a new document or an acknowledgement of the rights of the transferee. Clearly, the use of the electronic document is compatible with the current use of the non-negotiable document.

For purposes of a good-faith purchase, however, the electronic document poses problems, and most commentators agree that, to the extent that the negotiable document is used in the marketing of goods, the electronic document is no substitute for the paper one. Buyers that agree today to pay against documents expect to receive a piece of paper that stands for the goods without having to inquire into records, authority, and so forth. The fast-paced transfer of negotiable documents standing for fungibles such as grain, ores, and petrochemicals is not possible under the electronic regime. The non-negotiable paper document does not play a role in that kind of regime, however; and the electronic document does not appear destined to play a role in it either.

§32.4 THE FINANCING FUNCTION OF THE DOCUMENT OF TITLE

The third role of documents of title arises when the owner of stored goods or commodities wants to use them as collateral for a loan. That need for financing is usually short term, sometimes for a matter of days, but may, in the case of distilled spirits that are aging, last for years. In all cases, the owner is using the value of the goods to support its note, that is, to make it more marketable with the lender, so that the lender is more likely to take it (i.e., to make the loan) and more likely to take it at an attractive rate.

Importers and other brokers frequently buy shipments of goods whose value far exceeds the capital of the importer itself. The net worth of the borrower in this transaction, the importer, does not justify the amount of the loan it needs to finance its purchase of the shipment. A broker importing a supertanker of North Sea crude will need millions of dollars to pay its seller and may not be able to resell the oil until it arrives in, say, Bayonne. Someone will have to finance the transaction while the commodity is on the North Atlantic and, maybe, for a period of time while the oil is stored at a tank farm in Bayonne. Because the price of commodities fluctuates daily, there are some risks involved in financing this transaction, but generally the importer will be able to use the value of the oil so that a lender will advance it a significant portion, if not all, of the purchase price.

Remember, the importer knows the U.S. petroleum markets and probably has arranged to purchase the oil from a foreign seller at a price below the U.S. market price. If the foreign seller's price is $10 million, chances are that the value of the oil in the U.S. is above that amount. It would not be impossible, then, for a financial institution or other investor to lend virtually the entire purchase price to the broker, as long as the lender took back as collateral for repayment of the loan a security interest in the oil.

Because a negotiable bill of lading issued by the carrier stands for the oil and because the law generally provides that the supertanker must deliver the oil only to the person who holds the bill of lading, lenders are willing to make the loan in return for possession of the bill with the understanding that if the importer does not repay the loan, the lender will take delivery of the oil, sell it, and use the proceeds to satisfy the loan balance.

Thus, the parties may anticipate that the importer will not repay the loan until it resells the oil, and the parties may know that the resale will not occur until a period of time after it arrives. In that event, the parties arrange for the substitution of one document of title for another.

When the tanker docks in Bayonne, the lender, through its agent or, if it trusts the importer, through the importer itself, will deliver the bill of lading to the tanker and order delivery to a tank storage facility, which issues a new document of title, a warehouse receipt covering the oil. By taking possession of that receipt, the lender uses it to protect its interest in the oil. If the importer defaults after the oil is stored in the tanks, the lender surrenders the receipt to the tank farm against delivery of the oil, which the lender then sells, using the proceeds to satisfy the loan balance.

The use of the bill of lading to finance the sale and transport of goods depends to a considerable extent on the negotiability of the document. Negotiability in turn depends on the reification concept explained in Section 32.6. The process of inquiring into the identity of people sending messages and correcting unauthorized communications, or the process of making any inquiries of a central recordkeeper (all of which are probably necessary under electronically issued bills of lading or other documents of title) renders the EDI documents of title ill-suited to the negotiability functions of documents.

Under rules established for electronically issued bills of lading, the carrier can issue a bill electronically from its office to the computer terminal of any interested party. EDI bills, however, by definition are not in paper form and do not admit of easy transfer without notice to the issuer and subsequent reissuance or transfer acknowledgement. Most commentators are in agreement, therefore, that an electronic bill of lading cannot be negotiable and cannot serve the good-faith purchase functions of the negotiable bill. Electronic bills of lading, then, pose serious problems for those merchants that want to use the goods they are selling or shipping to finance the transaction.

Similarly, truncation of documents of title poses a problem for negotiability. Under truncation, the carrier issues a negotiable bill of lading in paper form in the name of the holder but delivers the bill to a central recorder of some kind, probably a bank. When the holder wants to transfer the bill to a buyer or a bank, the holder notifies electronically the central recorder who then acknowledges the transfer electronically. Ultimately, the goods arrive at their destination, and the carrier delivers them to the party to whom the recorder's record indicates delivery should be made.

While these electronic innovations are efficient in some contexts, they are not suitable to the use of goods-in-transit as collateral for advances or to the traditional payment-against-documents sale. Some writers argue that the use of goods in this fashion is diminishing in any event, and that the failure of the electronic document or truncation to satisfy good-faith purchase needs does not render it impracticable in the marketplace. That point is probably well taken. The electronic bill's failure to satisfy negotiability concerns does not render it unfit to serve the function of the non-negotiable document, the document to which it is a true analogue.

That is not to suggest that the non-negotiable bill of lading plays no role in international trade in general and in North Atlantic trade in particular. To the contrary, there is evidence that the use of the non-negotiable bill, sometimes referred to as a "waybill," is appearing with increased frequency in that trade. If the commercial parties know each other and do not need to finance the goods during transit, negotiability is not necessary and can even be unattractive. Carriers require indemnity when a party loses a negotiable bill but will deliver cargo covered by a non-negotiable bill against the consignor's instructions. As enterprises come to know and rely on each other, they will not need the protection of the negotiable bill; neither will the banks need it if they are not financing the transaction. There is increasing evidence that larger enterprises are now using a freight forwarder's receipt, a kind of non-negotiable bill of lading, in their international sales transactions.

§32.5 BONDS AND REGULATORS: PROTECTING THE PUBLIC

This discussion should conjure up in the reader's mind all sorts of analogies between bailees and banks. Warehouse receipts and bills of lading are to bailments what certificates of deposit are to banking. Bailments resemble deposits. Delivery orders are analogous to checks and drafts; accepted delivery orders to certified checks. Documents of title are "commodity" paper, paper that stands for an obligation to deliver a commodity; checks, notes, and drafts are financial paper, paper that stands for an obligation to pay money.

In both of these systems, the reliability of the paper depends in part on the financial strength of the issuer. Certified checks lose their attractiveness if the bank that certifies is insolvent. Warehouse receipts lose their value if the market has doubts about the integrity of the warehouse. It would not advance commerce if any dishonest warehouse operator could issue a warehouse receipt for phantom goods and sell them to a gullible market. The states and the federal government have enacted legislation regulating bailees and providing for unannounced audits similar to those conducted by state and federal bank examiners.

Not all audits are successful, however. In the past, bailors have issued receipts for commodities they did not receive, and from time to time we read in the newspapers of insolvent grain elevators that have sold grain that they were supposed to be holding and of vegetable oil tank farms that fooled auditors by filling tanks with water and a film of oil. Insurance can, of course, protect against some of these losses, and some states have established insurance funds to protect bailors and others who sustain losses as a consequence of a bailee's overissuance of documents of title.

The bailment system is like the banking system. It works only as long as commodity paper is sound. To some extent the market assures that soundness. By accepting paper issued by bailees of good repute and rejecting paper issued by those without it, the market fosters good bailment practices. The market has not proved a sufficient policeman by itself, however. To a degree the state must regulate bailees as it regulates financial institutions.

§32.6 REIFICATION

The law merchant long ago accepted the idea that a piece of paper can embody an obligation. A negotiable draft was not merely a contract, not simply evidence of the underlying obligation, it was the obligation itself, and transfer of it constituted transfer of the obligation. This is the merchant idea of reification, and it was and to some extent still is indispensable to some branches of commerce.

For documents of title, reification is the notion that the document stands for the goods. In fact, when a negotiable document of title issues, the goods cease to exist and become "mere simulacra" — a mere shadow. As long as the negotiable document remains outstanding, anyone desiring to deal with the goods must deal with the document.

Note that this reification notion serves the marketing and financing functions of the document but is not necessary for the contract function. Commercial parties that are not interested in using the document for financing or marketing purposes may decide that they do not want to bother with a document that stands for the goods. Thus for these parties the electronically generated bill of lading and the electronically issued warehouse receipt are satisfactory.

There are serious problems with documents that stand for the goods. First, the bailee will not deliver goods subject to such a document without its surrender. If bailees delivered goods without obtaining and canceling the document, no one could rely on the document, and it would lose its reification character. In many transactions, surrender of the document becomes problematic. If a Los Angeles seller of goods transports them to his Boston buyer by a carrier that issues a document that stands for the goods, the seller will have to get the document to Boston in order for the buyer to take delivery when the goods arrive. Getting the document to Boston may not be easy, quick, or inexpensive. If the goods travel by air they may well arrive before the document. Sometimes, documents are lost or stolen. Buyers of goods can arrange to indemnify a carrier against loss incurred by the carrier's delivery of goods without surrender of the document. A bank indemnification agreement can be used by a buyer who wants to take delivery of goods from a carrier without surrendering all copies of a bill of lading that is issued in multiple originals. Indemnification bonds and the like are expensive, however, and procuring them takes time.

In order to avoid the transaction costs that lost or delayed documents entail, merchants decided that it would be advantageous to create a document of title that did not stand for the goods. This document is evidence of a shipment or of a storage contract. It often is sufficient to satisfy a buyer that goods have been shipped or stored and sometimes is satisfactory evidence for lenders. Above all, it is evidence of the bailment, and governs the contractual relationship between the bailor and the bailee. Merchants called this modified document of title "non-negotiable" in order to distinguish it from the document that embodies the goods. In the transport industry, parties take some pains to distinguish negotiable and non-negotiable bills of lading. The negotiable bill is an "order" bill, the non-negotiable bill a "straight" bill.

Document 32-1. Truck Bill of Lading (Non-negotiable)

OP-097 11/95

FREIGHT CHARGES ARE COLLECT UNLESS MARKED PREPAID BELOW

☐ STRAIGHT BILL OF LADING—ORIGINAL—NOT NEGOTIABLE

ROADWAY

ROADWAY EXPRESS, INC. (RDWY)
GENERAL OFFICES: AKRON, OHIO
(DUNS 00-699-8397)

DATE _____ PRO. NO. _____

B/L NO. _____ PAGE _____

THANK YOU FOR USING ROADWAY.

USE THE *ROADWAY VOICE RESPONSE SYSTEM*
FOR TRACING, ROUTING, RATE AND CLAIM INQUIRIES,
AND THE LATEST ROADWAY NEWS.

CALL 1-800-ROADWAY
(1-800-762-3929)

SHIPPER NO.	TRAILER NO.		CONSIGNEE NAME AND ADDRESS		
SHIPPER NAME					
ADDRESS					
CITY	STATE	ZIP CODE	DESTINATION CITY	STATE	ZIP CODE
ORIGIN CITY (IF DIFFERENT THAN ABOVE)	STATE	ZIP CODE	PHONE NO.		

INVOICEE			CUSTOMER NO.	STORE NO.	DEPT.
ADDRESS			P.O. NO.		
CITY	STATE	ZIP CODE	SPECIAL INSTRUCTIONS		
ATTN.					

NOTICE: FREIGHT MOVING UNDER THIS BILL OF LADING IS SUBJECT TO TARIFFS ON FILE WITH THE INTERSTATE COMMERCE COMMISSION OR MAINTAINED AT THE CARRIER'S PRINCIPAL PLACE OF BUSINESS. THIS NOTICE SUPERSEDES AND NEGATES ANY CLAIMED ORAL OR WRITTEN CONTRACT PROMISE, REPRESENTATION, OR UNDERSTANDING BETWEEN THE PARTIES, EXCEPT TO THE EXTENT OF ANY WRITTEN CONTRACT SIGNED BY BOTH PARTIES TO THE CONTRACT.

COD FEE PREPAID ☐ COLLECT ☐ **COD AMT** $ _____

CUSTOMER CHECK OK FOR COD AMOUNT? YES ☐ NO ☐

NO. SHPNG UNITS	KIND OF PKG	HM	DESCRIPTION OF ARTICLES, SPECIAL MARKS, AND EXCEPTIONS	NMFC ITEM NO.	CLASS	WEIGHT (LB) SUBJ. TO CORR.	RATE	CHARGES CARRIER USE ONLY

HAZARDOUS MATERIALS EMERGENCY CONTACT NUMBER:

NOTE—WHEN THE RATE IS DEPENDENT ON VALUE, SHIPPERS ARE REQUIRED TO STATE SPECIFICALLY IN WRITING THE AGREED OR DECLARED VALUE OF THE PROPERTY.

THE AGREED OR DECLARED VALUE OF THE PROPERTY IS HEREBY SPECIFICALLY STATED BY THE SHIPPER TO BE NOT EXCEEDING.

$ _____ PER _____

RECEIVED, SUBJECT TO THE CLASSIFICATIONS AND LAWFULLY FILED TARIFFS IN EFFECT ON THE DATE OF THE ISSUE OF THIS BILL OF LADING, THE PROPERTY DESCRIBED ABOVE IN APPARENT GOOD ORDER, EXCEPT AS NOTED (CONTENTS AND CONDITION OF CONTENTS OF PACKAGES UNKNOWN), MARKED, CONSIGNED, AND DESTINED, AS INDICATED ABOVE WHICH SAID CARRIER (THE WORD CARRIER BEING UNDERSTOOD THROUGHOUT THIS CONTRACT AS MEANING ANY PERSON OR CORPORATION IN POSSESSION OF THE PROPERTY UNDER THE CONTRACT) AGREES TO CARRY TO ITS USUAL PLACE OF DELIVERY OF SAID DESTINATION, IF ON ITS ROUTE, OTHERWISE TO DELIVER TO

I HEREBY DECLARE THAT THE CONTENTS OF THIS CONSIGNMENT ARE FULLY AND ACCURATELY DESCRIBED ABOVE BY PROPER SHIPPING NAME AND ARE CLASSIFIED, PACKED, MARKED AND LABELLED PLACARDED AND ARE IN ALL RESPECTS IN PROPER CONDITION FOR TRANSPORT ACCORDING TO APPLICABLE INTERNATIONAL AND NATIONAL GOVERNMENTAL REGULATIONS.

FREIGHT CHARGES ARE:
☐ COLLECT ☐ PREPAID

TOTAL CHARGES $

SUBJECT TO SECTION 7 OF CONDITIONS, IF THIS SHIPMENT IS TO BE DELIVERED TO THE CONSIGNEE WITHOUT RECOURSE ON THE CONSIGNOR, THE CONSIGNOR SHALL SIGN THE FOLLOWING STATEMENT

THE CARRIER SHALL NOT MAKE DELIVERY OF THIS SHIPMENT WITHOUT PAYMENT OF FREIGHT AND ALL OTHER LAWFUL CHARGES.

SIGNATURE OF CONSIGNOR _____

ANOTHER CARRIER ON THE ROUTE TO SAID DESTINATION. IT IS MUTUALLY AGREED AS TO EACH CARRIER OF ALL OR ANY OF SAID PROPERTY OVER ALL OR ANY PORTION OF SAID ROUTE TO DESTINATION AND AS TO EACH PARTY AT ANY TIME INTERESTED IN ALL OR ANY OF SAID PROPERTY THAT EVERY SERVICE TO BE PERFORMED HEREUNDER SHALL BE SUBJECT TO ALL THE CONDITIONS NOT PROHIBITED BY LAW WHETHER PRINTED OR WRITTEN, HEREIN CONTAINED INCLUDING THE CONDITIONS ON THE BACK HEREOF, WHICH ARE HEREBY AGREED TO BY THE SHIPPER AND ACCEPTED FOR HIMSELF AND HIS ASSIGNS

SHIPPER	CARRIER **ROADWAY EXPRESS, INC.**	
PER	PER SPECIMEN DATE	H/U RECEIVED

1 MARK "X" IN "HM" COLUMN FOR HAZARDOUS MATERIAL

SINGLE SHIPMENT PICKUP ☐

Reprinted with the permission of Roadway Express, Inc. Only the front page of the document is reproduced.

Document 32-2.   Truck Bill of Lading (Negotiable)

OP-098 6/94

FREIGHT CHARGES ARE PREPAID UNLESS MARKED COLLECT

☐   ORDER NOTIFY BILL OF LADING—ORIGINAL—DOMESTIC

ROADWAY EXPRESS, INC. (RDWY)
●GENERAL OFFICES: AKRON, OH   (DUNS 00-699-8397)

DATE _____   PRO. NO. _____

B/L NO. _____   PAGE _____

THANK YOU FOR USING ROADWAY.

USE THE *ROADWAY VOICE RESPONSE SYSTEM*
FOR TRACING, ROUTING, RATE AND CLAIM INQUIRIES,
AND THE LATEST ROADWAY NEWS.

CALL 1-800-ROADWAY
(1-800-762-3929)

SHIPPER NO.	TRAILER NO.	CONSIGNED TO ORDER OF		
SHIPPER NAME		ADDRESS		
ADDRESS				
CITY	STATE ZIP CODE	DESTINATION CITY	STATE	ZIP CODE
ORIGIN CITY *(IF DIFFERENT THAN ABOVE)*	ZIP CODE	NOTIFY *(NAME)*		
SPECIAL INSTRUCTIONS		ADDRESS	CITY	
		PHONE NO.	CUSTOMER NO.	
		P.O. NO.	STORE NO.	DEPT.

NOTICE: FREIGHT MOVING UNDER THIS BILL OF LADING IS SUBJECT TO TARIFFS ON FILE WITH THE INTERSTATE COMMERCE COMMISSION. THIS NOTICE SUPERSEDES AND NEGATES ANY CLAIMED ORAL OR WRITTEN CONTRACT, PROMISE, REPRESENTATION, OR UNDERSTANDING BETWEEN THE PARTIES, EXCEPT TO THE EXTENT OF ANY WRITTEN CONTRACT SIGNED BY BOTH PARTIES TO THE CONTRACT.

NO. SHPNG UNITS	KIND OF PKG	HM	DESCRIPTION OF ARTICLES, SPECIAL MARKS, AND EXCEPTIONS	NMFC ITEM NO.	CLASS	WEIGHT (LB) SUBJ. TO CORR.	RATE	CHARGES CARRIER USE ONLY

HAZARDOUS MATERIALS
EMERGENCY CONTACT NUMBER:

NOTE—WHEN THE RATE IS DEPENDENT ON VALUE, SHIPPERS ARE REQUIRED TO STATE SPECIFICALLY IN WRITING THE AGREED OR DECLARED VALUE OF THE PROPERTY.

THE AGREED OR DECLARED VALUE OF THE PROPERTY IS HEREBY SPECIFICALLY STATED BY THE SHIPPER TO BE NOT EXCEEDING:

$ _____ PER _____

FREIGHT CHARGES ARE PREPAID UNLESS MARKED COLLECT.
CHECK BOX IF CHARGES ARE *COLLECT* ☐

TOTAL
CHARGES $

SUBJECT TO SECTION 7 OF CONDITIONS, IF THIS SHIPMENT IS TO BE DELIVERED TO THE CONSIGNEE WITHOUT RECOURSE ON THE CONSIGNOR, THE CONSIGNOR SHALL SIGN THE FOLLOWING STATEMENT:

THE CARRIER SHALL NOT MAKE DELIVERY OF THIS STATEMENT WITHOUT PAYMENT OF FREIGHT AND ALL OTHER LAWFUL CHARGES.

SIGNATURE OF CONSIGNOR:

RECEIVED, SUBJECT TO THE CLASSIFICATIONS AND LAWFULLY FILED TARIFFS IN EFFECT ON THE DATE OF THE ISSUE OF THIS BILL OF LADING, THE PROPERTY DESCRIBED ABOVE AND IN APPARENT GOOD ORDER, EXCEPT AS NOTED (CONTENTS AND CONDITION OF CONTENTS OF PACKAGES UNKNOWN), MARKED, CONSIGNED, AND DESTINED, AS INDICATED ABOVE WHICH SAID CARRIER (THE WORD CARRIER BEING UNDERSTOOD THROUGHOUT THIS CONTRACT AS MEANING ANY PERSON OR CORPORATION IN POSSESSION OF THE PROPERTY UNDER THE CONTRACT) AGREES TO CARRY TO ITS USUAL PLACE OF DELIVERY OF SAID DESTINATION, IF ON ITS ROUTE, OTHERWISE TO DELIVER TO

ANOTHER CARRIER ON THE ROUTE TO SAID DESTINATION. IT IS MUTUALLY AGREED AS TO EACH CARRIER OF ALL OR ANY OF SAID PROPERTY OVER ALL OR ANY PORTION OF SAID ROUTE TO DESTINATION AND AS TO EACH PARTY AT ANY TIME INTERESTED IN ALL OR ANY OF SAID PROPERTY, THAT EVERY SERVICE TO BE PERFORMED HEREUNDER SHALL BE SUBJECT TO ALL THE CONDITIONS NOT PROHIBITED BY LAW, WHETHER PRINTED OR WRITTEN, HEREIN CONTAINED, INCLUDING THE CONDITIONS ON THE BACK HEREOF, WHICH ARE HEREBY AGREED TO BY THE SHIPPER AND ACCEPTED FOR HIMSELF AND HIS ASSIGNS.

THIS IS TO CERTIFY THAT THE ABOVE NAMED MATERIALS ARE PROPERLY CLASSIFIED, DESCRIBED, PACKAGED, MARKED, AND LABELED AND ARE IN PROPER CONDITION FOR TRANSPORTATION ACCORDING TO THE APPLICABLE REGULATIONS OF THE DEPARTMENT OF TRANSPORTATION.

SHIPPER	CARRIER ROADWAY EXPRESS, INC.		
PER	PER SPECIMEN DATE	PIECES RECEIVED	

1

MARK "X" IN "HM" COLUMN FOR HAZARDOUS MATERIALS
THE SURRENDER OF THE ORIGINAL ORDER NOTIFY BILL OF LADING PROPERLY ENDORSED SHALL BE REQUIRED BEFORE THE DELIVERY OF THE PROPERTY. INSPECTION OF THE PROPERTY COVERED BY THE BILL OF LADING WILL NOT BE PERMITTED UNLESS PROVIDED BY LAW OR UNLESS PERMISSION IS ENDORSED ON THE ORIGINAL BILL OF LADING OR GIVEN IN WRITING BY THE SHIPPER.

SINGLE SHIPMENT ☐
PICKUP

Reprinted with the permission of Roadway Express, Inc. Only the front page of the document is reproduced.

ENTRY NO.

DATE | OUR REF NO

| IMPORTING CARRIER | LOCATION | FROM PORT OF ORIGIN AIRPORT |
| B L OR AWB NO | ARRIVAL DATE | FREE TIME EXP | LOCAL DELIVERY OR TRANSFER BY (DELIVERY ORDER ISSUED TO) |

THIS DOCUMENT, ALTHOUGH A CARBON COPY IS AN ORIGINAL DELIVERY ORDER AND THE ONLY ORIGINAL DELIVERY ORDER PRODUCED TO COVER RELEASE OF THIS MERCHANDISE. IT IS VALID WHEN IT CONTAINS AN ORIGINAL SIGNATURE.

DELIVERY CLERK: PLEASE DELIVER TO

| MARKS & NOS. | DESCRIPTION & WT. |

SPECIMEN

| CUSTOMS PERMIT | LODGED WITH | PKG NOS HELD BY U S CUSTOMS—TO FOLLOW | GO # |
| ☐ ATTACHED | ☐ U.S. CUSTOMS | | |

ORIGINAL DELIVERY ORDER

PER

Form 15-515 Printed and Sold by UNZCO 190 Baldwin Ave., Jersey City, NJ 07306 • (800) 631-3098 • (201) 795-5400

DELIVERY CLERK: ALL DEMURRAGE FOR ACCOUNT OF DRAWEE OF THIS ORDER

ORIGINAL

Reprinted with the permission of Unz & Co., 700 Central Ave, New Providence, NJ 07974-1139.

Using the Warehouse Receipt

§33.1   STORING DOMESTIC GOODS

John and Mary face retirement with a measure of optimism. They have worked hard most of their lives, raised two children, paid off a mortgage, and purchased a mobile home that will permit them to see the country they never had time or spare money to see. They sell the house and set off for two years of travel to the Grand Canyon, Alaska, and the Great Lakes. When they finish their travels, they plan to buy a condominium in Florida and move into it. Until then, for the next couple of years, they will store their household goods in a warehouse. Their contract of storage is set out in the warehouse receipt the warehouse company issues them.

Note that this receipt is important to the relationship between the couple and the warehouse, but it will probably not be of concern to third parties. No one anticipates that John and Mary will use this receipt as collateral for a loan or that they will sell their furnishings by selling the receipt. If they lose the receipt, the warehouse will still deliver the goods to them when they return from their travels, provided, of course, that they pay the storage charges. This receipt is non-negotiable, and the warehouse may not even require its surrender upon redelivery of the furnishings. The warehouse may require John or Mary to sign a receipt acknowledging that

Figure 33-1. Consumer Bailment

redelivery, however. Figure 33-1 illustrates this simple and common bailment.

§33.2 STORING AGRICULTURAL PRODUCTS

It would be nice if each month farmers produced commodities in quantities that approximated the market's needs for the next month. Food brokers and processors could then adopt just-in-time inventory controls and save lots of money for themselves and their customers. Unfortunately, farm production does not work that way. Each fall, farmers harvest billions of bushels of grain and legumes, and the industry must accommodate itself to storage of those commodities while they are consumed over the entire year.

Grain elevators, maintained across the nation's grain belt, store the commodities until grain companies, processors, and chemical producers need them. Farmers traditionally deliver the grain to the elevator in their own trucks. The elevators, located along a railroad siding, load the grain onto rolling stock for shipment when the time comes.

In the interim, the grain owners, the farmers themselves, or the elevator, which may purchase some grain for its own account, may want to sell the grain or borrow against it.

If the farmer holds the receipts, he can use them to sell the grain himself, by indorsing the receipts and selling them through a broker. The broker relies on the receipt and takes delivery of the grain later or resells the grain by transferring (negotiating) the receipt to a buyer. During these transactions, the grain, having been dried and stored in a clean elevator, remains out on the prairie free from insects, rodents, mold, and other deleterious effects. It all works rather well. Document 33-1 is an example of a negotiable warehouse receipt, and Figure 33-2 illustrates a transaction with multiple buyers.

§33.3 THE TERMINAL WAREHOUSE

Some middlemen (brokers, dealers, jobbers, and the like) purchase goods or commodities that are in transit. These buyers do not usually have warehouse capacity of their own and must turn the goods around, that is,

Figure 33.2.   Marketing Grain

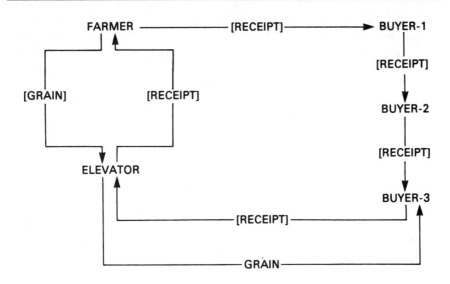

find a buyer for them, quickly. Sometimes, they do not find a buyer who can take delivery when the goods arrive at their destination, and in that case it is necessary for the middleman to store the goods until it does find a buyer. **Terminal warehouses,** often located along rail lines in metropolitan areas, provide a way for the middleman to take delivery of the goods from the carrier and store them during that period. Often, though not always, the terminal warehouse will issue a receipt for the goods. Sometimes the bailor and the warehouse will enter into a warehouse agreement, a contract.

§33.4 THE FIELD WAREHOUSE

While the terminal warehouse, being located at the railroad terminal, requires the owner of goods to get them to the warehouse, the **field warehouse** industry takes the warehouse to the goods; hence its name. This warehouse is in the field. Field warehousing occurs when an owner of goods desires to finance them with a seller or an institutional lender of some kind. The creditor, in these transactions, is uneasy about leaving the goods in the borrower's control. Generally, commercial law protects buyers of goods from merchants. Those buyers usually take from the merchant free and clear of any security interest, even when that interest is perfected. Lenders are aware of that rule, and sometimes they are unwilling to make a loan unless they can deprive the borrower of the power to sell the goods. The field warehouse is an efficient and rather ingenious device for effecting that deprivation.

321

In the field warehouse, the owner of the goods usually has them stored at its own facility. A distiller may have thousands of barrels of aging whiskey stored in its own warehouse. The distiller does not want to sell the whiskey until it has aged sufficiently and may need to use it as collateral for a bank loan. By turning its own warehouses into a field warehouse, it can effectively deprive itself of possession of that collateral and satisfy the bank's concerns that the distiller not be able to sell the whiskey to a buyer who would have greater rights in it than the bank. Seller-creditors can use the field warehouse to similar effect.

A sawmill that sells millions of board feet of lumber to a lumber company on credit may not want the buyer to be in a position to resell the lumber to sub-buyers without the mill's permission. In this case, the lumber company turns its sheds and open storage areas into a field warehouse, depriving the lumber company of the ability to sell the lumber.

In these illustrations, the owner of the collateral, the distiller or the lumber company, enters into a lease of its own premises with the field warehouse company. The field warehouse company then takes possession of the premises, the warehouse of aging whiskey or the sheds of lumber, and locks them up. The warehouse company usually then issues a non-negotiable warehouse receipt in favor of the creditor, the bank in the first illustration, the sawmill in the second.

At this point, the creditor is in possession of the collateral through an agent, the field warehouse. When the owner wants to sell some of the collateral, it must seek the creditor's permission. If some of the whiskey has aged sufficiently and is ready for bottling, the distiller asks the bank to release a certain number of barrels from the warehouse. The bank usually issues a delivery order to the field warehouse authorizing the delivery. Since the whiskey is covered by a non-negotiable receipt, it is not necessary for the bank to surrender any documents to the warehouse. A distiller in Kentucky, therefore, may do business with a bank in New York, and the bank can issue its delivery orders over the phone or by other teletransmission. The creditor, of course, does not authorize the deliveries if the borrower is in arrears on its loan or is otherwise in default on its loan agreement. The arrangement gives the creditor a measure of protection that a nonpossessory security interest does not give it.

There is a danger in the field warehouse transaction that the field warehouse employee will deliver goods when he is not supposed to. Often, the field warehouse employs as its man on the spot an inventory control officer of the borrower. In the sawmill example, the field warehouse may take the yard manager off the lumber company's payroll and put him on the warehouse company's payroll. The parties guard against the yard manager's malfeasance by bonding him. In the event the manager delivers lumber without having a delivery order or other authorization from the creditor, the unpaid sawmill, the bonding company will make good the sawmill's losses.

There is also danger in the field warehouse arrangement that the borrower will circumvent the field warehouse's security measures. Grain elevator operators have been known to "hot wire" locked-up augurs and empty a grain elevator while the field warehouse managers are miles away. Similarly, sawmill operators can cut through chain link fences and disarm burglar alarms in order to remove collateral from the field warehouse and sell it. Such activity, of course, is unlawful, but business people desperate for cash to save their businesses have done worse.

Note also that there is a considerable measure of activity in the field warehouse transaction. First, there is paperwork: the lease, the change in the yard manager's employment, the warehouse receipt, and delivery orders. All of this documentation results in costs that are, in the last analysis, borne by the borrower. It is in the best interests of the borrower to find a lender or a seller that will extend credit without any field warehouse. The borrower, whose credit is good enough and reputation strong enough that its creditors are willing to trust it, is going to save field warehousing costs. On the other hand, the costs of the field warehouse may not be too great for the new entrant or the troubled business to pay when no one will extend it credit otherwise. Figure 14-7 illustrates the field warehouse transaction.

Unfortunately, recent liberalization of liability rules has rendered field warehouses common targets for banks and finance companies that lend and then find that the borrower has thwarted the field warehouse's security measures, taken the goods, and sold them. The number of active field warehouse companies has diminished, and the amount of field warehousing has fallen to a level that may not sustain the industry. The idea is a good one, however, and it is probably only a matter of time and a matter of forging more realistic liability rules until borrowers and lenders find a need once again for the field warehouse.

One law teacher (me) announced the demise of the field warehouse industry altogether only to hear from a lawyer that his client, a bank, had set up a field warehouse in Helsinki for Mercedes Benz automobiles that the bank was financing for a Mercedes dealer in St. Petersburg. When the dealer found a customer in Russia and received the money, the dealer repaid the bank's loan on the vehicle; and the bank ordered the field warehouse to deliver the vehicle to the dealer.

VAN DE HOGEN MATERIAL HANDLING INC.
2590 Dougall Avenue
Windsor, Ontario N8X 1T7

RECEIPT NO.

N

_____ 19____

THIS IS TO CERTIFY that we have received in Storage Warehouse, _____

for the Account of _____

NUMBER	PACKAGES	SAID TO BE OR CONTAIN	MARKS

EX.

Storage _____ per _____ per month from _____ 19____

Handling _____ per _____ in and out inclusive

UNDER THE FOLLOWING CONDITIONS: — The above described property subject to all terms and conditions contained herein and on the reverse hereof, such property to be delivered to _____ order, upon the payment of all charges, and the surrender of this Warehouse Receipt properly endorsed.

NEGOTIABLE

VAN DE HOGEN MATERIAL HANDLING INC.

claims a lien for all lawful charges for storage and preservation of the goods, also for all lawful claims for money advanced, interest, insurance, transportation, labour, weighing, coopering, and other charges and expenses in relation to such goods.

VAN DE HOGEN MATERIAL

BY _____

Herald Press Ltd. 31691

SPECIMEN SPECIMEN

Reprinted with the permission of Van de Hogen Material Handling, Inc.

324

Document 33-1. (continued)

The goods mentioned below are hereby released from this receipt for delivery from warehouse. Any unreleased balance of the goods is subject to a lien for unpaid charges and advances on the released portion.

DELIVERIES

DATE	QUANTITY RELEASED		SIGNATURE	QUANTITY DUE ON RECEIPT

LIABILITY — (a) The warehouseman is liable for damage for loss of or injury to the goods caused by its failure to exercise such care and diligence in regard to the goods as a careful and vigilant owner of similar goods would exercise in the custody of them in similar circumstances, but unless otherwise agreed in writing, it is not liable for damages which could not have been avoided by the exercise of such care. The warehouseman shall not be liable for loss damage, delay or demurrage caused by acts of God, civil or military authority, insurrection, riot, strikes, picketing, any other labour trouble, disturbance or interference of whatever cause or nature, whether primary, secondary or tertiary etc., or enemies of the government, or by odors, sprinkler leakage, flood, wind, storm, fire, moths corruption or depredation by rats, mice, insects, parasites or other vermin, or by any other cause beyond the control of the warehouseman or by any cause not originated in the warehouse. No liability is, or will be attributed to or assumed by the warehouseman for loss of weight, for breakage, or for insufficient cooperage, boxing, crating, car bracing, bagging or packing or for wear and tear. The warehouseman shall not be held responsible for loss of goods by leakage or through failure to detect same or for concealed damage. All storage and handling charges must be paid on goods lost or damaged.

(b) The Warehouseman shall not be responsible for any seizure of goods by any court, agency, agent or officer of the federal, state or local government.

LIMITATION OF LIABILITY - THE LIABILITY OF THE WAREHOUSEMAN AS TO EACH ARTICLE ITEM OR UNIT STORED IS LIMITED TO THE ACTUAL VALUE OF SUCH ARTICLE, ITEM OR UNIT.

CLAIMS AND SUITES - (a) The warehouseman shall not be liable for any loss or damage unless the claim therefore has been presented in writing within a reasonable time, and, in any event, not later than thirty (30) days from the date of shipment from the warehouse or, within thirty (30) days from the date the storer requested delivery in the event that shipment is not made. Such notice of claim shall be presented to the warehouseman in person, or by certified mail.

(b) No action at law or in equity shall be brought in connection with any loss or damage prior to the expiration of sixty (60) days after presentation of claim therefor, nor shall such action be brought at all unless brought within one year from the expiration of the sixty day period last mentioned.

34

Using the Delivery Order

§34.1 IN GENERAL

Delivery orders are curious in a number of ways. They can arise out of nonbailment situations, may be issued by strangers to a bailment, are transformed at times by acceptance into warehouse receipts, and sometimes the parties use them when the original bailee has not issued a document of title.

Delivery orders can occur in any transaction involving the storage of goods, whether as a bailment with a third-party bailee or as an on-premises storage arrangement. In a sense, whenever a sales officer of a company issues directions to the plant or warehouse for the delivery of product to a customer, that officer has issued a delivery order.

Delivery orders are somewhat unique in that anybody may issue one. A stranger to the bailment may issue the delivery order, and sometimes the bailee will obey it. Most of the time, the bailor or its agent issues the delivery order. In any case, whether the bailee will honor the delivery order is far more important than the identity of the issuer, though at times the unaccepted delivery order may be valuable to a holder. Generally, a party that issues a delivery order stands behind it if the bailee dishonors.

Delivery orders may be negotiable or non-negotiable. The delivery order that begins as non-negotiable becomes, on acceptance, a non-negotiable warehouse receipt; while the delivery order issued in negotiable form becomes, on acceptance, a negotiable warehouse receipt.

§34.2 BILL-AND-HOLD SALES

In some industries, the textile industry being an example, manufacturers tool up for a product once a year and make a short production run. Customers that expect to use such a product during that year must place early orders and then hope that they find sufficient business to satisfy their projections. Because manufacturers in these industries are financially strong relative to their customers, they are in a position to dictate these early-order arrangements. The system is optimal, however, since it keeps the down time of the producer's plant to a minimum. The program has much the same inefficient effect, however, that the seasonal harvest has on the agricultural commodity industry. It leaves a large surplus of goods at the beginning of the selling season, a surplus that must be stored.

Manufacturers relieve some of the burden the short production run imposes on their customers by selling the product on a bill-and-hold basis. Under this marketing arrangement, the producer enters into a contract with each of its customers at the time the customer orders the merchandise and before the producer manufactures it. After production, the producer holds the product at its mill and bills the customer. The customer, not having much or any warehouse space of its own, leaves the product at the mill until it needs it.

This situation lends itself to the delivery order. If the customer decides that it needs 25 percent of its order in April, it issues a delivery order to the mill directing delivery during that month to the customer's facility or to the plant of the customer's sub-buyer. Sometimes, the customer sells the goods to a third party before the third party wants to take delivery. In that case, the third party or the customer may issue a delivery order to the mill. Note that the mill may not know whether to honor the delivery order without some inquiry. Usually, however, a telephone call to the customer is sufficient to determine whether the customer has in fact authorized the delivery order. The number of customers is limited, so that the producer is not dealing with a large universe of customers. Unlike the bank that has thousands of customers, the producer may have only a few dozen or perhaps a few hundred. Authenticating delivery orders is not an onerous task.

Third-party buyers from the customer who issue a delivery order themselves to the mill or who take a delivery order from the customer are not in a position to know whether the mill will honor the order. It may be that the customer has yet to pay for the product or that it has already taken delivery of all that it ordered. In those cases, the mill dishonors the delivery order. Thus, the third party that issues a delivery order or takes one from the customer must inquire of the mill whether it will honor. The mill may signal its willingness to honor by accepting the delivery order. That acceptance, of course, renders the delivery order a warehouse receipt, but the mill will usually not accept until it has verified that the customer wants it to accept.

These features of the delivery order give it considerable flexibility. If the customer's buyer wants to be assured of receiving product stored in Georgia, the buyer can hasten payment and delivery by using a check and a delivery order. By sending the check to the seller through the bank collection system, the buyer can instruct the presenting bank in Georgia not to give the check to the seller until the seller has the delivery order accepted by the bailee. Once the buyer obtains the accepted delivery order, the Georgia bank releases the check and returns the accepted delivery order to the buyer, who presents it to the bailee when he wants to take delivery.

Alternatively, the parties may use the bank-collection system to pay funds to the mill for the customer's account. In that case, the sub-buyer will send the check to the mill through the system with instructions to the bank to deliver the check upon the mill's acceptance of the delivery order. Document 32-3 is an illustration of a delivery order that might be used in such circumstances. Figure 34-1 illustrates the bill-and-hold transaction.

§34.3 PIPELINE SALES

Large volumes of natural gas and natural gas derivatives move from production facilities in western Canada and the southwestern United States to all parts of the country. The pipeline companies that control the flow

Figure 34-1.   Bill-and-Hold Transaction

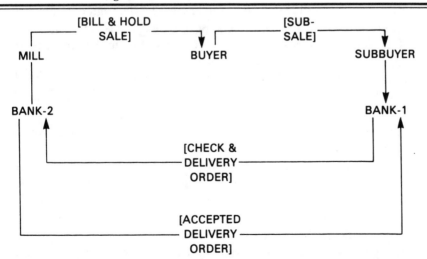

of these products are common carriers that issue bills of lading to their customers. Refiners that sell the product are located at the pipeline source. They maintain underground storage facilities that they constantly replenish from their refineries. In addition to these sellers, there are bailees that maintain storage facilities at some point along the line. The final party in the pipeline transaction is the wholesaler that buys from the refiner.

Thus, a refiner in Tulsa, Oklahoma, stores gas with a bailee in Conway, Kansas. The refiner sells product to the wholesaler and ships it through the pipeline from the refinery to the underground storage facility. Later, when the wholesaler orders delivery, the refiner ships from the underground storage facility to the buyer's own storage facilities, probably above-ground tanks. Note that the sale may occur at any point before delivery: (1) before shipment to the underground facility, (2) after storage in the facility, or (3) while moving through the pipeline.

Pipelines are expensive operations, and it would be far from efficient for them to lie idle for any appreciable period of time. One pipeline can handle several products at different times but can handle only one product at a time. A pipeline company in Tulsa wants to keep product moving through its pipe without interruption and contracts with various parties to keep the line fully active, sometimes transporting natural gas, at other times propane or some other natural gas derivative. The product seller, of course, cannot keep product moving without customers who place orders.

There is, then, a commonality of interests at work here. Pipeline companies want product to be moving through the line constantly. Sellers want to sell product through the line. Buyers want to get product through the line at low prices.

These three players in the gas industry have worked out an efficient arrangement. First, the refinery seller undertakes to supply as much product as the market will need. The local gas wholesalers agree in advance to acquire product, but they may not want to take delivery immediately. The pipeline will transport the product to Conway for storage and will store some product for the wholesaler in the pipeline itself.

Unfortunately, local wholesalers may not know how much product they will need during a given marketing period, and they sometimes buy too much or too little. In fact, sometimes they speculate by purchasing more than they know they will need. There arises, then, a need for pipeline customers, the wholesalers, to be able to buy and sell product that is in the pipeline or in storage. (Note the similarity between this marketing system and that in the textile industry described in the previous section.)

Third-party information systems have facilitated that buying and selling by maintaining a computer-accessed market through which wholesalers can indicate their willingness to buy or sell product at quoted prices. In the event two wholesalers strike an agreement over the computerized

Figure 34-2.   Pipeline Transfer Orders

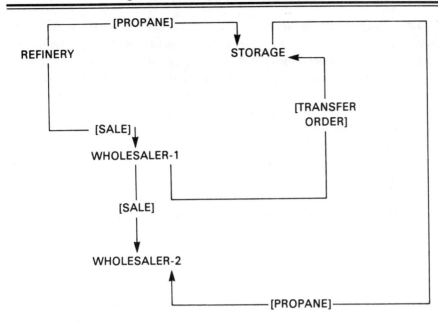

market, by telecommunications, or otherwise, the selling wholesaler transfers its product rights in product in the pipeline or in storage at Conway to the buying wholesaler with documents the industry has developed for these purposes. The wholesalers effect delivery of product in storage or in the pipeline by delivery order. Figure 34-2 illustrates the use of pipeline transfer orders.

§34.4 OCEAN SHIPMENTS

From time to time, shippers of **bulk cargo,** such as ore, petrochemicals, or grain, want to sell it or portions of it to traders while the goods are in transit. Parties sometimes use negotiable bills of lading for that purpose. At other times they use delivery orders. If the carrier is transporting the cargo under a non-negotiable bill, the shipper sells portions of the cargo to buyers and issues delivery orders to the carrier instructing delivery at the port of destination.

An importer of bauxite from Georgetown, Guyana, directs its Guyanese seller to ship the cargo on a **bulker** under a non-negotiable bill of lading. The importer arranges to sell portions of the shipment in the metals market by issuing delivery orders to the carrier directing delivery of portions of the cargo to various buyers.

If the cargo is in transit under a negotiable bill, the importer might issue delivery orders to the holder of it. Thus if the bauxite cargo is subject to a negotiable bill of lading that has been indorsed to a New York lender as collateral for an advance used to pay the bauxite seller in Georgetown, the importer may sell portions of the cargo and issue delivery orders to the lender for each portion sold.

In these cases, the buyers must realize that the delivery orders do not bind the carrier or lender until they are accepted and that the carrier and lender might, before acceptance, dishonor with impunity. In the normal course of affairs, however, buyers utilizing these arrangements either trust the importer or take steps to ensure that the bailee will honor or has honored before they part with value.

If the shipper ships under a non-negotiable bill, the carrier will honor delivery orders issued by the shipper. Thus an importer shipping the bauxite under a non-negotiable bill issues delivery orders to her customers who take delivery when the bulker arrives in port.

35

Domestic Transport

§35.1 BY BARGE, RAIL, OR TRUCK

Much domestic transport, especially local deliveries, occurs in vehicles owned by the shipper itself. When a retailer delivers merchandise to a customer, it uses its own fleet of trucks that pick up the merchandise at the retailer's warehouse and cart it off to the customer's home or office. Wholesalers also frequently maintain their own delivery equipment. Beer distributors, home heating oil suppliers, and some oil refineries load their trucks and make deliveries at each retail establishment or home that orders product. The same is true for many manufacturers and processors and for farm producers that traditionally haul produce to the grain elevator, the market, or the barge or rail terminal.

In addition, many buyers use their own vehicles to transport merchandise or commodities. It is often more efficient to send one's own truck to the lumberyard to take delivery of plywood than to wait for the lumberyard to make delivery.

Some shippers contract with cartage or **drayage companies** to haul merchandise or commodities, often in **containers** or **trailers** that belong to the shipper. A computer parts manufacturer might load its own trailers or a railroad company's containers at the manufacturer's plant. When the trailers or containers are ready for transport to a rail terminal, the shipper calls a **cartage company** and arranges for that company to transport the trailer or container to the terminal. If trailers are involved, the cartage company sends a tractor to the shipper's plant, connects it to the trailer, hauls the trailer to the terminal, and delivers the trailer to the railroad. The railroad then loads the trailer, by means of a crane, onto a railroad car. If the shipper is loading containers, the cartage company sends a **chassis** to the shipper's plant, where the shipper places the container onto the chassis for transport to the terminal. There, the railroad offloads it from the chassis onto a railroad car. Under these arrangements, the cartage company does not issue any document of title.

In short, a good bit of the business of transporting goods proceeds without the need to bring a document issuer into the transaction. As a consequence, some of this transport occurs without any bill of lading or equivalent. When a seller delivers from its own truck, the sales department forwards a shipping order to the dispatcher, who supervises the loading of the goods and gives directions to the employee driver for their delivery. By the same token, the purchasing officer of the buyer that takes delivery at the seller's loading dock sends his truck or his cartage company's truck to the seller's premises usually with a copy of the shipping order or of the purchase order or invoice, such latter documents frequently being generated by carbonless copies of the original sales order or from computerized systems that capture the information from one form, manipulate it somewhat, and reproduce it on another.

In a significant number of transactions, however, it becomes necessary for the parties to engage the services of an independent carrier. In fact, many of the short haul transportation arrangements described above are preliminary to the long haul out of which the bill of lading arises. In a long haul, the shipping department must decide which arrangements are superior for getting the merchandise to the buyer. In the United States, with its vast network of rail, truck, air, and barge facilities, a shipping manager has a number of options. In most cases, he contacts independent haulers who send a truck to his loading dock, though at times the shipper must transport the merchandise by its own vehicle or cartage company to a barge, air, rail, or truck terminal. Upon delivery of the merchandise to the independent carrier, the shipper receives a bill of lading. In the vast majority of domestic transport bailments, that bill of lading is non-negotiable in form. Document 35-1 is an example of a non-negotiable rail bill.

There may be occasions, however, when the seller and buyer arrange for a domestic sale involving payment against documents. In that transaction, a negotiable bill of lading is necessary. Chapter 4 discusses the documentary draft transaction.

§35.2 BY AIR

Air transport is more expensive than ground transport, but it is, of course, generally much quicker. The manufacturer whose production line is closed for want of a replacement part, the hospital that has an emergency need for supplies, and, above all, the lawyer who must get that contract to the client by 8:00 A.M. on Monday morning avail themselves of air transport to the point that it is a booming, profitable business.

Air transport of goods or documents does not lend itself to the documentary sale for a number of reasons. First, the goods that parties ship by air often arise out of isolated transactions in which special arrangements are necessary. If the goods are of high value, as they sometimes are in air shipments, the seller may have a representative at the destination to take delivery from the carrier and hold the goods against payment. Often, of course, the shipment is on open account, and there is no need to obtain a negotiable document. Finally, since the air shipment often arrives at the destination as quickly or more quickly than the air **waybill,** delivery against surrender of a negotiable document is not practical. In air shipments, therefore, the parties use non-negotiable waybills. Document 35-2 is an air waybill.

Some air carriers specialize in emergency shipments and utilize their own aircraft, which make unscheduled departures on an as-needed basis. Other air freight carriers pick up and deliver merchandise through a hub-and-spoke system. Under this arrangement, an air carrier designates certain airports as hubs for a national or international distribution system. Scheduled flights from the hubs move freight to cities along the spokes. If cities are located on spokes from different hubs, the carrier will move the freight along a spoke to the hub of the first city, then to another hub, and from there along a spoke to the second city.

§35.3 FREIGHT CONSOLIDATION

There is a measure of inefficiency in the shipment of small items of merchandise that the industry has overcome by consolidating freight shipments.

When a patient in Nome, Alaska, needs a kidney from a donor in Los Angeles, there is little concern about saving a relatively few dollars by consolidating shipments. In all probability this transportation arrangement will entail sending a flight directly to Nome to pick up the patient for transport to Los Angeles.

Transporting six cartons of tulip bulbs from Holland, Michigan, to Austin, Texas, however, does not command that kind of extravagance. Thus, the tulip seller delivers the freight to a **forwarder** who arranges to transport it by rail, truck, or air after consolidating this small shipment with other small shipments. By consolidating the freight, the forwarder or **consolidator** can take advantage of rates that favor large shipments in trailers or containers that can be handled by automation.

Freight forwarders that receive merchandise issue a bill of lading specifically designed for them as nonvehicle-owning common carriers (NVOCC).

§35.4 MULTI-CARRIER AND MULTI-MODAL TRANSPORT

Transhipment is the process of taking freight from one carrier and giving it to a second. For a Los Angeles seller to ship merchandise from California to Detroit by rail, it must arrange to have the goods shipped by more than one carrier, there being no railroad that travels from Los Angeles to Detroit. It makes little sense for each railroad that handles the merchandise to issue a separate bill of lading, though in fact, there is something illogical about the Burlington Northern Railroad's issuing a bill of lading to transport goods across the country when it cannot itself carry the goods to the destination. In theory, the Burlington, when it takes delivery of the goods, acts as a carrier and as a freight forwarder, for it carries the goods part of the way to the destination and arranges for the carriage of the goods for the balance of the way.

The Burlington may carry goods from Los Angeles to Chicago and there deliver them to the Grand Trunk Western for transport to Detroit, but the entire transaction will proceed under the bill issued by the Burlington. The document the industry developed for this transhipment of goods is the **through bill of lading.** Document 35-1 is an example of a through bill.

Sometimes, the transhipment of the goods will involve their offloading from one mode of carriage to another. A shipper of coal from Pittsburgh, Pennsylvania, to a steel mill in Bartonville, Illinois may arrange for a railroad to transport the coal from the deep mine in western Pennsylvania to a barge terminal on the Ohio River. From there, a barge will transport the coal down the Ohio and up the Mississippi to the Illinois River and up the Illinois to a terminal in Peoria. From the Peoria terminal, trucks will haul the coal to the steel mill in Bartonville.

Although a coal company may have sufficient transportation management to arrange for each of these shipments, some shippers on **multimodal** journeys will ask a forwarder to arrange for the transhipment in each case.

Uniform Domestic Straight Bill of Lading, adopted by Carriers in Official, Southern, Western and Illinois Classification Territories, March 15, 1922, as amended August 1, 1930 and June 15, 1941

UNIFORM STRAIGHT BILL OF LADING
ORIGINAL—NOT NEGOTIABLE.

Shipper's No.

Company .... Agent's No.

RECEIVED, subject to the classifications and tariffs in effect on the date of the issue of this Bill of Lading.

At .... ____ 19 ____ From ....

the property described below, in apparent good order, except as noted (contents and condition of contents of packages unknown), marked, consigned, and destined as indicated below, which said company (the word company being understood throughout this contract as meaning any person or corporation in possession of the property under the contract) agrees to carry to its usual place of delivery at said destination, if on its own road or its own water line, otherwise to deliver to another carrier on the route to said destination. It is mutually agreed, as to each carrier of all or any of said property over all or any portion of said route to destination, and as to each party at any time interested in all or any of said property, that every service to be performed hereunder shall be subject to all the conditions not prohibited by law, whether printed or written, herein contained, including the conditions on back hereof, which are hereby agreed to by the shipper and accepted for himself and his assigns.

(Mail or street address of consignee—For purposes of notification only)

Consigned to ....

Destination .... State of .... County of ....

Route ....

Delivering Carrier .... Car Initial .... Car No. ....

NO. PACKAGES	DESCRIPTION OF ARTICLES, SPECIAL MARKS AND EXCEPTIONS	*WEIGHT (Subject to Correction)	CLASS or RATE	CHECK COLUMN	
	SPECIMEN				Subject to Section 7 of conditions, if this shipment is to be delivered to the consignee without recourse on the consignor, the consignor shall sign the following statement: The carrier shall not make delivery of this shipment without payment of freight and all other lawful charges.
					(Signature of Consignor.)
					If charges are to be prepaid, write or stamp here, "To be Prepaid."
					Received $ to apply in prepayment of the charges on the property described hereon.
					Agent or Cashier.
					Per (The signature here acknowledges only the amount prepaid.)
					Charges Advanced:

*If the shipment moves between two ports by a carrier by water, the law requires that the bill of lading shall state whether it is "carrier's or shipper's weight."
Note.—Where the rate is dependent on value, shippers are required to state specifically in writing the agreed or declared value of the property.
The agreed or declared value of the property is hereby specifically stated by the shipper to be not exceeding $ .... per ....

Shipper, Per .... AGENT .... PER .... ①

Permanent postoffice address of shipper ....

The Fibre Boxes used for this shipment conform to the specifications set forth in the box maker's certificate thereon and all other requirements of Rule 41 of the Consolidated Freight Classification.

TOPS FORM 3040 LITHO IN U. S. A.

Document 35-2. Air Waybill

AIRPORT OF DEPARTURE

016- 5'2 32.6   016- 5'2 3 '6

SHIPPERS NAME AND ADDRESS	SHIPPERS ACCOUNT NUMBER	

NOT NEGOTIABLE

AIR WAYBILL (AIR CONSIGNMENT NOTE)

UNITED AIRLINES
P.O. Box 66100 Chicago, Illinois 60666

Copies 1, 2 and 3 of this Air Waybill are originals and have the same validity.

CONSIGNEE'S NAME AND ADDRESS	CONSIGNEE'S ACCOUNT NUMBER

It is agreed that the goods described herein are accepted for carriage in apparent good order and condition (except as noted) and SUBJECT TO THE CONDITIONS OF CONTRACT ON THE REVERSE HEREOF. ALL GOODS MAY BE CARRIED BY ANY OTHER MEANS INCLUDING ROAD OR ANY OTHER CARRIER UNLESS SPECIFIC CONTRARY INSTRUCTIONS ARE GIVEN HEREON BY THE SHIPPER, AND SHIPPER AGREES THAT THE SHIPMENT MAY BE CARRIED VIA INTERMEDIATE STOPPING PLACES WHICH THE CARRIER DEEMS APPROPRIATE. THE SHIPPER'S ATTENTION IS DRAWN TO THE NOTICE CONCERNING CARRIER'S LIMITATION OF LIABILITY.

TO EXPEDITE MOVEMENT, SHIPMENT MAY BE DIVERTED TO MOTOR OR OTHER CARRIER AS PER TARIFF RULE UNLESS SHIPPER GIVES OTHER INSTRUCTIONS HEREON.

ISSUING CARRIERS AGENT NAME AND CITY	ACCOUNTING INFORMATION, ALSO NOTIFY

AGENTS IATA CODE	ACCOUNT NO.

AIRPORT OF DEPARTURE (ADDR OF FIRST CARRIER) AND REQUESTED ROUTING

INTERNATIONAL

TO	BY FIRST CARRIER	ROUTING AND DESTINATION	TO	BY	TO	BY	CURRENCY	CHGS CODE	WT/VAL PPD COLL	OTHER PPD COLL	DECLARED VALUE FOR CARRIAGE	DECLARED VALUE FOR CUSTOMS

AIRPORT OF DESTINATION	FLIGHT DATE FOR CARRIER USE ONLY	FLIGHT DATE	AMOUNT OF INSURANCE	INSURANCE-If shipper requests insurance in accordance with conditions on reverse hereof, indicate amount to be insured in figures in box marked "Amount of insurance."	TC

HANDLING INFORMATION These commodities licensed by US for ultimate destination. Diversion contrary to US law is prohibited.

SCI

NO. OF PIECES RCP	GROSS WEIGHT	Kg lb	RATE CLASS COMMODITY ITEM NO.	CHARGEABLE WEIGHT	RATE / CHARGE	TOTAL	NATURE AND QUANTITY OF GOODS (INCL. DIMENSIONS OR VOLUME)

PREPAID / WEIGHT CHARGE / COLLECT / OTHER CHARGES

A.

VALUATION CHARGE

D.

TAX

I.

TOTAL OTHER CHARGES DUE AGENT

Shipper certifies that the particulars on the face hereof are correct and that insofar as any part of the consignment contains dangerous goods, such part is properly described by name and is in proper condition for carriage by air according to applicable Dangerous Goods Regulations.

TOTAL OTHER CHARGES DUE CARRIER

G. COD → CURRENCY

SIGNATURE OF SHIPPER

TOTAL PREPAID	TOTAL COLLECT	EXECUTED ON

CURRENCY CONVERSION RATES	C.C. CHARGES IN DESTINATION CURRENCY	(Date) (Time) at (Place)	SIGNATURE OF ISSUING CARRIER OR ITS AGENT

FOR CARRIERS USE ONLY AT DESTINATION (ALL COLLECT CHARGES IN DESTINATION CURRENCY)	CHARGES AT DESTINATION	TOTAL COLLECT CHARGES

016- 5' 3 ' (

FORM UAC 4365B REV. 1/95 INTERNATIONAL AIR WAYBILL PRINTED IN U.S.A.

COPY 3
ORIGINAL FOR SHIPPER

Reprinted with the permission of United Airlines, Inc. Only the front page of the document is reproduced.

36
International Shipping

§36.1   INTRODUCTION WITH A FEW DISTINCTIONS

This chapter deals essentially with imports and exports. Import transactions generally mirror export transactions, since one country's export transaction is another country's import transaction. Domestic lawyers tend to see only one side of each, however. Because international trade, especially that among the western industrialized countries, enjoys a considerable measure of uniformity, what is said here about U.S. exports tends to be true about British or Brazilian exports, though there are certainly many differences. The differences, however, pertain more to legal rules than to industry practices.

Exporters utilize many marketing methods. To the extent that they sell products overseas through subsidiaries or related corporations, their shipping arrangements are rather simple. They may ship on their own freighters or tankers or arrange for shipment on a third-party carrier in much the same fashion that an exporter ships goods it is selling on open account to an unrelated buyer. This chapter assumes that the exporter is selling to a third party, for that is the setting in which the complicated and interesting questions arise.

In all of these exporting transactions, the shipment stems from an underlying sales contract and is governed, in large part, by that contract. In addition, there is a considerable body of law that governs international shipping. There are international conventions governing sea and air transport, and there are shipping associations that set rates and adopt standardized forms for bills of lading and other **transport documents.**

Often, the character of the goods shipped will determine shipping arrangements. Since the early 1950s, containerization has altered the transport industry's practices significantly. Today, many manufactured goods are shipped in containers that may be filled at the seller's plant and not unloaded until they arrive at the buyer's plant. The container makes transhipment easy, since cranes or other mechanized facilities can load and unload containers with little risk of cargo damage, spillage, contamination, and pilferage. Some containers are on wheels and roll on and off a ship, barge, or railroad car. Others sit on trailers for over-the-road transport and off-loading onto barges, railroad flatcars, or ocean-going vessels.

Still other containers are collapsible, so that they may be returned empty to the shipper. Some ocean-going vessels are designed solely for containers. Companies that own such vessels often own the containers. The ship owners send the containers to the shipper's or the buyer's plant or to a freight forwarder for loading (sometimes called "stuffing") or unloading. Containers may be refrigerated to carry easily spoiled agricultural commodities that otherwise could not be transported long distances.

Containers also streamline the paperwork for exports. Formerly, goods from an inland point might have to be loaded first on a truck or railroad boxcar for transport to the port of exit in the seller's country, then onto an ocean-going vessel for transport to the port of entry in the buyer's region, and then to a truck or railcar for transport to the inland destination. For each leg of the journey, there might be a separate document of title. Transporting by container allows a single document to be issued by a forwarder for the entire voyage.

Some transport activity does not lend itself to containerization. Many agricultural commodities (such as grain and soybean oil), petrochemicals, and similarly bulky commodities are still shipped in bulk either on "bulkers" or tankers. Frequently, these commodities must be off-loaded and on-loaded at every transhipment point. Thus, grain moving down the Missouri and Mississippi Rivers from Omaha to New Orleans for transport to Vladivostok would have to be loaded on a barge in Omaha and would be unloaded in New Orleans onto the ocean-going vessel. This kind of **breakbulk cargo** is much more susceptible to contamination and loss than manufactured goods shipped portal to portal in sealed containers.

There are a couple of distinctions to keep in mind in reviewing the activity of the transport industries described in this chapter. The first relates to ship-owning companies. Such companies generally fall into one of two categories: lines and **tramps.** Lines are members of a shipping **confer-**

ence, such as the Baltic and International Maritime Council (BIMCO). They own **liners,** which are ships that follow published schedules over established routes and charge agreed-upon rates. Tramps are ships that wander from port to port in search of business and whose itinerary is determined by the destinations of the cargoes they take on. Often, tramps are subjects of **charter parties.**

Any industry that achieves a degree of sophistication and complexity gives rise to the expert. The ocean transport industry involves more than just shippers, people who want to ship merchandise, and shipping companies, the people that carry the merchandise. There are important middlemen in the industry. The first is the freight forwarder, the second is the **loading broker,** and the third is the **customs broker.**

Generally, freight forwarders are agents of the shipper. They arrange for the shipment by finding a carrier and, frequently, they consolidate the shipment with other shipments in order to take advantage of containerization or other economies of scale. Loading brokers are generally agents of the ship owner. Their function is to find cargo for the ship and to issue the documents in connection with the shipment. Sometimes, freight forwarders, who are supposed to be the agent of the shipper, are also loading brokers, that is, agent of the ship owner. If that arrangement troubles you, you are not alone, but it does not trouble the shipping industry and appears to be working rather well, as arrangements that startle lawyers so often do. Loading brokers may also act as ship brokers that arrange for charter parties. Customs brokers take charge of import shipments and see them through customs.

§36.2 SHIPPING TERMS

There has been a measure of standardization in ocean shipping by virtue of the efforts of various organizations, the most successful of which is currently the International Chamber of Commerce (ICC), which has published *Incoterms*. Generally, *Incoterms* sets out a lexicon that covers arrangements for delivery of goods, including delivery at the seller's works, multi-modal transport of goods portal to portal, and arrangements for single-mode transport of goods from one port to another. The most common export arrangements for shipping goods come under CIF, C&F, or FOB headings, all of which are described in detail in Incoterms.

"CIF" stands for "cost, insurance, freight," with "cost" being the price of the goods, "insurance" being the cost of marine insurance, and "freight" being the charges levied by the carrier for transporting the goods. "C&F" stands for "cost and freight," terms calling for the same arrangement as CIF without the insurance. A buyer that has its own coverage under a blanket policy would not ask its seller to ship CIF but C&F. "FOB" stands for "free on board" and means that a party must arrange to have the goods loaded on board a named vessel. In each of these cases, additional information is necessary.

A New York importer may order specialty steel from an Italian producer "CIF Cleveland." In that event, the producer must arrange for transport of the steel from its plant to an Italian port, thence by ocean/lake freighter to Cleveland. In the alternative, the producer may be able to arrange for transport on its own trucks to an Italian port with loading on a vessel there that can carry the steel directly to Cleveland. In a sale "FOB Genoa," the producer would have to arrange for loading of the steel on board a ship at the Italian port, but the buyer must arrange for the shipment and must advise the producer of the ship and the schedule.

Under the 1990 version of *Incoterms*, there are 13 incoterms, and the ICC publication spells out their meaning and the duties of the seller and buyer under each.

The international shipping industry and shippers have fashioned other terms for their contracts. "Pier to House," "House to House," and "Pier to Pier" are examples of phrases that parties use in international shipping by container. While these are not incoterms, they have meanings that the industry assigns to them, with a lesser measure of certainty than in the case of the incoterms.

Despite these efforts at standardization, sometimes shipping terminology has the disconcerting tendency to have one meaning in one region and a different meaning in another. The Uniform Commercial Code, for example, does not always follow international usage. The shipping industry, furthermore, is dynamic; practices and terminology change from time to time. The incoterms have themselves undergone revision and undoubtedly will undergo revision again.

The United Nations Conference on Trade and Development (UNCTAD) and the International Chamber of Commerce (ICC) have fashioned rules for multi-modal transport documents and something of a lexicon for the parties to the multi-modal transaction. The rules contain liberal opt-in provisions and will apply most frequently in the international shipment setting.

§36.3 THE OCEAN BILL OF LADING

In classic ocean transport, the shipper (the seller or exporter of goods) prepares the goods for transport by packaging them and delivering them to the carrier. The ship owner's agent that receives the goods may be the "mate," (i.e., the captain of the ship or his subordinate) or a loading broker. Upon delivery of the goods, the seller delivers a bill of lading it has prepared on the ship owner's bill-of-lading form. The ship owner's agent examines the goods to determine, to the extent that he can, whether the goods conform to the description in the bill. He then issues a **dock receipt** for the goods. Document 36-1 is a dock receipt.

At this point, the goods are not on board, and there is still considerable risk involved in their loading. They or their packages may be damaged or lost in loading, and, importantly, marine insurance coverage does not apply until the goods pass the ship's rail. Once the goods are loaded on board, the mate compares his receipt with the bill of lading the seller prepared. If everything appears to be in order, the mate then signs the bill of lading. If things are not in order, the mate signs a claused bill, that is, a bill that contains a clause advising, for example, that the goods were damaged upon loading or receipt or that the packages are damaged or dirty. This clausing of the bill is significant because under most letters of credit, banks do not accept claused bills.

Quite often, the ship owner issues a "received for shipment" bill of lading when the seller delivers the goods at the dock. That bill of lading is generally unacceptable to banks and overseas buyers because of the loading and insurance risks mentioned above. Once the goods are loaded on board, however, the ship's agent stamps the received-for-shipment bill with an **on-board stamp** and dates and signs the stamp, thereby rendering the bill of lading an on-board bill acceptable to buyers and banks.

The description of the goods in a bill of lading is often not reliable. Carriers are not inspectors; they do not open cartons or sealed containers to examine merchandise, and they are not expert enough to determine whether breakbulk cargoes such as grain or tankerload cargoes such as turpentine pass in the trade. Bills of lading, therefore, usually contain disclaimers such as **"said to contain"** or **"shipper's load and count"** (SLC). These disclaimers are not always accorded full effect by the courts, especially U.S. courts, but if they comply strictly with governing law, they are generally effective.

From the standpoint of efficiency, disclaimers make sense. Many sellers and buyers do not want to pay for third-party examination of the goods. They are satisfied with a bill of lading containing such disclaimers. Even banks, which take the bills of lading for value and may look to the goods in the event a buyer fails to reimburse the bank, are generally willing to accept bills with disclaimers. The buyer or bank that wants an examination should pay for it by arranging for an independent inspector's certification that the goods conform to industry standards or to the terms of the contract. Thus, the industry practice is optimal. Those who want inspection must pay for it; those who do not want it do not have to pay for it.

In some industries, especially those involving goods sold on spot markets or goods whose value fluctuates rapidly, traders who ship want to be able to sell or borrow against the cargo while it is in transit. In the oil industry while North Sea crude is being transported from Britain to Latin America, traders buy, sell, and borrow against the oil at breakneck speed. In fact, during the ten days or so that a tanker of oil traverses the North Atlantic, its cargo may be the subject of hundreds of transactions. Other commodities, such as grain, metals, and some raw materials, may change hands several times. In all of these cases, moreover, even when there is no sale of the cargo during transit, parties need to finance the goods.

In these transfers of cargoes to buyers or financers, the negotiable bill of lading may play a crucial role. By virtue of the fact that the carrier delivers the goods only to the holder of the bill, the bill stands for the cargo, and buyers and banks are willing to give value for it.

Traditionally, in order to guard against the loss of the bill, carriers issued ocean bills of lading in a set. Such bills were issued in multiple originals. The carrier would honor any one of the originals. That original having been honored, the outstanding bills became worthless. Bills issued in a set were separated and forwarded to the appropriate party (usually a buyer or a bank) by separate cover, so that if one was lost, at least one would arrive, permitting the buyer to take delivery of the goods. This practice of issuing bills in a set, though not so critical as it once was, survives in many transactions.

It also survives in bank forms, particularly drafts used in the documentary-draft transaction. Such draft forms may contain a clause reciting "**First of exchange** (Second of same tenor and date being unpaid)." That language appears on the first of the two drafts and indicates that the drafts are issued in duplicate and that one being honored, the other would stand void. The second copy of the draft would recite "**Second of exchange** (First of same tenor and date being unpaid)."

Sometimes, a bill is issued in single copy and becomes lost or arrives after the goods do. In that event, the carrier does not deliver the goods unless the bank or buyer seeking delivery agrees to indemnify the carrier against loss in the event the bill turns up in the hands of a third-party holder. When a bank's customer seeks such a guaranty, the bank will insist, of course, on indemnity from the customer so that the bank can recoup its loss in the event it is called upon to honor its guaranty.

§36.4 CHARTERS

Often, especially in full-capacity shipments, the shipper charters the vessel for a period of time or a voyage. Charters are governed by a contract called a "charter party." Charters may be by demise, in which case the shipper has to hire its own crew for the ship, but most of the time, the charter party leaves the operation of the ship in the owner's control, and the shipper merely delivers the goods for transport.

Charter parties are for a period of time (a time charter party) or for a voyage. In the former, the shipper bears the cost of delays caused, for example, by crowding at a port or unavailability of stevedores or docking facilities. These losses ("demurrage") are borne by the shipper in a time charter party. In a voyage charter party, however, the shipping company undertakes to transport the shipper's goods from one port to another, and the cost of demurrage falls on the shipping company.

When a shipper ships under a charter party, the charter party controls the shipping company's duties to transport and deliver the goods. Bills of lading are sometimes issued by the shipping company, but they customarily recite, and should recite, that they are subject to the charter party. Because third-party buyers and banks do not have the charter party, they are unaware of any terms in the charter party that may be burdensome or contrary to the usual arrangements for the carriage of goods under a bill of lading issued in the form established by a liner conference or a carriers' association. For that reason, charter-party bills of lading, even when they are denominated negotiable, are generally not acceptable to banks and buyers.

§36.5 FORWARDERS

Exporting goods often involves considerable expertise. The occasional exporter or the small operation that ships in less than container loads (LCL) often wants to assign the responsibility of obtaining the necessary **export licenses,** letters of credit, inspection certificates, transport documents, and the like to a freight forwarder that offers such services. Freight forwarders know liner schedules and charges and may even be loading brokers for one or more ocean carriers. In addition, some large forwarders own their own containers and maintain container freight stations remote from the docks to which they ultimately deliver the container.

Probably the most significant commercial function of the freight forwarder is its consolidation of shipments. Frequently, LCL sellers want the advantage of container rates and the advantages of container shipment — freedom from risks of loss, spoilage, pilferage, and the like. By engaging a freight forwarder, a number of LCL shippers can deliver their cargoes to the forwarder who consolidates them into full container load (FCL) shipments and delivers the containers to an ocean carrier for transport.

Often, of course, since some freight forwarders are located at places remote from the docks of ocean-going vessels, freight forwarders offer multi-modal transportation arrangements to their customers. A shipper in Grand Rapids may ask a freight forwarder in that inland city to arrange for truck, rail, and steamship transport of goods to Buenos Aires. On other occasions the freight forwarders facilities are alongside the docks. A San

Francisco exporter delivers its merchandise across the Bay in Oakland where a forwarder holds it until it can ship FCL on a **container ship** that travels between Oakland and Yokohama.

In the multi-modal situation, the forwarder issues a document of title to the shipper at the time the shipper delivers the goods to the forwarder. That document will probably be a **combined transport document** that anticipates shipment by various modes of transportation from the time of delivery to the forwarder until delivery to destination. The freight forwarder is not, in fact, a carrier, and the notion that a noncarrier may issue a bill of lading is a curious one. In such transactions, the forwarder styles itself "NVOCC." "NVOCC" means "nonvehicle-owning common carrier," and the banking and transportation industries have pretty much accepted bills of lading issued by such forwarders in that form. Such combined transport bills of lading are not **marine bills,** since they may cover carriage of goods by rail or over the road and perforce are not on-board bills. Thus any contract or letter of credit calling for an on-board bill or an ocean bill would not be satisfied by the forwarder's combined transport bill.

In a typical transaction involving a shipper and a freight forwarder, the shipper prepares the forwarder's bill of lading and delivers the goods to the forwarder, who examines the goods in a manner sufficient only for the purposes of satisfying the bill's disclaimer language (e.g., shipper's load and count) and ascertaining that containers are sealed and that there is no apparent damage to the goods or their packages. The forwarder issues its bill and then arranges with vehicle-owning carriers for the transport of the goods pursuant to its obligations toward the shipper.

In another typical arrangement, the freight forwarder receives an LCL shipment from the shipper, consolidates it with other merchandise into a full container load, prepares the export documents, and delivers the container to the carrier, which issues the bill of lading.

Freight forwarders often arrange shipment by more than one mode of transport, and multi-modal transport documents often arise in international trade. While shipments of goods from New York City to southeastern Asia will proceed by ship from New York through the Panama Canal to Singapore, shipments of goods from New York City to Japan and Korea may entail rail shipment from New York to Seattle and oceangoing vessels from Seattle to Yokohama or Inchon.

Containerization efficiencies have continued during the 1980s and 1990s. Container ship companies have constructed much larger transports to carry containers for ocean carriage and introduced double decking in rail transport. Some carriers have engaged in the sharing of vessels, so that a portion of the containers on a ship may belong to one carrier and the balance to another. Smaller importers and exporters have banded together to avail themselves of volume discounts. These innovations reduce transportation charges.

§36.6 MARITIME INSURANCE

When the owner of goods holds them for sale, they are usually covered under the owner's property-damage insurance coverage. When goods leave the premises of the owner, however, that coverage may terminate, and when the goods pass into the hands of a bailee, the cost of extending that coverage to them can become prohibitive. Goods on ocean-going vessels, moreover, may no longer be the property of the seller but that of the buyer or, in effect, that of the bank that is financing the transaction. It becomes efficient, then, that after the goods move out of the bounds of the seller's facility and before they move into the bounds of the buyer's, the insurance coverage be related to the goods themselves rather than to the identity of the person who has an interest in them.

Goods in transport may be the subject of sales and financing, and their value is clearly enhanced if potential buyers and lenders do not have to inquire of the seller or borrower as to insurance during transport.

Long ago, the transport and insurance industries responded to this problem with marine insurance policies that are transferable. Under such coverage, the shipper may indorse the policy to a buyer or lender, who then becomes the insured.

Sometimes the shipper cannot obtain a copy of the policy from its insurance broker in time to forward it to the bank or buyer. In that case the parties need to obtain evidence that the policy has, indeed, been contracted for and will issue in due course. **Binders** or insurance **covernotes** are issued by insurance brokers as evidence of that coverage. Some shippers, those doing a significant amount of exporting, may have an **open cargo policy** — a form of blanket coverage that, unlike the marine insurance policy, covers more than one shipment. In the event of that kind of open cargo coverage, the shipper is not in a position to make a policy available to the buyer or bank and uses instead a certificate of insurance.

Of these documents, the policy itself discloses the most information about the coverage — its effective date, the perils insured against, deductibles, limits, etc. The certificate contains somewhat less information, and the binder or covernote even less. Buyers and lenders are more inclined, then, to accept policies and certificates than they are covernotes or binders.

Note that the transfer of maritime insurance fulfills its anticipated role in these settings only if the transfer is free of equities. If the insurance company could deny coverage to a transferee by virtue of the company's right of setoff against the transferor, the maritime insurance apparatus would not work. For that reason, maritime insurance policies, which travel with the goods, are akin to negotiable instruments. In fact, maritime insurance is some of the oldest insurance that we have, and the negotiability feature of it is similar to the negotiability features of the document of title and the bill of exchange (draft) that also come to us out of maritime commerce.

There is a great deal of learning in and a considerable lexicon for maritime insurance. Some terms occur with sufficient frequency that they are worth mentioning here, especially because they arise in connection with the letters of credit and payments that the exports generate.

Average is the maritime insurance concept of partial damage, as opposed to total loss of the goods. **General average** is the concept that in the event of extraordinary danger to the ship's cargo, the master may deliberately sacrifice some cargo to save the rest. In that event, cargo that is saved must participate in the loss, which contributed to its being saved. **Particular average** is a partial loss caused, for example, by seawater leaking into the hold and not caused by such deliberate decision by the master of the ship to sacrifice cargo.

Some insurance coverage is described as **FPA,** that is, free of particular average. That coverage would not protect the insured from partial losses caused by accident. A marine policy covering particular average is **WA** or **WPA,** that is, with average or with particular average.

Often, marine policies contain a deductible expressed as a specified **franchise.** WPA subject to a 10 percent franchise would require the insurer to protect against partial losses exceeding 10 percent of the amount of the loss.

The term *all risks* modifying coverage in a marine policy does not mean that the policy covers all risks. Losses caused by a malfunction of refrigeration equipment or by virtue of the inherent nature of the goods (e.g., bananas that rot because of delays) and similar losses are not included in all-risks coverage.

§36.7 EXPORT DOCUMENTS

Exports are the subject of considerable regulation by the federal government. In order to advance certain political agendas and to restrict the transfer of technology that might be harmful to the national defense, the government requires the licensing of all exports. Most exports, however, fall under the general license procedure. Only those commodities that are listed on the Export Administration's Commodity Control List and that are destined for countries to which exports are restricted fall within the more burdensome validated license procedure. While the government provides administrative personnel to assist exporters in determining whether they must obtain a validated license and what they must do to obtain it, the process is bureaucratic and subject to delay, paperwork, and all of the other headaches that such procedures inevitably entail.

Exporters that ship goods of a value in excess of $500 or that are subject to a validated license must file a **shipper's export declaration** (SED). General licenses are issued automatically, without application, but validated licenses must be applied for. The process of obtaining a validated license may be accelerated by a procedure whereby the importer or importing country verifies that the goods will not be re-exported to a restricted country or that the goods will not be used for military or other restricted purposes.

§36.8 MARITIME FRAUD

With international trade's great distances, time changes, language and currency differences, and communications difficulties, the rogue finds opportunities to ply his trade. Sellers guard against that fraud with documentation and the letter of credit. Those procedures are sensitive, however, to maritime fraud, of which there is a considerable amount.

Maritime fraud can arise in a number of ways. In the most egregious case, a fraudulent ship owner of a rusty tub issues bills of lading for nonexistent merchandise and scuttles the ship at sea. False bills of lading can sometimes give rise to insurance fraud, when the ship owner or its agent issues bills of lading for nonexistent or worthless cargo, which it sells or, in the previous case, for which it obtains maritime insurance.

When third world countries ordered more goods than their ports could handle, some shipping companies, in order to avoid demurrage, off-loaded merchandise at the wrong port or even sold cargoes to third parties.

Sellers, buyers, and banks are victims of these acts of fraud and take a number of steps to avoid them. The first and most important step is to avoid commerce with rogues. Shippers are well-advised to investigate the creditworthiness of shipping companies or to engage experienced freight forwarders to represent them. Buyers and banks that are taking documents of title from questionable carriers can insist on independent cargo surveys to determine the seaworthiness of the vessels or independent loading certificates to determine that cargo has, indeed, been loaded on board.

§36.9 IMPORTS

Often, the U.S. party to an international sale is not an exporter but an importer. In these cases, the foreign seller usually arranges for the transport of the goods, though the buyer's foreign agent or employee may perform that task.

Those arrangements do not include the all-important task of seeing the goods through customs. That task usually falls to the importer, and generally customs brokers, who are often freight forwarders, perform those functions for the inexperienced or infrequent importer. Getting goods into the country can be an expensive, slow, and exasperating task. The multitude of goods and commodities that pass in international trade make it difficult for government customs inspectors to classify goods and impose customs duties, though efforts at international uniformity in the classification of goods and commodities are proving helpful.

It is a tribute to the ingenuity of all concerned that the system works as well as it does. Graft in U.S. customs activity is remarkably uncommon. It might even be fair to say that delays are rather uncommon, though they do occur, as do disputes that must be resolved with litigation, lawyers, and all the expense that goes with that activity.

Under customs statutes and regulations, only the owner of goods or their purchaser or a customs broker may enter goods into the country. There may be difficulty in determining the identity of a party and its relationship to the goods. Anyone holding a duly indorsed negotiable bill of lading will satisfy the Customs Service that he is entitled to enter the goods. In the absence of such a bill of lading, a carrier may certify the identity of the person with authority to enter the goods.

When merchandise arrives at a port in the United States several things might happen. First, the merchandise might be entered for consumption, that is, the goods might be entered by a party that is going to use or consume it in the country. Second, the goods might "arrive" at a port but not be entered there. If goods arrive in New York but are going to be transported to Chicago for "entry," New York is only the port of arrival: Chicago is the port of entry, that is, the port where the goods will be classified under the Harmonized Tariff Schedule and where the duty will be paid. Third, merchandise might be brought into the country to be warehoused for a period of up to five years during which the goods are stored in a bonded warehouse until the importer brings them into the country for consumption or re-exports them. Fourth, goods might be brought into a U.S. foreign trade zone or subzone. Under U.S. law, goods that are going to be subjected to a manufacturing process and re-exported are not subject to duty if the manufacturing facility is in a foreign trade zone or qualifies as a foreign trade subzone.

Once the Customs Service is satisfied that the duty on goods will be paid, it will release the goods, subject to later determination of the duty — a process that sometimes takes time, especially if the importer and the Service disagree on the classification of the goods. The Service requires a commercial or **pro forma invoice** and an entry summary form, so that it can compute duties and collect statistical information concerning imports. Document 36-2 is a pro forma invoice. In addition, the importer must file an entry **manifest**.

In all events, the Customs Service will not permit entry of goods without payment of the duty unless the importer posts a bond. If the importer is using a customs broker, the broker's blanket bond may stand for the obligation to pay the duty. After the Service determines the appropriate classification of the imported goods, of course, the duty must be paid. Failing that payment, the Service resorts to the bond. If the importer does not arrange for release of the merchandise pending resolution of any dispute with the Service, the merchandise remains in a bonded warehouse.

DOCK RECEIPT

2. EXPORTER (Principal or seller-licensee and address including ZIP Code)		5. DOCUMENT NUMBER	5a. B/L OR AWB NUMBER
		6. EXPORT REFERENCES	
	ZIP CODE		
3. CONSIGNED TO		7. FORWARDING AGENT (Name and address — references)	
		8. POINT (STATE) OF ORIGIN OR FTZ NUMBER	
4. NOTIFY PARTY/INTERMEDIATE CONSIGNEE (Name and address)		9. DOMESTIC ROUTING/EXPORT INSTRUCTIONS	

12. PRE-CARRIAGE BY	13. PLACE OF RECEIPT BY PRE-CARRIER	
14. EXPORTING CARRIER	15. PORT OF LOADING/EXPORT	10. LOADING PIER/TERMINAL
16. FOREIGN PORT OF UNLOADING (Vessel and air only)	17. PLACE OF DELIVERY BY ON-CARRIER	11. TYPE OF MOVE

11a. CONTAINERIZED (Vessel only) ☐ Yes ☐ No

MARKS AND NUMBERS (18)	NUMBER OF PACKAGES (19)	DESCRIPTION OF COMMODITIES in Schedule B detail (20)	GROSS WEIGHT (Pounds) (21)	MEASUREMENT (22)	D OR F (23)

DELIVERED BY:

RECEIVED THE ABOVE DESCRIBED GOODS OR PACKAGES SUBJECT TO ALL THE TERMS OF THE UNDERSIGNED'S REGULAR FORM OF DOCK RECEIPT AND BILL OF LADING WHICH SHALL CONSTITUTE THE CONTRACT UNDER WHICH THE GOODS ARE RECEIVED, COPIES OF WHICH ARE AVAILABLE FROM THE CARRIER ON REQUEST AND MAY BE INSPECTED AT ANY OF ITS OFFICES.

LIGHTER
TRUCK _____

ARRIVED— DATE _____ TIME _____

UNLOADED— DATE _____ TIME _____

CHECKED BY _____

PLACED IN SHIP / ON DOCK LOCATION _____

FOR THE MASTER

BY _____

SPECIMEN

ONLY CLEAN DOCK RECEIPT ACCEPTED.

PROFORMA INVOICE

PRO FORMA INVOICE NO.	DATE ISSUED

TERMS AND CONDITIONS OF SALE

SHIPPER

MODE OF TRANSPORT	CARRIER
AIR/OCEAN PORT OF EMBARKATION	LOADING PIER
AIR/OCEAN PORT OF UNLOADING	CONTAINERIZED

SOLD TO

☐ Yes   ☐ No

MARKS:

SHIP TO

GROSS WEIGHT:

QUANTITY	U/M	DESCRIPTION OF MERCHANDISE	UNIT PRICE	AMOUNT

SPECIMEN

FREIGHT
EXPORT PACKING
INSURANCE
MISC

TOTAL

WE HEREBY CERTIFY This Invoice Is True and Correct and that the merchandise described is origin of the United States of America.

Authorized Signature   Title

Form 10-080 Printed and Sold by UNZCO 190 Baldwin Ave., Jersey City, NJ 07306 • (800) 631-3098 • (201) 795-5400

Reprinted with the permission of Unz & Co., 700 Central Ave., New Providence, NJ 07974-1139.

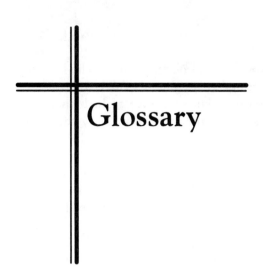

Glossary

PART I. SALES

Acceleration — in installment obligations, the right of the obligee, in certain circumstances, to declare all installments due. [The obligee will invariably insist on the right to accelerate payment obligations in the event of the obligor's default on one payment. In an installment promissory note, for example, the holder will want to declare the full balance due upon the default of the maker on one payment. Otherwise, the obligee of an installment obligation must wait until each installment is due before it can bring an action against the defaulting obligor.]

Acceptance — a negotiable instrument that is payable a stated period of time after its "acceptance." [In the **documentary draft** transaction, a seller draws a **draft** on the buyer. If the sales contract between the buyer and the seller calls for credit, the buyer will have a number of days, say 60, to pay the draft. When the seller's agent, usually a collecting bank, presents the draft to the buyer, the buyer will signal its undertaking to pay the draft upon maturity by signing the draft on its face. That signature is an act of acceptance and the negotiable draft becomes a negotiable acceptance.] (*See also* **banker's acceptance, trade acceptance.**)

Adverse selection — a concept derived from experience in the insurance industry in which an insurance product is priced so high that it attracts an unsustainable mix of bad risks. If life insurance, for example, is priced so high that it is an attractive product only for older or ill people, the insurance issuer will fail. In order to avoid adverse risk, insurers must price life insurance so that healthy and younger people will see it as attractive and buy it, thereby giving the insurance com-

355

pany an adequate mix of younger and older insureds. The concept finds application in other settings. A tire manufacturer, for example, might grant an extended warranty but at a price so high that only those whose use of the tires is abnormally risky will pay the price. The end result is that the manufacturer has an unsustainable level of warranty claims.

Adviser — in letter of credit transactions, the party (usually a bank) that notifies the beneficiary of the credit that it has in fact issued form the office of the **issuer**. Banks traditionally have issued letters of credit through their correspondents who advise the credit to the beneficiary. When a Dutch bank issues a credit in favor of a New York seller, the Dutch bank, the issuer, notifies its New York correspondent (the **correspondent bank**) of the issuance of the credit. Interbank communications of this sort are secure, but nonbank beneficiaries usually rely on a bank in their market to give the notice of issuance.

Agreement — the bargain of the parties in fact. (*Compare* **contract**.)

Allowance — credit due a buyer for returns, damages to delivered goods, and short shipments.

Arbitrage — the practice of buying in one market and selling in another. [If the price of a commodity, in New York, for example, is higher than the price of the same commodity in California, arbitrageurs will buy in California and sell in New York. Sometimes a seller will attempt to maintain price differentials by restricting resales of its commodities in a particular market. If A sells to B in the North with an understanding that B will not sell in the South, A will be able to charge higher prices in the South than B charges its customers in the North only so long as C, an arbitrageur, does not learn of the price disparity. Once C learns the facts, he will buy from B and resell in the South at a price lower than A is charging.]

Attornment — acknowledgment of another's rights in property. [In feudal times, a tenant recognized a new landlord by attorning — the act of acknowledging that the tenant held the real estate through the lord. The concept of attorning survived to some extent in **bailments**, by virtue of the fact that the law treated as significant a **bailee's** acknowledgment that he held for a new owner. To a degree, notice to a bailee has displaced attornment. It is not necessary in general for the bailee to attorn, notice to the bailee being sufficient.]

Bailee — one who takes possession of goods and holds or transports them for another. [Bailees may, in turn, bail goods with a third party, a sub-bailee, or may hold goods that are transferred from the original bailor to a second full or part owner, such as a secured party.]

Bailment — delivery of property by the **bailor** to an agent, the **bailee**, for storage, transport, service, or other purpose. [It is sometimes difficult to distinguish a bailment from a sale. Common bailments include personal property leases, storage arrangements with commercial warehouses, and shipment by common carrier.] (*See also* **bill of lading** and **warehouse receipt**.)

Bailor — one who delivers goods to a **bailee** for storage, transport, services, or other purposes. (*See* **bailment**.)

Banker's acceptance — an acceptance made by a bank, rather than by a merchant. (*Compare* **trade acceptance**.)

Basing point pricing system — determining price to include the cost of shipment from a base point even though shipment may be from a different point.

Bid bond — undertaking of a surety company to pay a percentage of the contractor's bid to the owner if the owner accepts the contractor's bid and the contractor does not enter into the construction contract and supply **performance** and **payment bonds**.

Bill of exchange — synonym for **draft**. [The term derives from the earliest function of the draft as a medieval instrument of international trade that served, in part, to exchange one currency for another. The term survives in England and other common law jurisdictions.]

Bill of lading — a **document of title** issued by a carrier evidencing a contract of carriage of the goods and setting out delivery terms.

Bond — an undertaking whereby one party (1) acts as surety for another's obligation to a third party or (2) agrees to hold a party free from loss. (*See also* **bid bond, performance bond, payment bond**.)

Boot — in a trade, something given in addition to the item traded.

Broker — middleman that undertakes to sell frequently odd lots and usually not on a continuing basis. [Brokers may represent any number of sellers in an industry or in related industries. Brokers usually do not take title to the goods they sell for their principals but "broker" the merchandise, real estate, or securities. Often, brokers do not even take possession of the property they sell but traditionally bring together sellers and buyers that do not regularly do business with each other. Sellers of odd lots and distress merchandise and occasional sellers often resort to brokers. Owners of real estate and securities traditionally use brokers to find buyers, and, conversely, buyers of real estate and securities use brokers to find sellers.]

Bulk sale — traditionally, a sale of more than one-half of inventory out of the ordinary course of business. [Bulk sales are extraordinary, and they attract the attention of the law because they were used at times in the past as a method to avoid creditors' claims. A merchant that had obtained credit on the strength of his inventory might sell out in bulk, abscond with the sale proceeds and leave his reliance creditors with nothing. The advent of credit reporting agencies, audited financial statements, and filing systems have largely put an end to the bulk sale fraud. Today's creditors rarely extend credit on the strength of a merchant's stock in trade. The Bulk Sales Law, Article 6 of the Uniform Commercial Code, survives in most jurisdictions, nonetheless, and the notion of a bulk sale is still important to the extent that it is not a sale in ordinary course, so that the bulk sale buyer does not qualify for the favored treatment of the **buyer in ordinary course.**]

Buyer in ordinary course — a buyer who buys out of inventory in good faith and without knowledge that his purchase is in violation of the ownership interest of a third party. [The advantage of buyer in ordinary course status lies in the **good-faith purchase** doctrine, that is, the notion that the buyer in ordinary course takes free and clear of most claims and defenses.]

Capital lease — one of many terms used in commerce (in this case by accountants) to refer to a lease that is truly a credit sale and one, therefore, that must be so recognized on the financial statements of the lessee.

Cartel — a horizontal combination of independent sellers or producers for the purpose of restricting output and increasing prices.

Cashier's check — a **check** drawn by a bank on itself. [The act of the bank's drawing on itself raises conceptual questions. Some courts view the cashier's check as an "accepted" item, since it contains the signature of the drawee, just as an acceptance does. Other courts see the cashier's check more in the nature of a promissory note. The commercial advantage of the cashier's check over the regular check is the fact that it involves the undertaking of the bank, which cannot stop payment, except in unusual circumstances. The cashier's check reduces significantly the risks of insufficient funds and of stopped payment.]

Cash sale — sale not on credit. [In every sale, the seller, consciously or unconsciously, decides whether (1) he will deliver on the credit of the buyer's promise to pay or (2) insist on delivery against payment. The former is a **credit sale**; the latter is a **cash sale.** To some extent, there is always a measure of trust on both sides of a sale. If the seller hands the goods to the buyer, while the buyer fills out a check, the seller has, in a sense, entered into a credit transaction. By the same token, the buyer that hands cash to the seller as the seller prepares to hand the buyer goods has extended credit to the seller by prepaying. As a matter of commercial and legal necessity, the law and merchants have distinguished these substantially contemporaneous transactions from those in which payment or delivery is deferred. Payment by a check post-dated by a single day creates a credit sale. The distinction between cash and credit sales is important. Mercantile fairness demands that the credit seller shoulder the risks inherent in his decision to trust the buyer and that he not be able to shift the risk to innocent third parties that rely on appearances created by the seller's delivery of merchandise to the buyer. Yet, the law, in order perhaps to encourage the use of certain negotiable instruments and to reward transactions that are regular, treats the seller that takes a check that is not post-dated, i.e., a check that is payable on demand, as a cash sale.] (*Compare* **credit sale.**)

Caveat emptor — "let the buyer beware." [The rule that the buyer should beware originated in the **security of property** concept that the buyer could take no greater interest in the property sold than the seller enjoyed. The first crack in the caveat emptor doctrine was the **good-faith purchase** exception to security of property.]

Certified check — check drawn by a customer on his bank and accepted by the bank, the act of acceptance constituting certification. [The commercial advantages of the certified check are that it virtually eliminates the risks of insufficient funds and stopped payment.] (*See also* **cashier's check.**)

Channel of distribution — method of marketing products. [Each seller must decide which method of distributing its goods is most efficient. Large firms may seek economies through **vertical integration.** Smaller firms may use **direct sales** efforts, **distributors, manufacturers' agents,** or a combination of these and other distribution methods.]

Chattel — item of personal property.

Check — a **negotiable instrument**, being an order (i.e., a **draft**) drawn on a bank and payable on demand. [Formerly, some checks were "counter" checks that permitted a depositor to use a blank check supplied by a merchant. With the advent of reader sorter machines in the bank collection system and the need for microencoded ink character recognition (MICR) symbols that the reader sorter equipment reads, preprinted checks with symbols that route the check during the collection process and that identify the drawee bank and the drawer's account became indispensable. At that point, the counter check disappeared. There are a number of items in the bank collection system that are "near checks." The thrift industry in the 1970s introduced the **negotiable order of withdrawal** and the share draft. While these items are not technically checks (since they are not drawn on banks), they generally function as checks do, and most courts seem inclined to treat them as such. Current efforts at legislative reform are catching up with these financial industry innovations.]

Chose in action — right to bring an action to enforce an obligation. [At early common law, prompted by fears of fraudulent claims, courts were adamant in their opposition to the alienability of a chose in action. Only the original obligee could maintain the action. That view unduly inhibited the marketability of obligations (notes, **drafts, bonds,** etc.), and eventually, after a long struggle and with the prodding of the legislature, the courts abandoned it.]

Claim — an assertion of a property interest. [The true owner of goods that brings an action to recover them from a thief is making a claim. By the same token, a secured party that sues for the value of security that has been disposed of by a third party is making a claim. Causes of action in replevin and conversion are classic claims. One of the benefits of **good-faith purchase** status is that it cuts off the claims that arise most often.]

Coase theorem — the theorem that in a world without **transaction costs**, regardless of the legal allocation of risks, contracting parties will opt for a **pareto optimal** risk allocation.

Commercially reasonable security — procedures established by an **electronic messaging system** to ensure that transmissions are authorized.

Commission merchant — similar to a **broker**, except that the commission merchant traditionally does take delivery from its seller and may store and transport the merchandise and sell in its own name.

Commodities exchange — organization of merchants or brokers, usually at a given location, that trade commodities represented by contracts or other documents.

Confirmer — in letter of credit transactions, the party (usually a bank) that notifies the beneficiary of the credit (1) that it has in fact issued from the office of the **issuer** and (2) that adds its undertaking to that of the issuer that the beneficiary will be paid. (*See* **adviser**.)

Consignment — seller's delivery of goods to buyer for resale with the understanding that **title** will remain in seller and buyer will return to seller any goods that are not resold. [The law has some difficulty distinguishing true consignments from disguised inventory financing arrangements.]

Consumer — any party that uses up, rather than resells, services, raw materials, or products. [A utility company consumes raw materials and uses motor vehicles. In the broad sense, the utility is a consumer. The concept is often used more narrowly to cover individuals who are using goods or services for personal, family, or household purposes. It is important for commercial law to maintain the distinction between the consumer and the nonconsumer, and especially between the consumer and the **merchant**. Law fashioned to meet the exigencies of the merchant setting often does not suit the consumer setting, and, conversely, law fashioned to protect consumers often does not suit the marketplace's needs for celerity and certainty.]

Contract — legal obligation that arises from the **agreement** of the parties. [The distinction between *agreement* and *contract* is a basic Llewellynism grounded in the Uniform Commercial Code and in the dogma of legal realism—the jurisprudence he, in his role as chief reporter, enshrined in much of the Uniform Commercial Code.]

Cost — a nebulous and often troublesome concept in sales transactions relating to the expenses incurred by a seller in producing a product or service. [Buyers sometimes agree to buy on a seemingly simple "cost plus basis." In fact, there are significant difficulties in computing the cost of a manufactured or processed commodity or of services. Allocation of overhead is frequently the subject of dispute. Tooling-up costs and labor costs are very much subject to the whim of the manufacturer, unless the sales contract specifies matters in great detail. By making short production runs at times when employees are working at overtime rates and by using raw materials and parts that are the highest priced of those items in inventory, a producer can pass high costs on to its cost plus buyer. Even the most scrupulous seller and buyer will find themselves at odds over cost allocations, as cost accountants themselves frequently disagree over those allocations.]

Credit sale — sale not for cash. [When a seller delivers goods or provides services without substantially contemporaneous payment, it has extended credit to the buyer, and the law frequently imposes burdens on it. The act of extending credit is not commercially unreasonable and, in fact, is economically desirable. There inheres in the credit transaction the risk of the buyer's default, and the law generally takes account of that reality by depriving the seller of certain rights that the cash seller, who has not extended credit, still enjoys.] (*Compare* **cash sale.**)

CRS (*See* **commercially reasonable security.**)

Currency risk — the risk of loss occasioned by fluctuation in the relative value of two currencies. For example, if a U.S. seller and a Japanese buyer agree to the sale of construction equipment for delivery in 120 days at a designated price, there is a risk that the relative value of the U.S. dollar and the yen may change during that period. If the parties designate the price in yen, a fall in the value of the yen against the dollar during the 120-day period will yield a real loss for the seller, who will not be able to obtain as many dollars with the purchase price as it would have been able to obtain at the time the parties entered into the contract. One of the ways the parties can guard against currency risk is to hedge against that risk. Thus the U.S. seller could, at the time it entered into the sale with the Japanese buyer, enter into a corresponding agreement in the currency futures market to sell yen at a dollar price roughly equivalent to the then-value of the yen. If the yen falls relative to the dollar, the counterparty (a speculator, bank, or dealer, able to hedge against the risk it undertakes under the futures contract) will bear the loss, rather than the seller, who is not a speculator and is not otherwise able to hedge against a fall in the yen.

Dating — the practice of extending the time for payment beyond the customary credit period. [In the brass industry, for example, foundries that serve as parts **vendors** may sell on 30-day credit terms. If a brass parts buyer's business is seasonal, it may not be able to pay within 30 days, and the foundry may extend the time for payment to 60 or 90 days. EOM (end of month) dating is the practice, common in some industries, of having the credit term start at the end of the month in which purchases are made. Under EOM dating, a 30-day credit term will begin to run at the end of the month. Buyers who purchase at the beginning of a month will have more than 30 days, perhaps as many as 60 days, before payment is due.]

Dealer — a retailer, the last seller in the **channel of distribution.**

Death of contract — the idea that formal contract rules, especially the Statute of Frauds, the perfect tender rule, and the doctrine of consideration, are unimportant relics that courts largely ignore in deed, if not in word. [In reaction to the formalism that characterized contract law in the eighteenth and nineteenth centuries, courts began in this century and to some extent in the last to relax the enforcement of contract provisions and even to challenge the notion that contracts needed consideration to be binding. By invoking estoppel in all its guises, opening the parol evidence rule and the Statute of Frauds to numerous exceptions, inferring "missing terms," fashioning unconscionability and bad-faith defenses and standards, and generally rendering contract enforcement problematic and uncertain, courts have, in the words of Professor Grant Gilmore, given the death to contract. While Gilmore generally applauded this retreat from formalism, the development left commercial parties with serious problems. The issue in contract drafting became one not so much of spelling out the agreement but of predicting whether the courts would enforce the agreement as written. Merchants and business people have adapted in a number of ways. They have, in many cases, deprived the courts of jurisdiction by agreeing to commercial arbitration. To some extent, they have modified the contractual relationship by introducing commercial specialties such as standby letters of credit and first demand guaranties. It is axiomatic, furthermore, that they have increased their prices to cover the cost of doing business with contractual uncertainties.]

Defense — legal argument excusing nonpayment or other nonperformance of a contract or other obligation. [Defenses become important in commercial and contract law when the obligee transfers the **chose in action** to a third party. If that third party enjoys **good-faith purchase** protection, it takes free of commercial defenses, that is, personal defenses, but takes subject to real defenses. The law of each state determines which defenses are real and which personal, but it is the law in all jurisdictions that the good-faith purchaser takes free of the defenses of failure of consideration and fraud in the inducement. Since these two defense are the defenses that arise most commonly in commercial transactions, by protecting the good-faith purchaser from them, the doctrine of good-faith purchase provides significant protection. Real defenses usually cover such matters as incompetence, fraud in the execution, illegality, and the like, i.e., defenses arising out of rather uncommon settings.]

Delivery terms — terms in a sales contract that specify the place, time, and manner of delivery of goods or services. (*See also* **Price terms.**)

Demand — in economics, the quantity of a product that will be sold at a given price.

Demand curve — in economics, graph on which the *y* axis is the price and the *x* axis is the quantity of **demand.** (*Compare* **Supply curve.**)

Derivation principle — the first rule of conveyancing law, a synonym for the **shelter principle**, based on the notion that the taker derives all of his rights from the transferor. (*See also* **nemo dat rule.**)

Direct sales — sales by a manufacturer or other supplier to its customers without using a **commission merchant, manufacturer's agent,** or the like.

Discount —

(1) reductions in the price, usually by virtue of early payment, volume purchase, or early order. [In an open account sale, for example, sellers might offer 60-day credit terms with a 5 percent discount for payment within 30 days. Seasonal businesses, anxious to even out their production schedules, to increase cash flow during slow periods, and to reduce inventory costs, will offer special discounts to customers that place orders early in the season or off season. Many manufacturers offer discounts to special customers, such as **OEM** or fleet buyers. Sometimes, sellers in an industry publish their price lists and give trade discounts off the list price. Trade discounts are determined by the market, and the trade discount arrangement is designed to obviate the need to republish price lists.]

(2) purchase of **dealer** paper at a price below face. [Formerly, banks performed an important function called the "discount function," which consisted of taking a merchant's paper (obligations, usually promissory notes, of the merchant's customers) and collecting it. When the bank took the paper, it paid less than par, i.e., less than the face value of the paper. The difference between par and the amount the bank paid was the discount. Today, banks and other lenders discount retail installment contracts and receivables for dealers and sometimes discount a seller's time draft.]

Distributor — enterprise that buys from manufacturers, transports, stores, and resells to **original equipment manufacturers,** governmental units, mining, transportation, communications, retailers, and similar firms. [Distributors are **wholesalers.** Distributors that deal in products that are not sold at retail are sometimes called "industrial distributors."]

Documentary draft — a **draft** accompanied by a **document of title.** [The documentary draft arises in the documentary draft transaction and the letter of credit transaction. Usually the document that accompanies the draft will be a **bill of lading** or a **warehouse receipt.**]

Document of title — document issued by or to a **bailee** involving the carriage or storage of goods. [The most common documents of title are the **bill of lading, the warehouse receipt**, and the **delivery order**, of which the first two also serve as a contract between the **bailor** and the bailee. Documents of title may be negotiable or non-negotiable. In the former case, they generally stand for the goods; in the latter they do not.] (*See also* **Bailment, Documentary draft, Negotiability.**)

Draft — an instrument, usually negotiable in form, by which the drawer of the draft orders the drawee to pay the payee. ["Sight" drafts are payable on demand, i.e., "at sight." "Time" or "usance" drafts are payable a period of time after presentment or date, i.e., "at usance." Drafts arise in the **letter of credit** transaction and the **documentary draft** transaction. A **check** is a draft drawn on a bank and payable on demand.]

Drop shipping — delivery of goods not to buyer but, at buyer's request, to buyer's sub-purchaser. [Frequently manufacturers or other suppliers will enter into contracts with buyers, such as **group buyers,** that do not take delivery of the merchandise. The buyer, who has located a sub-buyer, will direct the supplier to deliver to the sub-buyer, that is, to drop ship to the sub-buyer. Drop shipping is a common practice, and its significance to the supplier can be overemphasized. The typical seller will treat drop shipment instructions as ordinary delivery instructions, and courts should not, though they sometimes do, attach significance to the drop shipping arrangement.]

EDI (*See* **Electronic data interchange.**)

Elasticity — in economics, the direct response of one factor (e.g., price or supply) to the increase or decrease of another factor. [When demand or supply tends to react to price or income change, that demand or supply is said to be elastic. If, for example, the demand for French wine tends to increase as the price decreases or tends to increase as income increases, the demand for French wine is elastic. (In the first case "price elastic," in the second case "income elastic.") If the demand for bread does not decrease when the price increases or does not decrease when income decreases, the demand for bread is inelastic. Similarly, the supply of some agricultural commodities is inelastic, that is, when the price decreases, the supply may increase; while the supply of oil is traditionally seen to be elastic, since the supply of oil will usually increase as the price increases.]

Electronic data interchange — technological development, much ballyhooed of late, that permits information to be transmitted by computer technology. [Commercial activity is often subject to documentation, thanks in no small part to us lawyers. That documentation slows the process. It may take three days for a purchase order to travel by mail from Boston to San Francisco and three days for the order acknowledgment to get back. It takes seconds for information to be transmitted by computers using satellite and telephone communications systems. Buyers and sellers with access to electronic data interchange (EDI) systems can often conclude a **contract** in seconds, rather than days. EDI systems may be quite sophisticated. SWIFT, an international bank communication system, for example, uses switching centers, so that banks need access SWIFT only and need not have direct access to the hundreds of banks in the system. The switching center, acting like the hub of a hub-and-spoke system, can relay information from any sender to any bank connected to the system. Part III explains EDI in the Payments System, and Chapter 27 of that Part explains SWIFT.]

Electronic messaging systems — in **EDI**, the network that the parties to the interchange use to transmit their signals. Automated clearinghouses (discussed in Section 28.5) and SWIFT (discussed in Section 27.7) are electronic messaging systems.

EMC   (*See* **Export management consultant.**)

EMS   (*See* **Electronic messaging systems.**)

Estimated residual value — value at the time of entering into the lease that the parties to an equipment lease attribute to the equipment at the end of the lease. The parties use the estimated residual value as an incentive and reward for the lessee to maintain the equipment properly. If the actual residual value exceeds the estimated residual value, the lessor refunds a portion of the lease payments. The term has more application in the finance lease than in the true lease setting.

ETC (*See* **Export trading company.**)

Ex ante — before the fact. [In many executory contract situations, a party will attempt to take full advantage of the benefits accorded him under the contract at the outset (ex ante) but to deprive the other party of the benefits of the arrangement later (**ex post**).]

Export management consultant — a sales representative that provides expertise on document preparation, evaluation of foreign accounts, letter of credit facilitation, transport, and other matters often unfamiliar to domestic producers. (*Compare* **Export trading company.**)

Export trading company — exporter that purchases goods from a domestic producer and sells them abroad. Traditionally, export trading companies are thinly capitalized ventures, classic middlemen, that need credit to facilitate their purchase of the domestically produced goods and to enable them to provide their foreign buyers with credit terms.

Ex post — after the fact. (*Compare* **Ex ante.**)

Express warranty — obligation relating to the nature of goods or services imposed on a party, usually a seller, by virtue of terms in the agreement between the parties. (*Compare* **Implied warranty.**)

Externalities — consequences of economic activity that are not included in the cost of that activity. [If the cost of pollution from a garbage incinerator is borne by the residents in the vicinity of the incinerator rather than those who produce the garbage or use the steam generated by the incinerator, the pollution costs are externalities.]

Fabricator — manufacturing enterprise that takes a manufactured product and refashions it. [An aluminum fabricator, for example, takes aluminum ingots produced by a mill that refines bauxite (aluminum ore) into ingots. The fabricator takes the ingots and makes aluminum products, such as framing for storm doors and windows.]

Factor — formerly, a merchant that holds and sells the goods of others, today usually called a **commission merchant**. [For many centuries until the beginning of this one, manufacturers would use a factor to market their goods away from the place of manufacture, and agricultural producers would use factors to market their produce in the cities. A New York manufacturing firm would deliver merchandise to a factor who would transport the goods to Tennessee, for example, and sell them to retailers. Tennessee farmers would deliver grain to factors who would transport them to New Orleans, for example, and sell them to exporters or mills. Today, the term *factor* usually refers to finance companies that buy and collect or lend against receivables. The literature sometimes refers to the selling agent as the "old factor" and the company that finances receivables as the "new factor."] (*See also* **Supercargo.**)

Finisher — an enterprise that takes a product and transforms it in some way. [A textile finisher, for example, buys materials produced by a mill and, using dyes, creates patterns and colors in the product.]

Fixed cost — cost that does not increase with increases in sales. The cost of heating a manufacturing facility is a fixed cost, since it does not increase as productivity increases. (*Compare* **Variable cost.**)

Fordism — the manufacturing processes, developed by Henry Ford, involving a separation of intellectual work from repetitive assembly line work, with large inventories, mass production, and interchangeable parts. Now largely replaced in the U.S. manufacturing sector by **lean manufacturing.**

Forward contract — agreement for the sale of a specific quantity of goods or securities at an agreed-upon price, delivery and payment to be made at a subsequent date. (*See also* **Futures contract.**)

Franchise — the right to market a manufacturer's goods or to use a trade name or mark in a designated territory, often on an exclusive basis. [When an organization grants special marketing privileges, such as an exclusive territory and the use of marks or names, to a buyer, the arrangement is termed a franchise, the buyer being the franchisee and the seller the franchisor.]

Fraudulent conveyance — the third rule of conveyancing law under which the taker receives less than his transferor. [Under this third rule of conveyancing law, **security of property** and the **good-faith purchase** doctrine being the first two, in order to serve some public policy, usually one against fraud, the taker receives fewer rights than his transferor enjoyed in the property. If, for example, Transferor holds goods free and clear of any **claims** but owes money to Creditor, and if Transferor conveys to Transferee in a fashion that offends a fraudulent conveyancing statute or common law fraudulent conveyancing rule, Transferee takes the property subject to Creditor's claims. In short, even though Transferor held the property free of Creditor's claims, Transferee takes subject to them.]

Futures contract — agreement to sell a commodity or security at a future date. [A grain producer may enter into a contract in June with a local elevator to sell his corn for delivery and payment in October. The elevator will obtain the price of October corn from a commodity exchange and will immediately, unless the elevator is speculating, resell the contract on the exchange. The producer, in turn, has locked in the elevator at the agreed-upon price. Futures contracts have been the subject of litigation when the price of the commodity rises or falls dramatically after the parties enter into the contract. As a general rule, courts have recognized that parties entering into futures contracts assume that the buyer bears the risk of a falling market and the seller of a rising market and have enforced the contracts despite dramatic price fluctuation.]

Good-faith purchase — the second rule of conveyancing law, to the effect that a taker receives greater rights in the property transferred than the transferor enjoyed. [Conveyancing law has three basic rules: (1) the **security of property** principle, (2) the good-faith purchase principle, and (3) the doctrine of **fraudulent conveyance**. Under the first rule of conveyancing law, the transferee receives everything that his transferor had to convey, under the second he receives more, and under the third he receives less. Good-faith purchase is rooted in the market's need to provide for free movement of goods. By protecting the good-faith purchaser, the second principle of conveyancing permits the honest **purchaser** who acts in the ordinary course of business to give value without inquiring as to the transferor's **title**, that is, he cuts off **claims**. The one exception to the protection afforded the good-faith purchaser arises when he takes from a thief, for the thief cannot give the good-faith purchaser good title. The good-faith purchase doctrine also protects the purchaser from **defenses**. When the good-faith purchaser takes a **chose in action,** he generally cuts off those defenses of the obligor on the chose that arise by virtue of failure of consideration or fraud in the inducement.]

Gray market — market for goods in violation of some resale restrictions. [Some strong manufacturers will require their distributors to purchase periodically a minimum number of units or volume of product. A distributor that cannot sell all of the units or the volume at its customary price faces the problem of selling below that price or selling to distributors that are not authorized distributors of the manufacturer. Often, the authorized distributor is unwilling to cut its price. Once it does so, it becomes difficult to enforce the customary price. The distributor, therefore, resorts to the unauthorized distributors who comprise the gray market.]

Gresham's law — the principle that when bad money competes with good money in circulation, debtors will hoard the good money and pay their debts with the bad money, that is, the principle that bad money drives out good money. [The term now has a broader meaning and applies whenever lower standards in an industry drive out higher standards by putting the party that maintains the high standards at a competitive disadvantage.]

Guaranty — usually, a secondary obligation, contingent on default of the principal obligor. [A guarantor of principal's debt undertakes to pay the debt if principal fails to pay it when due. In some areas of commerce, there are primary guarantees. These undertakings, often issued by banks or other financially strong institutions, serve to guarantee the obligation of a principal but are payable not on the principal's default but on the presentation of documents.] (*Compare* **Independent guaranty**.)

Hedging — the practice of matching sales and purchases in order to reduce market risks. [In order to protect themselves against price fluctuation, parties that deal in commodities and that are not willing to speculate will match one purchase or sale with another purchase or sale. For example, an Iowa propane gas **wholesaler** that knows it will need product in February may buy February propane on the futures market. If the price has risen in February when the wholesaler needs the propane, it will purchase locally at the higher price but make a profit on the futures contract, which it will sell on the exchange. The wholesaler might not take delivery of the propane under the futures contract because the delivery point under the contract could be in Houston. On August 1, a manufacturer of corn meal will buy corn from a seller to make into product and agree at the same time to sell the same quantity of corn at the same price to a buyer on August 30, the day the corn meal will be ready for market. If the price of corn increases, the manufacturer will not enjoy any profit on the corn, since it will have to buy corn in the market to fill its contract to sell on August 30. If, on the other hand, the price of corn falls, the manufacturer will have avoided the loss on his meal, which will now sell at a lower price given the drop in the raw material cost. Even though the manufacturer will not be able to sell its meal at a price that reflects its cost, it will make money on the August 30 sale, since it will buy at market (low) and sell at the contract price (high). Hedging will occur whenever there is a recognized market. The practice is common in the securities industry and in banking as well as the commodities markets.]

Identification — determination that certain goods will be used to satisfy a contract of sale. [By designating certain goods to a contract for sale the seller alone or the buyer and seller together have identified the goods. Identification is a critical time in the sales transaction. It is the first moment at which the buyer has an interest in the goods. That interest is an insurable interest and a **special property.**]

Implied warranty — obligation imposed by the law on a party, usually a seller, relating to the nature of goods or services. [The implied warranty arises even though the parties' agreement is silent as to warranties and may survive efforts by the obligor to disclaim the warranty if the disclaimer fails to meet statutory requirements.] (*Compare* **Express warranty.**)

Indemnity agreement — primary undertaking of the indemnitor to hold the indemnitee harmless from losses. [A buyer of goods, for example, may need to take delivery of them from a carrier before the buyer has obtained the **bill of lading** covering them. The buyer will ask the carrier to release the goods against an indemnity agreement, which the buyer will obtain from a financially strong institution.]

Indenture — (1) agreement between the obligor on bonds or debentures and the holders of those obligations; (2) a real estate deed to which there are two parties, rather than simply a grantor.

Independent guaranty — a guaranty (sometimes spelled "guarantee") that secures an obligation but that is payable against the presentation of documents rather than against the fact of breach of the underlying obligation. Because the independent guarantor must pay against the presentation of conforming documents, courts generally will not permit the guarantor to dishonor the independent guaranty for reasons based on the equities of the underlying obligation. The rule of **guaranties** is "argue now, pay later." The rule of the independent guaranty is "pay now, argue later." An independent guaranty is for all practical purpose the equivalent of a **standby letter of credit.**

Installment — partial performance or payment. [Sales contracts frequently call for delivery of goods or services in discrete increments over a period of time. Also, sales contracts and other obligations sometimes call for payment in increments.]

Invoice — a record of the charges and a description of the goods or services provided by the seller and rendered to the buyer. [In lay parlance, the invoice is the seller's bill for goods sold or services rendered.]

ITC pass-through lease — investment tax credit pass-through lease, that is, a lease under which the lessor passes the investment tax credit (assuming the income tax laws were to create one again) to the lessee.

Jobber — middleman in the **channel of distribution** who traditionally buys from a manufacturer, distributor, or importer, often in small or odd lots, and resells to **dealers** or other retailers.

Just-in-time inventory — an inventory control practice under which buyers order parts or raw materials for delivery at the time that the buyer expects to use them in its production run. A just-in-time inventory program entails considerable coordination between a manufacturer and its suppliers but potentially reduces the cost of holding inventory, that is, the interest charges on loans the manufacturer needs to pay for parts and raw materials and the cost of storing the parts and raw materials.

Kaldor-Hicks efficiency — notion that the reallocation of resources is efficient if society in the aggregate is better off, without regard for the fact that one party may be made worse off by that reallocation. [Kaldor-Hicks efficiency differs, then, from **pareto** efficiency, which does not favor reallocation that makes one person worse off.] (*Compare* **Pareto optimal.**)

Lean manufacturing — the process of manufacturing with modern inventory control practices, including **just-in-time inventory** and **quick-response** programs, all with a view of keeping inventory carrying costs low and avoiding inventory obsolescence. Lean manufacturing is arguably the first significant departure from **Fordism**, the process of mass production initiated by Henry Ford in the first decade of this century.

Lease — agreement for the use of property under which the lessor permits the lessee to use the property in return for a stipulated rent. [Real estate and equipment are the most common subjects of leases. Equipment leases may be true leases or disguised sales contracts with a security interest reserved to the seller.] (*See also* **Net lease.**)

Leaseback   (*See* **sale and leaseback.**)

Letter of credit — an undertaking, usually issued by a bank, in favor of a beneficiary and on behalf of the issuer's customer, to honor **drafts** or demands for payment, often on the condition that they be accompanied by other documents.

Limited partnership — partnership made up of one or more general partners and a number of limited partners. [The limited partnership is a device used to syndicate real estate developments, oil and gas exploration, equipment leasing ventures, and the like. The general partner is the syndicator or a cognate that plans the venture and carries it out. The limited partners are usually just investors with only their investment at risk.]

Liquidated — determined, fixed. [A **claim** is liquidated when there is no bona fide dispute over the amount due, though there may be a dispute over the validity of the claim itself.]

Lock box — collection facility that permits a collecting bank or other party to intercept a payee's mail, remove **checks** or other instruments, and collect them. [Corporations with widespread sales face the problem of consolidating their funds efficiently. The lock box assists the company's comptroller in that process by permitting the company to collect payments at diverse locations and deposit them at nearby banks, thereby reducing float and making the funds available for the company's cash needs more quickly.]

Loss leader — merchandise sold by a retailer at a loss in order to attract customers for other merchandise.

Manufacturers' agent — independent enterprise that represents two or more manufacturers, usually of related products, and services customers on a continuing basis. [Unlike **wholesalers** and **distributors**, manufacturers' agents generally do not purchase and store merchandise, except for samples, and do not provide repair or maintenance service.]

Manufacturers' representative   (*See* **Manufacturers' agent.**)

Manufacturers' sales branch — a vertical extension of the manufacturer's operation involved in wholesaling and, therefore, different from manufacturers' **direct sales** operations. [Sometimes the branch will not stock merchandise but operates solely as a sales office and not as a wholesaler.]

Marginal cost — increase or decrease in a producer's total cost of production by producing one more unit, i.e., the cost of the last item produced. [Theoretically, marginal cost determines the rate of production, since producers should increase production as long as doing so reduces the marginal cost and should reduce production when doing so decreases marginal cost. In normal economic times, most producers do not reach optimum output, the point at which marginal cost equals the average cost of producing a unit and at which the producer's profits are maximized per unit of production. For some producers, however, and in times of shortages, for many producers, production has reached a level that makes further economies of scale impossible. Such producers, if they increase production, will lose more on the increase than they make, because, for example, they have to hire additional workers who will not be utilized efficiently or because they have to add warehouse or shipping capacity that will not be used efficiently.]

Market overt — market in which purchasers take free of **claims**. [For a long time the merchants of England had chafed under the **security of property** rule that made it necessary for buyers to investigate the **title** of their sellers or bear the risk that the title was defective. Eventually, they established the notion of market overt, whereby sales made at designated places and at designated times were not subject to the security of property notion but to the doctrine of **good-faith purchase**. Eventually the term came to include all sales that benefit from good-faith purchase.]

Market value — a nebulous concept that assumes that property has an inherent value abstract from any actual sales price. [From time to time it is necessary to determine the value of property without selling it. If the property is similar to that traded on a recognized market, market value is the same as market price. If A holds 100 shares of common stock in X Corporation, whose common stock is traded publicly on the New York Stock Exchange, the market value of A's stock is computed by using the price at which X Corporation common trades on the exchange. As the market price goes up or down, the market value of A's stock goes up or down. This perfectly rational concept has given rise to an irrational myth — the idea that property that is not traded in a recognized market still has market value and that some expert can determine it. There are times when it is imperative that the law determine property values without a sale. In eminent domain cases, for example, the parties and perhaps ultimately the court, must place a value on the property that the state takes. Similarly, it is necessary to place a value on property for property tax purposes. The use of experts who give their opinions in those cases (nontransaction situations) should not give rise to the mistaken notion that their opinions are more than that — opinions. Opinions of market value are not market price. Unfortunately, courts have often been seduced into thinking that because the law recognizes those opinions in nontransaction situations, the law is justified in assuming that those opinions are the equivalent of market price. In some cases, for example, courts will hear testimony of market price and conclude that the contract price is unfair or unrealistic or unconscionable and therefore unenforceable. In fact, contract prices agreed to in arm's-length settings are the market price, the opinions of the experts are usually the source of the unrealistic prices.]

Materialman — in the construction industry, a subcontractor of the **prime contractor** or another subcontractor that agrees to supply materials for the project. (*See also* **Mechanic's lien.**)

Mechanic's lien — claim against property and, sometimes, against funds due for work done on or materials supplied for construction of improvements to real estate or personal property.

Mercantile agency — generally, a credit reporting agency that sometimes also does collections. [The advent of mercantile agencies made open account selling possible. Dun & Bradstreet and TRW are two of the larger mercantile agencies.]

Merchant — person or entity that deals in goods or services of a kind or holds itself out as having expertise peculiar to the goods or services or to whom such expertise may be attributed by virtue of its engagement of a merchant. [The merchant is often held to a higher standard than the nonmerchant. Much of the tension in commercial law today results when (1) parties attempt to enforce against nonmerchants rules fashioned for the market place and (2) courts apply to merchants rules whose proper application should be limited to situations involving consumers or other nonmerchants. The distinction between merchants and nonmerchants does not resolve all of the difficulty, since the line between the two is often blurred. Most commentators prefer a broad reading of the term *merchant*.]

Money order — **draft** usually on or payable at a bank, sold by the bank to a customer who pays cash for the draft and uses it in lieu of a **check**. [The postal service also sells money orders.]

Moral hazard — unintended consequence, consisting of an incentive to behave in an economically inefficient fashion, usually arising out of a system designed to allocate losses. [If a system permits A at no cost to himself to incur costs for B, the system poses a moral hazard. Casualty insurance is an efficient device for spreading casualty losses, but it poses the moral hazard that one party owning an asset that she cannot sell will fake an accident, that is, the existence of the insurance may create the moral hazard that owners will destroy their property. Similarly, the existence of liability insurance may lead parties to act with less care, since the losses their carelessness produces are covered by insurance. Welfare benefits provided by the state can yield similar moral hazards.]

Negotiability — in negotiable instruments law, the **good-faith purchase** rule. [Under the doctrine of negotiability, the holder in due course and a person having the rights of a holder in due course cut off **claims** and **defenses**.]

Negotiable order of withdrawal — a customer's order, widely adopted by the thrift industry, for transferring deposits. [Traditionally, thrift industry deposits were not demand deposits, that is, they were not available to the depositor by **draft** or **check**. With the advent of deregulation in the banking and thrift industries, thrifts initiated competition with commercial banks by offering thrift customers the negotiable order of withdrawal and its ability to transfer deposits (financial institution credits) to third parties.]

Nemo dat rule — the principle that a taker by voluntary conveyance cannot take more than his transferor had to convey. [This is a corollary of the **security of property** principle. It is an old idea, rooted in logic, that one cannot give what one does not have. It comes from a Latin maxim: *nemo dat quod non habet.*]

Net — said of an amount calculated by subtracting charges of one kind or another. [List prices and specified prices in a contract are often subject to adjustments for discounts, returned merchandise, and the like. Rents specified in a lease are subject to similar adjustments for taxes, maintenance charges, and insurance. Net prices and net rents are prices and rents so adjusted.]

Net lease — lease under which the lessee pays property taxes, insurance, and maintenance costs, sometimes referred to as a "triple net" lease.

Net net — said of any arrangement that involves more than one netting process. [If, for example, a settlement system is "netted" it is bilateral, so that each party to the system nets against the other. If the system calls for all parties to settle with a central party, the netting takes two steps for two parties to net against each other. They each net against the central party. CHIPS (*see* Chapter 27) involves net net settlements, since the CHIPS switch acts as a central clearing agent.]

Nominal — said of prices and interest rates expressed in figures that do not reflect inflation or deflation. [Nominal prices or interest rates may be misleading. The nominal interest rate on a bond may be 10 percent over one year, but inflation will make the *real* interest rate something below 10 percent. A seller may list a nominal price for merchandise but with various discounts may never charge that price.]

Nominated bank — in letter of credit practice it is common for the issuer of a credit to nominate some other bank to (1) honor the credit obligation and (2) seek reimbursement from the issuer. A Dutch bank that issues a credit payable in Australian dollars to a Sydney seller may nominate a Sidney bank to honor the beneficiary/seller's draft or demand for payment. The Sidney bank will have Australian dollars to pay the seller and will reimburse itself through an interbank arrangement that permits easy set off and exchange of bank obligations.

OEM   (*See* **Original equipment manufacturer.**)

Operating lease — an equipment lease under which the lessor services the equipment and, sometimes, agrees to update the equipment in the event of product improvements. [Users of high technology equipment are often reluctant to make large investments in equipment that may have a long useful life but that might become obsolete as a consequence of improvements made by the manufacturer. The operating lease is a device manufacturers and users have implemented to give the manufacturer greater accessibility to the market and the user more security in the event the manufacturer improves its product.]

Opportunity cost — cost incurred when a person chooses one activity over another. [Law students not only pay tuition and expenses while they go to law school, they also incur an opportunity cost — the loss of income they would have earned had they entered the work force full time instead of attending law school.]

Option — the right to obligate another to perform, usually, a contract for sale. [In the securities industry, the right to require another to sell is called a *call option*; the right to require another to buy a *put option*. Options also frequently arise in real estate transactions.]

Order acknowledgment — the seller's indication that it has accepted the buyer's offer to purchase. (*Compare* **Purchase order.**)

Original equipment manufacturer — designation sellers give to their buyers that take the sellers' product and incorporate it into a new product. [A manufacturer of hose, for example, may sell to distributors, retailers, and industrial and household consumers that use the hose as a discrete product. The seller may also have a customer that uses the hose, say, in a washing machine or motor vehicle that it manufactures for sale. The seller would refer to this customer as an original equipment manufacturer and would often make special discounts and other sales terms available to it.] (*See also* **Vendor.**)

Ostensible ownership — the concept that possession of personal property connotes ownership. [In personal property law, **title** is not a matter of record and may be difficult to determine. To some extent, the concept of possession has supplanted the concept of title: "Possession is nine points of the law." The law recognizes, furthermore, that possession often raises reasonable expectations on the part of third parties. A true owner, for example, will not be heard to say that he owns the horse he delivered to a horse merchant at a horse auction, if the merchant sells the animal to a **good-faith purchaser**. The merchant has ostensible title to the horse and gives good title to the buyer.]

Overhead — costs that are not directly related to the production of a product or the provision of services. [Insurance and taxes are part of a manufacturer's overhead; raw material expenses are generally not.]

Pareto optimal — in **welfare economics,** said of the allocation of property that has achieved the maximum efficiency of distribution, i.e., when no change in that allocation can benefit one person without damaging another. [If under allocation A every one is as well off as under allocation B and at least one party is better off, allocation A is pareto superior to allocation B.] (*Compare* **Kaldor-Hicks efficiency.**)

Payable-through draft — **draft** drawn on someone other than a bank and payable through the bank that, rather than paying the item, presents it to the person on which it is drawn. [Self-administered insurance plans use payable-through drafts. An employer providing insurance to its employees, for example, will draw a draft on the insurance company for the amount of an employee's loss. When the payable-through bank presents the payable-through draft to the insurance company, the company will check to see that the draft is in order. If it is, the insurance company will authorize payment of the draft. Credit unions use payable-through drafts as their share drafts.]

Payment bond — surety company's undertaking to pay all suppliers and subcontractors in the event the purchaser of those supplies or services does not pay for them. [In real estate construction, owners are concerned that the **prime contractor** may complete the work but not pay all of the suppliers or subcontractors. The owner will insist that the prime contractor obtain a payment bond to insure that there are no liens on the property.] (*See also* **Performance bond.**)

Performance bond—surety company's undertaking to complete performance of a contract in the event the obligor fails to perform. [In the construction industry, owners traditionally require contractors to supply a performance bond. In the event of the contractor's default, the surety company engages another contractor to complete the work.] (*Compare* **Payment bond.**)

Prepaying buyer—buyer that pays the seller in advance of delivery of goods or services. [In the simplest transaction of sale, the seller delivers the goods against the buyer's payment of the price. The demands of modern commerce do not always permit simple sales transactions, and sellers frequently sell on credit. On the rare occasion, the seller and the buyer will agree upon prepayment. Such prepayment raises questions concerning the buyer's rights in the goods. Some courts have concluded that the prepaying buyer is a **buyer in ordinary course**; others have taken the position that the prepaying buyer is really a lender who has no interest in the goods other than an unperfected security interest. Generally, the prepaying buyer should bear the risks his prepayment creates, but courts and commentators do not always agree.]

Present value—the value today of a future payment or payments. [Present value is computed by discounting the future payment in a calculation that presumes the rate of interest (compounded) on funds over the period in question. To compute, for example, the present value of $10,000 to be paid ten years from today, it is necessary to assume an interest rate that the discounted sum will earn that will yield $10,000 of principal and interest in ten years. If the assumed rate is 10 percent per year, the present value will be $6,145; if the assumed rate is 5 percent per year, the present value will be $7,722.]

Price elasticity—the degree to which price is a direct function of demand or supply. [When the demand for a product (e.g., imported wine) increases and decreases as the price decreases and increases, the demand is price elastic. If the demand for a product (e.g., bread) remains relatively steady in the face of price changes, the demand is price inelastic. If supply of a product (e.g., oil) increases and decreases with increases and decreases in price, the supply is price elastic; if supply of the product remains steady when prices increase or decrease (or even increases when prices decrease as in the case of agricultural commodities), the supply is price inelastic.]

Price terms — terms in a sales contract that describe the financial compensation of the seller and also may include discount, credit, and method of payment terms. [The shipment terms "C.I.F." and "C&F" are price terms. They determine the remuneration that the buyer must provide to the seller. "F.O.B." and "F.A.S." are **delivery terms.**]

Prime contractor — in the construction industry and under government contracts, the contractor that enters into a contract with the owner of the project or the government. [Contractors who enter into contracts with the prime contractor to do portions of the prime contractor's work are subcontractors.]

Production sharing — the practice of exporting from the United States partially manufactured goods for further manufacture, followed by reimportation of the product into the United States for resale or further manufacture.

Pro forma invoice — an invoice usually prepared in advance of shipment of the goods subject to a contract for sale that is not the actual or commercial **invoice** but that approximates the terms of the actual invoice and can be used to obtain import documents or as a benchmark against which the commercial invoice can be measured.

Progress payments — in the construction industry and under other contracts, especially government contracts, payments by the owner to the contractor periodically for work done.

Purchase — transfer by voluntary conveyance. [As a general rule, in contract and commercial law, a voluntary conveyance is a purchase transaction. Buyers, donees, and secured parties are purchasers. Some purchasers, such as secured parties and buyers, are purchasers for value. Some purchasers, such as secured parties or mortgagees, are purchasers of less than the full interest. The law also distinguishes between the **good-faith purchaser** and the purchaser who takes out of the ordinary course (such as the buyer under a **bulk sale**) or with notice of title infirmities. Persons who take by involuntary conveyance are not purchasers. A buyer at a sheriff's sale and a lien creditor are not purchasers, since they take their interest in property by operation of law rather than by voluntary transfer.]

Purchase order — the form in which the buyer customarily makes its offer to purchase the seller's goods or services. [In many industries, seller's publish price lists. Potential purchasers take information from the price list and incorporate it into a purchase order. Traditionally, the purchase order was in writing, but often parties take purchase orders by telephone or **EDI**. Some sellers confirm the purchase arrangement with an order acknowledgment. In the fast pace of domestic sales, the paperwork may lag behind performance. When a sales office is busy, the sales manager may be more concerned about getting orders shipped than about getting the papers out. Lawyers, of course, are always more concerned about the papers. That is one of the reasons that the president of a company is usually more respectful of his sales vice president than he is of his lawyer.]

Quasi lease — not a true lease, but a credit sale disguised as a lease or a security agreement securing a loan to purchase the equipment that is the subject of the lease.

Quick-response — an inventory control practice under which retailers or others who hold inventory for sale keep track of that inventory with computer technology and replenish inventory on the basis of data generated by that technology. A retailer that stocks 10,000 items, as some mass merchandisers do, can achieve significant efficiencies by keeping moment-to-moment track of inventory levels in order to determine which items need to be reordered and which items should not.

Regression analysis — in statistics, the determination of the extent to which a dependent variable relates to an independent variable. [For example, a manufacturer may want to know whether rainfall in a geographic area is related to sales of irrigation equipment in that area. The process of determining the relationship between rainfall (the independent variable) and sales (the dependent variable) is regression analysis. If the relationship is perfect and direct, the correlation coefficient is 1, that is, a 100 percent increase in rainfall yields a 100 percent increase in product sales. The coefficient is \-\1 if an increase in rainfall yields an identical decrease in sales. If there is no correlation between rainfall and sales, the coefficient is 0.]

Reinsurance — that part of an insurance risk that one insurance company transfers to a second company (the reinsurer). [Reinsurance is the insurance analogue to the banking industry's practice of transferring parts of loans, i.e., loan participations.]

Requirements contract — sales agreement under which the buyer agrees to take all of its need for a product from the seller. [When a buyer wants to protect itself against shortages and price increases, it may agree to give an exclusive contract to a supplier by promising to purchase all of its requirements from that single supplier. If the contract fixes a price, the arrangement deprives the buyer of any advantage it might realize if the market price of the product supplied goes down. The quantity term of a requirements contract is open, and disputes sometimes arise if the buyer's needs for the product increase dramatically. Sometimes, the price term remains open in a requirements contract. In that case, the buyer is attempting to assure itself of a source of supply but does not have any protection against a rising market.]

Resale price maintenance — the manufacturer (or supplier) practice of specifying the prices above or below which a customer may not sell products.

Risk — the possibility of loss. [There are many kinds of risk, and parties frequently allocate risks in their contracts. Among the kinds of risk that may be allocated are risk of accidental loss, exchange rate fluctuation, political upheaval, insolvency, market increases or decreases, material shortages, unforeseen developments, and litigating in a foreign jurisdiction. Unhappily, some courts do not understand that commercial, as opposed to consumer, parties almost always allocate risk in their contract, and those courts are wont to reallocate the risks based on the courts' views of what is fair.]

RISK (*See* **Retail installment sales contract** in Part II glossary.)

Risk-averse — said of a party that is willing to pay more than the market price in order to avoid a risk. Some parties may be willing, for example, to buy insurance against a 1 percent chance of sustaining a $1 million loss from the destruction of a building from an earthquake at a price that is greater than the probability of such loss times the value of the building ($0.01 \times \$1,000,000 = \$10,000$). Such an owner is risk-averse. The same owner might not be risk-averse (**risk-neutral**), however, in the case of a 10 percent chance of sustaining a $100,000 loss ($0.1 \times \$100,000 = \$10,000$), even though the risk is the same in both examples. (*Compare* **Risk-neutral.**)

Risk-neutral — said of a party that is unwilling to pay more than the cost of a risk determined by multiplying the probability of that loss by the amount of the loss. (*Compare* **risk-averse.**)

Sale and leaseback — arrangement under which the owner of property, usually real estate or equipment, sells the property to a party that leases it back to the original owner.

Security of property — the first rule of conveyancing law, the principle that a party may transfer an interest in property freely. [The first and necessary corollary of this rule law is the **shelter principle** — the idea that the taker receives all of the transferor's interest. The second and equally necessary corollary is the idea that the taker receives no greater rights than those of the transferor. This is the **nemo dat rule**. The net effect of the two corollaries is that the taker will receive exactly the same interest that the transferor enjoyed. It is important to bear in mind that the first principle of conveyancing law with its two corollaries is the starting point in any conveyancing analysis. If the transaction does not qualify for treatment under the second (the **good-faith purchase** principle) or third (the **fraudulent conveyance** principle) rules, the first rule always applies.]

Selling agent — an independent enterprise similar to the **manufacturer's agent** but with more authority for determining prices and other sales terms with its customers and often with the exclusive right to handle the entire production output of the manufacturer.

Shelter principle — a corollary to the first rule of conveyancing law (**security of property**) — the notion that the transferee obtains exactly the same interest that the transferor conveyed. [Under the first corollary, the shelter principle, the taker enjoys all of the interests in the property conveyed that the transferor enjoyed. Under negotiable instruments law, for example, a transferee from a holder in due course generally will have the rights of a holder in due course, even though the transferee does not itself meet the requisites for holder in due course status. Similarly, a buyer in ordinary course, having bought without notice of **claims**, usually cuts off those claims and can convey that power to its transferee even though the transferee knows of the claims at the time it takes. The shelter principle has an important obverse feature. Just as the taker under the shelter principle takes every thing that the transferor enjoyed, so he can take no more. This feature is the **nemo dat** principle.]

Specialized market — market in which there are few substitutes. The market for artificial heart valves is a specialized market. (*Compare* **Thick market.**)

Special property — an interest in property, but not **title** and not a security interest. [When goods are **identified** to a contract for sale, the buyer has a special property in them. That special property is not the same as title; it is something less than title. It is an interest that gives the buyer rights in the goods. That is not to say that the buyer's rights by virtue of the special property are superior to those of the seller or some third party. They may not be. The fact that a buyer has a special property in goods under a contract for sale, for example, even though it arises before the time for delivery, does not relieve the buyer from its obligation to pay the seller the price.]

Specialty — at early common law, a contract under seal. [Bonds, for example were usually under seal. They needed no consideration to be binding, and the paper itself, the bond, rather than any underlying promise, was the source of the obligation. The term "specialty" has developed to encompass any obligation embodied in an instrument that is independent of the transaction out of which it arises. **Letters of credit** are said to be specialties because they are peculiarly independent of the transactions out of which they arise. To some extent, negotiable instruments are specialties. With the **death of contract**, courts have declined to enforce contractual obligations vigorously, and the distinction between **contracts** and specialties has taken on a significance that it did not have at early common law or even as recently as the beginning of this century. As commercial parties became aware of the imprecision that courts had given to contractual undertakings and the slow, painful, and often unpredictable process that attended the enforcement of contracts, those parties (primarily merchants and bankers) began to rely increasingly on tools of international trade that had retained their commercial rigor. The letter of credit and the first demand guaranty, both of which are arguably specialties, have grown in importance as a consequence of these developments and of the commercial need for undertakings that can be enforced with celerity and certainty. Regrettably, courts are not always inclined to observe the distinction, so that the death of contract may be followed by the death of specialty.]

Specialty manufacturer — a manufacturer that fabricates goods, often machinery, at the request and to the specifications of the buyer. [The specialty manufacturer is often a rather small concern relative to the buyer and may be thinly capitalized.]

Speculating — buying and selling in the hope of being able to profit from changes in market price. [While most buyers and sellers buy and sell in connection with their activity in a line of commerce in a fashion that reduces the risk of price fluctuation, some buyers and sellers are speculators, that is, they buy and later sell with a view at the outset of playing the market. While a grain elevator, for example, may buy and sell grain, it usually **hedges** in a way to reduce the risk of price decreases, realizing that such hedging wipes out any profit that might accrue because of price increases. The grain speculator, on the other hand, buys grain when it thinks the price will go up and sells grain, usually on the futures market, when it suspects that the price will go down. Some observers feel that speculators are an unworthy branch of the **merchant** profession. In fact, speculators play a critical role in stabilizing prices. By virtue of their willingness to play the market, other buyers and sellers are able to **hedge** and to find sources of supply and outlets for product when otherwise there would be limited sources and outlets. To some extent, nearly all merchants must speculate, since they can never protect themselves completely from the vagaries of the market, but the existence of speculators renders market vagaries more manageable.]

Spot delivery — immediate delivery.

Spot market — over-the-counter market (i.e., one conducted by telephone or similar wire communication) for commodities that are bought and sold for cash and immediate delivery. (*Compare* **Futures contract.**)

Statement — summary of periodic activity of a customer's account.

Strategic behavior — engaging in behavior that advances self-interest at the cost of a counterparty. A seller, for example, under a contract for sale with weak delivery requirements, may deliver at times inconvenient to the buyer but advantageous to the seller, all contrary to what a buyer might reasonably expect. Such a seller is engaging in strategic behavior.

Supercargo — formerly, a ship's captain that took on merchandise and transported it, often from port to port, looking for a buyer. [**Title** to the goods remained in the seller, the supercargo being an agent. The arrangement might have misled creditors of the supercargo if it had not been clear that his authority over the goods entrusted to him included the power to sell them but not to borrow against them, i.e., the supercargo had no power to "mortgage" the goods.] (*See also* **Factor.**)

Supply curve — graph on which price is the y axis and quantity of supply is the x axis. (*Compare* **Demand curve.**)

Take or pay contract — in the oil and gas industry a contract in the nature of a term supply arrangement under which the seller guarantees that it will supply product and the buyer guarantees that it will take product with the understanding that in the event the buyer does not have the storage capacity or otherwise cannot take delivery, the buyer will pay the seller the purchase price.

Telex — telecommunications device that permits communication, often internationally by translating telephonic signals into words and printing them on a receiving machine. [Often, the parties refer to the message as printed by the telex machine as a "telex."]

Teller check — an official check, i.e., one issued by a financial institution, rather than a **merchant** or **consumer.**

Thick market — a market in which there are many substitutes. In the restaurant industry, there are many suppliers of pasta, so the market for pasta is thick. (*Compare* **Specialized market.**)

Title — the notion of property ownership and its concomitant, the power to exclude others from its use or possession. [Title is a metaphysical concept embedded in the psychology of the individual, as any witness to sibling or schoolyard disputes can attest. It is difficult to imagine that the title notion did not antedate sophisticated legal systems. Primitive jurisprudence may give ownership to the strong and take it from the weak, but the concept of title is nonetheless present. Karl Llewellyn, the chief reporter for the Uniform Commercial Code, felt that the law, especially sales law, was burdening the title concept too much. He argued against deciding issues of risk of loss and the like on the basis of title and fashioned a statute that largely dethroned that ancient concept. Whether he succeeded in depriving courts and lawyers of a notion that is as much psychological as legal and that may be stronger than any legislative enactment remains to be seen.]

TRAC lease — true lease containing a terminal rental adjustment clause. [Automotive leases often contain a terminal rental adjustment clause under which the parties specify a value for the vehicle at the end of the lease term. Upon the termination of the lease, if the vehicle is worth more than the specified value, the lessee receives a return of rent payment equal to the excess. If the terminal value is less than the specified value, the lessee must account to the lessor for the deficit.]

Trade acceptance — an **acceptance** on which the acceptor is a merchant rather than a bank. (*See also* **Banker's acceptance.**)

Trading partner — the two parties (usually a buyer and a seller of goods or services) that have entered into an agreement for the use of **EDI.** Such an agreement will include the adoption of standards, security procedures, systems operation, and other matters peculiar to the EDI relationship.

Transaction costs — costs incurred in order to effect a transaction as opposed to the cost of the goods themselves. [If a buyer spends $5,000 to learn of the location of goods that he needs and to arrange the contract for their purchase and then pays $100,000 to the seller for the goods, the transaction costs are $5,000.]

Turnkey project — a project sold to a customer with the understanding that the seller will set it up so that the buyer can walk in and operate the project. [A seller of car wash equipment may offer a turnkey operation to its customers who would expect to be able to operate the car wash without start-up costs after the seller installs the equipment.]

Tying — marketing practice whereby the seller refuses to sell the tying product (presumably an attractive product) unless the buyer agrees to buy the tied product (presumably a less competitive product). [Sometimes the tying seller does not require the buyer to buy the tied product but insists that the buyer promise not to buy the tied product from anyone else. Motion picture distributors, for example, might "blockbook" their products by requiring movie houses to take less attractive films in order to get the box office successes.]

Umbrella rule   (*See* **Shelter principle**.)

Usance   (*See* **Draft**.)

Variable cost — expense that varies directly with activity. [For a taxicab company, the cost of fuel would be a variable cost.] (*See* **Fixed cost**.)

Vendor — firm that supplies parts to a manufacturer. [A company that makes lighting fixtures, for example, may need brass fittings and plastic parts for its product. Because the manufacturer does not have brass foundry or plastic extrusion capabilities, it will order the fittings and the plastic parts from parts suppliers that it will refer to as its "vendors."] (*See also* **Original equipment manufacturer**.)

Vertical integration — consolidation of various operations from supplying to manufacturing, distribution, and sales. [In order to achieve economies, some concerns do not use independent entities in the **channel of distribution** but provide their own wholesale and retail functions. This vertical integration of the firm can extend forward into sales and distribution or backward into raw material supply and parts vending. Vertical integration is distinct from horizontal integration, the merging of competitors or of potential competitors.]

Voucher — usually, a receipt evidencing payment.

Warehouse receipt — **document of title** issued by a commercial **bailee** of goods and specifying the terms of the **bailment** and of the redelivery of the goods. [Warehouse receipts may be negotiable or non-negotiable. In the former case, they are said to stand for the goods.]

Warranty (*See* **Express warranty** and **Implied warranty.**)

Warranty disclaimer (*See* **Implied warranty.**)

Welfare economics — theory of economic analysis based on the assumption that the economic system should maximize human welfare.

Wholesaler — firm that buys merchandise, usually from one or more manufacturers, stores the merchandise, and resells it to **retailers,** other wholesalers, or **distributors.** [Wholesalers often perform financing and product service functions and in some industries do product research for their customers. Wholesalers may enjoy exclusive territories and may agree to exclusive distribution arrangements.]

PART II. SECURED LENDING

ACA (*See* **Agricultural Credit Association.**)

Acceleration — the act of declaring all installments of an installment obligation due. [In the event of a **default** under the **loan agreement** or the **security agreement,** a secured lender usually has the right to declare all obligations due immediately. This power to accelerate the debt of the borrower is essential to the secured party, who otherwise would have to wait until the maturity date under a term loan or until each of the installment dates under an installment loan before proceeding against the collateral.]

Acceptance corporation — a **finance company.**

Account — right to payment, for the sale of goods or for services, not evidenced by **paper.**

Account debtor — the obligor on **paper** or an **account** that is assigned to a lender. [When a **dealer** discounts a **retail installment sales contract** to a lender, the consumer buyer is the account debtor. When a seller grants a lender a security interest in the seller's **accounts,** the seller's buyers, the obligors on the account (usually for sold goods or services) are the account debtors.]

Add-on interest — interest computed at a nominal rate multiplied by the original principal balance without allowance for prior payments of principal, often expressed in language such as the following: "$4 per hundred per year." (*Compare* **Annual percentage rate, Discount interest rate.**)

After-acquired property — collateral acquired by the borrower after the date of the **security agreement.** [Under the **floating lien** of many security agreements, especially those involving **inventory** and **accounts,** the creditor's **security interest** will attach to the property owned by the debtor at the time he enters into the agreement and to property acquired thereafter. Such security agreements may describe the collateral as property "now owned or hereafter acquired."]

Agricultural credit association (ACA) — part of the **farm credit system,** a lender that makes federally subsidized, short-term and long-term loans directly to farmers. (*Compare* **Production credit association.**)

Annual percentage rate — nominal rate of interest expressed in a percentage computed on the basis of an annual rate applied to a declining principal balance to yield the finance charge. (*Compare* **Add-on interest, Discount interest rate.**)

APR (*See* **Annual percentage rate.**)

Asset-backed issue — issuance of obligations that are secured by assets such as consumer related receivables. (*See* **Asset securitization.**)

Asset-based lender — traditionally, a **finance company** or other lender that takes a **security interest** in property of the borrower and relies on that interest as an important potential source for repayment of the loan.

Asset securitization — practice of selling, usually in the **secondary market,** obligations that are secured by collateral, such as mortgages, automobile loans, or credit-card receivables.

Assignee — in secured lending, the transferee of **paper** or **accounts** from a **dealer** or other seller. (*See also* **Assignment, Assignor.**)

Assignment — in secured lending, the transfer of **paper** or **accounts** to a lender by a **dealer** or other seller. (*See also* **Assignee, Assignor.**); in letter of credit transactions, the beneficiary's transfer of the right to receive the proceeds of the letter of credit.

Assignor — in secured lending, the seller who transfers **paper** or **accounts** to a lender. (*See also* **Assignee, Assignment.**)

Attachment — the secured lending concept that describes the creation of the **security interest.** [Under the Uniform Commercial Code, a security interest is not enforceable until it has attached. The Code spells out the requirements for attachment and the rules for determining the time that attachment occurs — a time that may be crucial for determining the priorities of conflicting claims to the same collateral.]

Auditor — in secured lending, independent accountant that audits, reviews, or compiles information concerning the financial status of the borrower and, in the first case, certifies its financial statements.

Aval — a guaranty, often of an obligation, written on the obligation itself with the words *par aval.*

Balloon — the last payment in a loan that is repayable in a number of installments, the last of which is relatively large and equals the unpaid principal balance. [A balloon loan is in essence an agreement to finance the obligation for a short term only with the understanding that the borrower will have to refinance the obligation by "financing the balloon" at the time the balloon payment comes due.] (*Compare* **Bullet note.**)

Bank holding company — business corporation that owns one or more commercial banks.

Basis point — a measure of interest, being .01 percent, that is, one percent of one percent.

Blanket security interest — **security interest** that covers all or virtually all of the borrower's personal property. [Often, especially in the financing of middle-market operations, secured lenders insist that they have a security interest in all of the borrower's property. They take a blanket security interest and make a **broad form filing** that effectively ties up all of the borrower's assets. The lender's insistence on that arrangement may strike some as overreaching, but the request for a blanket security interest is usually reasonable and efficient. In loans that are marginal, that is, where the value of the collateral is questionable, the credit history of the borrower is relatively weak, or the borrower's business prospects are problematic, lenders may be unwilling to make a loan unless they know that, in the event of default, they will have unfettered control of the borrower's assets. For example, in the event of default, the secured creditor will want the option of selling the borrower's business as a going concern or piecemeal, whichever in the judgment of the lender will yield the greater return. If the lender does not have a security interest in some of the borrower's assets, or if another secured party has a prior position with respect to some of those assets, the lender loses one of its options or must negotiate with a third party (the other lender) before acting. By respecting the right of a borrower to grant blanket security interests, commercial law increases the marginal borrower's prospects of obtaining financing.] (*See also* **Working capital lending.**)

Bond — evidence of an obligation to pay interest and principal, sometimes secured by assets of the obligor, say, real estate (in the case of a corporate bond) or by designated revenues (in the case of a municipal bond).

Book entry security — a certificateless security, that is, a corporate or governmental obligation that is evidenced not by the issuance of a bond, debenture, or promissory note but by a "book entry," i.e., by a computer record reflected in a paper record that is only a receipt or acknowledgment and is not itself the obligation. [Book entry obligations are not reified in a piece of paper.]

Broad form filing — **financing statement** that covers all or virtually all of the borrower's personal property. [In order to protect its **blanket security interest,** a secured lender must file a financing statement that covers all of the borrower's assets. The broad form filing is such a financing statement and merits enforcement as an indispensable part of the blanket-security-interest arrangement.]

Bullet note — **promissory note** with principal and interest payable in a single designated payment at maturity. (*See also* **Balloon.**)

C & I Loans — commercial and industrial loans.

Cashier — an officer of a bank, the analogue to the business corporation's secretary.

Chapter 7 — describing a form of bankruptcy relief for a debtor under which the debtor's debts are discharged and its assets liquidated.

Chapter 11 — describing a form of bankruptcy relief under which the debtor is reorganized with a view to keeping the debtor in business. [Chapter 11 proceedings are often unsuccessful, in which case, the debtor is liquidated under Chapter 7.]

Chattel lease — security agreement disguised as a lease. (*See also* **Lease purchase agreement.**)

Chattel mortgage — type of security agreement under pre-Code chattel mortgage statutes, the term sometimes still being used to refer to a security agreement covering goods.

Chattel paper — usually, a **retail installment sales contract** or a lease.

Claim — in secured transactions, an assertion of a property interest. [The notion is akin to the claims that prospectors make in Hollywood westerns and is essentially different from the claims that law students deal with in tort courses. The common law fashioned a number of writs or causes of action by which a claimant could proceed. Among them are trover, replevin, and (most important) conversion. Conversion is an important commercial remedy. It is, of course, a strict liability cause of action, and it is a claim. When commercial law decides that a purchaser in good faith cuts off claims, it prevents these claimants from asserting such claims against the purchaser.]

Cleanup — in **working capital loan** the requirement that once during a period, usually once a year, the debtor reduce its borrowings to zero.

Clearance — in the securities markets, the practice of comparing, matching, and confirming trades. *See also* **Settlement.**

Closed-end lease — finance lease under which the lease payments are sufficient to cover the lessor's cost of the equipment and interest charges, so that the lessor is not exposed to the risk that the **estimated residual value** is insufficient to protect the lessor's investment.

Closing — the exchange of documents and funds that are the subject of the **loan agreement**.

Collateral — the goods or other property in which the borrower conveys an interest to the lender under the **security agreement**.

Collection agency — firm that specializes in the collection of delinquent **accounts**.

Glossary

Collections — in secured lending, the activity of pursuing delinquent accounts.

Commercial — pertaining to business as opposed to **consumer** activity.

Commercial bank — traditionally, a "full service" financial institution that accepts time and demand deposits, provides payments and collections services, a trust department, and commercial and consumer loans. (*Compare* **Thrift** and **Finance company.**)

Commercial loan officer — bank employee that has authority to make commercial loans, that obtains that authority from the **loan committee** in some cases, and that attends to the loan documentation, the loan closing, and, in some cases, workouts and loan collections.

Commercial paper — short-term (not usually longer than nine months) **promissory notes** issued by large borrowers who borrow directly from investors rather than from financial intermediaries.

Comptroller of the Currency — primary regulator of nationally chartered banks (national associations).

Consumer — pertaining to sales or loans for personal, family, or household purposes.

Consumer goods — goods used primarily for personal, family, or household purposes. [Goods that lay people may consider consumer goods may not be such for purposes of secured lending. A refrigerator, for example, in the kitchen of a homemaker would be consumer goods. The same refrigerator in the kitchen of a restaurant would be **equipment** and on the showroom floor of an appliance store would be **inventory**.]

Consumer paper — generic term for paper usually generated by **dealer** sales to consumers, now generally confined to **retail installment sales contracts** and leases.

Contract right — in secured lending, a concept (rendered archaic by the 1972 revisions to Article 9) referring to the right to payment under a contract for the sale of goods or services before the seller has performed. [Contract rights are now generally **accounts** or **general intangibles**.]

Correspondent bank — bank with which another bank maintains a relationship that may involve corresponding account balances, referral of business, loan participations, and the routing of checks for collection. [**Nonmember banks,** for example, will use a correspondent that is a member of the **Federal Reserve System** when the nonmember bank wishes to avail itself of the System's collection apparatus.]

Cosigner — one who signs a borrower's obligation in order to provide a guaranty to the lender or credit seller. [The term comes from negotiable instruments practices, which sometimes involved a requirement that an obligor, say, the maker of a note, obtain a cosignature by a second obligor, usually someone of strong credit repute.]

Credit bureau — firm that maintains credit records on individuals and firms in a given area and discloses credit information for a fee.

Credit department — that part of a financial institution that analyzes the credit information relating to a potential borrower.

Credit enhancement — said of any effort to increase the acceptability of an obligation in the market. [This is an old concept that merchants and bankers seem to rediscover from time to time. In the earliest of commercial transactions, we read of the merchant who could not obtain credit because his paper was not marketable. A trader whose credit repute in seventeenth-century London, for example, was not widely known and favorable could not get other traders and merchants to accept his promissory notes and drafts. The new entrant was forced to take measures to increase the attractiveness of his paper. He did so generally by obtaining the signature on the paper or elsewhere of someone who enjoyed the requisite financial reputation. He could obtain the signature of an accommodation party (a cosigner), or he could ask the drawee of his draft to announce in advance his willingness to accept (a virtual acceptance or letter of credit). These practices of enhancing the paper of the borrower exist today. The consumer borrower frequently obtains a cosigner in order to render his promissory note acceptable to a lender. Corporations that borrow directly from investors through the financial markets often use **standby letters** of credit, credit insurance, or **securitization** to enhance the marketability of their **commercial paper** or **bonds.**]

Credit reporting agency — a form of **credit bureau.** [In addition to credit bureaus, there are commercial credit reporting agencies, such as Dun & Bradstreet and TRW that secure credit information from firms and their creditors and make it available to subscribers.]

Credit scoring — the financial institution practice of evaluating credit applications by assigning numerical values to the categories that the lender considers in evaluating the loan application and determining whether or how much to lend on the basis of the potential borrower's total "score." While the practice of credit scoring has traditionally been confined to large lenders with high volumes of loans, smaller lenders that traditionally prided themselves on evaluating loan risk on a personal basis are now beginning to report to credit scoring.

Cross collateralization — using collateral to secure more than one advance, so that, for example, collateral granted to the lender to secure an **inventory** loan will also secure loans made against **accounts**.

Dealer — any retailer that sells on credit and generates **accounts** or **paper**.

Dealer reserve — in **consumer-paper** borrowing **with recourse,** lenders frequently insist that a small percentage of the sums collected on the paper be allocated to a reserve account that will be used to satisfy consumer defaults.

Debenture — unsecured, interest-bearing obligation of business or municipal corporation.

Default — failure on the part of an obligor to fulfill a legal obligation. [It is essential that a **loan agreement** spell out with some specificity those events that constitute default and give the lender the right to **accelerate** the debt and to proceed against the collateral. As a general rule, the default provision is broadly drawn, so that breach of any **warranty** or **negative covenant** or default on any other obligation to the lender will give the lender such rights.]

Deposit liability — obligation of financial institution to repay sums to depositors. [In banking, deposits are liabilities of the bank; loans are the bank's assets.]

Deregulation — generally, the process of breaking down the legal barriers that distinguish the banking, **thrift,** insurance, securities, and other components of the financial services industry.

Direct loan — loan made directly to a borrower, rather than indirectly by acquiring his obligation from a **dealer**. [In dealer financing, the lender can buy the **consumer paper** from the dealer and indirectly lend money to the consumer, or the dealer can send the consumer to the lender to arrange a **direct loan.**]

Discount interest rate — rate of interest applied to principal balance of loan and collected at the time of the loan closing. In a $100 loan for one year at 4 percent discount, the lender will disburse $96 to the borrower and collect $100 in loan payments. (*Compare* **Add-on interest** and **Annual percentage rate.**)

Discrete lending — lending against a single asset or single group of assets, usually with the idea that the asset is sufficient to serve as collateral for the debt. [While some lenders engage in **working capital** lending and take security interests in **revolving collateral,** there are still many instances of lending against a discrete item of collateral. Banks and **equipment** leasing companies, for example, often enter into finance leases under which the only security they have in the event of the lessee's default is the leased equipment. Similarly, lenders or credit sellers that take purchase-money security interests from consumer borrowers are engaging in discrete lending.] (*See also* **Floating lien, Revolving collateral, Working capital lending.**)

Disintermediation — movement of funds out of **banks** and **thrifts** (**financial intermediaries**), an economic phenomenon that occurs when it is more efficient for investors to lend directly to borrowers rather than to utilize financial intermediaries such as banks and thrifts.

Document — in secured lending, (1) a **document of title** or (2) papers executed in connection with the documentation of the loan, e.g., **promissory note, security agreement, financing statement.**

Document of title — generally, a bill of lading or other transport document or a warehouse receipt.

Dragnet clause — provision in a **security agreement** that defines broadly the obligations secured by the debtor's property, so that, for example, the property secures not only the advance made at the time of the loan transaction in question but also any future advances and all other obligations due from the debtor to the **secured party**.

Equipment — usually, office or production machinery but also any goods that do not fall within the Article 9 definitions of **consumer goods, farm products,** and **inventory.**

Estimated residual value — parties' estimate at the time of entering into a lease of the value of leased equipment at the termination of the lease. Thus, in order to provide incentive to the lessee to maintain leased equipment properly, parties to a lease may estimate the value of the leased equipment at the termination of the lease. When the lease terminates, the lessor disposes of the equipment and pays a premium to the lessee if the sales price is greater than the estimated residual value or charges the lessee a premium if the sales price is less than the estimated residual value.

Estoppel certificate — certificate by a creditor often used in connection with a loan closing certifying the amount of the debt as of the date and time of the closing.

Eximbank — a bank that is part of the federal government's program to subsidize international trade. The Eximbank guarantees loans made by commercial banks that finance such trade, makes intermediary loans directly to commercial banks for such purposes, and makes direct loans to foreign buyers.

Factor — in secured lending, a lender that takes **accounts** from a **dealer,** manufacturer, or other seller and collects them.

Factoring — the practice of conveying an interest in accounts receivable to a party that collects the accounts.

Farm Credit System — broad structure of federally subsidized organizations that generally service the agricultural sector of the economy and that includes the **Farm Service Agency, agricultural credit association**, and **production credit association**.

Farmers Home Administration — federal agency whose functions have been assumed by the **Farm Service Agency** that formerly insured loans made to farmers and that acquired the loans in the event of the borrower's default. **FmHA** loan officers, who were located in rural areas, were often intimately involved in loan decisions and loan documentation.

Farm products — usually crops and livestock but, in both cases, only as long as they are in the possession of a person engaged in farming operations, i.e., in the possession of a farmer.

Farm Service Agency — federal agency that has assumed the functions of the **Farmers Home Administration** and that makes loans and guarantees loans to farmers, loggers, and fishermen.

FCIA   (*See* **Foreign Credit Insurance Association.**)

Federal Deposit Insurance Corporation — primary federal regulator of state **nonmember banks,** insurer of bank and thrift deposits, and receiver for failed banks and thrifts.

Federal Housing Finance Board — supervisory authority for the system of Federal Home Loan Banks.

Federal Reserve Bank — privately owned (by member financial institutions) bank that comprises one of the 12 federal reserve banks in the **Federal Reserve System.** [**Member financial institutions** utilize the federal reserve banks as sources of credit and as the primary vehicle for the presentation and collection of checks and wire transfers of funds.]

Federal Reserve Board — the central bank of the United States, that is, the federal agency charged with the primary role in shaping and effecting government economic policy, and the federal regulator of **bank holding companies** and state chartered banks that are members of the **Federal Reserve System.**

Federal Reserve System — system of 12 regional **federal reserve banks** and their 24 branches, governed by the **Federal Reserve Board.**

Field warehousing — form of secured **inventory** loan under which an independent warehouse in the field, i.e., at the borrower's place of business, takes control of the inventory and permits sales of it only upon authorization from the lender.

Finance charge — cost of credit, including interest, points, and other charges. (*See also* **Time price differential.**)

Finance company — traditionally, an **asset-based lender** that would make loans that were, for whatever reason, unattractive to **commercial banks.** [Finance companies pioneered **consumer** lending by taking **consumer paper** from **dealers.** Large manufacturers have their own finance companies, such as Chrysler Credit Corp. and General Motors Acceptance Co., which may be larger, in terms of assets, than the largest U.S. commercial banks. Finance companies have been strong in **equipment** and lease financing as well. At the present time, many finance companies are subsidiaries of **bank holding companies.**]

Finance lease — traditionally, a lease arising out of a transaction in which the lessor is strictly a financing party, usually one completely unfamiliar with the leased equipment. In a finance lease transaction (typically one involving any aircraft, ship, or other large industrial equipment) the lessee selects the equipment and may even have it manufactured to the lessee's own specifications. Although title to the equipment passes from the manufacturer to the lessor (usually a bank or other financial institution) when the lessor pays for the equipment, the manufacturer ships the equipment directly to the lessee. The function of the lessor in the transaction, therefore, resembles that of a financer rather than that of a seller; and warranty and other liability is accordingly limited. The term *finance lease* is now also statutory and carries with it certain statutory requirements. *See* UCC §2A-103(1)(g) (1989).

Financial intermediary — an institution that accepts funds from investors and lends them to borrowers. [Bank depositors have invested their money in checking accounts and various kinds of time deposit accounts. When the bank lends those funds to borrowers, it is engaging in the classic role of financial intermediation. **Thrifts,** brokers, **investment bankers,** and insurance companies are also financial intermediaries.]

Financing buyer — buyer that prepays a portion of the purchase price in order to enable the seller to obtain raw materials or supplies necessary to fill the buyer's order. [Sometimes the prepaying buyer takes a **security interest** in the **goods,** at other times it argues that it has an interest in the goods as a buyer of them.]

Financing statement — short document identifying the "debtor" and the "**secured party**" and the collateral in which the debtor has granted or plans to grant the **security interest.** [The secured party files the **financing statement** in the office of a public official.]

Fixed rate — rate of interest that does not vary throughout the life of the loan.

Fixture — a vague concept: Personal property, not including building materials incorporated into a building on the real estate, that has become, by virtue of its affixation to the real estate or real estate improvements, under the real estate law of the jurisdiction, part of the real estate.

Floating lien — **security interest** that extends to **after-acquired property.** [When lenders make **working capital loans** or finance **inventory** or **accounts,** it is inconvenient for them to lend against discrete items of collateral. It is more efficient to permit the borrower to grant such lenders a security interest in collateral "now owned or hereafter acquired." Such a security interest "floats," that is, it attaches to new inventory or **equipment,** as those items are acquired by the borrower and to new accounts as the sale of goods and services gives rise to them.]

Forbearance agreement — agreement between lender and borrower executed in the event of borrower default under which (1) lender agrees not to exercise default rights and (2) borrower undertakes to comply with certain duties in addition to those set out in the **loan agreement.**

Foreclosure — **secured party's** exercise of its rights under the **security agreement** to resort to the borrower's property. [When a secured party forecloses on the collateral to satisfy the borrower's debt, it may take the collateral in satisfaction of the debt or may sell it.]

Foreign Credit Insurance Association — agency of the **Eximbank** that insures foreign accounts receivable against political risk. Domestic sellers often find that they cannot finance their foreign accounts, with banks being uneasy about the collectability of those accounts. By providing insurance, the Foreign Credit Insurance Association (FCIA) renders the accounts more marketable, that is, more attractive to domestic lenders.

General intangible — any property interest that does not fall into one of the specific categories of property described in Article 9 (**goods, accounts, chattel paper, documents, instruments,** or money), *e.g.,* an inheritance, sums due under a copyright license, the right to have stock issue under a preincorporation agreement.

Goods — in secured lending, personal property, which falls into one of four classifications: **consumer goods, equipment, farm products,** and **inventory.**

Government-sponsored enterprise — a privately owned corporation chartered by the federal government to effectuate a public purpose. The Federal National Mortgage Association (Fannie Mae), the Federal Home Loan Mortgage Corporation (Freddie Mac), and the Student Loan Marketing Association (Sallie Mae) are three GSEs. Generally, these enterprises borrow funds in the money markets and lend them for purposes defined by their charters. They also guarantee loans.

Grace period — period during which a defaulting party may cure the **default.** [In the event of default under a **loan agreement** or a **security agreement,** the borrower would like to have a period of time during which the lender may not proceed against the collateral or otherwise enforce its **security interest** while the borrower attempts to cure the default. For example, most loan agreements stipulate that it is an event of default for a borrower to be late with an interest payment. If, because of a misdirected wire transfer or an error in mail delivery, an interest payment is late, a healthy borrower will be able to cure the default promptly and will want the right to do so. Many creditors will refuse to grant any grace period in the loan agreement or security agreement. In the event of default, delay is problematic for the secured party. A grace period of one week or even two days may seriously imperil the value of collateral. Such creditors are not without constraint, since the duty of good faith in the enforcement of the agreement stands as a general barrier to overreaching creditor conduct.]

GSE (*See* **Government-sponsored enterprise.**)

Indirect loan — loan made by a financial institution not directly to the borrower but by acquiring the borrower's obligation from a **dealer**. [In dealer financing, when the dealer refers the customer to the lender to arrange the financing, the loan is direct; when the dealer sells on credit and then discounts or finances the **paper** with a lender, the lender has made an indirect loan to the purchaser.]

Installment loan department — in a **commercial bank,** the department that generally deals with **consumer** as opposed to **commercial** loans.

Installment loan officer — bank employee who makes direct **consumer** loans and who makes **indirect loans** to consumers by acquiring **consumer paper** from **dealers.**

Instrument — usually, a negotiable instrument or a certificated security.

Inventory — **goods** held for sale or lease, including work in process, raw materials, and supplies (such as stationery or gasoline for trucks) used up in the course of the affairs of an enterprise, but not **equipment**.

Investment banker — **financial intermediary** that, among other activities (1) underwrites the issuance of securities, that is, agrees to purchase securities from the issuer and resell them, itself or through brokers, to the investing public or (2) arranges the sale of securities by the issuer to others.

Lease purchase agreement — **security agreement** disguised as a lease.

Lender liability — a broad term encompassing various causes of action against lenders all of which assume that the lender's unconscionable, bad-faith, or capricious conduct injured the borrower. [Such claims generally arise when the lender refuses to renew a loan or to extend additional credit.]

Leverage — the act of using relatively small equity to generate credit. [There is a measure of tension in any loan situation. The lender tends to seek as much security as it can get, while the borrower will usually try to limit the amount of security it must transfer. In **discrete loan** situations, the first step the lender takes in securing itself is often an insistence that the borrower commit itself significantly to the transaction by investing money of its own. Real estate development lenders, for example, will only lend 80 or 90 percent of the development cost and will insist that the developers come up with the balance as the developer's equity. Similarly, purchase money sellers often require buyers on credit to make a down payment. These efforts on the part of the lender reflect lender concern that the loan be properly secured. The correlative concern on the part of the borrower is to keep as much property for itself. The borrower's success in that regard is his ability to leverage a small amount of investment or a small amount of collateral into a significant loan. A relatively large loan secured by relatively little collateral or investment is highly leveraged.]

LIBOR (London Interbank Offered Rate) — nominal interest rate large international banks charge each other.

Lien — an interest in property, usually taken, voluntarily or involuntarily, to secure an obligation. [There are a number of property interests in the Uniform Commercial Code: **title,** the **special property,** the **security interest,** and the lien. The last, is a catch-all category that generally includes any property interest that does not fit one of the other categories. Generally, liens, in the catchall sense of the UCC, are possessory, that is, the lienor loses the lien absent possession by itself or its agent. Government liens, such as tax liens, are not possessory. In the broadest sense, of course, liens can be possessory or nonpossessory.] (*See also* **Lien creditor.**)

Lien creditor — (1) an unsecured creditor of the borrower who has obtained a judicial **lien** on the borrower's property; (2) under the Bankruptcy Code, the trustee in bankruptcy who has the rights of a hypothetical lien creditor. [By statute or common law writ, creditors may obtain a lien on their debtor's property either simply by obtaining a judgment or, in most states, by causing a state official to seize the property. Such seizure is sometimes symbolic. The sheriff, for example, may simply disable a piece of equipment or lock it up after marking it as having been subjected to levy.]

Line of credit — authorized amount of borrowing against which a borrower may draw, as its cash needs dictate.

Liquidity — measure of ease with which an asset can be converted into cash. [Money-market instruments such as bankers' acceptances or short-term corporate debt instruments with a recognized market are highly liquid. Long-term subordinated debt is not.]

Loan agreement — the entire agreement between the borrower and the lender. [The **security agreement** may be part of the loan agreement.]

Loan committee — committee of bank loan officers and, sometimes, board members that evaluate those loan applications that exceed the loan authority of individual loan officers.

Loan documentation — all of the documents that a loan officer obtains in connection with a loan, including the **promissory note,** loan agreement, security agreement, financing statement, corporate certificate of good standing, corporate resolutions, opinions of counsel, etc.

Loans & discounts — in banking, the department that generally deals with **commercial,** as opposed to **consumer** loans. (*See also* **Installment loan department.**)

Long term — said of an obligation whose term exceeds one year. (*Compare* **short term.**)

Mass market — the **consumer** portion of a **commercial bank's** customer base that uses the bank for check writing and personal loan services.

Match book — in the securities or any other market the broker practice of matching sellers with buyers. A broker that makes a market in, say, government securities can avoid risk by matching buyers and sellers. Thus, the broker will accept a seller's offer to sell only if it has located a match, a buyer willing to buy at the seller's price. In this type of market it is not necessary for the broker to introduce the seller and buyer, who will remain ignorant of each other's identity, and it is not necessary for the broker to buy for its own account. Risk remains, for one of the contra parties may default, but the risk is less than it would be if the broker buys for its own account and holds the securities until it finds a buyer.

Member financial institution — a financial institution that is a member of the **Federal Reserve System.** [Prior to deregulation, only banks could be members of the system.]

Merchant bank — financial institution, common in foreign countries but unusual in the United States, that engages in some **investment banking** functions and also assists, through counseling and negotiation, and participates in merchant activity such as the buying and selling of commodities, especially in international transactions.

Middle market — that portion of the loan market consisting of medium-sized businesses that presently account for a considerable portion of a commercial bank's secured-loan portfolio.

National association — **commercial bank** chartered under the National Bank Act, a federal statute.

National Credit Union Administration — federal agency that insures and regulates credit unions.

Negative covenants — promises in an agreement by a party under which it undertakes not to engage in certain activity or not to permit certain acts to be taken. [In a **loan agreement,** the creditor will usually secure from the borrower a series of negative covenants, that is, a series of representations that events have not occurred. For example, a lender may insist that the borrower covenant that there are no **liens** on any of its property or that certain financial ratios (e.g., total liabilities to net worth) will not exceed a specified figure. Such covenants survive the loan closing, and if the borrower suffers any of the events to occur, he is in **default** and subject to having the secured debt **accelerated.**]

Negative pledge — promise in the nature of a **negative covenant** under which a borrower agrees not to grant a security interest in designated property or in any of its property to anyone other than the lender in question. [In many **loan agreements** and **security agreements,** secured creditors exact a promise from the borrower not to grant security interests in the same collateral or, perhaps, in any of the debtor's property, without the creditor's prior approval. These negative pledges are not instances of creditor overreaching but are reasonable attempts to put the creditor in a position to obtain the best price for the collateral in the event of the borrower's **default.**]

New value — value given not by virtue of taking a security interest on account of an antecedent debt. [Sometimes, secured lending law distinguishes "value," a concept defined in the Uniform Commercial Code, from "new value." "Value" includes taking security for a preexisting debt. "New value" is anything that would be value under the Code definition other than taking collateral as security for a prior debt.]

Nonmember bank — bank that is not a member of the **Federal Reserve System** and that must use a **member financial institution** in order to avail itself of the benefits of the system.

Office of Thrift Supervision — primary federal regulator of **thrifts**.

Open-end lease — lease under which the lease payments do not satisfy the lessor's acquisition and interest cost. In the open-end lease transaction, the parties do not anticipate that the lessee will use the equipment for its useful life and that there will be significant residual value at the termination of the lease. In fact, these leases usually contain the lessee's guaranty of the residual value, so that the lessor's risks are minimal. In the event that there is no such guaranty, the lessor must find a second lessee; and if it does not find a second lessee, the lessor will bear the unsatisfied acquisition costs. Therefore, unless the lessor is an enterprise that can use the equipment itself or one that is in the equipment rental market, an open-end lease without a residual value guaranty entails market risks that many financial institutions are unwilling to take, especially when they are unfamiliar with the market for the equipment and are acting primarily as a financer.

Operations officer — employee of a **commercial bank** that is concerned with payments and collections, investment of bank funds, and other administrative duties. (*Compare* **Commercial loan officer.**)

Overdraft financing — practice, common in some foreign jurisdictions, of generating loans by honoring overdrafts.

Paper — traditionally, any debt obligation evidenced by a piece of paper, such as a **promissory note,** draft, or installment contract. (*Compare* **Account.**)

Participation — a share of a loan. [A lead bank, that is, one that has made a loan commitment to a borrower, may be unwilling or unable to fund the entire loan and will ask other banks to participate in the loan by taking a piece of it and of the collateral that secures it. The lead bank then "participates" out portions of the loan to the participating banks.]

PCA   (*See* **Production Credit Association.**)

Perfection — the act of rendering a **security interest** superior to any sub-sequently acquired judicial **lien.** [Once a security interest has become effective, that is, once it has **attached,** third parties need to know whether they are bound by the conveyance. Article 9 of the Uniform Commercial Code uses the concept of perfection to determine the answer to that question. Generally, perfection occurs when there is notice of some kind that will warn the diligent third party that the owner does not hold an uncluttered interest in the property. Article 9 fashions generally clear rules for determining whether perfection has occurred, when it has occurred, and the three means by which it can occur: filing, taking possession, and doing nothing. Perfection rules are also critical in determining the **priority** of competing **secured parties.**]

Pledge — **security interest** effected and perfected by the **secured party's** possession of the collateral. [The oldest secured transaction is probably the pledge. In ancient times, obligors pledged their servants, their first son, or even their royalty as security for repayment of debts or performance of other obligations. Transfer of possession is the essence of the pledge, but the law quickly realized that the transfer can be to the agent of the secured party as well as to the secured party himself. In fact, sometimes the property will be in the possession of a third party, and mere notice to that party or acknowledgment by him will serve to effect the pledge. Two conclusions are inescapable from the premise that the pledge involves a transfer of possession from the owner to the secured party. First, only tangible property can be the subject of a pledge. Second, any retransfer of possession to the owner or other activity that gives the owner power to control the possession of the property destroys the pledge.]

Points — interest charge expressed in terms of a percentage of the loan amount (one percentage point being one point), usually collected at the time of the loan closing.

Prime rate — traditionally, the interest rate banks charge their best customers; now, an indicator against which interest charges on loans are often pegged.

Priority — the concept that one party's rights in property rank ahead of that of another. [In order to avoid uncertainty, the Uniform Commercial Code establishes a wide-ranging scheme for determining the relative positions of each party claiming an interest in collateral.

These priority rules often depend on the concepts of **attachment** and **perfection.**]

Private banking—a marketing concept under which a bank reserves special attention (e.g., service at a desk rather than at a teller window) to upper-income customers.

Production credit association (PCA) — part of the **farm credit system,** a lender that makes federally subsidized, short-term loans directly to farmers. (*Compare* **Agricultural Credit Association.**)

Promissory note — instrument (usually negotiable) signed by the borrower and evidencing a repayment obligation. [If the note is negotiable, the repayment obligation is embodied in the instrument, with significant consequences.]

Purchase — to take by voluntary transfer. [A voluntary conveyance, including transfers by way of sale, gift, or **pledge,** is a transfer by purchase, and one who takes by such voluntary conveyance is a purchaser. Involuntary conveyances, such as transfers by operation of law under judicial **lien** statutes or the Bankruptcy Code are not transfers by way of purchase, and lien creditors and the trustee in bankruptcy are generally not purchasers.]

Purchase-money lender — lender that advances funds to a buyer who uses them to acquire property.

Purchase-money security interest — a **security interest** that secures credit granted in order to enable the borrower to purchase the collateral. [There are two kinds of purchase-money loans: (1) those made by the seller of goods and (2) those made by a lender who advances funds that the borrower uses to purchase the goods.]

Purchase-money seller — seller on credit.

Real-bills banking doctrine — an economic theory that banks will create the proper amount of money only when they make commercial loans that are short-term, self-liquidating loans against goods with market value sufficient to liquidate the loan. [Under this theory of banking, when a loan officer made a loan it was **discrete** and often related to a single piece of equipment or, more probably, a specified quantity of inventory covered by a single sales transaction or a specified document of title. This theory rejects the idea that a borrower's ability to repay a loan depends as much on its value as a going concern with a strong history of good credit and earnings than on the value of a discrete item of collateral. Under the old theory, loans were short term, and the inability of the borrower to repay the loan at maturity was a serious default. Modern bank theorists take a different view. They often see collateral as a secondary source of protection against **default** and see the general financial and managerial competence of the borrower as the primary source of loan repayment. Under this view, borrowers may substitute collateral and may repay their loans, not according to a preordained schedule, but in accordance with cash flow.]

Regulation Z — Federal Reserve Board regulation promulgated under the Consumer Credit Protection Act chiefly governing the advertising and documentation of **consumer** lending.

Repo — (1) a **repurchase agreement** or (2) **equipment** or other property that a lender has repossessed from a defaulting borrower.

Repurchase agreement — a **security agreement** disguised as a sale with an obligation on the part of the seller to repurchase the property that is the subject of the sale, often referred to as a "repo" agreement.

Retail installment sales contract — credit sales contract between a retailer and a **consumer** calling for payment of the purchase price in installments and reserving a **security interest** in the retailer.

Reverse repo — a repurchase agreement viewed from the perspective of the buyer. [In a repurchase agreement, a seller of securities undertakes to repurchase them, usually at a specified time for a specified price. The arrangement is, in reality, a loan from the "buyer" under the agreement to the "seller." In the parlance of the industry, the agreement is a repurchase agreement in the eyes of the seller, who has a repurchase obligation. However, in the eyes of the buyer, that is, the lender, the arrangement is a reverse repurchase agreement.] (*See* **Repurchase agreement.**)

Revolving collateral — collateral (**inventory** or **accounts**) that the borrower sells and acquires, usually without the interference of the lender. [When a lender's security agreement includes an **after-acquired property** clause, the collateral revolves. As original inventory, for example, is sold by the borrower, it passes into the hands of buyers free of the security interest, so that the lender loses that collateral. At the same time, the borrower is acquiring new inventory, and the security interest **attaches** to that inventory as soon as the borrower acquires an interest in it.]

Rule of 78s — formula for computing interest rebate to installment borrower who prepays a loan. [The formula assumes that the installments are in equal amounts and that interest payments comprise an increasingly smaller portion of each subsequent payment as the loan balance is reduced by prior payments. Based on those assumptions and using the sum-of-the-digits method, the earned interest in the first month of a one-year loan is $^{12}/_{78}$ths, in the second month $^{11}/_{78}$ths, etc. The sum of the digits 1 through 12 is 78; hence the name of the rule.]

Sale as secured transaction — secured transaction disguised as a sale. [Traditionally, many **dealers** entered into transactions with **factors** or other finance companies transferring their **accounts** or **chattel paper** to the factor for **collection.** Those transfers were either **with recourse** or **without recourse.** Sometimes in the with-recourse transfer and most of the time in the without-recourse transfer, the parties considered the transaction a sale of the accounts or chattel paper. At other times, they thought of it as a secured transaction. In order to avoid confusion, the Uniform Commercial Code generally treats transfers of accounts and chattel paper as secured transactions, without distinguishing those that the parties consider a sale from those that the parties consider to be a loan secured by a transfer of collateral.]

Savings and loan association — a **thrift** that traditionally financed home mortgage loans and real estate development.

Savings bank — a **thrift** institution. [The statutes of some states use this term to refer to institutions that are called **savings and loan associations** in most states.]

Secondary market — market in which originating institution sells or wholesales its loans in order to obtain fresh funds to meet borrowers' needs. [For example, **commercial banks** that generate significant volume of automobile loans may sell those loans in the secondary market at rates that yield a profit to the bank and provide the bank with funds.]

Secured party — creditor that has taken a **security interest** in property of the debtor. [A creditor that extends credit on security is referred to under the **security agreement** as the secured party. Secured creditors are often **asset-based lenders** but may also take security in the form of **side guaranties** or **standby letters of credit.**] (*Compare* **Unsecured creditor.**)

Securities entitlement — in the securities industry, the property interest of a person whose securities are held by a financial intermediary.

Securitized — said of obligations (**bonds** or notes) that are backed by collateral. [Some large borrowers, including **commercial banks** and **finance companies,** have begun the practice of marketing their loans by packaging them and using them as collateral for bonds or other debt obligations. This practice of, for example, securing paper with automobile loans or **consumer** credit card receivables is called "securitization" or "collateralization."]

Security agreement — a contract of conveyance whereby the borrower grants to the lender an interest in personal property to secure performance of the borrower's obligation to the lender.

Security interest —

(1) (Article 9) — the interest in personal property granted a lender by a borrower in the **security agreement,** an interest created by agreement, rather than by operation of law. [It is often important in secured lending situations to distinguish the security interest, an Article 9 concept, from other property interests that creditors of the owner may assert. Usually, those other interests will be **liens** of some sort, but they may also be a **seller's right to reclaim** or a nonvoluntary security interest under Article 2 of the Uniform Commercial Code. In secured transactions under Article 9, the security interest is one voluntarily created by a conveyancing agreement called a **security agreement.** The distinguishing features of the security interest are (1) that it results from a voluntary conveyance by the owner (or, in some situations, of the buyer's agreement that the seller retain a security interest) and (2) that it secures a debt, that is, the creditor's interest in the property is limited by the amount of the debt. The "voluntary" feature distinguishes the security interest from most liens, which arise by operation of law. The second limitation distinguishes the security interest from the seller's right to reclaim or **seller's lien,** which gives the seller the right to take the property and keep it. The secured creditor cannot take the property and keep it but must account to the owner for any excess in the value of the property over the amount of the debt.]

(2) (Article 2) — **security interest** created by operation of law, namely, by operation of provisions in Article 2 of the Uniform Commercial Code. [In two instances, Article 2 creates a statutory right in a party, which the Code calls a security interest. This security interest differs from the Article 9 security interest in that it arises not by voluntary conveyance but by operation of law, but it resembles the Article 9 security interest in that it secures an obligation of

the owner of the goods and does not give the secured party the right to keep the goods without an accounting. A seller who ships goods under reservation has a security interest in the goods by operation of law to secure payment of the contract price. A buyer who holds non-conforming goods has a security interest in them to secure costs it incurs in connection with the caring of them.]

Seller's lien — **lien** arising (1) by virtue of the seller's right to stop delivery if buyer fails to pay the agreed upon consideration or (2) under provisions of Article 2 codifying common law, antifraud rules that give a defrauded seller rights in goods that it has delivered to the buyer. [In some cases of buyer breach at common law, sellers who had already granted rights in goods to the buyer could reassert an interest in the goods to the point of selling them to a third party free of the buyer's interest. By giving the seller the right to resell in that fashion, the seller's lien became a powerful interest, since it permitted a seller to retain any sales proceeds over and above the loss the seller incurred by virtue of the buyer's breach and relieved the seller of the proof burden of showing that it did not receive a benefit from the buyer's breach.]

Seller's right to reclaim — a manifestation of the **seller's lien,** in this case, arising by virtue of the buyer's fraud. [In some cases involving buyer fraud, the seller's lien extended to goods it had delivered to the buyer. Since liens are almost always possessory in nature, this right is extraordinary and reflects the depth of commercial law's animus toward fraud.]

Settlement — in the securities markets the practice of transferring the securities against payment. (*Compare* **Clearance.**)

Short term — said of an obligation whose term is less than one year. (*Compare* **long term.**)

Side guaranty — guaranty given by a party under an agreement that is separate from the primary obligation, i.e., the **promissory note** that the principal debtor executes. [In order to avoid the traps and pitfalls of surety law, most sophisticated lenders no longer take **cosignatures** from parties that lend their credit as security for the debt of the principal borrower but take a side guaranty agreement with strong provisions that generally close the escape routes developed by surety law and that courts have generally, though less often now than formerly, enforce.]

Signature loan — usually, a small unsecured loan made to a borrower with a good credit record upon the signing of a **promissory note.**

Small loan company — **consumer** lender that traditionally made short-term loans in small amounts and took **security interests** in consumer **goods** or in the form of wage assignments. [Now heavily regulated, small loan companies are not an important source of secured credit.]

Standby letter of credit — letter of credit used to secure a repayment or other obligation, often used to enhance the obligation, be it a **promissory note, commercial paper,** or **bond.** [Commercial letters of credit, which arise in sales transactions, provide the model for the standby credit. In the commercial-credit transaction, the seller draws a draft on the credit issuer to obtain payment for goods sold. In the standby credit transaction, the holder of an obligation, such as a promissory note, draws on the standby in the event the obligor **defaults** on the note.]

Structured finance — another term for **asset securitization.**

Subordinating — the act of moving a **claim** or interest from a higher **priority** to a lower one. [At times it may be convenient for a creditor to subordinate itself to the position of a creditor over which it enjoys priority. If, for example, a **working capital** lender has taken a **security interest** in all of its borrower's **accounts** and has perfected properly, there is no way that the borrower can grant a second creditor a security interest in those accounts prior to that of the first creditor. The first creditor, however, may not have any objections to the arrangement that the borrower and the second creditor propose and may be content to have the new creditor pump fresh funds into the borrower's enterprise. A small manufacturer may have $400,000 in overdue accounts. Its bank, a working capital lender, advances funds from time to time and feels secure by virtue of its **blanket security interest,** which covers valuable **inventory, equipment,** and current accounts. The manufacturer has located an accounts receivable financer that is familiar with the industry and with these particular accounts and that is willing to "buy" the overdue accounts for $.50 on the dollar but is willing to do so only if it can take them free of the bank's security interest. By entering into a subordination agreement, the bank and the accounts-receivable financer can agree on their relative positions with respect to the overdue accounts.]

Subordination agreement — agreement whereby one creditor agrees to surrender its **priority** over another creditor.

Syndication — selling of obligations to investors. [For a variety of reasons, among them a desire to keep its loan portfolio diversified and to comply with lending limits, a bank will sometimes refuse to make a large loan by itself and will ask other banks to join it in a syndicate. Syndicated loans may take a number of forms. The simplest is the loan **participation** arrangement.]

Thrift — financial institution, such as a savings bank, savings and loan institution, or credit union, that traditionally was limited by law to the making of mortgage loans and some **consumer** loans and that could pay a higher interest rate on deposits than that allowed to **commercial banks,** but that could not accept demand deposits, i.e., checking accounts. [With the advent of deregulation, federal law abolished the deposit interest rate disparity, permitted thrifts to accept demand deposits, and expanded the legitimate area of thrift loan activity to encompass commercial loans. Deregulation notwithstanding, thrifts have largely continued to dominate in the area of real estate lending and have not generally competed in the commercial lending area, though they have offered checking accounts or their equivalent (e.g., share draft or negotiable order of withdrawal accounts). At the present time, thrifts are not subject to regulation by the traditional bank regulators (**FDIC, Comptroller of the Currency,** and **Federal Reserve Board**) but are part of a different scheme of regulation under the aegis of the **Office of Thrift Supervision** or the **National Credit Union Administration.** The latter insures the deposits of **credit unions.** The **Federal Deposit Insurance Corporation** currently insures the deposits of **savings banks** and **savings and loan associations** and administers the Savings Association Insurance Fund (SAIF).]

Time price differential — difference between the cash price and the credit price. [At times when usury laws prevented the charging of competitive rates for consumer borrowing, merchants invented the concept of the time price differential, which some courts took to be something other than interest and, therefore, not subject to the usury limitation.]

Unsecured creditor — (1) sellers or lenders that extend credit to a buyer or borrower without taking a **security interest** in any property, i.e., nonasset-based lenders; (2) sellers or lenders who attempt to take an interest in the property of the buyer or borrower but who fail to follow the rules of the Uniform Commercial Code and who therefore fail to effect an enforceable security interest. [The former category of creditor probably comprises the single biggest source of short-term credit in the economy and consists of (1) open account sellers of merchandise and (2) public utilities. The creditor without security usually is a party that relies not on the assets of the borrower but on its credit history. Trade creditors, usually open account sellers, generally do not ask for collateral and do not rely on the buyer's assets but look to the buyer's history as a good credit risk. The unsecured creditor is the opposite of the **asset-based lender.** Unsecured parties often complain, after the fact, when assets are unavailable to satisfy their claims. The trustee in bankruptcy, who represents unsecured creditors in a debtor's bankruptcy, attempts to increase the pool of assets that are not subject to security interests in order to augment the bankruptcy dividend that will be paid the unsecured creditors. Unsecured commercial creditors who have not relied on the debtor's assets have convinced some commentators that their claim to those assets in bankruptcy is meritorious. There are some noncommercial creditors that are unsecured. These are mostly tort claimants, whose claims are usually covered by liability insurance.]

Value   (*See* **New value.**)

Variable rate — said of an interest rate that varies with some indicator, such as the **prime rate** or **LIBOR.** (*Compare* **fixed rate.**)

Warranties — in secured lending, representations by the borrower as to facts usually relating to its financial or legal status. [In a **loan agreement,** the lender will require the borrower to represent as true certain facts that are important to the efficacy of the agreement. A corporate borrower's loan agreement, for example, will include a warranty that all corporate actions necessary to authorize the borrowing have been taken and that the corporation is in good standing in all jurisdictions in which it is authorized to do business. In the event a representation proves to be untrue, the borrower will have breached a warranty, which, in turn, will be an event of **default** under the agreement and permit the lender to **accelerate** the debt and proceed against the collateral.]

Without recourse — said of the transfer of **paper** or **accounts** under an agreement that does not require the transferor to buy back any paper or account on which the **account debtor** defaults.

With recourse — said of the transfer of **paper** or **accounts** under an agreement that requires the transferor to buy back any paper or account on which the **account debtor** defaults.

Working capital lending — lending, usually in the **middle market,** for working capital needs. [With the demise of the **real-bills doctrine**

of banking, lenders gradually realized the benefit of letting collateral turn over via the **floating lien** and of letting the borrower draw down on the line of credit to satisfy its credit needs and to pay against the debt balance as cash flow permitted. With some flexible limits, the working capital lender does not concern itself with the borrower's use of loan proceeds, and gives the borrower significant discretion in determining the time to draw against the line of credit and the time to pay off loan principal.]

PART III.   PAYMENTS SYSTEMS

Accept — the **drawee's** act of executing a **time draft,** usually on its face, as a method of undertaking to pay the **draft** according to its **tenor** at the time it becomes due.

Acceptance — a **time draft** that has been **accepted** by the **drawee.** (*See* **Banker's acceptance** and **Trade acceptance.**)

Acceptor — a drawee that has **accepted** a **time draft.**

ACH   (*See* **Automated clearinghouse.**)

Acquirer — in the **bank** credit card industry, the **merchant bank,** that is, the bank that acquires the merchant seller's **sales slips** and processes them or forwards them to a data processor for collection through the bank credit card association.

Affinity card — credit card issued under a marketing strategy that takes advantage of the cardholder's loyalty to an organization by including on the card itself the mark or logo of an organization (e.g., social fraternity, bar association, professional baseball club, or March of Dimes) that receives a fee of a few cents for itself or a designated charity upon each use of the card. [Marine Midland Bank of New York offers a New York Knicks Mastercard. Citibank offers a National Football League Visa card under a program that permits the cardholder to pick his favorite team's logo. Affinity cardholders sometimes obtain discounts on items associated with the designated organization.]

Association of Reserve City Bankers — trade group of large banks that, among other things, competes with the Federal Reserve System for check-collection business.

Automated clearinghouse — **wire transfer** facility permitting (1) **payors** to transfer funds to multiple payees and (2) payees to draw funds from multiple payors. [Parties utilize the automated clearinghouse in connection with recurring payments or collections such as social security payments or insurance premium collections.]

Bank — usually a commercial bank, as opposed to a **thrift, credit union,** or other financial institution, but now frequently in the payments context any financial institution that accepts deposits and permits the transfer of them.

Bank credit — **bank** deposits, usually **demand deposits** (checking accounts) that are transferred in the payments system.

Bank draft — **draft** drawn by a **bank** on an account it maintains at another bank, frequently, a bank in another country.

Banker's acceptance — **draft** drawn on and **accepted** by a **bank,** frequently in connection with a commercial letter of credit transaction.

BankWire — a private **wire transfer** network that competed with **Fedwire** and that is no longer in operation.

Beneficiary — in **electronic funds transfer,** the party to whose account the funds are to be transferred, usually, the creditor of the party that originates the funds transfer.

Bill of exchange — in the United States, an anachronistic term for **draft;** in Great Britain and other Commonwealth countries, a synonym for *draft.*

Board of Governors of the Federal Reserve System — independent agency of the federal government consisting of a seven-member board that governs the **Federal Reserve System,** serves as the principal regulator of state **banks** that are members of the system and of bank holding companies, and acts as the nation's central bank.

Book transfer — in electronic payments systems, a wire transfer initiated by a customer of the same bank to which the transfer order is directed. The analogue to an on-us item in checking collection practice.

Cashier's check — **check** drawn on a **bank** by itself. [A cashier's check bears the **drawee's** signature as **drawer.** It is, in the act of **utterance,**

both a **draft** or check and an **acceptance,** since at the time of issuance, it bears the drawee's signature.]

Cash item — a demand instrument for the payment of money drawn on a **bank** as it proceeds through the payments system, e.g., a **check.** (*See* **Collection item.**)

Cash letter — document accompanying a batch of **checks** and containing a dollar total of the checks.

Certified check — a **check** that the **drawee bank** has certified. [The certified check differs from the **cashier's check** in that a depositor of the bank draws the former, while the bank itself draws the latter.]

Check — a negotiable **draft** drawn on a **bank** and payable on demand.

CHIPS — Clearing House Interbank Payment System, a creature of an association of New York **banks,** the New York Clearinghouse Association, designed for settlement of international, dollar-denominated payments.

Clear — payment of an **item** or **wire transfer.**

Clearinghouse — traditionally, a meeting place at which members of an association of **banks** exchanged **items** drawn on each other; now, often, an association of such banks.

Collecting bank — **bank** in the collection chain other than the **payor.**

Collection item — **item** that is deposited in the **bank** collection system for collection but that does not require payment by a bank without some authorization and one, therefore, for which the bank of first deposit usually does not give credit until final payment. [**Documentary drafts** drawn on a buyer are often deposited in the banking system. Such **drafts** would be collection items, since they are not payable by any bank but are to be honored by a buyer. Similarly, payable-through drafts are collection items, since they are not payable by the payable-through bank, which must first obtain the authority of the **drawee.**]

Correspondents — **banks** that maintain a continuing relationship. [Often, such banks maintain corresponding balances in accounts with each other, but sometimes, a smaller bank (country bank) will maintain a correspondent relationship with a larger bank (city bank) in order to avail itself of the larger bank's facilities, such as its access to **CHIPS** or an **automated clearinghouse.** In such a case, the smaller bank will maintain an account with the larger bank, but the larger bank will not maintain any account with the smaller bank. In international banking relationships, both correspondents usually maintain exchange accounts with the other.] (*See* **Nostro account** and **Vostro account.**)

Counter check — an imprecise term usually used to refer to a blank check form supplied, prior to the advent of magnetic ink character recognition (**MICR**) symbols, by a teller to a customer but sometimes used to refer to checks drawn on the bank at the counter of the bank for payment directly to the drawer/customer. Prior to the advent of MICR technology and reader sorter machines, depositors could use blank check forms that did not contain the preprinted name of the drawer or even of the drawee bank. Customers obtained such forms at the teller window of a bank or from a retailer. The customer would then complete the form by inserting the usual information (amount and name of payee) and also the name of the drawee bank. MICR technology and the automation of bank check collections have rendered that type of counter check obsolete.

Countertrade — the practice of selling goods not for cash but in return for goods (barter) or for cash but on the condition that the seller will purchase output or other goods at a later time.

Credit cap — limit on **overdrafts** a participant in a transfer system may incur at any given time in the system, among all systems, or against another participant.

Credit item — an **item** sent by an **originator** for debit to the originator's account and, therefore, as a credit to the account of another. (*Compare* **Debit item.**)

Credit sale — sales transaction that does not entail immediate payment. [Open account sales, deliveries against postdated **checks,** and sales against **time drafts** are credit sales.]

Credit transfer — funds transfer that enters the payment system at the payor's institution as an order to that institution to transfer funds into the account of the payee and thus pushes the funds. The European **giro** system involves credit transfers, as do electronic transfers of dividends, social security benefits, and payroll in **automated clearinghouses,** as well as most wire transfers. (*Compare* **Debit transfer.**)

Credit union — financial institution that accepts deposits from and makes loans, usually for personal, family, or household purposes, to a closed group, e.g., employees of a school district or members of a parish.

Debit cap   (*See* **Credit cap.**)

Debit card — plastic card, usually with magnetic stripe, that activates computer terminal or similar equipment to effect payment.

Debit item — an **item** sent by an **originator** for credit to the originator's account and, therefore, as a debit to someone else's account. (*Compare* **Credit item.**)

Debit transfer — funds transfer that enters the payment system at the payee's institution as an order to the transferor's bank and thus pulls the funds into the account of the payee from the transferor's account. Funds consolidation transfers and the collection of insurance premiums through the **automated clearinghouse** are debit transfers. Payments by check are also debit transfers. (*Compare* **Credit transfer.**)

Delayed disbursement — the ethically questionable practice of delaying payment of a debt by drawing a **check** or other **item** on a **payor** located in an area distant from the payee. [Cash managers desire to hold funds as long as they can. Some of them follow the practice of using delays in the payments system to effect longer holds than would otherwise arise. A securities broker, for example, with offices in Detroit and New York might pay its New York customers with checks drawn on a Detroit **bank** and its Detroit customers with checks drawn on a New York bank. Because it takes longer for the Detroit payee to collect a check drawn on a New York bank than it would for him to collect a check drawn on a Detroit bank, the **drawer** has managed to keep his funds for an extra day or perhaps longer. The practice also tends to burden the check-collection system since it requires the system to move two checks through the **Federal Reserve System,** which may involve two **Federal Reserve Banks,** while clearing local items might be effected through the local **clearinghouse.**]

Demand deposit — deposit subject to withdrawal on demand, as opposed to a **time deposit,** which is subject to withdrawal only with notice.

Demand draft — negotiable order payable at sight, as opposed to an order payable at a fixed date or after a period of time.

Depositary bank — the first **bank** in the collection chain.

Depositary institution — in the **Federal Reserve System,** a financial institution that maintains a deposit with a **Federal Reserve Bank** and, therefore, that may avail itself of **Fedwire,** the Federal Reserve check-collection system, and other Federal Reserve System services.

Deregulation — the legislative and regulatory process of removing legal inhibitions on the activity in which financial institutions may engage in order to permit them to compete with nonregulated industries that had invaded their traditional markets. [In the 1970s, when the trend began for the securities, insurance, and retail industries to compete with **banks** and **thrifts** for deposits and other traditional banking services, regulators and legislators responded by removing restrictions on bank activity such as the rate of interest that could be paid on deposits and the types of assets that an institution could hold.]

Discount — a function performed traditionally by commercial **banks** that consists of taking paper, e.g., chattel paper or promissory notes, for a discounted price, that is, for a price below par or face value.

Documentary draft — a **draft** accompanied by a document of title such as a bill of lading or a warehouse receipt.

Draft — a negotiable instrument, being an order on a **drawee** to pay (1) bearer or (2) the order of a designated payee.

Drawee — the person designated as the **payor** on a **draft** or **check,** the person who receives the order to pay.

Drawer — the person who draws a **draft** or **check,** the party who gives the order to pay.

EBT (*See* **Electronic benefits transfer.**)

EFT (*See* **Electronic funds transfer.**)

Electronic benefits transfer — transfer by wire of food stamps, welfare payments, and other government benefits to persons who do not have bank accounts of the sort that entail use of **ATMs.**

Electronic funds transfer — transfer of **bank** or other credit by telephone, telex, or similar telecommunications, as opposed to transfer by a paper instrument for the payment of money such as a **check** or **draft.**

Eurocheck — a form of **check** that is guaranteed by a **bank** and that is in use in western European countries.

Exchange — converting the currency of one state into the currency of another state.

FDIC (*See* **Federal Deposit Insurance Corporation.**)

Federal Deposit Insurance Corporation — insurer of **bank** and **thrift** deposits through two insurance funds, the Bank Insurance Fund (BIF) and Savings Association Insurance Fund (SAIF), and primary regulator of state banks that are not members of the **Federal Reserve System.**

Federal Home Loan Bank Board — former federal agency that regulated **thrifts** and served as their lender of last resort, superseded by the **FDIC,** which now insures thrifts, and the **Office of Thrift Supervision,** which supervises them.

Federal Reserve Bank — a privately owned, federally chartered **bank,** one of twelve that comprise the **Federal Reserve System.**

Federal Reserve Board (*See* **Board of Governors of the Federal Reserve System.**)

Federal Reserve District — one of the 12 districts into which the **Federal Reserve System** is divided. [There are 12 **Federal Reserve Banks,** each serving a district. In addition, there are 25 Federal Reserve branches, 11 nonbranch offices, and 46 regional check processing centers.]

Federal Reserve float — float that results when a **Federal Reserve Bank** makes funds available to a **depositary institution** before the **bank** debits the account of the **payor** bank. [The Federal Reserve Banks make funds available to depositary institutions that submit **checks** to the Federal Reserve Banks for collection according to a funds availability schedule. Since the maximum delay in funds availability under the Federal Reserve Banks' schedule is two banking days, frequently those funds are available to the depositary banks before the Federal Reserve Bank has presented and collected the check from the payor bank. For example, the Federal Reserve Bank of Chicago might make funds available to Second National Bank on Tuesday for a check transferred to the Federal Reserve Bank on Monday. At the same time, the Federal Reserve Bank might not be able to charge the account of the drawee-payor bank (Third National) until Wednesday. For one day, then, Second National and Third National are using the same funds. Hence, the **Federal Reserve System's** efforts to accelerate the collection of **items** has the effect of creating float. In recent years, the Federal Reserve has taken steps to reduce the amount of federal reserve float with considerable success. While federal reserve float averaged $6.7 billion per day in 1979, by 1982 reforms had reduced that figure to $1.8 billion. Under the Monetary Control Act of 1980, the Federal Reserve has reduced that float even further and now prices float, so that any bank that receives the benefit of federal reserve float must pay for it.]

Federal Reserve System — system of 12 **Federal Reserve Banks,** their 25 branches, and 46 regional check processing centers that, among other activity, operates a nationwide check-collection system and **Fedwire.**

Fedwire — a **Federal Reserve System** program for **electronic funds transfer.**

FHLBB   (*See* **Federal Home Loan Bank Board.**)

Float — funds in the collection system that, because of collection inefficiencies, belong to one party but are available for use by another party, such as (1) collected deposits that, by virtue of delayed funds availability schedules, are not available to the depositor, (2) funds against which payment orders have been issued but that have yet to be paid, and (3) uncollected funds available for use. ["Holdover" float occurs when computer breakdowns or heavy volumes of **checks** cause processing delays. Bad weather, accidents, and vehicle breakdowns yield "transportation" float. "Disbursement" float occurs when a payor in one area writes a check on a **drawee** in a distant, and often remote, area.]

Floor release limit — in credit-card transactions, the threshold, above which the sales person must obtain authorization from the credit-card system before proceeding with the credit sale.

Funds availability — in a system of **pull orders,** such as **checks** and **drafts, depositary institutions** do not know when an **item** clears and must establish schedules for making deposits available to the depositor or permitting withdrawals on a credit basis. Pursuant to federal legislation, the **Federal Reserve Board** has promulgated schedules for the availability of deposits.

Funds consolidation — the practice of bringing widely scattered funds to a central point or points in order to enable the consolidator to utilize them efficiently.

Giro — a **push order,** common in European countries, for the transfer of funds. [Giro accounts are frequently offered by a country's postal service and often by commercial and savings **banks.**]

Image processing — scanning of documents optically to produce digital images that can be stored on disks or in computer memory and manipulated electronically. [Image processing is a recent and largely untested innovation that may have application in the **check** and the credit-card collection systems. The process has two advantages: (1) it eliminates paper from the collection apparatus, and (2) it facilitates the capture of information from paper, where information is difficult to access and manipulate, and its transfer to computer memory or optical disks, where it is easy to access and manipulate.]

Interchange fee — the fee, a percentage of the transaction amount, paid by the **merchant bank** to the **credit card bank** in each credit card transaction. Usually, the merchant bank passes this cost on to the merchant as part of the fee it charges the merchant in connection with each transaction.

Issuing bank — in credit-card systems, the **bank** that issues the credit or **debit card** to and enters into a revolving-credit contract with the customer.

Item — an instrument for the payment of money. [**Checks, drafts,** and promissory notes are items.]

Lock box — a facility offered by financial institutions for **funds consolidation** whereby a party's customers mail their **checks** to a lock box, i.e., a **bank** or other financial institution local to the customer in order to accelerate the collection of the check. [A mail-order business in Massachusetts, for example, does not want its California customers to mail checks drawn on California banks to the mail-order house in Massachusetts. Since most California buyers would draw checks on California banks, checks received at the mail-order house would have to be collected by depositing them in a Massachusetts bank, which would forward them through the banking chain to California for collection. The mail-order house prefers to have its

California customers' checks collected at a bank in California. That bank acts as the lock box and collects the checks for the mail-order house by indorsing them and sending them to the payor banks. When the payor banks honor the checks, the lock-box bank forwards the proceeds to Massachusetts. The lock-box system accelerates the collection and thus saves the seller interest charges.]

Magnetic ink character recognition — (often abbreviated "MICR") said of symbols on **items,** usually **checks** and the like, which pass through the **bank** collection system and are read by reader-sorter machines. [Checks bear preprinted MICR symbols designating the **Federal Reserve District** and the identity of the **payor** bank and the **drawer's** account number. When a payee deposits a check, the **depositary bank's** data-entry clerks print MICR symbols on the check indicating the amount of the check, so that thereafter reader-sorter machines can "read" the amount as well as the preprinted information.]

Merchant bank — (1) in credit-card systems, the **bank** that solicits merchants to accept credit cards and agrees to acquire the **sales slips** generated by the merchant's sales; (2) in Europe and now somewhat in the United States, a financial institution that engages in investment banking and business counselling, especially with regard to exports and imports.

Merchant processing — the activity of installing terminals and collecting credit card charge information from retailers whose customers have used their cards to pay for purchases.

MICR   (*See* **Magnetic ink character recognition.**)

Negotiable order of withdrawal — demand **item** offered by savings **banks** and savings and loan institutions. [Prior to the deregulation of financial institutions, **thrifts** could not offer demand accounts. In the early 1970s, however, some states began authorizing thrifts to accept deposits that would be available by negotiable order of withdrawal. Rather quickly, the practice gained widespread approval, and the thrift industry gradually accepted negotiable order of withdrawal deposits and began facing the problem of fashioning a national collection system for its demand-account items.]

Net — balance after computing all additions and subtractions. [In clearing, it makes no sense for institutions to shuffle payments back and forth all day. It is more efficient to settle only once a day. The **clearinghouse,** for example, usually settles once, late in the afternoon. The amount of that settlement is computed by adding all of the transfers to a party and subtracting all of the transfers from that party to arrive at the net settlement figure, which may be positive or negative.]

Netting — in **electronic funds transfer,** the practice of holding transfers for a period of time, computing net positions at the end of the period, and transferring funds in the net amount. [It is expensive to transfer funds, even over **wire transfer** systems. To the extent that two participants can avoid multiple transfers, they can reduce their transfer costs. Also, multiple transfers can create short-lived **overdrafts,** which are usually reduced by the end of the period but which increase system risks, may violate **debit caps,** and may result in penalties. Two participants in a wire transfer network may be able to avoid some of these problems by holding transfers, say, for a few hours. If, for example, First Bank will be transferring $4 billion to Second Bank during the first hour of a transaction day and Second Bank will be transferring $3 billion to First Bank during the second hour of that day, it may make sense for the two **banks** to hold mutual transfers until the end of the second hour, so that the only transfer expense incurred is for one $1 billion dollar transfer instead of several transfers aggregating $7 billion. The practice, which is not always possible, given the demands of the banks' customers, reduces the number and amounts of the transfers and reduces First Bank's overdraft from a high point of $4 billion to $1 billion.]

Noncash item — an **item** that is not payable by a **bank** in the **check** collection system without some authorization from its customer. [**Documentary drafts** and payable-through **drafts** are noncash items.]

Nostro account — in international banking, the foreign currency account of a domestic **bank** in a foreign country. [In order to facilitate payments to its customers' creditors, a New York bank might want to maintain a pound sterling account. Prior to 1988, domestic banks could not offer their customers accounts in foreign currencies, and most customers would prefer not to maintain such accounts in any event. The New York bank will open an account with its London correspondent. The New York bank will refer to that pound-sterling account as a nostro account. At the same time, the New York bank will offer dollar-denominated accounts to its foreign correspondents and will refer to those accounts as **vostro accounts.**]

NOW   (*See* **negotiable order of withdrawal.**)

Office of Thrift Supervision — primary federal regulator of **thrifts.**

Official check — said of a **certified, cashier's, teller's,** or other **check** drawn by a **bank** on itself or on another bank.

On-arrival draft — **draft** to be presented to the **drawee** upon the arrival of the goods covered by the accompanying bill of lading or other document of title. [Usually, a **documentary draft** arises in a transaction calling for payment against documents, in which case, the drawee does not have the opportunity to examine the goods before honoring the draft. Parties, however, are free to alter that feature of the transaction by utilizing the on-arrival draft, which allows the presenting bank to hold the draft and accompanying document of title until the goods arrive. At that point, the drawee-buyer will have an opportunity to examine the goods before it must honor the draft.]

Originator — in **electronic funds transfer,** the customer of a **bank,** a participant in a **wire transfer** system, that asks the bank to send a transfer order.

Originator's bank — in **electronic funds transfer,** the first **bank** in a **wire transfer** system to transmit a fund transfer order.

Overdraft — said of an account balance that shows a deficit or of an **item** or transfer that results in a deficit account balance.

Payor — the party designated by an instrument or a **wire transfer** as the party that will pay the order. (*See* **Drawee.**)

Personal identification number — computer-generated number given to a credit or debit cardholder for use in computer terminals or other equipment as a method of identifying the user as the person authorized to use the card.

PIN   (*See* **Personal identification number.**)

Point-of-sale terminal — computer terminal into which a cardholder can insert a **debit card** for the purpose of transferring funds.

POS terminal   (*See* **Point-of-sale terminal.**)

Preauthorized debit — in **automated clearinghouse** transactions, the authorization of a party for the clearinghouse to make periodic debits to his account. [Frequently, payees such as insurance companies and utilities that collect periodic payments from their customers utilize an automated **clearinghouse** to collect those payments. The **payor's** authorization of the payments is a preauthorized debit.]

Presentation — the physical act of submitting an **item** to a payor. [Presentation can be for payment or acceptance. In the **documentary draft** transaction, for example, if the seller draws a **time draft,** the presenting **bank** will present the **draft** for acceptance. After acceptance, the bank will present for payment. If the draft in such a transaction is a **demand draft,** there will be only one presentation, that for payment.]

Presenting bank — the **bank** in the bank-collection chain that transmits an **item** to the **drawee** or other **payor.**

Pull orders — **drafts** or **checks** that, by their nature, "pull" funds from the drawer's account. (*Compare* **Push orders.**)

Purchase — any voluntary transfer. [A transfer by gift is a purchase. A transfer by operation of law, such as the attachment of a judgment lien, is not a purchase.]

Push orders — wire order or **item,** such as a **giro,** which the sending party or **drawer** delivers to the institution issuing his account with instructions to transfer the funds to a designated beneficiary or account, hence, the order or item pushes the funds. (*Compare* **Pull orders.**)

RCPC (*See* **Regional check processing center.**)

Receiving bank — in **electronic funds transfer,** the **bank** that receives a transfer order. [If a bank receives a computerized instruction from its customer, the bank is a receiving bank. When it transmits the order to a second bank, that bank becomes a receiving bank, the first bank having also become the **originator's bank.** The last receiving bank is the beneficiary's bank.]

Regional check processing center — center that receives **checks** for collection through the **Federal Reserve System** for collecting checks. [Sometimes, **depositary banks** short circuit the normal collection chain. They bypass the **Federal Reserve Banks** and direct items to regional check processing centers that serve a region that may include all or parts of more than one of the 12 **Federal Reserve Districts.**]

Remitter — the party that supplies the funds represented by an instrument, e.g., the party that provides the funds to a **bank** that issues a **cashier's check.**

Remitting bank — any **bank** transferring funds through the check-collection system. [**Checks** pass from the **depositary bank** to the **drawee-payor** bank. Theoretically, the funds pass in the opposite direction, from the payor to the depositary institution. In fact, of course, the funds move by virtue of credits that each bank gives to the bank prior in the collection chain.]

Sales draft — in credit-card transactions, the piece of paper that bears the imprint of the cardholder's card, a description of the merchandise, the sales price, and the cardholder's signature.

Sales slip (*See* **Sales draft.**)

Same day presentment fee — in direct presentment situations, the charge levied by the **drawee-payor bank** against the depositary bank that is making the direct presentment.

Sender — in **electronic funds transfer,** the party that originates an order or transfers an order that it has received.

Share draft — negotiable order for the payment of money drawn by a customer of a **credit union.** [Prior to deregulation, credit unions could not accept **demand deposits,** that is, they could not accept checking accounts. As deregulation commenced and the **thrift** industry began using **negotiable orders of withdrawal,** credit unions commenced using the share draft. Share drafts are usually payable through a **bank** or other financial institution.]

Sight draft — a **draft** payable upon presentation, that is, within a specified short time after presentation. (*Compare* **Time draft.**)

Smart card — plastic card resembling a credit or **debit card** with an embedded silicon chip that stores information that can be read and altered by a merchant's or a financial institution's terminals. [The plastic credit card familiar to most U.S. consumers bears a magnetic stripe that contains relatively little information and that requires on-line terminals or human intervention for access to such data as the cardholder's credit line. Smart cards can be operated at terminals without on-line capabilities and can not only read data such as the cardholder's credit limits but can reduce the limit by the amount of a given purchase.]

Society for Worldwide Interbank Financial Telecommunication — Belgian cooperative owned by **banks** and dedicated to the international transfer of information between banks under a system that accepts coded information at terminals, transfers the information to a **switching center,** and relays the information to another bank's terminal where it is decoded.

SWIFT (*See* **Society for Worldwide Interbank Financial Telecommunication.**)

Switch (*See* **Switching center.**)

Switching center — a computerized component of a message system serving to accept signals from a terminal, store them, and retransmit them to a second terminal.

T&E card (*See* **Travel and entertainment card.**)

Telex — a system of (1) transmitting messages by electronic impulse over telephone wires and by satellite and (2) recording the message in printed form at a terminal dedicated to telex use.

Teller check — a **cashier's check** or other **check** drawn by a **bank** on itself or another financial institution.

Tenor — the terms of an instrument, i.e., date, amount, etc.

Thrift — usually, a savings and loan association or a savings **bank,** as opposed to a commercial bank.

Time deposit — debt of a financial institution that is payable to the depositor not on demand but at a given period of time after demand or at a specified date.

Time draft — **draft** payable not on demand but a given time after sight or date or on a given date. [Time drafts arise in connection with credit sales and may be payable a certain number of days (e.g., 90) after sight, after the date of the draft, or after the date on a bill of lading. Time drafts are honored twice: first, by acceptance, and second, by payment.]

Trade acceptance — a **time draft** that has been accepted by a merchant or trader as opposed to a time draft accepted by a **bank.** (*Compare* **Banker's acceptance.**)

Transaction account — an account against which the depositor may make withdrawals by **check, negotiable order of withdrawal, share draft,** or the like.

Transit item — an **item** for collection that is not an on-us item or one to be cleared through the **clearinghouse,** that is, an item to be cleared through the **Federal Reserve System.**

Transmitting bank — in **wire transfers,** a **bank** that transmits funds through a wire transfer system.

Travel and entertainment card — credit card that usually is (1) marketed by a nonbank entity, (2) requires payment in full at the end of a billing cycle, and (3) has no credit limits.

Truncation — any variant of a paper-collection system that provides for the interruption of the transfer of the paper and the substitution for it of an electronic signal or other form of **wire transfer.** Truncation in the check-collection system may occur at the **drawee bank,** the **depositary bank,** or the **clearinghouse.**

Unwind — in **electronic funds transfer,** the process of undoing a transfer that is partially or wholly complete.

Usance draft — synonym for **time draft.**

Utter — in negotiable-instruments law, the process of issuing a negotiable instrument. [A **drawer** utters a **draft** or **check;** a maker utters a promissory note.]

Value dating — issuing an **item** with instructions that value not be given immediately but at a later date.

Vostro account — in international banking, an account held by a domestic **bank** and owned by a foreign bank. (*Compare* **Nostro account.**)

Wholesale wire transfer — **electronic funds transfer** that is initiated by a nonconsumer. [By virtue of the facts (1) that the initial legislation in the field of **wire transfers** differentiated consumer transfers from nonconsumer transfers and (2) that some wire transfer systems entail transfer costs that are not economical for frequent low-dollar, consumer use, the electronic funds transfer industry, regulators, and some legislation have differentiated consumer from nonconsumer or wholesale wire transfers.]

Wire transfer — transfer of funds effected not by paper but by telephonic, telegraphic, computer, or other telecommunication.

PART IV.   TRANSPORT AND STORAGE

All risks—in maritime insurance, coverage that includes losses caused by fortuity but not all losses. [For example, damage caused by hooks or malfunctioning of refrigeration equipment or by delays are not covered by an all risks policy. The all risks coverage has been displaced by the Institute Cargo Clause A.]

Average—in maritime insurance, a partial, as opposed to total, loss. (*See* **General average, Particular average.**)

Bailee—the party to whom personal property is delivered under a **bailment**.

Bailment—arrangement between a **bailor** and a **bailee** for the transport, storage, or use of personal property. [In a bailment, the bailee has the right to hold the goods but does not acquire the "property," i.e., the title. There are many examples of bailment in commerce and private activity. Agisters, who graze cattle for the owner, are bailees. Lessees of equipment are bailees. A neighbor who borrows a pair of hedge clippers is a bailee. This Part deals primarily with commercial bailees: those who store or transport goods for compensation.]

Bailor—in a **bailment**, the party who causes goods to be put in the possession of a **bailee**.

Bill of lading—a **document of title** issued by a **bailee** who agrees to transport or arrange for the transport of the bailed goods.

Binder—in maritime insurance, the broker or agent's brief summary of the insurance coverage and certification that the insurance policy will issue in due course.

Breakbulk cargo—**bulk cargo** that is subject to separate **bills of lading.**

Bulk cargo—cargo that is not shipped in **containers.** [It is often not efficient to ship cargo in containers, the cost of loading and unloading the ship's hold or tanks being less than the cost of shipping in individual containers. Ores, crude oil, agricultural commodities, and many other fungibles are shipped in bulk.]

Bulker—a ship that carries bulk rather than **container** cargo.

Cabotage — a coastal trade or transport of goods, sometimes said of intranational transport or transport within a single state in the European Union.

Cartage company — a trucking company, often one that makes short hauls of goods, say, from a shipper's dock to a rail siding or dock. [Often cartage companies send their tractors to pick up **trailers** or send tractors with **chassis** to pick up **containers**.]

Cellular container ship — ocean-going vessel that is designed to carry large **containers**.

Charterer — the party that rents a ship to carry goods or passengers under a contract called a **charter party** with the owner.

Charter party — the contract between the owner of a ship and the party that undertakes to use it for a voyage or a period of time.

Chassis — a device on which a **container** may be placed for hauling by a truck tractor.

Combined transport document — a **document of title** covering the transport of goods by more than one mode of transportation, e.g., by truck and rail or by barge and ship.

Combined transport operator — a **bailee** that transports or arranges for the transport of merchandise on more than one mode of transport. [A combined transport operator may be a carrier that uses trucks and rail, for example, or may be a **freight forwarder** that arranges for such transport.]

Commercial invoice — document, prepared by the seller of goods, submitted to the buyer requesting payment. [The commercial invoice usually includes a number of important terms of the sales agreement: the description and quantity of the goods and the payment and delivery provisions. The commercial invoice is of interest to third parties such as customs officials and bankers who are financing the transaction. The seller must take care that the commercial invoice conforms to customs and banker usages. United States customs officials, for example, expect the commercial invoice to include all handling and shipping charges, the currency in which payment is to be made, and drawbacks or rebates that may come due, the country of origin, and other matters. Banks that issue letters of credit will not pay drafts accompanying commercial invoices that do not describe the goods as the letter of credit describes them. The commercial invoice, then, is

Glossary

an important document whose preparation requires considerable care and expertise.]

Conference — association of ship owners or **liners** that publishes schedules and sets charges.

Consignee — the party designated on a **bill of lading** as the party to whom the carrier should deliver the goods. [The term *consignee* is somewhat anomalous in negotiable **bills of lading,** since the party to whom the goods are to be delivered under a negotiable bill is the holder of it. Nevertheless, modern bill-of-lading forms use the term in both negotiable and non-negotiable bills.]

Consignment note — a non-negotiable receipt for goods with the terms for their transport. (*See* **Waybill.**)

Consolidator   (*See* **Freight forwarder.**)

Container — box, usually of corrugated steel, or tank into which merchandise is "stuffed" for shipment.

Container ship — ship designed for **container** rather than **bulk** cargo.

Covernote — in maritime insurance, an agent or broker's certification that insurance coverage has been purchased and that the policy of insurance will issue. (*See* **Binder.**)

Customs broker — party that offers importers the service of getting goods through customs. [A custom broker's services include preparing the documentation, seeing to the offloading of goods into bonded warehouses, and, sometimes, paying charges for the importer. Customs brokers may have blanket type bonds under which goods may be released by the customs service before the duty is computed. Many customs brokers are also **freight forwarders.**]

Customs invoice — special invoice prepared in order to satisfy the customs service of the importing country. [Some countries specify the terms to be included in the commercial invoice and accept that invoice for customs purposes. Other countries have, at times, required a special customs invoice on their own forms, and still other countries require the commercial invoice to be "consularized," that is, examined by consular official of the importing country in the exporting country. The consular official then stamps and signs the invoice, thereby consularizing it. In all of these cases, the government officials use the invoice information to determine import duties, to enforce import restrictions, and to generate statistical information.]

Data freight receipt (*See* **Waybill**.)

Delivery order — a **document of title** issued by any party, sometimes a stranger to the **bailment**, requesting the delivery of goods, usually that are the subject of a bailment. [Delivery orders arise in any number of transactions. Their independent value as documents of title depends on the parties that sign them. When they are accepted by a **bailee,** they become the equivalent of a **warehouse receipt**.]

Destination control statement — statement appearing on an invoice, **bill of lading**, or **shipper's export declaration** providing notice of the foreign destinations to which a shipment may be transported and used as a method of government control of exports.

Disponent owner — in a sub-**charter party**, the party granting the right to use the vessel to the **charterer**. [It is not uncommon for a ship to be the subject of more than one charter. The owner may charter the vessel to X, who in turn, subcharters it to Y. In the subcharter, X is the disponent owner.]

Dock receipt — receipt evidencing delivery of goods to an agent of the shipping company. [The shipping company's agent may take delivery of the goods prior to the issuance of the **bill of lading**. In that case, the dock receipt serves as a document covering the **bailment**.]

Document of title — commodity paper, that is, paper that (1) stands, in the event the document is negotiable, for the goods themselves while they are in the possession of a **bailee**, and (2) evidences the **bailment** arrangement between the **bailor** and the bailee. [Documents of title may be negotiable or non-negotiable. In the former event, they stand for the goods; in the latter, they merely evidence the bailment and the terms of it.]

Door-to-door — shipment term indicating that the goods will be shipped in **containers** stuffed at the seller's facility and delivered unopened at the buyer's facility.

Drayage company (*See* **Cartage company**.)

Equivalents — standard length measurements for **containers**, e.g., 20 ft., 40 ft.

Glossary

EWR — electronic warehouse receipt, presently confined to the cotton warehouse industry.

Export license (*See* **General export license** and **Validated export license**.)

FCL — full **container** load.

FIATA — acronym for the French name of international **freight forwarders** association: Fédération Internationale des Associations de Transitaires et Assimilés.

Field warehouse — company that operates a warehouse or warehouses at the premises of another party, usually, a debtor whose creditor desires to deprive the debtor of possession of its inventory, which is stored in the field warehouse.

First of exchange — recital on a draft used in international trade indicating that the draft is the first of two or more, the draft having been issued in multiple copies. [In the international documentary draft transaction, because of the risk that documents might be lost in the mails, it was common in the past and survives to some extent today for sellers to assemble two or more sets of documents in order to send them to the buyer by mail and by ship. If the documents arrived by mail, the buyer or bank to which they were directed would use them, and the duplicate set would be void. If the documents did not arrive by mail, the buyer or bank, as the case might be, would go to the steamship that carried the goods and ask the captain to deliver the duplicate set of documents that the **shipper** has entrusted to him and that he had carried in the ship's safe. Drafts drawn under the practice contained a recital indicating the draft as the first or the second in the set. Thus, "first of exchange" indicated that the draft was the first copy. **"Second of exchange"** indicated that it was the second. Customarily, following these recitals there was further language indicating the number of drafts drawn and the consequences of honor of one of them. After "first of exchange," the draft would recite "second of same tenor and date being unpaid." Thus if the duplicate draft had been paid, the drawee knew not to honor the first.]

Forwarder (*See* **Freight forwarder**.)

FPA — in maritime insurance, "free of **particular average**," that is, coverage that does not extend to particular average losses. (*Compare* **General average** and **WPA**.)

Franchise — in maritime insurance, a kind of deductible, expressed in a percentage or in dollar terms.

Freight forwarder — agent of the **shipper** who arranges for the transport of the shipper's goods. [Often, the forwarder is a **consolidator**, that is, he accepts **LCL** shipments from his clients and consolidates them into **FCL** shipments. Forwarders are also sometimes **customs brokers** and often are **loading brokers**.]

General average — partial loss allocated among surviving cargoes as a consequence of the ship captain's decision to sacrifice cargo in order to save ship or cargo from extraordinary peril.

General export license — U.S. export license covering all exports except those covered by a **validated export license**.

Gray-market goods — goods manufactured abroad in violation of U.S. registered trademarks and imported for resale in the United States.

Gross weight — weight of cargo including contents and packaging or **container**.

House bill of lading — said of a **bill of lading** issued by a **freight forwarder**.

IATA — International Air Transport Association.

Insurance binder   (*See* **Binder**.)

Insurance certificate — document certifying that there is coverage, usually under an **open cargo policy**, of a designated shipment.

LCL — less than **container** load.

Lighter — a small vessel or barge used to transport merchandise from ship to ship or from ship to dock and back in port.

Liner — ship that travels established routes under **conference** schedules and rates.

Loading broker — agent of the ship owner whose duty it is to obtain cargo for the ship. [In addition, the loading broker may perform some of the ship owner's functions in connection with the issuance of the **bill of lading**, the affixation of the **on-board stamp**, and the like.]

Manifest — ship's record of cargo the ship is carrying.

Marine bill of lading — bill of lading issued by an ocean-going carrier, as opposed to a **house bill of lading** or bill of lading issued by a **freight forwarder**.

Marks — (as in "marks and numbers") markings on goods or packages identifying the goods and their destination. (*See also* **Numbers**.)

MT document — the bill of lading issued by an **MTO**.

MTO — multi-modal transport operator. [Traditionally in the transport industry a carrier issued a bill of lading for each leg of the journey, one bill for the rail carriage from the manufacturer's facility to the docks, a second bill for the ocean carriage to a foreign port, and so on. Today, one carrier, the multi-modal transport operator, will arrange for this multi-modal shipment.]

Multi-modal — said of transport of goods by more than one mode, i.e., by rail and steamship. (*Compare* **Unimodal**.)

Net weight — weight of contents only, i.e., exclusive of weight of packages or **containers**.

Numbers — designation on a series of packages, when a shipment consists of more than one package.

NVOCC bill of lading — a **bill of lading** issued by a nonvessel-owning common carrier, a **freight forwarder**. (*See also* **Transport document**.)

On-board bill of lading — bill of lading indicating that the goods have been loaded on board. [For risk of loss, title passage, insurance, and other purposes, it may be critical for parties to know that the goods have been loaded on board the ship. **Received-for-shipment bills of lading** are issued by carriers or by **freight forwarders** and do not indicate that the goods are loaded on board unless the received-for-shipment bill contains an **on-board stamp**, signed and dated by the ship's agent.]

On-board stamp — notation superimposed on **received-for-shipment bill of lading**, signed and dated by the ship's master or agent, and indicating that the cargo has passed the ship's rail.

Open cargo policy — marine insurance policy in the nature of a blanket policy, that is, one policy that covers many shipments.

Order bill of lading — a negotiable **bill of lading**.

Packing list — detailed description of the contents of packages that contain the cargo.

Parallel goods — synonym for **gray-market goods**.

Particular average — in maritime insurance, an accidental, partial loss and specifically not a **general average** loss.

Pro-forma invoice — an invoice, incomplete in one or more respects, sometimes used as a seller's quotation or offer to sell. [The pro-forma invoice suggests that the buyer and seller have yet to conclude all of the terms of their sales contract, but the document permits the buyer to approach customs authorities or other officials and present documentation that will permit him to obtain preliminary approval of his imports and preliminary calculation of duties and other charges. When the **commercial invoice** issues, if its terms differ materially from the pro-forma invoice, the preliminary approval and calculations will be revoked, and the whole purpose of the pro-forma invoice will be frustrated. The pro-forma invoice, therefore, is usually a draft of the commercial invoice with the words "pro forma" superimposed. In the event the transaction proceeds as the parties plan, the terms of the commercial invoice may be identical to those of the pro-forma invoice.]

Received-for-shipment bill of lading — **bill of lading** issued by a carrier or **freight forwarder** indicating that the **bailee** has received the cargo but not indicating that the goods are loaded on board. (*Compare* **On-board bill of lading**.)

Roll-on, roll-off — said of **containers** that are on wheels and can roll on and off **chassis**, railcars, or other carrier equipment.

Said to contain — a carrier's disclaimer, often found in **bills of lading**, indicating that the carrier has not verified the description of the goods on the bill. (*See also* **Shipper's load and count**.)

Second of exchange   (*See* **First of exchange**.)

SED — shipper's export declaration.

Shipper — the **bailor**, the party that delivers the goods to a carrier or **freight forwarder** for shipment.

Shipper's export declaration — document required by the U.S. Department of Commerce for all export shipments of a value in excess of $500. [The shipper's export declaration permits the Commerce Department to enforce export control regulations and statutes and provides data for the Department's statistical reporting role.]

Shipper's load and count — (sometimes "shipper's load, weight, and count") a disclaimer, often found in **bills of lading**, indicating that the carrier is not vouching for the description of the goods in the bill of lading. [Disclaimers in **documents of title**, especially bills of lading, are common and reasonable attempts to avoid claims that the goods, which are often in sealed **containers** or packages, do not conform to the description in the document. In most transportation arrangements, for instance, the **shipper** fills out the bill of lading for the carrier's agent to execute. It is not efficient for the carrier to inspect all shipments. Most buyers, banks, and other parties that take the bill of lading are content to rely on the honesty of the shipper. The disclaimers, of which **SLC** is but one, are an effort to alert the amateur buyer or taker of the document that the carrier does not stand behind the description. If a buyer wants verification of the packages' contents, he must arrange for an independent inspector or require a document that does not contain the disclaimer. Some courts have been reluctant to enforce these disclaimers, and there is statutory and case law applicable to them in domestic and international shipments.]

SLC — shipper's load and count.

SRCC — in maritime insurance, "strikes, riots, and civil commotions," perils that may be included or excluded from the underwriter's insurance obligation.

Stale bill of lading — generally, a **bill of lading** that is outstanding more than 21 days after issue. [In the banking industry and among parties that take bills of lading as a method of purchasing goods, there is concern that the bill not cover merchandise that has already been unloaded. Sometimes, carriers will deliver goods without surrender of the bill. If the bill is lost, for example, the **consignee** may obtain a guaranty to indemnify the carrier against the possibility that the bill is in the hands of a holder who has rights in the goods. In order to balance the interests of all innocent parties (i.e., true owners, carriers, and indemnitors), the industry has fashioned the rule that any bill of lading that is more than 21 days old is suspect. Persons who take such a bill are warned, therefore, that something may be amiss and that they may not qualify as holders who take by due negotiation, in which event, they will not take a superior interest in the goods covered by the bill.]

Stevedore company — a company that loads and unloads ships.

Straight bill of lading — a non-negotiable **bill of lading**.

Survey — in the maritime industry, the evaluation by an expert of the seaworthiness of a vessel.

Tariff — a schedule of shipment charges. [Prior to the deregulation of the domestic transportation industry, virtually all shipments by truck and rail were made under tariffs that were published with a federal, state, or quasi-official agency. Those tariffs prevented what some saw as abuse by carriers, in particular the long haul-short haul differentials that have riled **shippers** since the great railroad era of the last century. Deregulation of the domestic transport industry permits carriers to negotiate freight rates, and more and more shipments are now handled by private contractual arrangements.]

Terminal warehouse — warehouse located at a rail, truck, or ship terminal, as opposed to a **field warehouse**, which is located "in the field."

Through bill of lading — a **bill of lading** that is issued by the initial carrier and that covers transport by that carrier and one or more subsequent carriers. [Under the through bill, the initial carrier acts as the agent of the **shipper** for the purpose of engaging other carriers to complete the transport of the goods. Thus if a Detroit shipper desires to ship merchandise from Detroit to Los Angeles, it may deliver the goods to the Grand Trunk Railroad in Detroit. The GT will transport the goods to the end of its line and deliver them to a Burlington Northern train, which will haul them to California. In the through-bill situation, the Grand Trunk collects the entire freight charge from the shipper and the Burlington draws on the Grand Trunk and collects its share of the charge through a clearinghouse maintained by the railroads.]

TPND — in maritime insurance, "theft, pilferage, and nondelivery," perils that may or may not be covered by the maritime insurance policy.

Trailer — a **container** that is on wheels and may be hitched to a truck tractor.

Tramps — ships that travel from port to port in search of cargo and do not follow a published route and schedule. (*Compare* **Liner.**)

Transhipment — (sometimes transshipment) the act of off-loading goods from one vessel, which completes part of a voyage, and on-loading them to a second vessel for another leg of the voyage. [Transhipment may be **unimodal** or **multi-modal** and may involve more than two legs to a single voyage.]

Transport document — the equivalent of a **bill of lading** issued by a non-carrier. [It offends the logic of some in the banking and transport industry that noncarriers, such as **freight forwarders,** may issue a bill of lading — a document indicating that the issuer will carry the goods. In some areas, therefore, noncarrier issuers do not issue bills of lading but "transport documents." In the United States, freight forwarders issue an **NVOCC bill of lading.**]

Truncation — in transport and storage, the practice of issuing a document of title, probably in paper form, to a central recordkeeper or depository that functions as a recipient and recorder of transfers and that subsequently issues, by paper or electronically, acknowledgements of transfers to the respective transferees.

Underwriter — in maritime insurance, the insurance carrier.

Unimodal — said of a shipment that will occur on one type of carrier only, e.g., by truck only and not by truck and rail or rail and ship. (*Compare* **Multi-modal.**)

Validated export license — government grant of authority to a specified exporter to export specified goods. [Validated licenses must be applied for and are used when the goods are national-security sensitive or are destined for a country that is, often for political reasons, the subject of U.S. export restrictions.]

WA — in maritime insurance, "with average," i.e., said of insurance coverage that extends to **average.**

Warehouse receipt — a **document of title** issued by a **bailee** and covering the storage of goods or commodities.

Waybill — non-negotiable document indicating the terms of a shipment. [In the air transport industry, the air waybill is the only document that the carrier issues. In the rail industry, the waybill is usually a carbon copy of the non-negotiable **bill of lading** that the carrier issues. The waybill is attached to the railroad car, so that railroad personnel will know where to direct the shipment.]

Weight note — document, executed by the seller of merchandise or by a third party, certifying the weight of the shipment.

WPA — in maritime insurance, "with particular average," i.e., said of coverage that extends to **particular average**. (*Compare* **FPA**.)

Master Word List

All references are to page numbers.

ACA
   See **Agriculatural Credit Assocation**
Acceleration   355, 388
Accept   235, 415
Acceptance   32, 235, 415
Acceptance corporation   388
Acceptor   247, 415
Account   94, 388
Account debtor   109, 388
ACH
   See **Automated clearinghouse**
Acquirer   415
Add-on interest   389
Adverse selection   355
Adviser   41, 355
Affinity card   415
After-acquired property   175, 389
Agreement   5, 356
Agricultural credit association (ACA)   202, 389
All risks   348, 431
Allowance   356
Annual percentage rate   389
APR
   See **Annual percentage rate**
Arbitrage   356
Asset-backed issue   389
Asset-based lender   389
Asset securitization   389
Assignee   147, 389

T&E card
See Travel and entertainment card
Take or pay contract   385
Tariff   307, 440
Telex   40, 386, 429
Teller check   386, 429
Tenor   429
Terminal warehouse   321, 440
Thick market   386
Thrift   94, 218, 413, 429
Through bill of lading   336, 440
Time deposit   429
Time draft   246, 429
Time price differential   413
Title   5, 386
TPND   440
TRAC lease   386
Trade acceptance   33, 247, 386, 429
Trading partner   386
Trailer   333, 440
Tramps   340, 441
Transaction account   429
Transaction costs   31, 386
Transhipment   441
Transit item   221, 430
Transmitting bank   430
Transport document   340, 441
Travel and entertainment card   291, 430
Truncation   236, 430, 441
Turnkey project   386
Tying   386

Umbrella rule
See Shelter principle
Underwriter   441
Unimodal   441
Unsecured creditor   203, 413
Unwind   430
Unwindable   258
Usance
See Usance draft
Usance draft   32, 430
Utter   430

Index

All references are to section numbers.

Index

Index

Index

Index

Index

Index